Radical Irish Priests
1660–1970

EDITED BY

Gerard Moran

with an introduction by

Donal Kerr

FOUR COURTS PRESS

This book was typeset by
Woodcote Typesetters
in 10 on 12 point Ehrhardt for
FOUR COURTS PRESS LTD
Fumbally Lane, Dublin 8, Ireland
e-mail: info@four-courts-press.ie
and in North America for
FOUR COURTS PRESS
c/o ISBS, 5804 N.E. Hassalo Street, Portland, OR 97213.

A catalogue record for this title
is available from the British Library.

ISBN 1-85182-249-6

Printed in Great Britain
by the Martins Printing Group, Bodmin, Cornwall

Contents

Editor's Preface

While biography is sometimes regarded as a side-track in history and of little merit, the recent contributions of R.F. Foster on the life of W.B. Yeats and Frank Callanan on Tim Healy have added greatly to our understanding of late nineteenth- and early twentieth-century Ireland. The inspiration for a collection of essays on the lives and works of Irish radical priests came from some of the contributors who suggested that such a book would be worthwhile and informative. I am indebted to all who have encouraged, stimulated and pushed for the completion of this project. I am especially grateful to the D'Alton Fund, Maynooth for the subvention which has brought this about. To those who have made sacrifices, in particular spouses and families, I am in gratitude and especially Clodagh, Eoghan, Cian, Cillian and Caoimhe. A special word of thanks to the staff of Four Courts Press, and in particular Ronan Gallagher, for their patience and continuous encouragement.

Abbreviations

Add. Mss	Additional Manuscripts
A.N.A.A.	Archives Nationales [Archives Anciennes]
A.N.M.G.	Archives Nationales [Ministere de la Guerre]
Arch. Hib.	*Archivium Hibernicium*
B.L.	British Library, London
B.O.	Bodleian Library, Oxford
Cambs.	Cambridge University Library
Coll. Hib.	*Collectanea Hibernica*
C.S.O.	Chief Secretary's Office
D.D.A.	Dublin Diocesan Archives
D.E.P.	*Dublin Evening Post*
F.D.J.	*Dublin Journal*
F.J.	*Freeman's Journal*
H.C.	Parliamentary papers, House of Commons series
H.M.C.	Historical Manuscripts Commission
I.E.R.	*Irish Ecclesiastical Record*
N.A.	National Archives, Dublin
N.L.I.	National Library of Ireland, Dublin
Journ. of Cork Hist. & Arch. Soc.	*Journal of the Cork Historical and Archaeological Society*
R.P.	Registered Papers (National Archives, Dublin)
P.R.O.	Public Record Office, London
P.R.O.N.I.	Public Records Office of Northern Ireland
R.A.	Royal Archives [Windsor Castle, Stuart Papers]
R.I.A. Proc	*Proceedings of the Royal Irish Academy, Dublin*
S.P.	State Papers
T.C.D.	Trinity College, Dublin
U.C.D.	University College, Dublin
U.C.G.	University College, Galway

Introduction

Donal Kerr

When Pope John Paul was welcomed at the airport by Ernesto Cardinal, the Minister for Culture, a press photograph showed him with his right index finger raised. Vatican wags interpreted it as the pope raising a scolding finger at the minister, a poet and a Trappist priest who had left his monastery to take part in the revolutionary Sandinista government. There are many others – the Berrigan brothers, Hans Kung in Germany, and most recently, Tissa Balasuriya, a Sri Lankan Oblate Father, to name but a few. The Catholic Church has always had its share of radical priests. Some were saints – Francis of Assisi would spring most readily to mind, though he was never ordained; others like Yves Congar and Henri de Lubac eventually became cardinals, and others still like Girolamo Savonarola, are even now in the process of being rehabilitated. Yet others, like Martin Luther, remain outside the fold. Most 'radical' priests were judged so because of their position on some point of Catholic doctrine. Others like the martyred Archbishop Oscar Romero and Latin American liberation theologians, such as Leonardo Boff, were social radicals.

Irish 'radical priests', have been more associated with social and political activity, rather than doctrinal radicalism – Walter McDonnell of Maynooth was an exception and so, in another way, was George Tyrrell – and few of them have ended up outside the Church. Reflecting this fact, the priests in this fascinating collection of essays are not theological radicals but social and political radicals. What unites this very diversified series of 'lives' in this volume, is that all nine priests come under the umbrella of 'radical'. This, in turn, begs the question of what radical means. Brian Murphy, in his chapter on 'The Stone of Destiny: Fr John Fahy (1894–1969) and clerical radicalism in independent Ireland' suggests that 'radicalism' might be too slippery a concept to be a trustworthy guide. Certainly, the rich variety of priests in this volume and their differing attitudes accentuate the polyvalence of 'radical'. A major mistake would be to confuse radical and liberal. Since radicalism normally implies blazing a new trail, it often implies revolutionary change. Sometimes, in keeping with its etymological meaning, it can betoken a prophetic return to the roots and can emerge as deeply social and conservative. On the whole, Irish clerical radicalism tends to fall into the second category, as befits ministers of a religion who believe in the enduring inspiration of the Christian message. A possible definition of a radical could be one who challenges the established order, political, social or cultural. The radical's perspective can be a personal one.

The two chapters that begin this volume provide an example of both innovative and conservative tendencies. In his chapter, Éamonn Ó Ciardha, gives us a picture of the poet, Father Liam Inglis, a mid eighteenth-century Jacobite poet. His study, 'A voice from the Jacobite underground', is important for it opens a gate to Irish-language poetry of the eighteenth century and provides a key for assessing the political content of Jacobite poetry in Irish. His chapter is a timely reminder to students of Irish history of the real danger of neglecting important, if difficult, material in Irish-language poetry. Inglis' poetry certainly provides an insight into the Irish Jacobite 'underground' (though given the amount of Jacobitism in the country perhaps 'underground' may not be an exact description) and shows the key-role of the priests (for Inglis was but one of a number) in keeping the Irish-speaking population aware of the fortunes of Jacobitism and its major protector, the French. It was remarkable how detailed a knowledge of the events of the Seven Years War, from the campaigns in Silesia in Poland to those in Quebec in Canada, Inglis' poetry provided. Put to popular airs, those poems were a powerful means of keeping the Irish-speaking majority informed and maintaining morale. In retrospect, by the 1750s, when Inglis was writing, the Stuart cause could be seen as lost, yet for nervous Irish Protestants, whose fears amply demonstrated the existence of a lively Irish Jacobitism, Inglis and his fellow-clerics, who fervently predicted for the hearers a French invasion, they were dangerous political radicals indeed.

Inglis was a conservative radical who hankered after the Stuart and Catholic monarchy. James Kelly's chapter is on Father Arthur O'Leary, an Augustinian friar, who was only thirteen years younger than Inglis. One can scarcely credit that they inhabit the same little island in much the same life-span, for the lasting impression from their writings is that they were living in different worlds. In contrast to O'Leary, Inglis' radicalism could appear reactionary, outmoded and even sectarian. O'Leary, for his part, instead of encouraging anti-Hanoverian feelings, was not opposed to the establishment but directed his efforts towards having his Catholic fellowmen accepted into it. What had happened was that by 1760 a major change had taken place. It was now clear that the Stuart cause was dead and Catholics were seeking new modes of accommodation with the existing state. O'Leary was one of the first to devote his great talents as a pamphleteer towards this goal. While vehemently condemning Enlightenment free-thinkers as a danger to church and state, he preached that the Christian religion, Catholic and Protestant, should unite rather than divide the people of Ireland. True religion, he wrote, 'instead of inspiring hatred and rancour, commands us to love'. O'Leary was a brilliant pamphleteer, taking on, in the interests of religious freedom, such powerful writers as John Wesley. This, too, was at a time when few if any Catholics, and priests in particular, dared raise their heads or write on controversial subjects. Unfortunately for O'Leary, his reputation has been permanently blemished by his acceptance later on of a pension from the government to report on his fellow-Catholics. Yet, as James Kelly's sympathetic study shows, he was a more complex character, and his plea for liberty of conscience was among the most striking and most radical statements in favour of religious and political forbearance during the whole of the eighteenth century. His convincing writings on 'tolerance' helped to prepare Protestant opinion for Catholic relief and stimulated Henry Grattan to work for a religiously and politically inclusive 'Irish nation', a radical enough concept for the time. Another, less successful, radical attitude was his approach to the agrarian unrest. While condemning the outrages of the Rightboys, he courageously defended their position, pleading that 'their actions was founded on ... poverty', their mode of proceeding 'moderate' and the tithes against which they rebelled 'oppressive'. This even-handed approach was too radical for the noblemen of Munster who denounced these 'seditious' publications. By the 1790s, confrontation and conflict began to prevail in Ireland, O'Leary's influence diminished and he retired from the scene. He welcomed the Act of Union, however, hoping, like most leading Catholics, that it would lead to Catholic Emancipation and would end the 'tumultary scenes which have distracted my ill-fated country for ages'.

Very different from either of those two priests again is the third in this section on the eighteenth century, Fr Nicholas Sheehy of Clogheen, county Tipperary. And yet, with the exception of the Father Murphy of Boolavogue, and perhaps Fr Patrick Lavelle of Partry, he is the best known of the 'rebel' priests. Unlike Inglis and O'Leary, there are no writings of his to indicate whether or not he held radical views. The perception that he is a radical comes later. On the application of radical to Fr Sheehy, Thomas Power, the author of this essay, explains that its use in regard to Fr Sheehy 'in part applies more to what was done to him by an ultra group among the Protestant gentry than to whatever involvement he may have had in agrarian agitation' and also 'to the fact that he was in part radicalised by the course of events and the charges brought against him'. Dr Power, in a thorough retelling and re-evaluation of his life, dismisses the accusation of murder, for which Sheehy was executed, as a trumped-up charge. Sympathetically disposed towards the plight of the peasants like O'Leary, Sheehy was more actively involved in helping them and paid the ultimate penalty exacted by a vindictive Munster gentry.

Like Sheehy, Fr Manus Sweeney of Newport, county Mayo, was caught up in a maelstrom that swept him away, the arrival of the French at Killala. Although educated in France and therefore familiar, as were many Irish priests, with the Enlightenment, of which the French Revolution was in part the fruit, there is no written work to show that Sweeney was a 'radical'. Like Sheehy, too, it is only afterwards that he was seen as a radical. The justification for his execution was that he spoke French and received the French officers. His hanging, and that of Fr Conroy of Laherdane, county Mayo, influenced that great 'radical' priest, John MacHale, who was to prove a thorn in the side of successive British governments for nearly half a century.

Insofar as it was born of sympathy for the poor, the radicalism of Fr Thaddeus O'Malley (1797–1877) bears some resemblance to that of Sheehy, for it was essentially a social radicalism. O'Malley rooted his radicalism in the Gospel. 'Until the lessons of the Gospel in reference to the relations of rich and poor are adopted as the preambles to our Christian legislation, Christianity shall have failed of its purpose.' In the 1830s, he and many others had called for a relief system for the poor but for O'Malley such a system, not as just a moral duty, but the people's right. 'I am talking of rights, not charity,' he insisted. O'Malley espoused the same cause in a letter on *The rights of labour*, and when the Revolution of 1848 broke out in France, he called on Irish workers to look to Paris where the working men had taken to the streets to fight for their interests. Long after the failure of the 1848 rebellion, he remained loyal to the cause of the worker and small farmer and, in 1851, he founded, edited and wrote *The Christian social economist*, a title that sums up his own stance. As late as the mid-1860s, he was still criticising the government's unfeeling social policy: 'the right to live of the prolétaire it surrenders to the discretion of some half-dozen gentlemen (so called) "guardians of the poor" who may too often be more truly called the guardians of their own pockets'. In politics, his main claim to fame was his espousal of Federalism of which he is rightly called the founding 'Father'. Sharman Crawford supported it, and O'Connell flirted with it but, under pressure from Young Ireland, dropped it, and it remained a dead-letter until revived in a different form by Isaac Butt's Home Rule movement which O'Malley supported. A talented man, poor O'Malley was regarded with suspicion for his part in the Hogan schism in Philadelphia and his endorsement of the Prussian education system and and never got the recognition or support he craved. Fergus A. D'Arcy's chapter foreshadows a long-overdue biography of this many-talented man.

Fr Patrick Lavelle's radicalism bore even more resemblance to Sheehy for he championed the small farmers against the tyranny of the landowners. Yet he is principally known for his defence of the Fenians and for the successful defiance, over the best part of a decade, he offered to Archbishop Paul Cullen. Gerard Moran's chapter, which gives us the quintessence of his recent pioneer work on Lavelle, highlights his involvement with the radical section of the Irish Church and places him as a bridge between the pre-famine radicalism of Fr John Murphy, Fr Manus Sweeney and Fr John Kenyon, on the one hand, and that of the post-famine radical priests, such as Fr David Humphreys, Fr James McFadden and Fr Michael Flanagan, on the other. For advanced nationalists, Lavelle became the symbol of Irish resistance to British injustice, whether in his opposition to the government or in his attacks on landlordism. Unlike the earlier radicals studied in this volume, Lavelle ably broadened his support by appealing to the Irish abroad, both in Britain and the United States, where his attacks on evictions and the landlord cruelty struck a ready chord. Lavelle's career illustrates the changing nature of 'radical' politics. Radical throughout the 1860s, history passed him by. After 1885, when Parnell came to dominate the scene, advanced nationalists no longer saw him as their champion. His radicalism was embedded in the past and history had voided it of relevance.

This transitory nature of radicalism comes out again in Breandán Mac Suibhne's account of 'an sagart mórh', Séamus Mac Phaidín, with both parallels and differences. Canon Mac Phaidin, or James McFadden, was revered by the smallholders of Gaoth Dobhair and he showed himself a fearless leader during the Land War and the Plan of Campaign. The historian of Gaoth Dobhair described him as 'the great hero of a man, who took the people of Gaoth Dobhair out of slavery, who put an end to hunger and hardship in the parish, who put backbone into them and who did not draw breath until he had put an end to rackrent, unjust laws and eviction'. Breandán Mac Suibhne's chapter makes the point that in addition to inheriting and using to the full the traditional leadership role of the priest, he was a charismatic leader regarded with awe and veneration by his parishioners. According to one of the crowds of reporters from England and further abroad flocking to Gaoth Dobhair to see him in action, the people had 'almost supernatural confidence in him'. As friend and foe, novelist and journalist, testified, by 1891, this 'indefatigable' (the epithet most commonly applied to him) priest had become 'a saviour'. For his vigorous resistance to eviction, he received a jail sentence, doubled on appeal, but imprisonment only strengthened his hold on the people and his own defiance of government. Fascinating though the recital of his exploits is, Breandán Mac Suibhne is less interested in MacFadden's radicalism than in the eclipse of his reputation once he was transferred to Inis Caoil in 1901. The novelist, Patrick MacGill, a native of Inis Caoil, bitterly satirised MacFadden in his trilogy *Children of the dead end – The autobiography of a navy*, *The rat-pit* and *Glenmornan*. For him, MacFadden was a townsman's priest, with a middle-class style of life paid for by the pennies of the poor country-folk. Mac Suibhne argues that the different images of Mac Fadden in Gaoth Dobhair and Inis Caoil stem from the differences between the social structure of the Catholic communities. Gaoth Dobhair's community was monolithic, for all were equally poor and they rallied behind the dynamic priest whose middle-class style of life they admired and expected rather than resented. In Inis Caoil, on the other hand, in a more divided community, that same style of life appeared to identify him with the townsman and the farmer against the poor 'mountainy man' and hand-knitter. 'Radicalism', then, would seem to have a geographical as well as a historical dimension. After his death MacFadden retained his reputation as the 'patriot priest'.

Canon Sheehan was different from all of the other radical priests in this volume. Not for him the public protest at the eviction, nor the defiance of the establishment in church and state, nor even the propaganda of the pamphlet. Yet as one of the greatest of Irish novelists, he used his writings to levy a critique of the state of the nation on the verge of attaining Home Rule. He was courageous enough to put forward his views on how it should be improved and, in doing so, he did not hesitate to oppose much of the current cant. Lawrence McBride rightly portrays him as a nationalist and a social critic. As a nationalist he wearied of the rhetoric of the public politician and the bullying bravado of the masses. A perceptive critic of the industrial age, he contrasted the redemptive power of spiritually grounded self-sacrifice with the decomposition of a populace hell-bent on materialist advancement. Like his heroes in *The Graves at Kilmorna*, James Halpin and Myles Cogan, the true Irishman must be willing to lay down one's life for the good of the commonweal. Against the blustering of the politicians, he insisted Irish political life had to be organised on real democratic principles. For the social ills of the time, he also offered a remedy – the Christian teachings on love and charity. Was he a radical priest? Insofar as he had a clear, indeed exceptional, intellectual vision of some of the profound evils that plagued Irish society and culture at the beginning of this century and had committed his great talent as a novelist to persuade people to advance the social, intellectual and spiritual welfare of the nation, he certainly was a reformer. While producing a fair quota of radical activists, Ireland has been short on radical thinkers and Canon Sheehan may find a niche there. Like many of the other priests in this volume, his radicalism was a conservative one, based on Christian and Irish values. Hesitant though the social analysis of this shy 'country priest' may have been, his was an effort towards encouraging a re-think of where and what we were.

The last priest in this series is almost of our own times – Fr John Fahy (1894–1969). A true republican and agrarian radical, Fr Fahy attacked the payment of land annuities, demanded the break up of large farms and gave support to the IRA, if indeed he did not recruit for them. Now, however, unlike Lavelle and MacFadden, Fahy took on the forces of an independent Ireland, both Cumann na nGaedheal and Fianna Fáil coming under the lash of his criticism. He comes across as strangely anachronistic, impractical, utopian. In Brian Murphy's account, this is the story of a man who pursued his principles to the limit. When the bailiff removed the cattle of a Miss Nevin, he led a crowd to recover them and when they proved afraid, he drove the cattle back himself. His bishop, Dr Dignan, a Sinn Féin supporter who had barely escaped with his life from the Black and Tans, tried his best to bring him to reason but with limited success. One of his pamphlets declared: 'For the lands do belong to the people .... Therefore CEASE PAYING RENTS'. He proposed a new state where the reign of virtue would render such institutions as the senate, the army, and the Garda superfluous! While this utopian pamphlet confirms his claim to radicalism, it raises the question as to his rationality.

Dr Murphy raises further interesting questions concerning other priests in the independent Irish state: How much political influence did they exercise? And were they radical? Which brings us back to the question with which this introduction began – Is radical too slippery a concept to cover this wide-range of clerics? That there is a certain rainbow quality to the radicalism that covers the 'martyr' Nicholas Sheehy and the novelist Canon Sheehan, the poet Liam Inglis and the pamphleteer, Arthur O'Leary, the Fenian Patrick Lavelle and the Republican activist John Fahy. Yet they all were radical in their pursuit of a goal not seen or not acted on by their contemporaries, a goal that involved attempting to change the social, political or cultural structure of their society.

This rich and absorbing volume makes one want to hear more of those clerics who from the eighteenth to the twentieth century exercised such influence on the people of Ireland. In his chapter on Lavelle, Gerard Moran mentions a half-dozen others and the list could be added to very considerably. It is to be hoped that its enterprising editor will issue a second volume or, in a second edition, expand on the present one to include Walter McDonnell of Maynooth, the Trinity College modernist, George Tyrell, John Murphy of '98 and John Kenyon of 1848, Archdeacon John O'Sullivan, who turned flour merchant to provide Famine relief, and perhaps Archbishop Daniel Mannix and Archbishop John MacHale.

A Voice from the Jacobite Underground:
Liam Inglis (1709–1778)

Eamon Ó Ciardha

In spite of the accumulating socio-economic and political disasters of the Reformation, Tudor and Stuart centralisation and the anglicisation and dynastic and
religious wars of the seventeenth-century, the Irish poets managed to keep their
fingers on the pulse of Irish political life. Although controversy has raged on the
usefulness of their literary output as a window on early modern Ireland the
ongoing debate has brought literary criticism and literary history to the fore-
front of Irish historical studies.[1]

The starting point for a more recent consideration of the importance of Irish
literature as a source for eighteenth-century Irish history is Corkery's 'Hidden
Ireland' or study of Gaelic Munster in the eighteenth century. This according
to Louis Cullen, was 'long established as an aspect of the interpretation of the
eighteenth-century economic and social history of Ireland'. Despite Cullen's
much-quoted reappraisal, Corkery's 'Hidden Ireland' still has merit: Irish historians have too readily used Cullen's thesis to justify ignoring Irish sources.
Indeed Cullen himself warned against this, and the general neglect of Irish sources
in a recent reprint of his 1969 article.[2]

With this in mind, the purpose of this present investigation is to seek to
demonstrate the importance of the Jacobite ideology in Irish political life in the

---

1 B. Bradshaw, 'Native reaction to the Western enterprise: a case-study in Gaelic ideology', in J.
Andrews, N. Canny and P. Hair (eds), *The Western Enterprise* (Liverpool, 1978), p. 65–80; N. Canny,
'The formation of the Irish mind: religion, politics and Gaelic Irish literature, 1550-1750', in *Past
and Present*, xcv (1982), pp 91–116; T. Dunne, 'The Gaelic response to conquest and colonisation:
the evidence of the poetry', in *Studia Hibernica*, xx (1980), pp 7–30; B. Ó Buachalla, 'Na Stíobhartaigh
agus an tAos léinn: Cing Séamas', in *R.I.A. Proc.*, 83 C (1983), pp 81–134; B. Ó Buachalla, 'Annála
Ríoghachta Éireann is Foras Feasa ar Éirinn: an Comthéacs Comhaimseartha', in *Studia Hibernica*,
xxii-iii (1981–2), pp 59–106; M. O'Riordan, *The Gaelic mind and the collapse of the Gaelic world*
(Cork, 1990); B. Ó Buachalla, *Aisling Ghéar: Na Stíobhartaigh agus an t-Aos Léinn 1603-1788* (B.Á.C.,
1997); M. Caball, 'Bardic poetry and the analysis of Gaelic mentalities', in *History Ireland*, ii, no. 2
(1994); B. Cunningham, 'Irish language sources for early modern Ireland', in *History Ireland*, iv,
no.1 (1996).
2 L. Cullen, *The Hidden Ireland: the reasssessment of a concept repr.* (Gigginstowne, 1988). See also B.
Ó Buachalla, 'Ó Corcora agus an Hidden Ireland', in *Scríobh*, iv (1979), pp 109–38; S. Ó Tuama,
Cúirt, tuath agus bruachbhaile (B.Á.C., 1990); M. O'Riordan, 'Historical perspectives on the Hidden Ireland', in *Irish Review*, iv (1988), pp 73–82. For a recent appraisal, see C. Buttimer, 'Gaelic
literature and contemporary Irish life', in C. Buttimer and P. O'Flanagan (eds.), *Cork: history and
society* (Dublin, 1993), pp 585–6.

mid-eighteenth century by focusing on the literary output of the priest, poet and Jacobite propagandist, Liam Inglis. I will also show that the optimism which pervades his verse reflects the hopes of his literary colleagues, his compatriots, his Irish *émigré* brethren and mirrors the fears of his Protestant contemporaries.

The staunch royalist, Inglis, seems an unlikely candidate for inclusion in a volume of essays on radical priests. However his poetry provides an insight into the radical world of the Irish Jacobite underground and an appreciation of the pivotal role of both the lower clergy and the Irish poets in the effusion of Jacobite rhetoric to the greater Catholic polity. The Catholic Church stepped into the breach created by the virtual destruction of the Irish Catholic aristocracy to patronise the poets as formidable moulders of public opinion. The poets were never found wanting in support of their exiled king and persecuted Church. The Church, for its part, appreciated this loyalty and held it as a *national* and *spiritual* duty to patronise native culture.[3] While Seathrún Céitinn and Pádraigín Haicéad were among the most prolific poets in seventeenth-century Ireland, the priest-poet was well represented in the ranks of the eighteenth-century Irish literati by Seán Ó Briain, Conchubhar Ó Briain, Dómhnall Ó Colmáin, Uilliam Mac Néill, Bhacaigh Ó h-Iárlaíthe and Liam Inglis.[4]

Inglis is in many ways typical of the key figures in the underground intellegensia of eighteenth-century Ireland, not least by his obscurity. Arguing from fragmentary evidence John O'Daly suggested that he was born in Newcastle, county Limerick and spent a considerable portion of his early life as a schoolmaster in Castleroach and in Charleville, county Cork. Risteard Ó Foghludha takes issue with this, opting for county Tipperary as his most probable place of birth. Little light can be shed on his earliest years up to 1730, but Ó Foghludha believed that he was educated in his native area, in a hedge-school. In 1733, at the age of 24 he is credited with composing a lament for Donnchadha Óg MacCraith of Cill Bhéine along with Liam Rua MacCoitir, although Ó Foghludha believed that Liam Rua was the sole author. In 1737 he wrote a lament for Séan MacGearailt, the young son of the knight of Glin who died in county Cork in the August of that year. By this time his reputation as a poet was well established among his literary brethren in Munster and he is listed as *Uilliam de Bhriotaibh* [William Briton] among the Munster literati by Liam Rua MacCoitir and Fr Seán Ó Briain. He continued the association with his literary colleagues throughout his career and Ó Foghludha's edition of his work includes commentaries, poems and verses composed by many of his Munster literary contemporaries, including Piaras MacGearailt, Éadhbhárd de Nógla, Pádraig Ó hÉigceartaigh, Muiris Ó Gríobhtha, Séan na Ráithíneach Ó Murchadha, Tadhg Gaelach Ó

3   R.A. Breathnach, 'The end of a tradition, a survey of 18th century Gaelic literature', *Studia Hibernica*, i (Dublin, 1961), p.133.
4   T. Ó Fiaich, 'Irish poetry and the clergy', in *Léachtaí Cholmcille*, iv (1975), pp 30–56.

Suilleabháin, Séan Ó Cuinneagáin and the priest-poets Dómhnaill Ó Briain, Séan Llúid and Bishop Risteard Breathnach.

Having composed a number of pieces in the 1730s, including verses for a certain Anne Price, and an *Aisling* in which he imagined himself visiting the house of the famous Jacobite poet, Séan Clárach MacDùmhnaill, Inglis opted for the religious life, entering the Dominican house at old Friary lane, near Old Fort St. in Cork city. Unable to endure the harsh Dominican penjury and as a direct result of a disagreement with the prior on the meaning of the vow of poverty, he 'was thrown out' and transferred to the Augustinians in Fishshamble St. He spent one or two years there until he left for the monastery of Merlano in Rome in 1743–4 where he eventually received holy orders in 1749. Although the poet is credited with a wide range of secular and religious verse, the national and international politics of the later 1750s provides his greatest inspiration and will be the main focus of this study. These included works on the political, religious and economic state of Ireland, the Jacobite question, the penal code and a continual report of the main engagements in the far-flung theatres of the Seven Years War.[5]

The fact that the poet gleaned much of his information on the Seven Year's War from contemporary newspapers, translated it to Irish and set it to well-known airs such as 'An Craoibhín Aoibhinn' and 'Séan Buidhe', 'Maidin Bhog Aoibhinn' and 'The Princess Royal', has implications for the poet's role in the effusion of European war-news and Jacobite retoric to a monoglot Gaelic audience.[6] Inglis was not an exception in this regard. Throughout the eighteenth century, a host of Irish poets, (among whom is to be numbered Aoghán Ó Rathaille, Séan Ó Neachtain, Séan Clárach MacDómhnaill, Aodh Buí Mac Cruitín, Aindrias Mac Cruitín, Tadhg Ó Neachtain, Séan na Ráithíneach Ó Murchadha, Séan Ó Tuama, Piarais MacGearailt, Eoghan an Mhéirín Mac-Cárthaigh and Peadar Ó Doirnín), continued to focus on the exiled Stuart king, the Irish Regiments in France and Spain, and the course of English and European politics in their song and verse. They were preoccupied with subjects ranging from the deaths of the O'Briens of Clare during the wars of the English and Spanish succession (*c*.1688–1713) to the political and military activities of the Jacobite duke of Berwick, Louis XIV of France and Philip V of Spain. During the Jacobite invasion scares of 1719 and 1722, and the subsequent Anglo-French *détente*, they followed the actions of the Jacobite dukes of Mar and Ormond and the pro-Jacobite Spanish Cardinal Alberoni, then mourned the death of Mary Beatrice, consort of James II, and welcomed the demise of the anti-Jacobite Regent of France (Philip d'Orleans) and his effective successor, Cardinal Fleury.[7]

5   R. Ó Foghludha (ed.), *Cois na Bríde* (B.Á.C., 1937), pp xv. 19; H, Fenning, *The Irish Dominican Province 1698–1797* (Dublin, 1990), p. 144; Buttimer, 'Gaelic life and literature', p. 589.
6   For an analysis of the main newspaper sources for Inglis' poetry, see Buttimer, 'Gaelic life and literature', pp 585–96.
7   MacCraith, 'Filíocht Sheacaibíteach na Gaeilge: ionar gan Uaim?', in *Eighteenth Century Ireland*,

Before considering the reaction of Inglis and his literary contemporaries to the 1745 rebellion it is necessary to consider the reaction of the Catholic and Protestant communities. As was the case at the outset of most eighteenth-century European wars, the anticipation of a Spanish-English war in 1739 (The War of Jenkin's Ear), and the War of the Austrian Succession (1743–9), gave encouragement to the Irish Catholics. In one instance in 1739 in county Kildare, the Quakers bore the brunt of their wrath in the aftermath of the 5 November celebrations of the 'Popish plot'. The insurgents: 'set up the Pretender, meaning, as the examinant believes the image of straw and they burned the house of William Hall'. The subsequent arrest of fourteen Catholics resulted in raising a Catholic Jacobite mob who issued threats against informants and promised speedy deliverance for their imprisoned confederates.[8] Contemporary newspapers also provided some inkling of approaching war, while intercepted correspondence from Madrid to Carrickmacross in August 1739 concurred with their reports. It promised war in Ireland and England within six months and showed the continued linkage between Irish *émigrés* and their native land. This may have been responsible for the high spirits of the Catholic populace in neighbouring Dundalk.[9]

The Protestants in Munster experienced similar fears. In a letter to Henry Hamilton in September 1739, the endemic smuggling of south Munster was linked to rumours of war and a French descent on Ireland with 2,000 men who were to be quickly joined by 50,000 more.[10] The correspondence of his contemporary, Robert Purcell, provided startling corroborative evidence of the apprehensions of Protestants, and the expectations of 'the common Irish' at the prospect of a Spanish or Franco-Spanish descent.[11] While war was enthusiastically proclaimed throughout the major towns of Ulster, Protestant self-confidence remained at a low ebbles in the Cork area where a real sense of Papist elation was intensified by the fear of a French descent. Lacking a militia, some Protestants felt powerless to deal with intestine revolt and external descent.[12] Historians have shown an inclination to dismiss such contemporary optimism as naive or unrealistic. However, when placed in the context of the earl of Newcastle's despairing contemporary despatch to the duke of Devonshire a different picture emerges. He described the triumph of the French in Germany, the inevitability of the elector of Bavaria becoming emperor and the continued prospect of Dutch

---

ix (1994), pp 57–75; Ó Buachalla, *Aisling Ghéar*, pp 231–395.

8 Devonshire to the Secretary of State, 12 Jan. 1739 (S.P. Irel. 63, 403 f. 7); see also (S.P. 63, 403 f. 9); P.O.,12–15 Jan. 1740; P.O. 20–24 Feb. 1738/9; B. Ó Buachalla, 'Irish Jacobitism in official documents', in *Eighteenth Century Ireland*, viii (1993), pp 128–38.

9 Intercepted letter from Madrid [from one Ward], 29 Aug 1739 (S.P. 63, 402 f. 13).

10 Richard Toler to Henry Hamilton, 25 Sept. 1739 (S.P. 63, 402 f. 16).

11 R. Purcell to Perceval, 21 Mar. 1739 (B.L. Add. Mss. 47, 001A f. 53); see also ibid., ff 20, 41, 69.

12 *D.J.*, 6–10 Nov. 1739; see also *F.D.J.*, 13–17 Nov. 1739; *F.D.J.*, 27 Nov.–1 Dec. 1739; (N.L.I. 2478 f. 73).

neutrality, and thereby justified Inglis' expectations and those of his Irish Catholic contemporaries.[13]

Such fears undoubtedly contributed to the expectation of their Catholic counterparts. Inglis's poem, 'M'atuirse traochta na fearchoin aosta', composed in 1742, reflects the tangible benefits of Franco-Spanish triumphs for the Irish Jacobite nation. He expresses the hope that the banishment of the villians would free 'our' towns from high rents [possibly quarterage] and end the use of nicknames for Prince Charles. His arrival and the reduction of yellow John [the Protestants] would return all the lost churches, reverse the status of the English and Irish languages and end the enforced silence of the poets:

> Do ghlanfadh as Éirinn mar dhanair na méirligh
> 'S ár mbailte a shaoradh ó árd-chíos;
> ... s is mairg do bhéarfadh leas-ainm ar Shéarlas
> Do bhainfeadh a réim cheart de Seán Buidhe.
> ... Do cailleadh le tréimhse le chéile ár gcealla ...
> Is araid tá an Béarla 'is gan tapaidh 's an Ghaedhilg
> Is balbh ár n-éigse ar gnáth-chaoidh ...;[14]

Inglis' literary colleague Muiris Ó Gríobhtha replies to these lines, promising that the honourable prince of the blood of the MacCarthy's of Cashel [Charles Edward] would crush the English Whigs and make the yellow Johns [the Protestants] howl:

> Gur dhearchas prionnsa dfhuil Chaisil Chuirc ionnruic
> Ar shleasaibh na srúill thùir ag rámhaidheacht;
> Is geallaid go mbrúghfaid an gall-whig ciontach
> Is bainfid sin liúgh ar na Seáin Bhuidhe.[15]

Although Inglis pursued his studies in Rome during the 1745 rebellion the arrival and subesquent exploits of Charles Edward in Scotland did not pass the attention of his literary contemporaries. The poetry of Peadar Ó Doirnín, Séan Clárach MacDomhnaill, Seán na Ráithineach Ó Murchadha and Aindrias

---

13 Newcastle to Devonshire, 17 Sept. 1741 (N.L.I. Special list 335 [1], Chatworth papers T.3158 ff 180,326).
14 Inglis, 'M'atuirse traochta na fearachoin aosta', in Ó Foghludha (eag.), *Cois na Bríde*, p. 40. Seán Clárach reflects this 'secrecy' in contemporary song to the tune of the 'White Cockade': 'I will not tell you who is my love' *Ní mhaoidhfid féin cé hé mo stór, / Tá innsint scéil 'n-á dheidh go leor;/* ; Seán Clárach, 'Bidhim-sé buan ar bhuairt gach ló', in J. Hardiman (ed.), *Irish Minstrelsy*, 2 vols repr. (Shannon, 1972), ii, p. 70. His colleague Piaras Mac Gearailt promises that 'a nameless hero will heal all our pain and suffering' *Is geallaim go réidhfidh laoch gan ainm, gach péin agus ceasna orainn*; Mac Gearailt, 'An gheallamhain', in R. Ó Foghludha (eag.), *Amhráin Phiarais Mhic Gearailt 1700–1788* (B.Á.C., 1905), pp 35–6.
15 M. Ó Gríobhtha, 'Trém Aisling do smóineas', in Ó Foghludha (eag.), *Cois na Bríde*, pp 41–3.

MacCraith preoccupied themselves with Louis xv, Philip v, the French commander Mareschal Saxe, the Jacobite general, George Murray, and his Hanoverian adversaries, George Wade and Johnny Cope.[16]

The expectations and unease of Irish Jacobites and Whigs continued to be reflected in the now ritual anti-Jacobite fulminations in the popular press. The episcopal censures of the Protestant bishops of Dromore, Elphin, Clonfert, Armagh and Tuam invoked familiar anti-Papist rhetoric against 'the pernicious tendency of popery, the numerical superiority of Irish papists and the potential threat from the long abjured Pretender and his Roman, French and Spanish confederates'.[17] The immediacy of this Jacobite threat was also reflected at a popular level in Protestant commemoration of the anniversary of the 1641 in Youghal, county Cork. Having been set up in effigy, the Pretender's son was dressed in the familiar trappings of Jacobitism the highland plaid, the blue bonnet and the white rose, and insulted with the allegations of illegitimacy, popery, the wooden sword, the rosary beads and warming-pan.[18] Moreover Cumberland's crushing defeat of the rebels was greeted with great rejoicing in Protestant circles and the destroyer of Jacobitism became an icon of Irish popular Protestantism.[19]

In his sermon preached in thanksgiving for the suppression of rebellion, Moses Magill effectively summed up the attitude of many Protestants in the aftermath of '45. Not only did he provide an insight into prevalent Protestant unease which later manifested itself in the Seven Years War, but he also showed an acute appreciation of the Irish Jacobite political underground and reflected

---

16 Ó Foghludha (eag.), *Seán Clárach*, pp 54–5, 94–5, 100–01, 113; T. Ó Donnchadh (eag.), *Seán na Ráithíneach* (B.Á.C., 1954), pp 255–7; Ó Foghludha (eag.), *Éigse na Máighe*, pp 203–4; Ó Foghludha (eag.) *Míl na hÉigse: Duanaire i gcomhair an Ard-teastas* (B.Á.C., 1945), pp 46, 204; S. DeRís (eag.) *Peadar Ó Doirnín* (B.Á.C., 1968), p. 13.

17 J. Brady, *Catholics and Catholicism in the eighteenth-century press* (Maynoth, 1965), pp 68–9; Anon, *Seasonable advice to the Protestants of Ireland, containing some means of reviving and strengthening the Protestant interest* (Cork, 1745); *The Free Briton's advice to the Pretender's declaration supposed to be wrote by His Grace the Abshp. of Yke* (Dublin, 1745), p. 5; B. Barrington, *A sermon preached at St Andrew's before the honourable House of Commons* (Dublin, 1745), p. 11; Anon, *Monsieur Pretendant and Signioro Pretenderillo, a poem* (Dublin, 1745); W. Henry, *A Phillippic oration against the Pretender's son and his adherents addressed to the Protestants of the North of Ireland* (Dublin, 1745), p. 4; A. Maclaine, *A sermon preached at Antrim December 18 1745 being the national fast* (Dublin, 1746), pp 20–2; Anon, *Loyalty to our king and the safety of our country against all Popish emissaries and Pretenders, as to his most sacred Majesty King George II* (Dublin, 1745), pp. 5, 18; Anon, *An answer to the Pretender's Declaration* (Dublin, 1745); J. Foulke,*The duty of subjects to a good prince considered* (Dublin, 1745); *The layman's sermon occasioned by the present rebellion which was or ought to have been published at St Paul's Cross on 1st of October 1745* (Dublin and Belfast, 1745); H. Brooke,*The farmer's six letters to the Protestants of Ireland* (Dublin, 1746).

18 *D.J.*, 29 Oct.–2 Nov. 1745.

19 *Nelson's Dublin Courant*, 19 Dec. 1747 (N.L.I. Ms.1539); J. Kelly, 'The glorious, pious and immortal memory: commemoration and Protestant identity', in *R.I.A. Proc.*, 94c (Dublin, 1994), pp 25–52. For post-war autopisies in the press, see Copy of the diary of J. Pratt of Agher Co. Westmeath, Sept. 1745-may 1747 (N.L.I. m.f. P. 4160); see also *P.O.*, 29 Apr.-3 May 1746; *P.O* , 3-6 May 1746; *D.J.* 8-12 July 1746; *P.O*, 11-15 Nov. 1746; *P.O*, 15-18 Nov. 1746; *P.O.* 29 Nov. 1746.

on the gravity of Charles Edward's affront to the Hanoverian dynasty by his capture of Scotland. It is difficult to understand how historians have ignored Jacobitism as a substantial influence upon the outlook of Protestants in both Britain and Ireland in the aftermath of '45, choosing to preoccupy themselves with the onward march of the Protestant nation.[20] That issue has been too often summarily decided, in the case of Ireland by citing the absence of Jacobite activity during '45 without reference to English or Scottish Jacobite opportunism and inactivity, and the content of Jacobite poetry and its antithetical Whig counterpart. It should be clear from the evidence provided here that the reality of the threat was not so easily dismissed by contemporary Protestants.

This is also borne out by the pivotal position which James III retained in Irish Catholic affairs and by the links which were deemed to exist between the Jacobitism and Catholicism in Ireland in the aftermath of '45. The author of the contemporary Protestant pamphlet *The axe laid to the root* considered that the lives and properties of King George's Protestant subjects in Ireland remained as insecure as ever in the aftermath of the 1745 rebellion.[21] His claims are justified by the psychological impact of '45 on the Irish Protestant nation, manifested by the proliferation of *Cumberland, Hanover* and *Culloden* societies.[22] Nonetheless his notion that the authorities failed to impose penal legislation is not borne out in the immediate '45 period, nor does it make allowance for the psychological effects of its continued existence on the statute books, attested in the letters of Irish clergymen and in the poems of Liam Inglis during the Seven Years War.[23] Protestant trepidation at the prospect of a French descent, the successive invasion scares which later prompted the vindictive witch-hunt against Fr Nicholas Sheehy, and the associations between Whiteboyism and Jacobitism in the late 1750s and early 1760 show that the author's opinions survived in the popular Protestant consciousness, especially in Munster.[24]

These fears of a French descent provide a mirror image of the optimism of the contemporary Jacobite literati. In his 'Ar maidin ag caoidh dham' Inglis meets 'the faithful messenger of the white hawk' (Charles Edward Stuart). She informs him that 'the leader would come with one thousand ships to banish the foreigners while the brave hounds of Louis XV [the Irish Brigade] would relieve

20 L Colley, *Britons: forging the nation, 1707–1837* (London, 1992); S. Connolly, *Religion, law and power: the making of Protestant Ireland, 1660–1760* (Oxford, 1992). For opposite view, see J. Black, 'Could the Jacobites have won?', in *History Today*, xlv (July 1995), pp 24–30.

21 Anon,*The axe laid to the root, or reasons most humbly offered for putting the Popish clergy in Ireland under some better regulations* (Dublin, 1749), pp 4–5; Moses Magill, *A sermon preached in the parish church of St Mary's Dublin in general thanksgiving for the suppression of the unnatural rebellion* (Dublin, 1746), p. 16; Brooke, *The farmer's six letters*, p. 16.

22 J. Kelly, 'Immortal memory', pp 25–52; see also (R.A. 295 f. 164).

23 For opposite views on the psychological effects of the penal laws see Connolly, 'Religion and history', in *Irish Economic and Social History*, x (1983), p. 79; Ó Buachalla, Aisling Ghéar, p. 594.

24 J. Kelly, 'The Whiteboys: a contemporary account', in *Journ. the Cork Hit. and Arch. Soc.*, xci, no. 53, Jan–Dec 1989, pp 19–26; (N.L.I., *Vigours papers*, private collection f. 2548); see also *P.O.*, 26–30 June 1753; (N.A Church misc. 1652-1795 f. 205, 2/447/17);

the Gaels'. Retribution would quickly follow. The 'black-haired fanatic and the mean-hearted, disagreeable wretch [George II] would be thrown in the dung':

[Is mé] teachtaire díleas an tSeabhaic Bháin ...
"Is dearbh a chaoin-fhir, 's a ghreann dáimh
Go dtaistealfá an taoiseach go teann tráth
le seascadh ar míle
de bharcaibh go buidheanmhar
Chum Danair do dhíbirt don tseann-áit ...
In ' fhochair do chífeas go lonn-lán
Gasra Gaoidhlach an antláis/Calm-choin Laoisigh ...
Níl Fanatic cíor-dhubh is gann-cháil
Cé ceannasach suidheann sin ag ceann chláir
Ná smalaire an chroidhe bhoicht
Is ceachardha i gcuibhreann
Ná caitheamh san aoileach dá bpleangcáil.[25]

In another song in this genre 'An tAodhaire Óg', written to the tune of the 'Princess Royal' after Charles Edward's expulsion from Scotland in 1746, Inglis laments the captive condition of Ireland, 'the sweet wife of Art who is in captivity, imprisoned and crying out every day'. While 'her heroes are weak and her clergy without justice, the muse had foresaken her weeping poets'. Harking back to the traditional function of the poet as the mediator between the king and his kingdom, (and similar to his English and Scottish Jacobite contemporaries), Inglis recapitulated the dreary decay which resulted from Éire's abandonment of the young shepherd: 'the salmon had deserted the waterfall, the birds shunned their songs, while the oak commanded no respect, its branches were twisted and the mountains were shrouded in mist':

Is dárach an bheart do chéile ghil Airt
bheith i ndaor-bhroid, i ngéibheann 's ag éigheamh gach ló.;
... A laochra go lag, a cléirigh gan cheart,
A héigeas gan dréacht, ag maothughadh a ndeór
"s a faol-choin gur scaip a tréada ar fad
Ó b'éigean dó tréigean,–an tAodhaire Óg.
Níl éigne ar eas, ná gaortha go glas,
Acht éanlaith go héadmhar ag séanadh a gceóil
Ar aon dair níl meas acht a ngéaga go cas
'S na sléibhthe in éinfeacht fé bhréidhibh ceóidh;[26]

25 Inglis, 'Ar maidin ag caoidh liom', in Ó Foghludha (eag.), *Cois na Bríde*, pp 22–3. See also ibid., pp 24–5.
26 Piaras Mac Gearailt, in a note written on a version of this poem in Maynooth from 1766, asks 'that

In another of his poem 'Póiní an leasa', Inglis follows the standard trope of
the brazen harlot, a favourite among Irish literati from Céitinn to Ó Rathaille.
The sorrowing woman 'formerly wedded to Eoghan and his father was now the
young harlot of British George'. The poet laments that 'the wife of the warlike
lion has yielded to the advances of this greasy, smug stranger'. He points out the
error of her ways, 'the decay and mist on her churches and the sorrow and
danger which affected her clergy'. However, he believes that her hour of deliverance approached as 'the young Caesar in Rome, of the race she had married
before, is coming across the sea and that he is the true spouse of Ireland':

Is baoth mo ghlórtha, is dóigh nár mheathas
Cé gur phósas Eoghan is a athair
Is gléigeal snódh'Mo ghéag ar ndóigh
'S mé im méirdrigh óig ag Seóirse Breatan.
Mo léan, mo bhrón, do ghlórtha mheabhail
A chéile chóir na leóghan lannach
A ghné mar rós
Is baoth an gnó
Duit géill ná góbhail le stróinse smeartha.
Féach-sa a óig-bhean mhódhmhrach mhaireach
T'fhéinnidh feóidhthe is ceó ar do cheallaibh
An chléir go deórach
Baol gach brónach
Tréig-se Seóirse, is geóbhair a mhalairt.
Tá Caesar óg sa Róimh 'n-a bheathaidh
Aon den phór úd phosais cheana
Ag gléasadh a shlóighthe
Ag teacht thar bóchna
Is é sin nóchar Phóiní an leasa.[27]

This consideration of the post-'45 religious and political context provided
the necessary background for an examination of the Seven Years' War. In a letter
to Newcastle in October 1747, Harrington, the new lord lieutenant of Ireland,
represented the uncertainty of public affairs and the need to put the country in
some state of defence in case of an invasion from abroad. These preparations
included orders for an immediate country-wide militia array, an exact report on
the state of the forts and fortresses in the realm and the recruiting of additional

God might bestow some sense on the half-wit who recited this verse for it was Liam Inglis' *go dtuga*
Dia ciall don leath-éarla adubhairt an duanóg seo, ó's é Liam Inglis é; ibid., p. 25.

27 Inglis, 'Póiní an leasa', in ibid., p.25. For a parallel in the Scottish Jacobite tradition, see J. Hogg
(ed.), *The Jacobite Relics of Scotland*, 2 vols (Paisley, 1874), i, p. 144.

forces in Great Britain with a warning to prevent the danger of admitting papists into the army.[28]

The arrival of suspected French officers raised the old bugbears of recruitment and treasonable machinations. This prompted Harrington to petition the duke of Newcastle for an extension of the powers granted during Chesterfield's government to detain and open suspected seditious correspondence.[29] His suspicions were not totally unfounded. James Dunne, in a letter to the Stuart court, alluded to a diversionary Irish invasion plot emanating from a Dubliner called Macallester who aided the '45 prisoners in London and had come to Paris to serve Eneas McDonnell the banker. He later provided a very long corroborative memoir to the French king in 1759 advocating a descent on Ireland on behalf of the Stuart king.[30]

Such fears resounded in the press and reinforced the popular Protestant opinions of Irish Catholic deception. According to one contemporary pamphleteer, the power of France, France's over-running Holland and possessing her naval ports and shipping, and effecting a descent on Ireland, would uncover the true sentiments of the papists. Such sentiments, often only evident in Jacobite poetry and secret correspondence to the exiled court, have been consistently ignored, as it is now proposed to show.[31]

Lionel Cranfield, the earl of Dorset, lord lieutenant of Ireland, (September 1751–April 1755) received other reports of Catholic disaffection in 1751, particularly in relation to the Jacobite agents 'Foley' and 'Colonel Mahony'. Foley had allegedly been involved in carrying correspondence between the Stuart court and its Irish sympathisers, while Mahony had recently gone into that kingdom.[32] Dorset also received intelligence relating to the activities of a group of Jacobites in Ennis, county Clare. Relating this information to the lord lieutenant, he advised him to use the utmost discretion 'in the use of letters of a very discreet nature'.[33] The note of alarm in these dispatches reflected the continued shock-value of Jacobitism and the contemporary fears in Protestant political circles.

Seditious Jacobite activity and plots continued to preoccupy the lord lieutenant in the late summer of 1752. Newcastle even reported to Dorset that Charles Edward was in Ireland as a part of a grand agitation related to the Pretender's

---

28 Harrington to Newcastle, 5 Oct. 1747 (S.P. 63, 410 f. 67).
29 Harrington to Newcastle, 8 Oct. 1747 (S.P. 63, 410 f. 72).
30 J. Dunne to James III, Paris, 6 Aug. 1747 (R.A 286 f. 59). He later turned out to be a Jacobite double-agent, see O. MacAllester, *A series of letters discovering the scheme projected by France in MDCCLIX for an intended invasion upon England with flat-bottomed boats*, 2 vols (London, 1762).
31 Anon, *The state of the nation for the year 1747 and respecting 1748 inscribed to a member of the present parliament* (Dublin, 1748), p. 27.
32 Holdernesse to the Lord Lieutenant, 10 Oct. 1751 (S.P. 67/12/10[5]); see also (S.P. 63, 414 f.192); Brady (ed.), *Catholics and Catholicism*, p. 80; P. Fagan (ed.), *Ireland in the Stuart papers*, 2 vols (Dublin, 1996), ii, pp 172, 178, 317; J. Hume-Weygand, 'Epic of the Wild Geese', in *University Review*, ii, no. 2 (1962), p. 31; L. Cullen, *The emergence of modern Ireland* (London, 1981), p. 32–3.
33 Holdernesse to Dorset, Whitehall, 4 Apr. 1752 (S.P. 67/12 f. 38 [19]); (S.P. 63, 412 f. 288).

removal to Avignon.[34] He urged Dorset to carry out the necessary private en-
quiries but again cautioned against raising unnecessary alarm.[35] The activities
of returned *émigrés*, French privateers and enlistees for the foreign service continued to capture the attention of the authorities in the midst of the drift towards war with France.[36] Rumours of a French invasion were subsequently circulated by Lord Inchiquin in April 1755 causing fears among the populace in
Dublin.[37] The real dangers of such a descent and the government's continued
unwillingness to antagonize Catholics became even more apparent in the correspondence of Sir Richard Wilmot to the duke of Devonshire. He advised caution against giving the Papists 'any handle for complaint at a critical time when
invasion from France was daily expected and accounts from America were bad'.[38]
Similarly, contemporary unrest in Dublin in this period had a distinctively Jacobite flavour; the assembled mob purportedly wore white cockades.[39]

Such sentiments are reflected in the correspondence of John Ryder, the Anglican archbishop of Tuam. Reporting between 1755–6, he asserted that the
leading Catholic gentry, while 'insisting that there were no plans for a rising,
(they) did not conceal from us their fears that the populace, of which 99 per cent
were Catholics, would not be restrained from violence at the landing of a foreign
force'.[40] Invasion rumours continued to circulate in early 1756. One reported
that a Prussian officer was engaged in recruiting for the French army.[41] Another
alleged that a French general and an engineer had allegedly visited Ireland to
extract information about the strength of the garrisons.[42] Horace Walpole, in
continued communication with the old Jacobite watch-dog Sir Horace Mann in
Florence, remained apprehensive, believing that the French designed to send a
body of troops and twenty-thirty thousand arms into the kingdom. He also
supplied the Lord Lieutenant, Devonshire with news of the movements of the
French army on the coast. Devonshire consequentially undertook the necessary
precautions to put the country in a better state of defence. A considerable quan-
tity of artillery was deployed at the coastal ports of Charles Fort, near Kinsale,
Duncannon and Passage, near Waterford, and Galway.[43] Other interested par-

---

34 Newcastle to Dorset, Hanover, 12/28 Aug. 1752 (S.P. 63, 412).
35 Newcastle to Dorset, Hanover, 12/28 1752 (S.P. 63, 412 f. 337); see also S.P. 63, 412 f. 341); (S.P. 63,
    413 f. 77).
36 Dorset to Sir T. Robinson, 5 May 1754 (S.P. 63, 413 f. 180); see also (S.P. 67/12/ 81 [41]); (N.L.I.
    Special list 335[2], *Chatham papers*, T. 3158/725).
37 Charles O'Hara to Lady Michael, 18 Apr. 1755, in Transcript of the O'Hara papers in P.R.O.N.I.
    (N.L.I 16, 943); Brady (ed.), *Catholics and Catholicism*, p. 86.
38 Sir R. Wilmot to Devonshire, St James's St, 24 Oct. 1755 (N.L.I. Special list 335[2], *Chatham
    papers*, T. 3158' 950). See also (S.P. 63, 413 ff. 212, 229, 327).
39 Hartington to the Sec. of State, 25 Aug. 1755 (S.P. 63, 413 f. 287).
40 Connolly, *Religion, law and power*, p. 245.
41 H. Fox to Devonshire, Jan. 1756 (S.P. 63, 414 ff 1-3).
42 Anonymous letter to the Lord Lieutenant, 21 Jan. 1756 (N.L.I. Special list 335[2], *Chatham papers*
    T.3158'1084).
43 Horatio Walpole to Devonshire, 26 Feb. 1756 (N.L.I. Special list 335[2], *Chatham papers* T.3158/

ties in Ireland were also in receipt of invasion news from abroad. Thus an intercepted letter from John Hetherington in Paris in February 1756 gave details of the movements of the Irish brigades towards the coast which was corroborated by an affidavit sworn by one Philip Dwyre. Captured on a French privateer from St Malo, taken before a judge at Morlaix and questioned regarding the state and situation of the king's forces in Ireland, Dwyre was assured that 'if he had a mind to join any of the French brigades' he might 'soon be in his own country as it was expected they should soon pay a visit there.'[44]

The popular press and the correspondence of major political figures in this period are filled with news of this possible French invasion and continuing Franco-English colonial rivalry, in particular the arrest, trial and execution of the English admiral, John Byng, for his failure to relieve Majorca.[45] Significantly Inglis' poetry offers a glimpse of Catholic reaction to the fate of the unfortunate admiral. A poem addressed to âadhbhard de Nógla [Edward Nagle] (son of the Jacobite lawyer, Patrick Nagle, close friend of the executed Jacobite leader, Sir James Cotter), alluded to Byng. It allowed Inglis the opportunity to engage in some clever word play at his expense: 'It is sweet [*binn*] for us to hear of Byng and his friends in sorrow'.[46]

Complementing the evidence of the press and contemporary poetry, *émigré* correspondence with the courts of the Stuarts and the French king also testifies to the centrality of Jacobitism as a feature of Irish political culture at this period. Its habitual optimism reflects is sometimes tempered in consequence of the estrangement of the French king from his would-be confederate, Charles Edward. Nevertheless it is a mistake to construe this disquiet with Charles Edward's intransigence as signifying a terminal cooling of Irish *émigré* Jacobite zeal. Rather sympathy for the French king's position reflects a realistic grasp of the military and political situation. It ultimately mirrored the Stuart patriarch's disquiet at the prince's continual snubs to the French king, and the over-riding political reality that Charles Edward needed Louis xv more than Louis xv needed him.[47] One commentator, Heguerty, reiterated his Jacobite principles and described the woes which had befallen Britain under the forty year-old Hanoverian yoke.

1151); see also (S.P. 63, 414 ff. 67, 136), 138); P. Cunningham (ed.), *Letters of H. Walpole to Sir H. Mann, in 9 vols* (London, 1891), i, pp 507–8; Lord Dover (ed.), *Letters of H. Walpole to Sir H. Mann*, 3 vols (London, 1833), iii, pp 98, 114, 319, 323, 325, 327, 339, 347.

44 John Hetherington to Dennis—, Paris, 7 Feb. 1756 (N.L.I. 9618 f. 21); affidavit sworn by Phillip Dwyre, 19 Oct. 1756 (S.P. 63, 414 f. 304).

45 Shannon correspondence (N.L.I. Special list 206[1]).

46 '*S is binn linn Byng is a chairde i mbrón!*/; Inglis, 'A Eadbháird aoibhinn uasail áluinn', in Ó Foghludha (eag.), *Cois na Bríde*, p. 42. Éadhbhard de Nógla mocked that 'we will not need Byng now as he is in sorrow' '*S ní dith linn Byng mar atá fá bhrón*, in R. Ó Foghludha (eag.), *Míl na hEigse: Duanaire i gcomhair an Árd-teastais* (B.Á.C., 1945), p. 51.

47 Heguerty to Edgar, Paris, 10 Nov. 1755 (R.A., Ms 359, f. 152). See also (R.A., Ms 360, f. 47). For discussion of Heguerty's relationship with Charles Edward, see M. Beresford, 'Ireland in the French strategy 1691–1789' (M. Litt thesis, T.C.D., 1975), pp 169–73, 195, 209–20.

The standard Jacobite arguments of spiralling indebtedness and the usurping house's territorial commitments on the continent justified his call for a French-inspired second revolution and an amalgamation of the powers of Europe against Britian's martial tyranny. In his opinion, the French-sponsored invasion of England must be 'headed by the only man who would make them welcome there' [Charles Edward].[48] He discussed ongoing rumours of a Stuart-led French invasion of either Scotland or Ireland as a prerequisite to the proclamation of Charles Edward as king. Although this proposal typified French opportunism and infuriated the Stuart prince, it cannot be interpreted as the termination of Heguerty's Jacobite loyalty. Like Charles Edward, he viewed such a move as nothing more than a stepping-stone to the subjugation of all three kingdoms.[49]

Other Irish Jacobites in France were confident of a favourable turn in Jacobite fortunes.[50] Thomas Lally, governor of Bologna (d. 1766), whose military judgement had been proven at Fontenoy and at Bergen-op-Zoom, remained convinced that the prince was still France's most powerful trump card. He advocated sending a diversionary force of eight or ten thousand men to Ireland or Scotland. He also shared the prince's opinion that the ailing condition of George II and the weakness of the Prince of Wales augured well for the Jacobite cause. Lally professed to believe that the prospect of a Stuart restoration never appeared brighter.[51]

While Lally provided a military assessment of the possibility of a Stuart Restoration, Father Bernard Rothe stressed the need for a concrete agreement to be made between James III and Louis XV in relation to a French landing in England. He advised that all matters pertaining to the choice of troops, generals and equipment should be left to 'His Most Christian Majesty'. His call for caution and discretion showed an appreciation of the delicate relationship between the French king and Charles Edward whom he urged not to come into French territory until called for.[52] His hopes for a favourable turn in the king's affairs appeared more realistic with the agreeable disposition of French affairs in Bohemia, Frederick the Great of Prussia's flight from Prague, the rupture between the Empress Maria Théresa and the elector of Hanover and the daily increase in dissent in England. Rothe believed that the ever-persecuted Catholics enjoyed the greatest peace and tranquillity since 1688 due to the level of Protestant trepidation in Ireland. However, his belief that this new-found freedom remained subject to Protestant perceptions revealed something of the con-

---

48 Heguerty to Charles, 25 Jan. 1756 (R.A., Ms 363, f. 65). See also (R.A., Ms 362, f. 167); (R.A., Ms 363, fol. 26); (R.A., Ms 365, f. 58); (R.A., Ms 364, f. 65); (R.A., Ms 367, f. 167). Fagan (ed.), *Stuart Papers*, i, p. 295.
49 Heguerty to Charles 21 July 1756 (R.A., Ms 363, f. 147).
50 For example Myles McDonnell to [Edgar], Corunna, 27 Dec. 1755 (R.A., Ms 360, f. 100); C. Rothe to James III, Paris, 4 Jan. 1756 (R.A., Ms 360, f. 162). See also Beresford, 'Ireland', p. 197.
51 Lally to Charles, 18 May 1756 (R.A 362, f. 146); Beresford, 'Ireland', p. 192.
52 Fr B. Rothe to James III, Paris, 10 Jan. 1757 (R.A., Ms 368, f. 27). See also (R.A., Ms 372, f. 55).

tinuing psychological burden of the penal laws on Irish Catholics in the period.[53]

Rothe's optimism was not totally unfounded. A 'tableau politique pour le campaigne de la present anneé 1757' proposed availing of England's present political difficulties to effect an invasion of England with thirty thousand soldiers and four thousand cavalry, backed up by a batallion of artillery. A diversion to Ireland by the Irish Brigades remained a mandatory requirement for the success of such a venture.[54] This optimism is also revealed in Fr James McKenna cryptic correspondence to the Stuart court which mirrored the hopes of Jacobites resident in Ireland:

> I had an account from the L. N. [Linen Hall] yesterday telling me that the *customers* cry out and they wish even for your factor [Charles Edward] with his friendly F.R. [France?] to come now to their relief. God grant them their desires and soon, as they really expect either this season or the farthest the next. Be well assured that your factor's place of abode is not yet discovered, but I do everywhere assure his friends that you and he are living and by God's blessing, well. Our youngster [Lord Lieutenant] is now every day expected here from East or Eutropia. I suppose you know him the *Hunter* of drofdeb [Bedford], and we begin to be very apprehensive of the same against you, and us, as were endeavoured in our last Change [Parliament] as the same spirits do still predominantly in each party of the *Dealers* [Patriot party] *Jobbers* [Court party] amongst us. The *Jobbers* and *Citizens* with their adherents look very demure especially since the late almost total *paid* or payment [defeat] of the Velvet Dresser of P.R.[Prussia] and of Mr Van Scheuter [Cumberland], which you all well know of by this time. Who if he returns to the East as he desires, we are thinking of his fate somewhat like to that of Gnib [Byng] …[55]

This international conflict had ramifications for the Stuart cause and it is no coincidence that both interlocking themes dominated contemporary political poetry. The Munster poets renewed their entreaties to Prince Charles and his partisans in the Irish Brigades. Seán Ó Cuinneagáin, composing in 1754, reiterated his trust in 'the birds who were called Geese who would help Prince Charles, the greatest warrior since Fionn MacCumhaill, to tear, destroy and scatter the rotten pigs':

53 Fr B. Rothe to James III, 4 July 1757 (R.A., Ms 373, f. 26). See also fn. 23 T. McLoughlin, 'A crisis for the Irish in Bordeaux in 1756', in M. O'Dea and K. Whelan (eds), *Nations and nationalisms: France, Britain, Ireland and the eighteenth century context* (Oxford, 1995), pp 135–8, 140–1; R. Hayes, *Irish swordsmen in France* (Dublin, 1934), p. 11.
54 'Tableau politique et militaire pour la campaigne de la present anneé 1757' (R.A., Ms 378, f. 53).
55 Fr James McKenna to James, 23 Aug. 1757 (R.A., Ms 374, fol. 49), edited in Fagan (ed.), *Stuart papers*, ii, pp 213–4.

Casfaidh na h-éanlaith dá n-gairmthear géanna
an arm go gleasda gan spár puinn
ag cabhair le Séarlas- an cathbhile is tréine
dár sheasaimh ó d'eagadar cnámha Fhinn
creichfaidh is ceasfaidh/'s scaipfidh na bréan-toirc.[56]

An examination of Inglis's poetry shows that he knew exactly what was going on. He espouses the cause of the king of France, the empresses of Austria and Russia, and the heroic deeds of their illustrious generals including Count Daun and Ulysses Browne who took the field against the king of Prussia. In his poem 'Leastar an Bhráthar' [1757], he provides an allegorical account of the progress of the Seven Years War, based, as Cornelius Buttimer has shown, on information gleaned from the local *Cork Journal*. According to the poet, 'The king of Prussia suddenly unsheathes his sword in his right hand and wages war against the gentle, amiable Empress Maria Théresa who sends (Marshal Ulysses) Browne like [the mythical Irish hero] Fionn [MacCumhaill] against him'. Meanwhile, 'the empress of Russia joins the fray as an important prop to her Austrian counterpart, while the clever French spread like a flood across the plains of Italy'. The poet rejoices that 'with all Europe in his [the French king's] pocket, the noise of the waves is annoying [Admiral Edward] Hawke whose fleet has been trapped in the Bay of Biscay'.

---

56 Ua Cuinneagán, 'Teacht na ngéanna fiadhaine', in J. O'Daly (ed.), *Poets and the poetry of Munster* (dubli, 1848), p. 168. See also 'Seán Clárach ar leaba a bháis go Éamonn de bhFál', in R. Ó Foghludha (eag.), *Seán Clárach, 1691–1754* (B.Á.C., 1932), p. 33. The poet Eoghan an Mhéirín places his hopes in 'the brave dragon of the true blood of McCarthy' *A dhragain Chuthaigh de Chárrth-fhuil úir*; in R. Ó Foghludha (eag.), *Eoghan an Mheirín MacCárthaigh, 1691–1756* (B.Á.C., 1938), p. 23; and 'those who did not abandon Spain and Louis' *an méid nach d'fhág an Spáinn 's Laoiseach*; in ibid., p. 31. Muiris Ó Gríobhtha longs for the arrival of 'radiant Louis as a prop for the troop, thousands of valiant heroes in accompaniment, leading warriors at their head from Britain and Gaels coming merrily from Scotland' *Tá Laoiseach lasmhar ina thaca ag an bhuidheansa / ag an Chraoibhinn aoibhinn álainn óg /'S na millte galach le gaisge dá choimhdeacht / atá Laochradh ceannais ó Bhreatain go bríoghmhar / Gaoidhil go greantadh a' sliocht Alban aoirde;* Ó Gríobhtha, in P. Walsh (ed.), *Reliques of Irish Jacobite poetry*, 2nd ed. (Dublin, 1866), p. 93. Aindrias Mac Craith praises 'Charles and his armed armada' *Carolus Lonn 's a chabhlach gleusta*; Mac Craith, 'Duain na Saoirse', in M. Comer-Bruen, 'Aindrias Mac Craith, An Mangaire Sugach. Tráchtas ar a shaol agus a shaothar' (M. Litt. thesis, T.C.D., 1967), p. 92. Seán Clárach lauds 'the gentle brave men of the noble race of Milesius' *na fir-chaoin chródha dhe chóir-sliochd Mhilésius*, 'Síle Ní Ghadhra', in Hardiman (ed.), *Irish Minstrelsy*, ii., p. 54, and 'the true Scots who would come back across the sea without doubt' *Fíor-Scoit na tíre do crádhadh le pléid / Fillidh gan mhaíll chughainn tar sáil 'gan bhréig*; 'A Shaoin ghlain de phríomh scoth', in Ó Foghludha (eag.), *Seán Clárach'*, p. 85. Eoghan Rua Ó Suilleabháin hopes that 'valiant Charles and his hearty troop will attack us easily by sea' *Tá Séarlas mear 'sa thrúip ghroidhe, D'ár n-íonsaidhe go h-Áasga ar seùl ; Filleadh Rí Séarlas'*, in Walsh (ed.), *Reliques*, p. 64. See also O'Daly (ed.), *Reliques of Jacobite poetry* (Dublin, 1844), p. 72. Ó Muirithe's translations of Seán Clérach's poetry also eulogised the Wild Geese; D. Ó Muirithe, 'Though not in full stile compleat: Jacobite songs from Gaelic manuscript sources', in *Eighteenth Century Ireland*, vi (1990), p. 98. Tadhg Gaelach Ó Súilleabháin praises 'the sharp, battle-hardened, fiercely determined warriors of the Gael' *gasra ghéirchatha Ghaodhlach dheaghghníomhach*; 'Ar maidin indé dham', in R. Ó Foghludha (eag.), *Tadhg Gaelach 1715–1795* (B.Á.C., 1929), p. 104.

Nochtann a cholg go hobann n-a láimh dheis
Is cuireann cogadh go hullamh ar Mháire-
An bhain-ímpire mhíonla, mhánla,
Chuir sí an Brúnach mar Fhionn 'san áth roimhe ...
Tá ag triall adtuaidh sluagh go táinteach
Ó Ríoghan Ruise ursa thábhachtach,
Tá ag triall andeas go prap le dásacht
Frangcaigh chliste mar thuile le fánaidh;
Tá anois ag triall ó iaith Iodáile
Curadh cathbhuadhach eacluath láidir;
Tá an Eóraip uile 'n-a chuimhil a mhála ...
Tá torann tonn ag bodhradh Hawke
Is é gan im, gan meidhg, gan bláthaigh
Tá a chobhlach uile i Muir Bhioscáine.[57]

Inglis' shows that the poets remained committed to the Jacobite cause in this period. He exhibits an awareness of the course of developments relevant to the Stuart cause in continental diplomacy. His poetry urged similar support for the Catholic clergy and aristocracy, maintaining a venerable poetic prerogative, continuing his allegorical narrative of the war in the woeful tale of the theft of his shoes, 'Mo ghearán crua le hUislibh Fódhla' [My hard complaint to the nobles of Ireland]. He satirically emphasised the difficulties of 'the king of Prussia and William, son of George [the duke of Cumberland], under oppression in Hanover'. The 'Butcher' was at that time 'in the grip of the brave Frenchmen, unable to move by coach or swift horse, and lying flat on his big arse':

Acht mac ár dtriath-na Uilliam mac Sheóirse
Atá fá chiach i ndiaidh Hanóbhar!
Atá sé i dteannta ag Frangcaigh chródha
In amhgar, in antart, i bpóna;
Ní tualaing é ar ghluaiseacht i gcóiste
Nó ar luath-each fá mhuar-phlaic a thóna.[58]

The continued woes of the elector of Hanover provides the main themes of his poem 'An eól díbhse a dhaoine i bhFionn Fáil' [Do you know, oh people of Ireland?]. The title of this poem is itself worthy of consideration. If 'they' did

57 Inglis, 'Leastar an bhráthar', in Ó Foghludha (eag.), *Cois na Bríde*, p. 27. Éadhbháird de Nógla replied to this poem in the same year, 'Mo chumha is mo dhanaidh', in ibid., p. 28; see also Buttimer, 'Gaelic literature and contemporary Irish life', pp 589, 591, 594, 596. C. Duffy, *The Wild Goose and the eagle: a life of Marshal Browne, 1705–57* (London, 1964). E. Sagarra, 'Frederick II and his image in eighteenth-century Dublin', in *Hermathena*, cxlii (1987), pp 50–8.
58 Inglis, 'Mo ghearán chruaidh le hUislibh Fódhla', in Ó Foghludha (eag.), *Cois na Bríde*, p.30.

not already know the intricate details of the Seven Years' War and particularly
the reversals suffered by King George, then Inglis addressed his poem to them.
This provides a further example of the poets' role in the diffusion of news to the
Irish-speaking public. To the poet's great joy, 'George was defeated and in such
great distress that if he soiled his trousers the tide would not clean his arse'. He
assures his listeners that 'Prague would not fall and that the king [Fredrick the
Great] would be scorched by Count Daun'. Inglis promises that 'thunder [mili-
tary might] was coming across the sea in the form of the French king and his
hosts to exalt the Stuart'. The poet hopes that 'the bright, brave, true-blooded
soldier [Charles Edward] would be surrounded by bishops and priests in abun-
dance':

> An eól díbhse i bhfonn Fáil
> Seóirse go claoidhte 's i lom-ghábha?
> Aiteas mo chroidhe istigh
> Mar theagmuig a bhríste
> 'S is Ní glanfadh an taoide a theampán!
> ... Geallaimse díbhse nár gabhadh Prág ...
> 'S do greadadh an Rí le Count Daun ...
> Tá tóirneach ar bóchna agus foghail ghnáth
> Agus gheóbhthar poll dóighte sa chómhlán
> Airgfidh Laoiseach
> A mbailte 's a dtíortha
> Is casfaidh an Stíobhart go ceann-árd:
> Faraire 'en fhíor-fhuil, tá fionn breágh
> Ba mhaise don ríoghacht é fé bheann cháidh;
> Beidh easpuig 'n-a thimcheall
> Is sagairt go líonmhar
> 'S mbeatha aca dílis go seang sámh.[59]

His colleague Pádraig Ó hÉigceartaigh, commended him on his poem, 'its
wealth of genuine truth, without exaggeration or joking on the wars in which
our enemies have been laid low'. Ó hÉigceartaigh's stirring compliments should
be borne in mind by historians who wish to evaluate the effects of the Seven
Years' War in Ireland and the political content of eighteenth-century poetry:

> Is acfuinneach aoibhinn do rann bhreágh
> 'S is dearbtha dílis gan antlás
> Is tarraigthe líonmhar

---

59 Inglis, 'An eól díbhse a dhaoine i bhfionn Fáil', in Ó Foghludha (eag.), *Cois na Bríde*, p. 32. See also
    Dover (ed.) *Letters*, iii, , pp 229–30.

Na cathanna coimeascair
'N-ar leagadh ár naímhide go fann tláth.[60]

In another of his poems, 'Atá an báire imeartha réidh', [the game is up] Inglis gloats on the strength of the warrior Daun who, with the strong Russians, would outmanoeuvre the Prussian king. He adds that 'the French general Constades will pursue the English and that the duke of Brunswick is without direction'. Not content solely with providing news of the European war, he turns to the Canadian and American theatres which, as Buttimer suggests, had become the main focus of the English war-effort in early-1758 under the overall leadership of William Pitt the Elder. In Canada, he notes 'the distress of the English Admiral [Edward] Boscawen in the straits of St Cassien'. He rejoices that 'in America the devil is on them altogether as they were left oppressed and afflicted after the battle at Ticonderoga where only one-third of them survived'. Moreover 'at Fort De Quesne they lay on their arses with the sun on the shattered timbers of their fallen flags':

Atá Daun an curadh go cumasach tréan
'S dár leat is dubhach atá a námhaid;
Ní tláth na Ruisigh i siomsa na bpléar,
Ní táir an ursa iad ag druidim le baoghal
Is breágh do chluicfidh an Prúiseach is a scaoth ...
Constades glacfaidh an t-amas go cóir
Is cionnárd a leanfaidh na Danair sa tóir,
Atá Brunswick i ríocht puic gan treóir
Is fágaimíd súd mar atá sé!
... Féach ar an amhgas n-a bhfuil cabhlach Boscawen
Féach an dteannta n-a raibh ag St Cas.
In Americe siar, tá an diabhal ortha ar fad,
Do fágadh 'san ngliadh iad fá chiach is fá cheas,
Ní tháinig leath a dtrian as, acht iarmhar beag lag
An lá san do bhíodar ag Ticonderoga;
Ag Fort Dhu Quesne ní léire bhí a mbail
Do thúrnadh gach n-aon ar an gcléir Senegal
Atá a dtóin leis an ngréin ag baoltaigh na mbrat
Is fágaimíd súd mar atá sé!.[61]

---

60 Ó hÉigcearthaigh, 'Is acfuinneach aoibhinn', in Ó Foghludha (eag.), *Cois na Bríde*, p. 33. In his poem 'An Fanuidhe', to the popular Jacobite tune 'over the water to Charlie', Tadhg Gaelach promises that 'Maria [Theresa] will have her crown and lands *'a coróin is a críocha ag Máire; in Ó Foghludha* (eag.), *Tadhg Gaelach*, pp 106–7.

61 Inglis, 'Atá an báire imeartha réidh', in Ó Foghludha (eag.), *Cois na Bríde*, p. 38. Ó Foghludha dates this poem from the year 1757 while Buttimer opts for 1758, Buttimer, 'Gaelic literature and contemporary Irish life', p. 594.

In his poem 'Do Mheidhbhín Ní Shúilleabháin' [To little Meabh Sullivan],
Inglis stresses that 'war-like bands were coming across the sea in slender ships
in black floods'. On their arrival, 'the songs of the clergy will be heard in the
church of Christ with the sweet knell to summon all, the progeny of the Gaels
will be in the fine houses and their inheritance, the group that is strong will be
reduced and the tables turned on the churls who extinguished poetry':

Tar bhóchna ghlais i luing chaoil
Go aoird gcrainn na ndubh-shruthain,
Tig slóighthe cliste i bhfeidhm claoidhimh
Le cruinn-ghaoith go lúthmhar lán,
... Beidh ceól na cléire i gcill Chríost
Agus creidhill bhinn dá mhúascailt tráth,
Beidh pór na nGaedhal n'a ndeigh-thigheas
'S a n-oidhrí n-a ndúthchas gnáth,
An slógh atá tréan gan puinn bríghe-
Na claidhrí do mhuc an dáimh-.[62]

The defeat of Cumberland in 1757 and the loss of George II's electoral lands
to the French king prompted his biting satire on King George, 'Is ró-dhian a
screadann'. He mocked George II 'for no longer having Hanover, Hesse Cassel
and his forefathers' ancestral lands and also that the elector no longer had the
shelter of Britain, nor the lands of Ireland, nor the fidelity of the Scots since he
cut their throats'. Inglis believes that George's defeat will 'spell death for the
clergy of Calvin while the learned clergy of [St] Peter would endure forever':

Is ró-dhian a screadann an sean-duine Seóirse
"Ó, a Dhia, cá racadh? níl agam Hanóbhar,
Ná fos Hesse-Cassel, mo bháile beag cómhgair,
Ná fód mo shean-athrach,Táid airgthe dóighte! ...
Níl dion dam Breatain ná fearanna Fódla,
Níl dílis dam Alba ó ghearras a scórnach, ...
Mo chiach! Mo lagar! Ní fheadar cá ngeobhaidh sin-
Iarmhar Chailbhin do sheachain na cómhachta-
I mbliana béam bascaithe leagaithe leóinte
Is cliar chliste Pheadair 's a mbeatha go deó aca!.[63]

62 Inglis, 'Do Mheidhbhín Ní Shúilleabháin', Ó Foghludha (eag.), *Cois na Bríde*, p. 41.
63 Inglis, 'Is ró-dhian a screadann', in Ó Foghludha (eag.), *Cois na Bríde*, p. 35. 'Séan Buidhe', a poem
    falsely credited to Séan Clárach (who died in 1754), attacks the duke of Cumberland after his defeat
    in Hanover in 1757, see (B.L., Add. Ms 31,874, fol.14). Piaras Mac Gearailt calls 'Little Molly
    [Ireland] to his side to tell her with great joy that George is crying and roaring' *Siúd a stóir, láimh
    liom a stór/ Is innseógadh duit le háthas/go bhfuil Seoirse ag gól is ag scairtigh*; 'A Mhalaí beag ó', Ó
    Foghludha (eag.), *Amhráin Phiarais Mhic Gearailt*, p. 30.

In his poem, 'Atá an fhuireann so thall gan amhras díleas', Inglis names the main benefactor of the elector's defeat, 'An craoibhín aoibhinn álainn óg' [The lovely little branch, Charles Edward]. His arrival will ensure that 'the poets would no longer be afraid to speak their treason, those who break the Friday fast [Protestants] would be under pressure and fear' and that 'before three months, the Gaels will get freedom of speech and our Catholic clergy will receive funeral offerings':

Dá dtigeadh an t-aon so ghaodhaim le hintinn
'S a thaisteal thar tuinn do gheóbhainn cead spóirt,
'S nár bh'eagal don éigse a dtréason d'innsint
Gur b'iad lucht briste na hAoine do thuill a ndóghadh;
... Súl a gcaithfeam trí mhí gheóbhaid Gaoidhil cead labhartha
Leis an gCraoibhín Aoibhinn Áluinn Óg.[64]

The optimism of Inglis, his literary conteporaries, his Jacobite audience and their exiled counterparts reflected the unease which reverberated at the highest level of English government circles in Ireland. Bedford, the lord lieutenant, appeared apprehensive at the prospect of a further reduction from the Irish military establishment in the light of a possible French descent.[65] Stressing the impossibility of the simultaneous deployment of the forces of the kingdom against a possible invasion, while at the same time protecting the major centres of population, he questioned the potential loyalty of native Irish regiments which he suspected were filled with papists. Having reiterated popular fears and expectations regarding the Irish brigades in the French army, he expressed unease at the numbers of Irish Papists, which he estimated at sixteen thousand men, who had knowledge of arms in consequence of such service.[66]

Shifting perspective once more, further testimony to the relevance of Jacobitism in this period is provided by the correspondence of the Irish *émigrés*. Richard Burke, writing from Naples to James Edgar, was optimistic that the war

---

64 Inglis, 'Atá an fhuireann seo thall gan amhras díleas', in Ó Foghludha (eag.), *Cois na Bríde*, p. 36. Inglis rejoices that 'the sound of the waves is deafening Hawke, *Tá torann tonn ag bodhradh Hawke*; in Ó Foghludha (eag.), *Cois na Bríde*, p. 27. The poet Seán Ó Cuinneagáin expects that 'Fr Uilliam [Inglis] will be providing for brothers since Hawke lost the battle' *Biaidh an tAthair Uilliam ag riar ar bhráthribh / Ó cailleadh a ngliadh no bh-fiann an hácach*; 'An Chraobhínn Aoibhinn', in O'Daly (ed.), *Poets and poetry*, p. 70. Tadhg Gaelach promises that 'the hosts of Silesia will be prepared and companion-like and Maria Theresa will have her lands and crown' *Beidh sloighte Shílisia go cóirithe cuibhrithe / A coróinn is a críocha ag Máire;* '*An Fánuidhe*', in Ó Foghludha (eag.), *Tadhg Gaelach*, pp 106–7. The continued reversals suffered by Britain and its allies in 1758 also gladdened Piaras Mac Gearailt, 'Duan na Saoirse' [A.D. 1758], in Ó Foghludha (eag.), *Amhráin Phiarais*, pp 24–5; An Caol-druineann Óg', in Ó Foghludha (eag.), *Amhráin Phiarais*, pp 39–40; Ó Foghludha (eag.), *Éigse na Máighe*, pp 211–12.
65 Bedford to the Rt Hon. Mr Pitt, Dublin Castle, 3 Jan. 1758 (S.P. 63, 415 f. 170).
66 Ibid.; Transcripts of the O'Hara papers in P.R.O.N.I (N.L.I. 16, 943).

in Europe would continue 'until the saddle is set upon the right horse'.[67] He wrote, it is clear, in the context of widespread rumours of a French-sponsored invasion. This situation also occasioned Dominic Heguerty's reproachful letter to Charles Edward, protesting against the latter's refusal to contemplate a French-sponsored invasion of Ireland. Heguerty appreciated that the prince's hopes were bound with the military plans of the French king:

> My heart is broken with grief to see you reject an invitation calculated to put a crown on your head which you throw under your feet, you disoblige a king who never forgets and seldom forgives. If you can do without His Majesty, in the name of God go on but if to the contrary what do you expect must be the consequence of your refusing this invitation ...?[68]

Heguerty's last correspondence to the prince has been interpreted as a stinging rebuke of Charles Edward's francophobia and as a disavowal of Jacobitism. Nevertheless O'Heguerty's letter should not be taken as the basis on which to build a thesis of popular anti-Jacobite sentiment among the Irish *émigrés* in France. Heguerty reminded his prince of the true value of his French-born Irish subjects, notwithstanding the continuing Francophobia of English and Scottish Jacobites. The letter may also have had the ulterior motive of a despairing last-ditch attempt to entice the prince into the latest French invasion scheme. In doing so, he accurately presented the stark facts of Charles Edward's hopeless political situation. However, he also reminded him of the impossibility of the Irish straying from their loyalty to his blood.[69]

Further light is thrown on the proposed invasion of Ireland by a memorial of the Chevalier Redmond to the duc d'Harcourt dating from July 1758. While Heguerty wavered in his loyalty to the Stuart cause, Redmond advocated the separation of Ireland from England. However this memoir cannot be taken as representative of *émigré* attitudes towards the Stuarts. Redmond was well aware of, and played upon, the frosty relationship between Louis XV and the French ministry towards Charles Edward, and, as he duly pointed out, his proposed separation of the two kingdoms would not have been acceptable to all his compatriots in France. He therefore chose to peripheralise Charles Edward in this latest venture, not by virtue of his relationship with the French king, but in terms of his abjuration of the Roman Catholic faith.[70]

67 R. Burke to Edgar, Naples, December 1758 (R.A., Ms 387, f. 145). See also (R.A., Ms 388, fol. 146).
68 D. Heguerty to the prince, 17 Nov. 1758 (R.A., Ms 387, f.[2]). See also (R.A., Ms 387, f. 17); (R.A., Ms 388 fol. 134). See also McLynn, *France and the Jacobite rising of 1745* (Edinburgh, 1981), p. 82.
69 D. Heguerty to Charles Edward, 10 June 1759 (R.A., Ms 390, f. 34); Beresford, 'Ireland', pp 208–20.
70 'Le Chevalier Redmond à Mr le duc D'harcourt, 2 Juillet 1758, in 'Recueil des lettres officelles de Mr le duc D'Harcourt, duc de Loiges et autres concernant la marine, la guerre en Europe pendant le mois de Juillet' (A.N., Ministère de la Guerre, vol 3534, vol. 2, fol. 4, N.L.I., mf. p. 154); Beresford, 'Ireland', p. 231.

His next invasion proposal to Marshal Belle-Isle on 13 July 1759 stressed that the advantages from the subjugation of Ireland far outweighed the risks. The richest and most advantageous ports of Cork, Waterford, Wexford and Dublin were in the south of the country and easily accessible to de Conflans by a sortie from Brest. The Irish people would eagerly embrace the French invasion force and maintain an establishment for themselves on the island after military success in an assault on England. The common Irish wanted nothing more than an army of Catholics in their country to deliver them from oppression and allow them the free exercise of their religion. Although Redmond's proposal to issue a declaration against the Pretender to the United Provinces showed his diffidence towards the Stuarts, it could also have been a shrewd political ploy to satiate a potentially hostile neighbour. He finally emphasised that all Irish hopes rested on the French and the great number of their compatriots in that service.[71]

While both Heguerty and Redmond were obliged to underplay or totally repudiate the Stuart cause, contrasting sentiments from the Irish *émigrés* in this period show the struggle for their political conscience between Jacobite sentimentality and French *Realpolitik*.[72] In his *Series of letters discovering the scheme projected by France in 1759 for an intended invasion upon England with flat-bottomed boats*, the double-agent Oliver McAllester provided a different view of the racial and ideological make-up of the officer-corps of Lally's regiment 'which had been reduced to a handful of skeletons in India'.[73] Having been 'recruited', 'made complete' and 'well-officered' after the disastrous French campaign in India, he believed that no 'regiment in France made a more brilliant or martial appearance with respect to uniforms, drums, muffs and officers'. He added that many of these comprised 'old veterans who had made their retreats after serving many campaigns but were now entered in the service again with hearts full of joy in hopes of seeing once more their native soil and leaving their old maligned carcases at home'.[74]

Final testimony that French preparations were taken very seriously both in Whitehall and Dublin is provided in the letter from Pitt to the duke of Bedford on his embarkation for Ireland as the new lord lieutenant. His most reliable intelligence from France suggested that the recent disaster which befell the Toulon fleet, and its increasing difficulties in eluding 'his majesty's fleet' and associated French despair, reinforced the possibility of the descent of the duc d'Arguillion's eighteen thousand man force into Ireland. While Bedford confirmed the loyalty of the Protestants he expressed misgivings about putting the

71 Le Chevalier Redmond à Mareschal de Belle Isle, 13 July 1759 (A.N. Ministère de la Guerre, vol. 3534 fol. 102, N.L.I., mf. p. 154); Cunningham (ed.), *Letters of Horace Walpole*, iii, p. 194.
72 Beresford, 'Ireland', pp 139, 197. See also (R.A., Ms 394, f. 66); (R.A., Ms 396, f. 118); (R.A., Ms 414, f. 11); (R.A., Ms 403, f. 201); McLoughlin, 'A crisis for the Irish in Bordeaux', pp 127–47.
73 J. C. O'Callaghan, *Irish brigades in the service of France*, repr. (Shannon, 1969), pp 505–79.
74 McAllester, *A series of letters*, ii, p. 186.

kingdom on full invasion alert to avoid unsettling Irish Protestants. While these invasion rumours ran the risk of depressing Protestant spirits, the optimism of their Catholic counterparts is undoubtedly mirrored in contemporary Jacobite literature.[75] This is clearly evident in the poetry composed by Inglis and his contemporaries between '45 and the end of the Seven Years' War.

Indeed the relationship between the Irish language and Jacobitism must be continually borne in mind and justifies the need to consider the singular importance of Irish sources as a window to the Irish Catholic Jacobite psyche. As late as 1764, when James III was in his death-throes, a memoir regarding Fr Egan, the parish priest of Clonmel, stressed the close links between the survival of Catholicism and the hatred of all things English, which could include their devotion to the House of Hanover:

> He is beyond reproach in public, he preaches well in English but as he does not know any Irish, he is not capable of instructing the people in the country district who, fortunately have no other language, this holds true for most of the Irish Catholics, the instructions given by the bishops when they were making their visitations, and especially on the occasion of their making their confirmation, are most necessary for the preservation of the faith and the good conduct of the Irish, whose dislike of the English language is one of the means used by providence for the preservation of the Catholic religion among them.[76]

This hatred of the English language which runs through Inglis's poetry embellished his disdain for the hated Hanoverian regime and his hopes for a Jacobite restoration. It is also evident that his Jacobite optimism was not lost on his Whig and Protestant contemporaries. Moreover the official despatches between Dublin and Whitehall, the paranoia of the popular Protestant pamphlet and sermon tradition reflect many of the same themes. This in turn showed that the Stuart Pretender and his French confederates retained the roles which they enjoyed throughout the first part of the eighteenth-century as both the messiahs and the *bêtes noires* of the respective Jacobite and Whig traditions. It is hoped that the foregoing review of Inglis' work together with no more that cursory glance of the corpus of writing of which it forms part indicates at least that.

---

75 Bedford to Pitt, 19 Oct. 1759 (S.P. 63, 416 f. 101); see also ibid. ff 130, 234–7.
76 Memoir concerning Fr Egan, P.P. of Clonmel, c. 1764, in Giblin (ed.), 'Catalogue of material of Irish interest in the Nunziatura di Fiandra', part 6, vols 133–135g, in *Coll. Hib.*, x (1967), p. 136.

'A Wild Capuchin of Cork':
Arthur O'Leary (1729–1802)

James Kelly

The prevailing view of Fr Arthur O'Leary is that he can more plausibly be described as a 'loyalist' than as a radical.[1] Considering O'Leary's acceptance of government patronage, his hostility towards the United Irishmen and his support of the Act of Union, it is hardly surprising that this term is employed to define him, or that he does not figure prominently in the Pantheon of 'radical' priests lionised by the powerful Catholic-nationalist historiographical tradition of the late nineteenth and early twentieth centuries.[2] O'Leary has attracted a number of biographers nonetheless, though their derivative quality and pietistic tone frequently occlude the real significance of his life and work.[3] There is, unfortunately, insufficient personal material with which to paint a clear picture of his 'useful life'.[4] But his writings offer vivid testimony to his dissatisfaction with the sectarian political and religious order that prevailed throughout most of western Europe and to the radicalism of his vision of a society in which politico-religious differences were transcended and toleration was acknowledged as the key to a harmonious society. This was an aspiration he shared with the United Irishmen, but compared with the United Irishmen, who provide the yardstick by which radicalism is measured in eighteenth-century Ireland, the radical implications of his writings remain largely unappreciated. Part of the reason for this is that he urged Catholics to work within rather than to overthrow the existing political order. But no less significant was the fact that his ideal of a tolerant society was rejected by a large section of the dominant Protestant interest in the mid-1780s and effectively sidelined in the crisis-torn 1790s

1 Dáire Keogh, *'The French disease': the Catholic Church and radicalism in Ireland, 1790–1800* (Dublin, 1993), p. 161. A brief, and overlooked, attempt at a contrary view is provided in Ignatius Murphy, 'Some attitudes to religious freedom and ecumenism in pre-Emancipation Ireland', *I.E.R.* 105 (1966), pp 94–5. The label 'a wild Capuchin' is Archbishop John Carpenter's (M.J. Curran, 'Correspondence of Abp. Carpenter with Bp Stweetman of Ferns' in *Reportium Novum*, i no. 2 (1956), p. 401).
2 J.O'M., 'Fr Arthur O'Leary' in *Journ. of the Cork Hist. & Arch. Soc.*, i (1892), p. 183.
3 T.R. England, *The life of ... Arthur O'Leary* ... (London, 1822); M.B. Buckley, *The life and writings of the reverend Arthur O'Leary* (Dublin, 1868). J.O'M.,'O'Leary', pp 183–9; Fr Paschal, 'Fr Arthur O'Leary,1729–1802: apostle of toleration', *Capuchin Annual*, 1961, pp 263–75; T.J.Walsh, 'Fr Arthur O'Leary: a Capuchin of Blackamoor lane', *Journ. of the Cork Hist. & Arch. Soc.*, 53 (1948), pp 88–94.
4 The phrase is Hugh Fenning's, 'The 'Udienze' series in the Roman archives of Propaganda Fide', *Archivium Hibernicum*, 48 (1994), p. 105.

when conflict and confrontation eclipsed his chosen *modus operandi* – co–operation and conciliation. However, in the late 1770s and early 1780s, when his influence was at its peak, Arthur O'Leary not alone helped to prepare Protestant
opinion for Catholic relief but stimulated liberal Protestants like Henry Grattan
to embrace the goal he so famously articulated in 1782 of a religiously and politically inclusive 'Irish nation'.

I

Arthur O'Leary's early years bear ample testimony to the restrictions under
which Irish Catholics lived their lives in the eighteenth century because of the
essentially sectarian legislation we term the penal laws. Born near Dunmanway
in 1729, he was obliged to go to France in his late teens to prepare for the priesthood.[5] It is not clear how he felt about this at the time, but subsequent reference
to these 'barbarous and Gothic laws' suggest that he was not unconscious of the
incongruity of his leaving one Catholic country for another to take orders.[6] He
spent a total of twenty-four years at the Capuchin College at St Malo, and while
there is little documentary evidence appertaining to his time in France, there is
no reason to challenge the claim of his first biographer that it was there that he
'imbibed the principles of ... learning, virtue and philanthropy' that informed
his actions throughout his life.[7]
    O'Leary maintained two years before he died that 'conscience was the rule
of my conduct', and that it was this which convinced him of the merits of the
principles of political and religious toleration by which he conducted his life,
and that he first demonstrated when he was appointed 'to superintend prisons
and hospitals during the wars of fifty-seven'. This involved ministering to prisoners of war, many of whom were Irish Catholics, and while the irony of Irish
Catholics serving in the British army being held prisoner by Catholic France
was not lost on him., he respected their decision. So when the duc de Choiseul
suggested that he should encourage them to desert the Crown for the standard
of France, he declined to do so. 'I thought', he explained later, 'it a crime to
engage the King of England's soldiers and sailors in the service of a Catholic
monarch against the Protestant sovereign'.[8] It was an emblematic moment. From
this point onwards he urged that all Christians should be allowed practice their
religion according to the dictates of their own consciences without fear or inter-

5   The standard sources for O'Leary's life are England, op.cit. and Buckley, op.cit., *passim*.
6   Arthur O'Leary, *Address to the Lords spiritual and temporal of the parliament of Great Britain ...*
    (London, 1800), p. 4.
7   England, op.cit., p. 17.
8   Cited in Buckley, op. cit., p. 18; England, op. cit., p. 17; O'Leary, *Address to the Lords spiritual and
    temporal*, p.4.

ference from the political authorities in the states in which they lived. Of course, O'Leary was by no means unique in western Europe in advancing such opinions. A significant range of powerful and influential people had reached the same conclusion, but they generally articulated their opinions in a less testing milieu than Ireland where, as the response to Thomas Leland's 1773 *History of Ireland* highlights, sectarian convictions continued to be strongly held.[9]

II

This was a matter of pertinence to O'Leary, who returned to Ireland to minister in Cork in 1771. He was an energetic and able priest, and he quickly established himself as one of the most popular members of the local Capuchin community. His most notable achievement was the construction of a small chapel on a site adjoining the Blackamoor Lane friary. This combined with his proficiency as a preacher to earn him local renown. The texts of his sermons do not survive, but the palpable thaw in denominational suspicion during the quarter century that he had been in France allowed him to comment from the altar on matters of current controversy.[10]

O'Leary's openness did not pass unnoticed. However, he wisely reserved his first public intervention for a theological rather than a political issue. The publication in 1775 by Patrick Blair, a Scots physician resident at Cork, of a tract entitled *Thoughts on nature and religion* in which he challenged several key articles of Christianity, including the divinity of Christ, excited deep resentment across the denominational spectrum. Normally, Catholic priests eschewed engaging in public disputation, but having encountered free thinking in France, O'Leary was disinclined to let its appearance in Cork pass unchallenged. Having first informed the Protestant ordinary of his intention, he produced a stylish, combative and informed defence of the doctrinal 'foundations of religion' which, he contended, provided the basis for a just and balanced society.[11] It was a well-judged tactic. By choosing to defend Christianity rather than Catholicism, O'Leary aligned himself with the bulk of Irish opinion which shared his conviction that no 'religion [was] more pure than that of the Christian' because it alone offered a comprehensible explanation of the human condition:

9 Joseph Liechty, 'Testing the depth of Catholic-Protestant conflict: the case of Thomas Leland's *History of Ireland*,1773', *Arch. Hib.* 42 (1987), pp 13–28.
10 Walsh, 'O'Leary', p. 89, and photographs facing pp 90, 92; Buckley, op. cit., pp 19–22; England, op. cit., p. 19.
11 England, op. cit., pp 20–7; Buckley, op. cit., pp 22–39; [Arthur O'Leary], *A defence of the divinity of Christ etc. or remarks on a work entitled Thought on nature and religion* (Cork, 1775), printed in *Miscellaneous works by Rev Arthur O'Leary* (Dublin, 1781).

Philosophers, in a strain of irony, may deride our Bible and catechism, and laugh at our folly for believing that an apple could entail such miseries on mortals: but let them seriously consider the multitude and greatness of the evils that oppress us, and how full of vanity, of illusions, of sufferings, are the first years of our lives; when we are grown up, how we are seduced by error, weakened by pain, inflamed by lust, cast down by sorrow, elated with pride – and ask themselves, whether the cause of those dreadful evils be the injustice of God or the original sin of man.[12]

O'Leary's articulation of fundamental Christian tenets here and elsewhere was not always doctrinally error free.[13] However, this did not bother most of his readers. They were swayed by his lucid prose, the vigour of his argument and the effectiveness of his defence of the application by religious-minded people of reason to faith to join with him in trumpeting the superiority of belief over the destructive contentions of sceptics, deists and freethinkers.

O'Leary was left in no doubt by the applause accorded his response to Blair that a pamphlet was a most effective means of communicating with the public. Despite this, he did not enter into print again until 1777 when he came out in support of the controversial oath of allegiance ratified by the Irish parliament in 1774. This oath provided a mechanism whereby Roman Catholics could avow their loyalty to the house of Hanover and disavow some of the more contentious doctrines attributed to them by Protestants. Because of this, it was perceived positively by O'Leary as a step towards full religico-political toleration. The problem was that the oath excited passionate differences within Irish Catholic ranks between those whose disposition was Gallicanist, who were well-disposed towards the oath, and those who were disinclined to do anything that reflected negatively on the Papacy. O'Leary did not describe himself as a Gallicanist, but he had little sympathy with the likes of Archbishop Carpenter of Dublin and Bishop de Burgo of Ossory who criticised the 1774 oath because it denied the Pope such controversial (and redundant) powers as the right to depose temporal princes.[14] He had even less time for Jacobitism which was also singled out for aspersive mention in the oath.

O'Leary presented his arguments in a pamphlet entitled *Loyalty asserted: or the new test oath vindicated.* Understandably, given its timing and subject, the bulk of the tract was given over to a clause by clause justification of the oath and to an ostentatiously erudite exposition of its compatibility with Catholic teach-

---

12 *A defence* ..., pp 17–18.
13 Buckley, op. cit., pp vi–iii; Walsh, 'O'Leary', p. 91.
14 See Patrick Wallace, 'Irish catechesis – the heritage from James Butler ii, Archbishop of Cashel, 1774–91' (Ph.D, Catholic University of America, 1975); Maureen Wall, 'Catholic loyalty to king and pope in eighteenth-century Ireland', in *Proceedings of the Irish Catholic historical committee, 1960* (Dublin, 1961), pp 20–4.

ing in respect to such topical issues as the Pope's 'deposing power' and the alleged right of Catholics 'to murder heretics'. It was in this context that O'Leary first maintained that there was no doctrinal or ideological reason why Catholics should decline to profess allegiance to the Protestant king of Great Britain: as subjects Catholics owed it to the king not to engage in 'conspiracies and treasonable practices "against his person, crown and dignity"', he pronounced. Taken in tandem with his naked hostility to the Stuarts, whose Irish policies he roundly criticised and whose restoration would, he forecast, result in the 'aggravation of our yoke and new calamities', O'Leary offered a more unconditional endorsement of the existing Protestant political establishment than had previously been advanced by a Catholic priest. He personally was of the opinion that since the Catholics of Ireland had suffered grievously as a consequence of their attachment to the Stuart cause since 1688, and because William of Orange had 'controuled the spirit of oppression' abroad in the 1690s, it was logical, as well as in Catholics' interest, to support the Hanoverian succession. Indeed, developing on a remark he made in his reply to Patrick Blair, he cited Dean Swift in support of his controversial contention that if Christians focused on their points of agreement rather than their points of difference, and emphasised 'charity' rather than 'religious inflammation' and 'evangelical spleen', it must result in the welcome attenuation of inter-denominational 'dissension' and greater social concord.[15]

O'Leary's plea that churches like the Roman Catholic and Anglican should overcome their traditional animosities and, as C.D.A. Leighton has put it, 'partner' each other in defence of 'an orthodox Trinitarian form of Christianity' was too radical for the adherents of the main denominations in Ireland to contemplate seriously, and it was not afforded the public discussion it deserved.[16] This did O'Leary's reputation little harm. He had made such a positive impression, that in late 1777 Charles O'Conor of Belanagare sought his participation in 'an Association for the refutation of invectives and for the publication of our grievances' as the Catholic Committee intensified its efforts to secure relief from the penal laws. Nothing came of this.[17] Indeed, we do not know what O'Leary thought of the 1778 Catholic Relief Act, but it is reasonable to assume that, like most Catholics who advocated cooperating with the state at this time, he felt the bill vindicated his stand. The likelihood that this is the correct conclusion is reinforced by the fact that when the kingdom was gripped by rumours of a French invasion in the summer of 1779, O'Leary consolidated his reputation as the

15 *Loyalty asserted or the new test oath vindicated and proved by the principles of the canon and civil laws and the authority of the most eminent writers with an enquiry into the Pope's deposing power and the groundless claims of the Stuarts* (Dublin, 1777), printed in *Miscellaneous tracts*; Buckley, op. cit., pp 65–9; C.D.A. Leighton, *Catholicism in a Protestant kingdom: a study of the Irish ancien régime* (Dublin, 1994), p. 57.

16 Leighton, op. cit., p. 154.

Catholic spokesman of the moment by winning the hearts of the Protestant community with an appeal 'to the common people of the Roman Catholic religion' to remain calm.

Forecasting, among other calamities, 'mangled bodies', 'scattered limbs', 'famine' and 'distress' should the country be precipitated into war, O'Leary recommended that the Catholic population should follow the 'example' of their bishops, clergy and gentlemen and support the Crown. The French, he admonished, had no interest in promoting Catholicism in Ireland:

> Expect ... nothing from the French on the score of religion, but remain peaceably in your cottages. Mind your business as usual, and be free from all groundless apprehensions. Work for those who employ you; for it is against the laws of war to molest or hurt any but such as oppose the enemy sword in hand.[18]

O'Leary was unrelenting in his insistence that a French invasion would disimprove rather than enhance the condition of the Catholic population. It would, he pronounced anxiously, result in the resuscitation of long dormant land claims and produce 'a thousand pretenders to every [e]state' – an eventuality he was most anxious to avoid because of his conviction that it would set back the hopes he increasingly entertained that an era of religious toleration was in prospect. Indeed, he urged the Catholic population to accept the existing land settlement, since any attempt to disrupt it would threaten the 'free exercise of religion' it currently enjoyed, and undo what he termed 'the glory of our days':

> the unhappy spirit of persecution dying away, and Christian charity succeeding the intemperate zeal, and unChristian superstition which, for many years, had disgraced religion and dishonoured humanity.[19]

As time was to show, this was an idealized perception of the prospects for improved inter-denominational relations in Ireland in the short-term. But such was the enthusiasm with which the tract was received, and the disposition of liberal Protestants to overcome their traditional denominational antipathies that O'Leary can be forgiven for concluding that rapid strides could be taken towards achieving the religious toleration that lay at the heart of his thinking.[20]

---

17 O'Conor to Ryan, 1 October, [11 November] 1777 in C.C. and R.E.Ward (ed.), *The letters of Charles O'Conor* (2 vols, Ann Arbor, 1980), ii, pp 106–7, 116.
18 *An address to the common people of the Roman Catholic religion, concerning the apprehended French invasion* (Dublin, 1779) p. 97 in *Miscellaneous tracts*.
19 Ibid., p. 104; Eamon O'Flaherty, 'The Catholic question in Ireland, 1774–93' (M.A. thesis, U.C.D., 1981), p. 44.
20 James Kelly, 'Inter-denominational relations and religious toleration in late eighteenth-century Ire-

III

Events in O'Leary's life continued to stimulate such hopes. In the spring of 1780, he became embroiled in a dispute with John Wesley following the latter's publication of a 'letter' 'concerning the principles of Roman Catholics', and 'A defence of the Protestant Association'. In common with many Protestants in Britain and Ireland, Wesley was profoundly agitated by the implications of recent concessions to Catholics arising out of his conviction that 'an open toleration of the Popish religion is inconsistent with the safety of a free people and a Protestant government'. He justified his assertion on traditional grounds. Since it was Catholic doctrine that 'no faith is to be kept with heretics' and the Pope reserved the power to 'pardon rebellions, high treason and all other sins whatsoever' and to 'dispos[e] ... with any promise, oath or vow' it was impossible for a Catholic to 'give any security for their allegiance to any government'. Therefore, no Protestant government could safely 'tolerate or encourage Roman Catholics' as long as they adhered to 'their intolerant, persecuting principles'.[21]

O'Leary was so taken aback that someone of Wesley's reputation should advance what he denominated 'false assertions' that he sought to expose them in a series of letters published in the *Freeman's Journal* in March.[22] In these, he made light of the history of Catholic coercion, intolerance and repression to which Wesley appealed on the grounds that the 'ransacking old books, canvassing legends of exaggerated massacres' served merely to 'haunt the living with the images of the dead'.[23] 'All our misfortunes', he pronounced earnestly, 'flow from long-running intolerance'. His mission was to mitigate the sectarianism he concluded Wesley was intent on perpetuating, and with this in mind he once again highlighted the doctrinal and ritual similarities of the main Christian religions, and suggested that if 'social harmony' was allowed prevail it would be to the population's economic advantage:

> The Roman Catholics sing their psalms in Latin, with a few inflections of the voice. Our Protestant neighbours sing the same psalms in English, on a

land: the 'paper war' of 1786–88' *Eighteenth-Century Ireland*, 3 (1988), pp 40–1, 54–5; John Brady (ed.), *Catholics and Catholicism in the eighteenth-century press* (Maynooth, 1965), p. 203. One negative commentary was provided by the fraudulent *Three letters of Father Arthur O'Leary to the people of Ireland, particularly to those of the Church of Rome* (Dublin, 1779). O'Leary publicly repudiated this (*FJ*, 20 Nov. 1779) in the course of which he reiterated his wish that 'banishment and prescription, on account of religious systems ... will not take place in Ireland and that people should 'love each other as Christians'.

21 John Wesley's *Defence of the Protestant Association*, p. 11; John Wesley's *Letter concerning the civil principles of Roman Catholicism*, pp 4–7. Both are reprinted in O'Leary, *Miscellaneous tracts*.

22 *FJ*, 14, 16, 21, 23 Mar. 1780.

23 *Remarks on Rev. John Wesley's letter on the civil principles of Roman Catholics and his defence of the Protestant Association* (Dublin, 1780), pp 77–8 reprinted in O'Leary, *Miscellaneous tracts*.

larger scale of musical notes. We never quarrel with our honest and worthy neighbours the Quakers for not singing at all; nor shall we ever quarrel with Mr Wesley for *raising his voice to Heaven*, and warbling forth his canticles on whatever tune he pleases, whether it be the tune of *Guardian Angels* or *Langolee*. We like *social harmony*, and in civil music hate *discordance*. Thus, when we go to the shambles, we never inquire into the butcher's religion, but into the quality of his meat. We care not whether the ox was fed in the Pope's territories, or on the mountains of Scotland, provided the joint be good; for though there be many *heresies* in old books, we discover neither *heresy* nor *superstition* in beef and claret. We divide them cheerfully with one another; and though of different religions, we sit over the bowl with as much cordiality as if we were at a *love-feast*.[24]

This measured approach served O'Leary well in his dispute with Wesley. It enabled him to deal judiciously with such perennially thorny issues as the 'violation of faith with' and the 'burning of heretics', the significance of the Council of Constance and the power of the Papacy without resorting either to abuse or apology. He was less patient in his observations on Wesley's defence of the Protestant Association, which was instrumental in fomenting the Gordon Riots.[25] But he could take heart from the fact that his commitment to the advancement of 'humanity' and to overcoming the legacy of centuries of religious animosity was widely applauded. As a consequence, it was O'Leary and not Wesley who emerged from the exchange with his reputation enhanced. This gave greater authority to his appeal for the repeal of the remainder of the penal laws, which he pilloried as 'a noxious humour' and 'a running evil ... [that] ulcerate every part of the body', on the grounds that Catholics had as vested an interest as Protestants in the stability of the British state.[26] The fact that his exchanges with Wesley were published in a pamphlet edition within weeks of their first appearance was also heartening. It encouraged him to press on with his most ambitious and radical work to date – a tract devoted exclusively to the issue of religious and political toleration.[27]

O'Leary's 'plea for liberty of conscience' – to cite the subtitle of his 'essay on toleration' – was one of the most radical statements in favour of religious and political forbearance published in eighteenth-century Ireland. Offering as its theme the proposition that it was desirable 'to throw open the gates of civil toleration for all Adam's children whose principles are not inconsistent with the peace of civil society, or subversive of the rules or mortality', he commenced his

24 Ibid., pp 25–6.
25 Ibid., pp 78–101.
26 Ibid., pp 31–2, 37–55, 59–61.
27 *FJ*, 28 Mar. 1780; Buckley, op.cit., pp 135–6.

exposition with an outline of 'the history of the calamities occasioned by difference in religious opinions' in which he pointed out that 'the partisans of truth,
forgetful of the moderation which reason and religion prescribe, committed the
same excesses with which they upbraided their oppressors'. It perturbed him
that Christians were guilty of such deeds; that throughout history priests 'gave
the sanction of heaven to the bloody mandates of the civil magistrates' and to
'persecution' that has 'thinned the world of fifty millions of human beings', but
he made no effort to deny their occurrence.[28] He likewise made no attempt to
elide over the complicity of the Papacy in the slaughter perpetrated by the In-
quisition since in this, as in the other cases of Christian persecution he enumer-
ated, it was his contention that it was 'the religion of time and place ... not the
religion of the Gospel' that was at fault. Such assertions rendered him vulnerable, he conceded, to the accusation that he was a 'latitudinarian, to whom all
religions are indifferent', but he was sufficiently secure in his Catholicism not
to be diverted by this. His object was to demonstrate that the state did not
possess the 'right to vindicate the Deity by fines, forfeitures, confiscations, oppression or the death of men, whose only crime is an erroneous religion ... whether
they be Jews, Mahometans, Christians, heretics or Catholics, provided they believe a Supreme Being'. The 'boundaries of religion and the concerns of the
civil magistrate' should, he contended, be kept distinct, and it was his conviction that 'true religion' served to mitigate rather than to justify human excess.
In this context, he introduced Montesquieu in support of his central contention that 'when many religions have got a footing in the state, they are to be
tolerated'.[29] This was O'Leary's argument reduced to its essence, and following
his consideration of the religious toleration practised in Germany, Switzerland
and Holland, he embarked on an extended discussion of the implications of the
existence of dissent in a state, in which he contrived to demonstrate that it was
incompatible with 'true religion' that believers should resort to oppression to
eradicate others:

> Those laws, then, that doom heretics to death, as well as the establishment of
> the Inquisition, are no parts of a Catholic creed, no more than [repressive
> anti-Catholic laws passed by the British] parliament are part of the Church
> of England's creed. The true religion should be preserved and perpetuated
> by the same means that established it – by preaching the Word of God, at-
> tended with prudence and discretion, the practice of all Christian virtues,
> boundless peace and charity.[30]

---

28 *An essay on toleration or Mr O'Leary's plea for liberty of conscience* (Dublin, 1780), pp 3–9. It is
    printed in *Miscellaneous tracts*.
29 Ibid., pp 10–25.
30 Ibid., p. 39.

It was by these means, and not by appeals to force, that Christ operated, he claimed, and he cited *patres* and saints in support of his contention. The equally vigorously reprobated those Popes, prophets and others who conducted them-selves contrariwise. 'Error in doctrine', he averred unhesitatingly, 'was never deemed a sufficient title to deprive a man of his life or property by the most pious and enlightened Christian legislators', and attributions such as heretic or Papist were 'too indeterminate a signification to become the object of legal venge-ance … To punish a man for Popery is to punish him because another pro-nounces a word of three syllables'. 'The most effective way to remove preju-dices', O'Leary concluded sagely, 'is to put oneself in other people's situations'.[31]

This provided O'Leary with an ideal opportunity to discourse at length on the merits of toleration in the Irish context, but he chose not to do so. His preference was to debate the issue at a more abstract level, and it was only after he had considered how 'the disputes of theologians have destroyed and fam-ished a good part of the creation' that he expressed his hope that

> our legislators, in whose power it is to ease the necks of their inoffensive subjects from the galling yoke of oppression …, will no longer consider dif-ference in religion as a sufficient reason for hindering the young gentleman from purchasing a pair of colors and fighting the battles of his king and country; the industrious citizen from realizing the fruits of his labor, in get-ting landed security for his money, and purchasing an estate descendible to his children; the physician, the opulent farmer, the man of property, from carrying a gun, a sword, a case of pistols, for their defence against the attacks of the midnight assassin or highwayman; the clergyman, who instils the prin-ciples of good morals into the minds of the ignorant, who would follow the fierce instinct of savage and uncivilized nature if they were deprived of their pastors, from the protection of the laws, which now leave them exposed to the caprice and fury of every ruffian, in whose power it is to shut up their chapels and get them transported; when it is obvious that such restraints arise from speculative points, disputed on a narrow ridge by the greatest men the world ever produced – when philosophers themselves are bewil-dered in their notions – and when the learned are at variance about matters far beyond the reach of the bulk of mankind.[32]

The people of Ireland deserved to be freed of such shackles, he pronounced, because it was their 'birthright' as human beings and because

---

31 Ibid., pp 40–60.
32 Ibid., pp 77–8.

the rulers of the earth, whether Catholics or Protestants, owe all social benefits to their loyal subjects of every denomination ... Honor, humanity, and the rights of mankind, should suggest to modern legislators to repair the losses caused by their predecessors' misguided zeal. And as the clergy of all denominations consider themselves the delegates of heaven, and invested with the commission to prescribe a mode of worship to man, let them propose it in a manner that may secure its triumph over the heart, brighten it up with the genial rays of humanity, benevolence, and love, and not cloud it with the sullen gloom of severity, oppression, and distress. For, Christ, who is the Creator of all, has not declared in His Gospel that one should be excluded from the protection of the laws, and persecuted for his worship, and the other authorized to famish, starve, and insult the weakness of a fellow-creature.[33]

This resounding clarion represented O'Leary's strongest affirmation to date of the benefactions of religious toleration. It was well-received, though once again few engaged fully with its radical implications. Many Irish Protestants, for instance, responded positively in a rather general way to the tract because they perceived O'Leary to corroborate the criticisms they had long levelled at Catholicism. They chose to ignore that what he wrote was as pregnant with implications for them as it was for Catholics. This was not a conclusion overlooked by liberal patriots. Encouraged by the possibilities of *de facto* as well as *de jure* toleration by the 1778 Catholic Relief Act, by O'Leary's appeal to Catholics for calm in 1779 and by his 'essay on toleration', most Volunteer corps in the early 1780s had little difficulty admitting Catholics to membership of the Volunteers or contemplating a further relaxation in the penal laws.[34] The high esteem with which O'Leary was held in these quarters is amply illustrated by the decision of the patriot club, the Monks of St Patrick, to admit him to honourary membership on the recommendation of Barry Yelverton. O'Leary did not, as far as one can tell, ever join in the social or political deliberations of the body, but his election to membership is testimony to the remarkable impact of his writings.[35]

IV

O'Leary sought to take advantage of his fame to ensure the widest possible dissemination of his opinions. His boldest initiative was the 1781 edition of his

---

33 Ibid., pp 80–1.
34 Kelly, 'Inter-denominational relations', pp 41–2.
35 Buckley, op. cit., pp 197–9; England, op.cit., pp 99–100.

collected works. Given the public profile and the impact of his writings, it is not surprising that the Irish Catholic Committee provided £40 towards the cost of the publication or that the English Committee paid for the distribution *gratis* of 100 copies. What is unexpected is that the prime minister, Lord North, subscribed and that the sternly Protestant Irish under-secretary, Edward Cooke, recommended that the lord lieutenant and chief secretary did likewise.[36] Cooke was prompted to make this suggestion by his belief that O'Leary could be of 'use to the Castle' because he 'has much influence' and '[is] well disposed to do what you wish'.[37] O'Leary had given Cooke no such assurance, but like others in government he misinterpreted O'Leary's advocacy of religious toleration as support for the political *status quo*. O'Leary did, it is true, nothing to disabuse Cooke of such illusions when he pronounced himself committed 'to cement the bands of society – to secure the safety of our country, by union and mutual confidence – to render the subject's allegiance firm' in the preface to the edition of his *Miscellaneous tracts*, which was published in 1781. But his main object, which he defined in the same preface, as 'induc[ing] Christians of every denomination to lay aside the destructive weapons which frenzy has so often put into their hands' in order that 'the sacred name of religion, which even in the face of an enemy discovers a brother, [should not] be any longer a wall of separation to keep us asunder' was fundamentally more challenging.[38]

Because it was so unusual for Catholic priests to express such opinions, many concluded that O'Leary's attachment to his Church was less than secure. This was not correct. His radical views on the cooperation of the Christian religions was not accompanied by any dilution in his Catholicism as his active involvement in the campaign in the early 1780s to safeguard the regular clergy against the imposition and enforcement of legal restrictions highlights.[39] O'Leary's role in this episode is too well known to need reiteration here, but it is significant to note that what has been presented as an example of his using his 'influence ... for the benefit of the Irish Catholics and particularly of his fellow friars' was also a fine practical illustration of his striving to advance religious toleration.[40] He was certainly better placed than any other regular or secular cleric to do so. Indeed, during a debate on Catholic relief in the House of Commons on 27

---

36 Buckley, op.cit., pp 200–2; R.D.Edwards, ed., 'The minute book of the Catholic Committee, 1773–92' in *Arch. Hib.*, ix (1942), p. 60; Cooke to Eden, 17 July 1781 (B.L., Auckland papers, Add. Ms 34417 f 392).
37 Cooke to Eden, 17 July 1781 (B.L.,Auckland papers, Add. Ms 34417 f 392).
38 O'Leary, *Miscellaneous tracts*, preface.
39 O'Leary to Callanan, [1 Apr. 1780] in Buckley, op.cit., p. 208.
40 Hugh Fenning, *The Irish Dominican province, 1695–1797* (Dublin, 1990), pp 457–67; idem, *The undoing of the friars: the novitiate question in the eighteenth century* (Louvain, 1972), pp 348–51; Buckley, op. cit., pp 208–19; England, op. cit., pp 123–40; O'Flaherty, 'The Catholic question', pp 59–60; Patrick Rogers, *The Irish Volunteers and Catholic emancipation, 1778–93* (London, 1934), p. 16; C. Giblin (ed.), 'Papers of Richard Hayes OFM', *Collectanea Hibernica*, 21&22 (1979–80), p. 113.

February 1782, both Henry Grattan and Barry Yelverton praised him for the purity of his motives.[41] Given that only a few days earlier, the Ulster Volunteer delegates who assembled at Dungannon approved Grattan's resolution in favour of Catholic relief, O'Leary became increasingly confident that the religious toleration he aspired to was within reach. He had certainly moved a long way, as his description in October 1782 of William of Orange as 'the first who scattered the seeds of liberty in this kingdom' and the king who 'never violated his engagements with the Catholics of Ireland' attests.[42] At the same time, he was no 'Castle Catholic'. He was, for example, ill-at-ease with what he characterised as 'the cringing language of servility' that was a feature of the public pronouncements of the Catholic Committee, though he declined to criticise it publicly. He was visibly more positive about the inclusiveness of the Irish Brigade corps of Volunteers which admitted 'all parties without distinction' to membership. Indeed, he not alone accepted their invitation to act as honourary chaplain, but recommended that they should further demonstrate their tolerance by nominating a dissenting minister as their 'third chaplain'.[43] O'Leary evidently regarded the Volunteers in 1782–3 as a key means of advancing religious toleration because he was present at the opening of the Grand National Convention of Volunteer delegates in Dublin in November 1783. However, the failure of the Convention to embrace Catholic enfranchisement and allegations that the radicals who took over the stewardship of the reform movement in 1784 sought to involve the French in Irish affairs prompted him to rethink his attitude and to take the fateful decision to succumb to official blandishments to report on the activities of the Catholic advocates of parliamentary reform.[44]

More than any other event, O'Leary's acceptance of government remuneration in 1784 has shaped his posthumous reputation. Considering the sensationalist manner in which the matter was exposed by W.J. Fitzpatrick this is hardly surprising.[45] O'Leary was, as we have seen, someone whom Dublin Castle had long believed could be of use to them, so when in the autumn of 1784 they convinced themselves that the French were conspiring with Irish political radicals, Catholics and Presbyterians 'to weaken the government and to sever the bonds of union between' Great Britain and Ireland, they looked around desperately for means to discover 'any secret intrigues of [the] French in this coun-

---

41 *The parliamentary register, or history of the proceedings of the House of Commons of Ireland* (17 vols, Dublin, 1781–97), i, 292–3.
42 O'Leary to Kirwan, 4 Oct. 1782 in W.J. Fitzpatrick, *Secret service under Pitt* (London, 1892), p. 374.
43 Ibid., pp 375-6; Buckley, op. cit., pp 202-03; England, op. cit., p.105.
44 Rogers, *The Volunteers*, p.119; England, op.cit., p. 105; James Kelly, 'The parliamentary reform movement and the Catholic question, 1783–5', *Arch. Hib.*, 43 (1988), pp 95–117.
45 W.J. Fitzpatrick, *Ireland before the Union* (Dublin, 1868), pp 105–06, 228; *idem, Secret service under Pitt*, pp 211–79; Buckley, op. cit., pp 203–4; England, op. cit., p. 118.

try'.[46] The key, the Lord Lieutenant, the duke of Rutland, and his chief secretary, Thomas Orde, both concluded was Catholic intentions, and Arthur O'Leary was identified as the means by which 'the real designs of the Catholics, from which quarter after all the real mischief is to spring', could be established. To this end, the secretary of state, Lord Sydney undertook on Rutland's instruction to invite O'Leary, who was in London in the autumn of 1784, to report on the activities of his co-religionists in Ireland. There is no minute of Sydney's meeting with O'Leary, but it is reasonable to surmise that the point that carried most weight with the Irish friar was the claim that the French were implicated, because the secretary of state reported to Rutland in September that he had secured O'Leary's service in return for an annual payment of £100 per annum.[47]

It is not clear precisely what O'Leary anticipated he could achieve when he yielded to Sydney's approaches because he was not a member of the Catholic Committee and he was regarded with reserve by moderates like Archbishop Butler.[48] It is possible that the allure of financial security was the decisive factor in his decision, since he had been obliged to teach rhetoric and 'other branches of the belles lettres' at the Brunswick Street Academy in Cork in 1783 for financial reasons.[49] If so, government employment did not answer either his fiscal or political needs. This was inevitable given that there was no plot to be discovered, but it was hastened by the distrust with which he was regarded by the Protestant political and religious establishment. It is not clear precisely what transpired, but it appears that Castle officials concluded either that he was no use to them or, in Primate Rokeby's estimation, that he was a double 'spy'. The fact that he had declined some time previously to write a history of the Gordon riots because he did not believe he could tell 'the truth' as long as penal laws remained on the statute book suggests further that he may also have concluded that what was asked of him was incompatible with his commitment to the advancement of toleration.[50] He had no hesitation, as his 1783 'caution to the common people of Ireland against perjury' in the courts and at the polls emphasises, requesting the people to honour the law. He was likewise prepared to deny that the taking of 'a false oath' was proper, even if 'the preservation of one's own or another's life was at stake', and to defend the compatibility of existing oaths with Catholic teaching. However, he was not prepared to ally himself with a

46 Orde to Pitt, 16 Aug. (N.L.I., Bolton papers, Ms 16355 ff 1–4); Orde to Nepean, 4 Aug. 1784 (P.R.O., *Chatham papers*, 30/8/329 ff 97–9); J.Kelly, 'The Irish parliamentary reform movement: the administration and popular politics 1783–5' (UCD, M.A. thesis, 1981), pp 225–7.

47 Sydney to Rutland, 4 Sept., Orde to Nepean, 8, 23 Sept. (P.R.O., H.O., 100/14 ff 94, 100, 123–4); Rutland to Sydney, 8 May 1784 in H.M.C., *Rutland*, iii, 94.

48 Butler to Troy, 2 Jan. 1784 (D.D.A., *Carpenter-Troy papers*, no. 140); Edwards (ed.), 'Catholic committee minute book', pp 93–112.

49 Brady, *Catholics in the press*, p. 221; Fitzpatrick, *Ireland before the union*, p. 228.

50 Rutland to Sydney, 8 May, Sydney to Rutland, 26 Sept. 1784 in H.M.C., *Rutland*, iii, 94, 140; England, op.cit., p. 119.

Castle administration which was opposed to religious toleration and to improving the legal circumstances of Catholics.[51]

If, as this suggests, O'Leary's relationship with Dublin Castle in 1784 was less consequential and personally advantageous than many commentators have suggested, he had the consolation of knowing that his credibility with the public was unaffected.[52] At the same time, there was no question, once parliamentary reform had disappeared off the political agenda, that the hopes he had entertained at the beginning of the decade of unlimited religious toleration stood any prospect of early realisation. Some leading Catholics continued to believe that they would secure 'additional benefits' at an early date provided they were compatible 'with the constitution and established religion',[53] but the firmly orthodox chord O'Leary struck when he intervened in a minor theological dispute in January 1786 suggests that he believed otherwise.[54] This may also explain his less than tactful response to the upsurge in agrarian discontent in Munster a month later.

V

Like many Catholics in the public eye, Arthur O'Leary was perturbed by the emergence of the Rightboys in the mid-1780s.[55] Impelled by 'the avarice of the priesthood and intolerable exactions of the tithe farmers', proctors and Church of Ireland clergy, the Rightboys' main object was to moderate the sums demanded by and paid to both the Catholic and Protestant Churches, and with this in mind they laid down a level of reduced fees which they enforced through a combination of communal solidarity and intimidatory violence. They were so successful that, by the spring of 1786, the rule of Captain Right prevailed over a large part of the southern half of the country to the dismay of Protestants who instinctively regarded any manifestation of agrarian unrest as a French-inspired insurrection against 'the Protestant establishment in church and, consequently,

51 Arthur O'Leary, *Caution to the common people of Ireland against perjury so frequent at assizes and elections* (Cork, 1783), pp 5, 17; O'Leary to [...], 15 Apr. [1784] (N.L.I., Ms 3936); James Kelly, 'The genesis of 'Protestant ascendancy': the Rightboy disturbances of the 1780s and their impact upon Protestant opinion' in G.O'Brien (ed.), *Parliament, politics and people* (Dublin, 1989), p. 108.

52 Arthur O'Leary, *A review of the important controversy between Dr Carrol and Reverend Messrs Wharton and Hawkins including a defence of Pope Clement in suppressing a late religious order* (London, 1786), preface; Brady, ed., *Catholics in the press*, p. 233; J.S.Donnelly, ed., 'A contemporary account of the Rightboy movement: the John Barter Bennet manuscript', *Journ. of Cork Hist. & Arch. Soc.*, 88 (1983) p. 20.

53 Kelly, 'Inter-denominational relations', p. 57; Butler to Plunkett, 11 Apr. 1786 in A. Cogan, *The diocese of Meath ancient and modern* (3 vols, Dublin, 1870), iii, 111–13.

54 O'Leary, *A review of the important controversy, passim*; England, op. cit., pp 141–5.

55 J.S.Donnelly, 'The Rightboy movement, 1785–8', *Studia Hibernica*, 17&18 (1977–78), pp 120–202.

56 Donnelly, 'The Rightboys', *passim*; O'Driscoll to Silver Oliver, 1 July 1786, printed in *Theophilus, An address to the nobility and gentry of the Church of Ireland* (Dublin, 1786) appendix, pp 110–12; *Parl. Reg.* (Irl.). vi, 85–7; Kelly, 'The genesis of 'Protestant ascendancy', pp 102–110.

in state'.[56] This was not the Rightboys' rationale, as the leaders of Catholic opinion knew, but they could not afford to be seen to make light either of Protestant fears or Catholic disorder. And given the success of his inspirational appeal for calm in 1779, it was no surprise that O'Leary was invited by friends in county Cork to repeat the exercise, or that he agreed to do so.[57]

To all intents and purposes, O'Leary's first two addresses 'to the common people' on the subject of the Rightboys, which were published in the *Cork Hibernian Chronicle* in February 1786, sought to achieve the same object as his 1779 *Address* – that is to promote calm and public order. To this end, O'Leary appealed to the Rightboys to obey the law and to desist from violence. He advised them that any gains they made would not be commensurate with the amount of disorder caused, and was at pains to emphasise the illegality of the Rightboy oath. However, it was not these remarks, which were anticipated, which attracted notice, but his ostensible legitimisation of the Rightboys' activities by his contention that their actions were 'founded on ... poverty'; that their mode of proceeding was essentially 'moderate'; that the 'manner' in which the tithe was collected was 'oppressive', and that the Church of Ireland clergy were not free of responsibility since 'the oppression of the poor and the love of sordid gain are inconsistent with the character of persons whose ministry is the condemnation of avarice, the contempt of riches and the recommendation of charity'.[58] These claims were well-received by liberal Protestants who favoured tithe reform, but conservatives, and they included a majority of churchmen, landowners or politicians, were deeply disquieted.[59] The chief secretary, Thomas Orde, maintained that O'Leary's 'very insidious letter' gave 'a sort of sanction' to the Rightboys, and his conclusion was supported by 'the noblemen and gentlemen of Munster' who resolved that 'seditious publications ... effecting to redress grievances ... ought immediately to be discountenanced'.[60]

The negativity of these responses puzzled O'Leary who was not opposed to the tithe *per se*, and who elsewhere described the Church of Ireland clergy as 'mild and tolerating'.[61] However, since nothing less than an unconditional repudiation of the Rightboys and everything they were seen to represent was sufficient for conservative Protestants, they chose, as Thomas Bartlett, has put it, to interpret his address 'as an elaborate jesuitical justification of the Rightboy depredations'. This was not O'Leary intention, but since he had *unwittingly* pro-

---

57   Kelly, 'Inter-denominational relations', pp 48–9; England, op.cit., p. 158; Donnelly, (ed.), 'The John Barter Bennett manuscript', p. 17.
58   The 'Addresses' are printed as an appendix to *Mr O'Leary's defence containing a vindication of his conduct and writings during the late disturbances in Munster with a full justification of the Catholics and an account of the risings of the Whiteboys in answer to the false accusations of Theophilus and the ill grounded insinuations of the Rt Rev Dr Woodward, Lord Bishop of Cloyne* (Dublin, 1787).
59   *Dublin Evening Post*, 2 Mar. 1786.
60   Orde to [Nepean], 10 Mar. (P.R.O.,H.O.,100/19 ff 59–60); Resolutions of the noblemen and gentlemen of Munster, 10 Mar. 1786 (N.L.I., *Bolton papers*, Ms 16350/77).
61   Fitzpatrick, *Secret service under Pitt*, pp 250–1.

vided the Rightboys with a number of arguments they were to make their own, and, equally unwittingly, convinced many Protestants that the Rightboys were part of a Catholic conspiracy, he now, and for the first time since he had embarked on his career as a controversialist, experienced the effects of unpopularity.[62]

This proved trying, and following the abject failure of the magistracy and the army to counter the intensified Rightboy activity that took place in the summer of 1786, O'Leary produced his third and final 'address to the common people' in November. He was, as might be expected, more unconditionally critical of the Rightboys on this occasion. But though he condemned their attempts to regulate labour and their interfere with the collection of the hearth tax on the grounds that such undertakings caused hardship and paved the way for scarcity and famine, his appeal against 'anarchy, disorder and confusion' was not unreserved.[63] This did his reputation little good with the fast growing ranks of his Protestant critics, and misleading rumours in September that he was about to convert to Protestantism did not help.[64] However, what was most ominous was the mounting support for the initiative of the proponents of 'Protestant ascendancy' to have the plans for tithe reform that had received official backing in 1786 jettisoned in favour of a law and order response, and the sustained effort to discredit him by portraying him as an apologist for Rightboyism.[65]

The most passionate of O'Leary's critics was the former fellow of Trinity College, Patrick Duigenan, who wrote under the pseudonym of Theophilus. A righteous bigot, as well as stalwart of the Church of Ireland, Duigenan was convinced that the Rightboy disturbances were part of a carefully planned premeditated Catholic assault on the Protestant establishment. Their purpose, he pronounced, was to undermine the Church of Ireland – 'the main pillar of the constitution' – and to reduce its clergy 'to absolute beggary' in order to pave the way for the destruction 'of the whole structure of our government' and its replacement by 'popery'.[66] Indeed, Duigenan contended that 'the insolent factious demands and pretensions' of the Rightboys were 'spirited up by agitating fryars and Romish missionaries sent here for the purpose of sowing sedition'. He cited the support afforded the Rightboys by priests, the fact 'that the popish laity are in general the slaves of their priests, and absolutely under their control' and the central importance of 'mass houses' in the swearing of the Rightboy

62 Resolutions of the Munster peasantry, 1 July 1786, cited in *Theophilus, An address to the nobility and gentry*, pp 110–12; Thomas Bartlett, *The fall and rise of the Irish nation: the Catholic question, 1690–1830* (Dublin, 1992), p. 176.
63 *Cork Hibernian Chronicle*, 20 Nov. 1786.
64 Brady, *Catholics in the press*, p. 244; Evelyn Bolster, *A history of the diocese of Cork from the Penal era to the Famine* (Cork, 1989), p. 125.
65 Kelly, 'Inter-denominational relations', pp 51–2; *idem.*, 'Genesis of 'Protestant ascendancy'', pp 111–12.
66 *Theophilus, An address to the nobility and gentry*, pp 4, 59.

oath as proof of this. More specifically, he identified Arthur O'Leary, whom he referred to as 'the Fryar with *the barbarous surname*', as 'the instructor of the peasantry in religion and politicks'. He assailed his February addresses for exuding a 'turbulent, factious and insolent spirit' that encouraged agitation, and attributed to him the pamphlet defence of the Rightboys written in the name of William O'Driscoll, the so-called 'secretary general to the Munster peasantry'.[67] O'Leary was distressed by this abusive misrepresentation.[68] But equally worrisome was Duigenan's citation of such traditional Protestant fears of Catholicism as the papal claim to depose heretic princes, the *auto-da-fé* and, in the Irish context, of Jacobitism, rebellion and massacre since it served to animate the denominational hatreds O'Leary was so anxious to ameliorate. Even more significantly, it attested to the envigoration of conservative Protestantism, which had been on the defensive since the late 1770s. According to conservatives, the challenge posed 'Protestant ascendancy' by the Rightboys was directly attributable to 'the hasty and improvident repeal of the most important part of that code of laws, called Popery Laws', and they were insistent, for this reason, that there should be no interference with the tithe as any attempt to commute or otherwise to alter its collection would prompt further Catholic demands leading inevitably to the repeal of all the penal laws, the transfer of land to Catholics, the accession of a Catholic monarch, and to a bloody war between Britain and Ireland.[69]

The publication of such an unregenerately intolerant tract troubled O'Leary, and his distress was intensified soon afterwards when Duigenan's views received the endorsement of Richard Woodward, the influential Church of Ireland bishop of Cloyne. Though a liberal on social issues, Woodward was possessed of a 'great but unnatural jealousy of the Roman Catholic religion' which led him publicly to oppose 'freedom of religion'. More pointedly, he upheld Duigenan's assertion that the Rightboy disturbances were precipitated by 'agitating friars and Romish missionaries' by alleging that O'Leary addresses were 'calculated to raise discontent and indignation in the Roman Catholick peasantry against the national clergy, the legislature, the executive power, and their Protestant fellow subjects'.[70] This was as violent a distortion of O'Leary's addresses as Duigenan had perpetrated, but it was avidly consumed by the Protestant population at large. Indeed, it was even alleged by 'a curate' that O'Leary was the instigator of

---

67 *Theophilus, An address to the nobility and gentry*, pp 15–17, 27–8, 63–4, 94–5; *Letter of William O'Driscoll, secretary general of the Munster peasantry to Silver Oliver* (Dublin, 1786).
68 O'Leary's anger is recorded by John Barter Bennett in marginalia on p. 17 of his copy of *Theophilus's Address* (N.L.I., pamphlets, p. 161).
69 *Theophilus, An address to the nobility and gentry*, pp 18–20, 22, 94–107.
70 Portland to Northington, 6 July 1783 (B.L., Northington Letterbook, Add, Ms 38716 ff 44–9); Richard Woodward, Bishop of Cloyne, *The present state of the Church of Ireland containing a description of its precarious situation* ...(4th edition), pp 105–8.

this Catholic plot 'to destroy our church ... an essential part of our constitution'.[71]

O'Leary's distress at the *ad hominen* nature of the criticism directed at him by Duigenan, Woodward and their acolytes in the winter of 1786–7 was compounded by the fact that it induced the Irish parliament in 1787 to abandon tithe reform in favour of a coercive response to the Rightboys. He was also troubled by the response of a number of Protestant friends who were so offended by his 1786 addresses that they cut off all contact with him.[72] The easiest decision for him in these circumstances would have been to have turned his back on the controversy and concentrated on his life as a priest. But, in common with Lord Kenmare and other leaders of Catholic opinion, he realised he could not let Duigenan's and Woodward's allegations go unanswered, even if the enthusiastic response of the Protestant population to their publication effectively signalled the end of his hopes for greater religious and political toleration in the short term. Having first consulted with Archbishop Troy, who commended some changes, O'Leary's eagerly awaited reply was ready for publication by March 1787.[73]

In contrast to James Butler, archbishop of Cashel, who focused on Woodward's criticisms of the Catholic Church in his *Justification* (1787), O'Leary's primary purpose was to 'vindicat[e] ... his conduct and writings' against Duigenan's and Woodward's 'garbled' and 'mangled' misrepresentations. To this end, he insisted that it was entirely appropriate for him to address the poor and oppressed people with 'sympathy and tenderness' as he had done in 1786. Indeed, he contrasted his actions pointedly with the 'harsh' and unChristian response of his Protestant critics. He did not, at the same time, overlook the disturbances themselves or Woodward's assertion that Catholicism was intrinsically intolerant, and he combatively argued that Protestant pamphleteers had resorted to 'the old game of popish plots and confederacies' simply to excite anti-Catholic alarm and 'to banish and drive away the dissenters, Catholics, Quakers; in a word, all Adam's children who do not profess his creed'. This was, of course, precisely what O'Leary's was about preventing, and having demonstrated to his own satisfaction that alarmist claims 'that the Protestant interest was now at stake' were

71 [A curate], *A few serious and seasonable observations on some matters that engage now the public attention* ... (Dublin, 1787), pp 61–2.

72 Kelly, 'The genesis of 'Protestant ascendancy'', pp 119–20; Donnelly, (ed.), 'John Barter Bennett manuscript', p. 10.

73 Kelly, 'Inter-denominational relations', pp 57–9; *Dublin Evening Post*, 15 Feb., 1 Mar.; *Volunteer Evening Post*, 27 Feb.; Kenmare to Moylan, 23 Feb. 1787 in Evelyn Bolster,(ed.), 'Moylan correspondence 1', *Coll.Hib.*, xiv (1971), pp 93–4; *Mr O'Leary's defence containing a vindication of his conduct and writings during the late disturbances in Munster with a full justification of the Catholics, and an account of the risings of the Whiteboys in answer to the false accusations of Theophilus and the ill grounded insinuations of the rt revd. Dr Woodward, Lord Bishop of Cloyne* (Dublin, 1787), *passim*.

groundless, he maintained that if the Church of Ireland clergy followed the example of their Catholic counterparts and reduced their charges this would do more to eradicate the Rightboys than their persistent cries of 'wolf'. This was not what the defenders of the Church of Ireland wanted to hear, but O'Leary was determined to demonstrate how burdensome the tithe was for the population at large. He was firmly of the opinion that its administration was irrevocably tilted in favour of those who received rather than those who paid it, and he offered persuasive evidence to show that the Rightboys were motivated by a wish to lessen the onerousness of the impost rather than by any wish to weaken the Church of Ireland. He was equally assertive on other points. Thus, he challenged both Theophilus and Woodward to produce even one of the 'agitating friars and Romish missionaries' they maintained so confidently were the instigators of sedition; he instanced Protestant support for the Rightboys to demonstrate that the disturbances were not anti-Protestant; he chided Woodward for his silence in 1785-6; he exposed lacunae in his narrative; and he justified the 1774 oath of allegiance in a fashion which made Woodward and other critics appear bigoted and intolerant.[74]

The frequency with which O'Leary accused Woodward of unChristian intolerance in his *Defence* provides the most visible testament of the extent of his disappointment at the rise in denominational animus in the mid-1780s. The fact that his animadversions on Duigenan and Woodward provoked howls of outraged protest from their supporters only served to intensify these feelings. This was highlighted by the proclivity of many critics of the *Defence* to resort to abuse rather than cogent argument. Ironically, several respondents, who rehearsed the spurious accusation that O'Leary was responsible for instigating this Catholic rebellion in an attempt 'to overthrow our happy constitution in church and state', decried O'Leary for his use of 'the most abusive and scurrilous language'.[75] A more imaginative, if no less morally bankrupt, response was provided by the author of *A letter to the reverend Dr O'Leary*, who congratulated O'Leary for his part in lulling Protestants into a false sense of security while Catholics readied themselves to replace the established church with Catholicism and 'English

74 *Mr O'Leary's defence ..., passim.*
75 For criticism of O'Leary's tone see Revd T.B. Clarke, *The second edition of Junius Alter's letter to Mr O'Leary with a short examination into the first causes of the present lawless spirit of the Irish peasantry and a plan of reform* (Dublin, 1787), p. 4 and A clergyman [Thomas Elrington], *A short refutation of the arguments contained in Dr Butler's letter to Lord Kenmare with a reply to the third section of Mr O'Leary's defence* (Dublin, 1787), pp 3–6; *Remarks on a letter lately published signed Arthur O'Leary stiled an address to the Protestant nobility and gentry of Ireland* (Dublin, 1787), pp 8–9, 13. He is echoed by Detector, *Observations on the indecent and illiberal strictures against the lord Bishop of Cloyne contained in a pamphlet lately published under the title of Mr O'Leary's defence etc.* (Dublin, 1787) who accused O'Leary of 'abusive scurrility' and by John Barter Bennett (see Donnelly (ed.), 'John Barter Bennett manuscript', pp 10–11).

domination' with 'a Catholic king'.[76] Few were so inventive. The Cork Protestant, John Barter Bennett, with whom O'Leary was on friendly terms until 1786, simply derogated his *Defence* as a work of 'the most notorious falsehoods and grossest misrepresentation'. Detector did the same, but what was most revealing about his response was his claim that Woodward's argument for continued Protestant ascendancy was 'the sentiments of every member of the established religion ', indeed every 'man who wishes well to the peace, subordination and tranquillity of society'.[77] The Revd Thomas Brooke Clarke concurred. He described O'Leary as the 'bold defender of the insurgents and champion of the Romanists against the Protestants in respect to their *religion* and *properties*', and cited his writings as demonstrable proof of how counter-productive it was to repeal the 'popery laws':

> Survey the present complexion of the Romanists! They rise from demand to demand. They have grown bold upon our indulgence, haughty on their success and imperious in their toleration. Would any Popish priest, till of late, have dared to smile inhumanly at the sufferings of the Protestant ecclesiastics, and not only to hold out a protection, but to halloo insurgents on, by laughing at acts that no necessity could warrant.

Since these were the words of an implacable opponent of both the Catholic Church and of Catholic relief, it was predictable that Brooke should suggest it might be necessary 'to draw tight again the religious restraints which we have relaxed ... to restore peace to both sects'.[78] Such explicit discussion of the merits of reintroducing the penal laws was uncommon. But conservative Protestants clearly hankered after the security they offered, because insecurity lay at the root of the persistent raising of such matters as the episcopal consecration oath of the Catholic Church, and warnings drawn from history that 'the bloody weapons of offence' would be used against Protestants if Catholics ever achieved political power in Ireland in the battery of replies to O'Leary's *Defence*.[79]

Liberal Protestants were more positive,[80] but whereas overwhelmingly lauda-

76 *A letter to the Rev Dr O'Leary [found on the Cloghnakilty Road]* (Dublin, 1787), especially pp 13–14. The author of this letter purported to be William O'Driscoll (the spokesman for the Whiteboys).

77 Donnelly, (ed.), 'John Barter Bennet manuscript', p. 11; Detector, *Observations on the indecent and illiberal strictures against the Lord Bishop of Cloyne*, p. 7.

78 Clarke, *The second edition of Junius Alter...*, pp 11–13.

79 Verax, *Remarks on a letter lately published signed Arthur O'Leary...*, pp 11–13; A clergyman [Thomas Elrington], *A short refutation of the arguments contained in Dr Butler's letter to Lord Kenmare with a reply to the third section of Mr O'Leary's defence* (Dublin, 1787), *passim*; Isaac Ashe, *A compendium of revealed religion...to which is added a concise and authentic account of the Reformation...with occasional observations...on the pamphlets...by...the Rev Mr O'Leary...*(Dublin, 1787); Philip Le Fanu, *An abridgement of the history of the Council of Constance with an appendix concerning Mr O'Leary...* (Dublin, 1787), pp 107–19.

80 *DEP*, 1, 3 Mar. 1787.

tory reviews of O'Leary's publications were the norm in the late 1770s and early 1780s, this was not so now. It is indicative of just how much opinion had changed, and of how hostile the political environment had become to his ideas that the mere introduction of his name into debate in the House of Commons in February 1787 prompted irreconcilable assessments of his work and its significance.[81] O'Leary effectively acknowledged this by publishing a reply to a critical article in the *Monthly Review* in July in which he reaffirmed the arguments he had made in his *Defence*.[82] This was well-received by the proponents of tithe reform and religious toleration. The advocates of Protestant ascendancy remained as implacable as ever, and the fact that they were able easily to reject Henry Grattan's attempt in 1788 to secure approval of a bill commuting the tithe indicates that it was they and not the proponents of religious toleration, were firmly in political command once more.[83]

VI

There is no surviving contemporary documentary account of how O'Leary responded to this comprehensive rejection of his goal of a more politically and religiously inclusive society by the majority of Protestant opinion. It is known that he disliked acrimony and was prone to depression. And it has been confidently and plausibly advanced that these synergised with his 'disgust ... with the condition of the country, and hopeless[ness] of doing anything by which it could be improved' to induce him to depart Ireland in 1789 for the 'freer' and more 'congenial' environment in England. He spent the final thirteen years of his life in London. His time there was not without incident or achievement as his biographers and the historian of English Catholicism in the late eighteenth century show.[84] However, it lacked the direction and purpose it had possessed in the eighteen years that he lived in Ireland as O'Leary acknowledged in his last work when he welcomed the Act of Union, because, he forecast,

---

81   *Volunteer Evening Post*, 6 Mar. 1787; *Parl. Reg.* (Irl.), vii, 357; England, op.cit., pp 187–8.
82   *Mr. O'Leary's letter to the monthly reviewers* (Dublin, 1787); *D.E.P.*, 13, 15 Sept. 1787; Daniel Thomas, *Observations on the pamphlets published by the Bishop of Cloyne, Mr Trant and Theophilus on one side, and on those by Mr O'Leary, Mr Barber on the other to which are added remarks on the causes of the late insurrections in Munster, a consideration of the grievances under which the peasantry of Ireland labours with a proposal of an adequate compensation for tithes* (Dublin, 1787).
83   *D.E.P.*, 28 Feb. 1788; Candidus, *A full display of some late publications on the subject of tithes and the sufferings of the established clergy in the south of Ireland attributed to those dues* (Dublin, 1788); *Parl. Reg.* (Irl.), vii, 336–60.
84   England, op.cit., p. 190ff; Buckley, op. cit., p. 304 ff; *A narrative of the misunderstanding between Rev. Arthur O'Leary and Rev. Mr Hussey* (Dublin 1791); Bernard Ward, *The dawn of the Catholic revival in England 1781–1803* (2 vols, London, 1909).

it will close the tumultary scenes which have distracted my ill-fated country for ages; and make the natives of every religious persuasion happy; a people *united*, not in a league against Great Britain, but *united* with her and amongst themselves in interest, prosperity and power; by a free and equal participation of all benefits and advantages arising in the state, and by the removal of those jealousies which ever subsist between kingdoms' situated as Great Britain and Ireland.[85]

O'Leary's hope was that the Act of Union would put an end to English exploitation of Ireland and lead directly to Catholic emancipation. He was confident that if this happened, it would pave the way for full religious tolerance because he remained as firmly of the view in 1800 as he had been in the early 1780s, when interest in his radical religious vision was at its acme, that true religion 'instead of inspiring hatred and rancor, commands us to love'.[85]

85 O'Leary, *Address to the Lords spiritual and temporal*, p. 6.
86 Ibid., p. 8.

Father Nicholas Sheehy (*c*.1728–1766)

Thomas Power

The execution of Fr Nicholas Sheehy of Clogheen, county Tipperary, in 1766 on a trumped-up charge of murder, stands out as one of the tragic events of Catholic Ireland in the eighteenth century, comparable to that of Sir James Cotter in 1720. Much of our knowledge of the case devolves on a consideration of the legal proceedings. Because the documentation is extensive, the details of the affair are well known, making an extended repetition of them here unnecessary. My purpose, rather, is to set the case within the economic, social and political context of the period.

At the outset it must be said that use of the term 'radical' with reference to Fr Sheehy in part applies more to what was done to him by an ultra group among the Protestant gentry of the county than to whatever involvement he may have had in agrarian agitation. It can also refer to the fact that he was in part radicalised by the course of events and the charges brought against him.

I

The Sheehy affair has been well written on, and moreover documentation on the episode is plentiful. Madden, in his multi-volume history of the United Irishmen, devotes a lengthy chapter to Fr Sheehy and the Whiteboys, and it is interesting to note its inclusion as a prelude to the emergence of radicalism in the 1790s.[1] Madden states that his information on the case came from a number of sources: contemporary printed accounts; older inhabitants of the Clogheen district at the time he was writing (1840s); and legal documents in the Crown Office in Clonmel, copied by him.[2] Burke, in his *History of Clonmel*, is largely dependent on Madden though he sought out additional information which he hoped would clarify some obscurities but this exercise proved elusive. Yet Burke's contribution has been to add local detail which has helped to fill in certain gaps.[3] Both Madden and Burke are invaluable sources because they reproduced origi-

---

1 R.R. Madden, *The United Irishmen, their lives and times*, i (Dublin, 1857), pp 21–89.
2 Ibid., i, pp 34, 36.
3 W. P. Burke, *History of Clonmel* (Waterford, 1907) (hereafter Burke, Clonmel), p. 361n. Burke had access to some important estate papers including those of the Perry family who were landowners in the parish of Newcastle where Sheehy officiated.

nal documentation, most of which is now destroyed. We are clearly in their debt for taking such an interest in the case and reproducing original material so extensively.

Froude's account of the case is based on assertion, on a scant and selective perusal of the sources of evidence (he is largely dependent on Musgrave), is inaccurate in some of its details, and is credulous and partisan in its tone.[4] Lecky, in contrast, is more balanced and objective in his treatment of the issue, in that he clearly recognised the arbitrary nature of the proceedings, and his information is better sourced, for instance he refutes the credibility assigned by Froude to the depositions reproduced by Musgrave.[5] Works on Sheehy in the present century indicate that though originally rejected by his fellow clergy and exalted only by the peasantry, Sheehy has come in time to be revered by middle- and upper-class Catholics as well.[6]

II

It appears that Sheehy's comfortable family status was one reason for him being targeted. A branch of the Sheehy family (originally MacSheehy) settled at Drumcollogher, county Limerick where they were large head tenants on the earl of Courtenay's estate.[7] They became wealthy graziers and were able to make loans to the Protestant petty gentry of the area. A younger son of the family, Francis Sheehy, son of John Sheehy (d.1740), married into the Power family of Bawnfune, parish of Kilronan, county Waterford, and inherited the property in right of his wife. They were head tenants to over 600 acres under Lord Midleton until 1848[8] and they were the parents of Nicholas the priest, who had a brother William (d.1775) and at least one sister, Catherine, who married a Burke of Clonmel. Something of the status of the family is indicated by the fact that two of Sheehy's first cousins married into important Catholic families in the region: two of the daughters of Roger Sheehy of Drumcollogher and later Cork city,

4   J.A. Froude, *The English in Ireland in the eighteenth century* (3 vols), i (New York, 1874), pp 29–34.
5   W.E.H. Lecky, *A history of Ireland in the eighteenth century* (5 vols), ii (London, 1892), pp 41–4.
6   P. Lonergan, 'The life and death of Father Sheehy', *I.E.R.*, 17 (July, 1896), pp 600–32; P.J. Boland, 'The trial of Fr. Sheehy'. *New Ireland Review*, 23 (June 1905), pp 215–22; P. O'Connell, 'The plot against Father Nicholas Sheehy: the historical background', *I.E.R.*, 108 (1967), pp 372–84; T.A. Murphy, 'Fr. Nicholas Sheehy, P.P. Clogheen' in P. O'Connell and W.C. Darmody (eds), *Siege of Clonmel: tercentenary souvenir record* (1950); and T. de Bhial, *Oidheadh an athair Uí Shíthigh* (Baile Átha Cliath, 1954).
7   The following details of the family are derived from: J. Begley, *The diocese of Limerick from 1691 to the present time* (Dublin, 1938), pp 72–3; *Burke's Irish family records* (London, 1976), 1018; and R.R. Madden, *The literary life and correspondence of the countess of Blessington* (3 vols) i (London, 1855), pp 13–15. For Courtenay: *Limerick Chronicle*, 28 Sept. 1780.
8   In 1758 William Sheehy is given as the tenant of Bawnfoune (303 in and Upper and Lower Sellyheene, barony of Glenahiry, county Waterford (N.A.: QRO Ledger: Clonmel, 1753–8, 142–3).

Anne and Catherine, married Bryan Keating of Bansha, county Tipperary (1768) and Patrick Nagle of Annakissy, county Cork (1775), respectively.[9] In a later generation, Marguerite Power of the Bawnfune family married the earl of Blessington.

Although the information is not definitive, it appears likely that Sheehy was born at Barrettstown near Fethard probably in 1728.[10] He was educated at Louvain, and ordained in Rome in 1752, factors which again indicate status since the Church was not cheap to enter, involving as it did a classical education and the financial support of one's family.[11] Upon his return he became *c*.1752 curate of Newcastle, county Tipperary close to his Bawnfune home; and later (possibly in 1755) parish priest of the united parishes of Shanrahan, Ballysheehan and Templetenny, which later became the parishes of Clogheen and Burncourt.[12] This area was the epicentre of Whiteboy unrest from its initial outbreaks in late 1761, a fact which was to play a vital role in Sheehy's ultimate fate.

III

One of the key questions regarding Sheehy is the degree to which he was involved with the social and radical issues of the day. He first came to the notice of the authorities when he was included in a list of priests who were obliged by the Catholic bishop of Cloyne, John O'Brien, to publicise in their respective parishes an edict of excommunication which he had placed on the town of Mitchelstown, county Cork in 1758.[13] The landlord of the district, Lord Kingston, an absentee, fearing the challenge to his authority and the loss of commerce to the town which publication of the excommunication would result in, offered a reward of £5 for the apprehension of each priest, including Sheehy, who had publicised the ban.[14] The affair may have initiated a strained relationship between Sheehy and his superior bishop, Pierce Creagh of Waterford and Lismore, who resided in Clonmel, the details of which are unclear.[15] However, it

---

9 *Burke's Irish family records* (London, 1976), p. 1018.
10 Lonergan, 'Father Sheehy', pp 600–32 at 602; P. Power, *Waterford and Lismore: a compendious history of the united dioceses* (Waterford, 1937), p. 134. His tombstone inscription declares that he died in his thirty-eight year.
11 Power, *Waterford and Lismore*, p. 134. T.P. Power and K. Whelan, (eds), *Endurance and emergence: Catholics in Ireland in the eighteenth century* (Dublin, 1990), p. 77.
12 P. O'Connell, 'The plot', *I.E.R.*, 108 (1967), pp 372–84 at 372.
13 For a summary of the Mitchelstown affair see Thomas P. Power, *Land, politics and society in eighteenth-century Tipperary* (Oxford, 1993) (hereafter Power, *Tipperary*), pp 240–1. For a lengthier treatment see James Coombes, *A bishop of the penal times: the life and times of John O'Brien, bishop of Cloyne and Ross, 1700–1769* (Cork, 1981).
14 *Cork Evening Post*, 11 Sept. 1758 (Quoted in J. Brady, *Catholics and Catholicism in the eighteenth-century press* (Maynooth, 1965), pp 94–5).
15 Burke, *Clonmel*, p. 389.

may be related to the fact that Sheehy was taking instructions from a bishop (O'Brien) who was not his superior, since Sheehy's parish lay within the diocese of Waterford and Lismore. Lord Taaffe said of Creagh that he 'behaved with all the severity he could towards the unfortunate priest Sheehy'.[16] Certainly, when Sheehy was in the midst of his troubles, Creagh did not intervene to speak on his behalf. This reluctance may have been motivated by considerations of self-protection, since as a bishop his status in the country was legally questionable and also his recent public involvement in the Mitchelstown affair may have raised his public profile more than was prudent.

The same reason may apply to the position of Sheehy's near neighbour the parish priest of Clonmel, William Egan, who was also vicar general of the diocese and coadjutor to Creagh. His reluctance to intervene on Sheehy's behalf can be interpreted as either clerical disapproval of his involvement, or a reluctance to become publically involved in a matter of controversy with the authorities. The most senior cleric in the region, James Butler, archbishop of Cashel, was equally deferential; while Sheehy's reputation as a trouble-maker was reported on disapprovingly to Rome.[17] This reluctance on the part of other clergy to be drawn into a defence of Sheehy is understandable in the circumstances given that a relaxation of the penal laws was hoped for, but at a popular level it was resented. Thus it was said that when Sheehy's body was being borne away for burial, his blood was sprinkled on Egan's door a symbol of how he was held responsible in popular eyes for the shedding of innocent blood.[18] A later lament perpetuated this tradition of clerical culpability in the fate of Sheehy, a line from one poem saying: 'Egan agus an Creach do dhíol thú' (Egan and Creagh sold you).[19]

To fully understand the events of the 1760s, the agrarian and sectarian dimensions need to be treated separately. In Sheehy's case, however, the two overlap. Clogheen, where he ministered, became the centre of Whiteboy activity. It was where the earl of Drogheda, who was sent to quell the unrest in 1762, had his headquarters; it was the centre of Whiteboy unrest; and it was the centre of Sheehy's parish. Thus agrarianism and sectarianism became enmeshed in time, place, circumstance, and personality.

Sheehy was charged with being involved with the Whiteboys. A sympathetic Catholic contemporary, in a cautiously worded estimation of Sheehy, conceded that he was predisposed 'towards relieving all those within his district, whom he

---

16 Taaffe to Beauchamp, 21 May 1766 (R.I.A.: Ms B.1.1., *O'Conor papers*).
17 See for instance his circular letter to the clergy and people dated 2 Feb. 1762 (Cashel Diocesan papers, Archbishop's House, Thurles: papers of James Butler I 1762/1-N.L.I., microfilm P.5998); C.Giblin, 'Catalogue of material of Irish interest in the collection Nunziatura di Fiandra, Vatican Archives pt.7, vols 135Hh-137' *Coll. Hib.*, 11 (1968), p. 52.
18 Burke, *Clonmel*, 390.
19 Quoted in Lonergan, 'Father Sheehy', p. 619.

fancied to be injured or oppressed'; otherwise he was considered a priest of 'unimpeached character'.[20] In the opinion of Amyas Griffith, a liberal Protestant, who was an excise officer in the area at the time, Sheehy 'was guilty of some irregularities ... perhaps he mixed with and countenanced the White-Boys. But it is absurd to suppose he was guilty of the murder for which he suffered'.[21]

Such a sympathetic predisposition towards Whiteboy aims may have derived from a decline in Sheehy's personal income, said by one source to be £200 which was substantial putting him on a par with smaller middlemen.[22] The enclosure of commons and the high rent for potato ground were the causes of population movement and even depopulation in the district. Since settlements in such areas were the source of income for priests like Sheehy, they were now left with nothing.[23] Villages with a hundred or so of cottages, each paying 6d. or 1s. annually, was a considerable loss. Such personal circumstances may have predisposed Sheehy to an acquiescence with Whiteboy objectives.

In addition, according to Madden, a novel claim was made in 1762 by a tithe farmer named Dobbyn on all Catholics for 5s. for every marriage celebrated by a priest in the Ballyporeen area.[24] If this is correct, it seems really innovatory since it was not the business of tithe farmers to make such arbitrary demands, rather that was the preserve of the priest of the area. Also, it would have had implications for Sheehy's own source of income. It is not surprising, therefore, that he publicly condemned the demand and that he encouraged resistance to its collection. On this particular issue, then, Curry's judgement on Sheehy concerning his 'unavoidable connection with those rioters, several hundred of whom were his parishioners', would appear to be substantiated.[25]

Sheehy also was said to have opposed the collection of church rates/tithes in the parish of Newcastle where, it was claimed that, there were no Protestant families, and was represented as someone who opposed tithes in principle where no service was rendered in return for their payment.[26] These facts may be the closest we can come to determining the degree of his involvement. In general, Sheehy can be viewed as a transitional figure in terms of clerical activism, between the relatively quiescent figures of the early eighteenth century and the more proactive clergy of the 1790s.

The inability of the grand jury in Tipperary to gain convictions on Whiteboy charges was an embarrassment to them.[27] A contemporary of Catholic sympa-

20 J. Curry, *An historical and critical review of the civil wars in Ireland* (London, 1786), ii, p. 274.
21 A. Griffith, *Observations on the bishop of Cloyne's pamphlet* (Dublin, 1787), p. 63.
22 Burke, *Clonmel*, p. 368; Power and Whelan, *Endurance*, p. 76.
23 *The Dublin Magazine* (Apr.1763), p. 199.
24 Madden, *United Irishmen*, i, p. 34.
25 Quoted in Burke, *Clonmel*, p. 368.
26 Madden, *United Irishmen*, i, p. 22. The census returns for 1766, however, show three Protestant families in the parish (W.H. Rennison, *Succession list of the bishops, cathedral, and parochial clergy of Waterford and Lismore* (n.p., [c.1920]).
27 Power, *Tipperary*, pp 214–16.

thies, conceded that during the Whiteboy outbreaks Sheehy was often indicted and tried as a priest but that he was always acquitted because of a lack of evidence.[28] Madden suggests that Sheehy was involved in collecting money for the defence of those accused of Whiteboy crimes who were his parishioners, and thus their acquittal was attributed to him.[29] This no doubt did not ingratiate him with the gentry of the county and was a contributory cause in him being targeted for destruction.

Another reason for his victimization is that he was a cousin to Edmund ('Buck') Sheehy, of Lodge, county Tipperary, gent., who successfully competed for preferential leases in the area and whose success was resented by Protestants who had been unsuccessful.[30] He, with two others, was executed two months after Sheehy.

IV

The traditional depiction of Sheehy's prosecutors has viewed them as motivated by purely sectarian concerns using a trumped-up charge of treason, rebellion, and murder to justify their cause. These were, however, the effects and manifestations of hysteria, for the causes were deeper and more complex. The judgements and perceptions of local Protestant society in general and a section of the gentry in particular, were informed by a series of crucial developments in the early 1760s. The 1760s, in fact, witnessed the coincidence in time and place of a novel set of circumstances which caused Protestants in the region to feel insecure in the face of, as they perceived it, a new assertiveness on the part of Catholics. These need to be elucidated if the actions of the gentry against Sheehy are to be understood. Already the Mitchelstown episode had shown how an internal ecclesiastical squabble had made Catholic bishops, who legally speaking had no status in the country, appear to be undermining the authority of the absentee landlord of the area. There may have been fears that such a challenge might be repeated elsewhere.

Secondly, the 1761 election in Tipperary was sharply sectarian.[31] Thomas Mathew of Thomastown, a convert, stood as a candidate in the Catholic interest, his opponent being his neighbour, Sir Thomas Maude of Dundrum, an improver and evangelical. Maude challenged the sincerity of Mathew's conversion and hence the validity of his candidature. The election was characterised by intimidation and partiality, but the amazing result was that Mathew gained a

28 Curry, *Historical and critical review*, ii, p. 274.
29 Madden, *United Irishmen*, i, p. 31.
30 Power, *Tipperary*, pp 250, 265.
31 For what follows see Power, *Tipperary*, pp 228–31.

narrow victory over Maude and was returned with Henry Prittie the other candidate. However, Mathew was unseated upon Maude's petition and the latter was returned instead. He played a key role in the events of the 1760s. Despite this ultimate victory, the election displayed the ability of Catholics to mobilise freeholders in favour of their candidate, Mathew, and to gain initial success. The ability of Catholics to influence the election so decidedly in favour of the convert, Mathew, served to unleash fears and concerns among Protestants about their political security.

Thirdly, a series of court decisions in 1759 and 1762 deriving from proceedings under the penal laws, had the effect of questioning the legal status of converts and the title of Protestants holding land under them.[32] Only with the passing of legislation in 1762 and 1764 was the situation regularised. Another act in 1764 confirmed Protestants who had purchased lands from Catholics in their title. This was particularly applicable in the Tipperary context in relation to the Bagwell purchase of the Dunboyne property. John Bagwell was a leading member of the group which targeted comfortable Catholics like Fr Sheehy.

Fourthly, there were fears among sections of Protestant society that if Catholics were permitted to loan money to Protestants with land as security, then the result would be a diminution of Protestant landownership in the event of default in repayment. As things stood already Catholic creditors held considerable sway over Protestant debtors, for instance it was said of Justin McCarthy of Tipperary that 'merely by the number of Protestants that were his debtors, [he] kept all persons of that religion in awe throughout the whole county and effectively prevented them by mere intimidation from putting any of the popish laws in execution for many years'.[33] Given these fears contemporary attempts to liberalise mortgage facilities to Catholics were defeated in parliament.

Fifthly, there was resentment at the success of a group of upwardly mobile Catholics, including the priest's cousin, Edmund Sheehy, in gaining preferential leases on the Butler (Cahir) estate in the early 1760s.[34] Sixthly, anti-quarterage agitation by Catholics in the towns in the early 1760s was seen, at least locally in towns like Clonmel, as treasonous and inspired by the Whiteboys.[35]

All this was taking place against the backdrop of the conflict with the French and the Whiteboy outbreaks which coincidentally broke out in the area. The hostilities of the Seven Years War between the British and the French concluded with the Peace of Paris on 10 February 1763. Prior to that the possibility of a juncture between the Whiteboys and the French coincided at least in terms of a time-frame; following it, however, less credibility could be attached to it, yet it was in the post-1763 period that the depiction of the Whiteboys as being in

32   For what follows see ibid., pp 242–5.
33   Quoted in Power, *Tipperary*, p. 248.
34   Ibid., pp 249–50.
35   Ibid., pp 251–2.

complicity with the French was most articulated by the Tipperary gentry. Never was it a possibility at any stage that the French would combine with the Whiteboys.[36]

This complex set of circumstances and developments informed the perceptions of the Protestant gentry of the county, whom one contemporary observer labelled 'red hot', a section of whom embarked on a course of radical action.[37] In the face of what this group perceived as multiple expressions of Catholic assertiveness, compounded by their inability to gain apprehensions for Whiteboy acts in the early stages, their nerve broke and the result was the hysteria and executions of 1766.

It is clear also that the events of the decade and the Fr Sheehy episode especially, caused a strained relationship between the local gentry and the central government. In the period 1761–6 Ireland had a succession of five lords lieutenant (Lords Halifax, Northumberland, Weymouth, Hertford, and Bristol). The weakness and instability which this situation implied was exploited to advantage by the local gentry. Government was concerned that the early growth of whiteboyism was due to a lack of resolve on the part of the local magistrates in the areas affected. In the event it was the Tipperary magistrates who first acted with resolve, and their example was emulated in adjoining counties.[38] Reflecting the seriousness with which the outbreaks were viewed, the lord lieutenant, Halifax, in 1762 granted the local justices the power to call in the military and to lead troops in apprehending suspected Whiteboys.[39] In addition, justices of the peace in Ireland had the power to enquire about treason, whereas their English counterparts could not.[40] It was the arbitrary exercise of these powers over the next four years which was to lead to the convictions and executions of 1766.

In the short term, however, though their efforts resulted in many apprehensions the gentry were to see all their endeavours come to naught when in 1762 Sir Richard Aston, the Lord Chief Justice of the Common Pleas, conducting a special commission at Clonmel, acquitted large numbers of those accused. This no doubt piqued the local gentry greatly, and was a marker along the way in their increasing lack of confidence in the central administration to see matters from their point of view. Indicative of the gulf that had been created by the time of Sheehy's execution is the fact that Sir Thomas Maude published a notice in which he publicly castigated the lord lieutenants, who had been in office during the course of the entire affair, for not taking firmer measures.[41]

---

36 L.T., *A candid enquiry into the causes and motives of the late riots in the province of Munster in Ireland* (London, 1767), pp 5–6.
37 Quoted in Power, *Tipperary*, p. 234.
38 Halifax to Egremont, 13 April 1762 (P.R.O., State papers, Ireland, vol. 421)
39 Ibid.
40 E. Bullingbrooke, *The duty and authority of the justices of the peace and parish officers for Ireland* (Dublin, 1788), p. 484.
41 L.T., *A candid enquiry*, pp 11–12.

V

The new powers given to the magistrates were immediately implemented and though several were apprehended, Sheehy and Fr John Doyle, parish priest of Ardfinnan, eluded capture.[42] By the end of May 1762, however, Doyle had been captured and he along with Sheehy and Fr Pierce Daniel of Cahir were presented by the grand jury at the summer assizes for being unregistered priests.[43] It was unusual to have this as a reason for prosecution, for although it was on the statute book since 1704 (2 Anne c.7) that priests had to be registered it had been largely unenforced for more than half a century.

In Sheehy's case the next known development was that at the Clonmel general assizes in May 1763 he was bailed in £2,000 on an indictment that he, 'with divers others, ill-disposed persons and disturbers of the peace', in March 1762 at Scarlap made William Ross swear never to inform against the Whiteboys.[44] Ross and his father, James, were large Catholic middlemen on Lord Cahir's estate, and by enclosing commonage on their lands of Drumlemmon, they had provoked the Whiteboy outbreaks initially. The Rosses, however, forfeited their recognizance (£100 each) allowing the charge against Sheehy to lapse for the reason, it has been suggested, that they were unwilling to proceed against him.[45] Whatever the level of his involvement at this stage, it was quite different from that later attributed to him in 1765–6. What characterised these particular assizes, however, was the large number of acquittals on Whiteboy charges, much to the embarrassment of the local gentry who had put up 300 guineas as a reward for securing the apprehension of suspects.[46]

In response to these frustrations, a crucial development in the proceedings took place in July 1763. It having been brought to the notice of the grand jury that threats had been made to the owners of tithes in various parishes of the county, they now gave public notice that 'we have got reason to suspect and believe that such unlawful practices have been encouraged and maybe prevented by several Popish priests illegally officiating in such parishes'. They vowed to prosecute any such priest in whose parish such threats occurred in future, offered a reward of 20 guineas for information, and invited all aggrieved by such threats to submit details at the next assizes.[47] This formulation has two points of interest: firstly, because of frustration at the large number of previous acquittals the grand jury targeted the priests as more easily identifiable for apprehension;

42 *Sleator's Public Gazetteer*, 8 May 1762 (Brady, *Catholics*, pp 104—5).
43 *Dublin Gazette*, 25–9 May 1762; *F.D.J.*, 22–6 June 1762.
44 Quoted in R.R. Madden, *The literary life and correspondence of the countess of Blessington* (2 vols.), i (London, 1855), p. 487.
45 Madden, *United Irishmen*, pp 36–7; Burke, *Clonmel*, p. 369.
46 *F.D.J.* 26–9 Mar., 31 May–4 June 1763.
47 Ibid., 26–30 July 1763.

and secondly, there is the explicit assumption that since the priests were attached to parishes where intimidation over tithes was taking place, that they were naturally involved.

While this development did not lead to a decline in tithe intimidation, it had important consequences for Sheehy.[48] On 28 March 1764, Sheehy with three others was indicted for unlawfully assembling with 200 others on 10 February 1762 for the purpose of high treason and rebellion.[49] At the summer assizes of that year, Sheehy with five others was indicted for on 7 March and 6 October 1762 assembling at Clogheen in white shirts for a rebellious purpose.[50] In a separate indictment at the same assizes, Sheehy and seven others were indicted for on 4 January 1764 assaulting John Bridge at Shanbally.[51] We do not know the outcome of these charges of treason, but presumably Sheehy was not brought to conviction at this time. The ensuing period, despite the vigorous efforts of the local gentry, witnessed their inability to bring Whiteboy leaders to full conviction because of a lack of evidence.[52]

By November 1764 two of the lord justices were advising the lord lieutenant that it was the opinion of the Privy Council that it would be preferable to have Sheehy privately apprehended by Cornelius O'Callaghan, a justice of the peace for the county, and conveyed to Dublin, than to have a proclamation issued which might be the signal for Sheehy to flee the country.[53] A warrant to this effect was issued to O'Callaghan with the request that 'he would cause the same to be executed with the greatest secrecy, care and despatch'.[54] By the time O'Callaghan received the warrant, however, Sheehy had fled apparently to his relatives in county Limerick, not to France where if he had been an agent he would likely have gone.[55] However a proclamation was eventually issued in February 1765 offering a reward of £300 for his capture.[56] As rewards went this was unusually high and it should be compared with the fact that his annual income was £200. The issuing of the proclamation reflects the ability of the local gentry, particularly the earl of Carrick (who with John Bagwell was on a Lords and

48 For further acts of intimidation over tithe in the Clogheen area: *F.D.J.*, 29 Oct.–1 Nov. 1763, 5–8 Oct.1765; Mount Melleray Abbey, county Waterford, Burke Ms 31 p.[269]; *Gentleman's and London Magazine* 35 (1765), p. 703.
49 Burke, *Clonmel*, pp 369–70. The bill of indictment was sworn to by Michael Guinan, who with his wife Catherine in 1759 converted to the established church (E. O'Byrne, *The convert rolls*, Dublin, 1981, p. 123).
50 Burke, *Clonmel*, p. 370.
51 Madden, *United Irishmen*, i, p. 37–8.
52 *F.J.* 21–25 Aug. 1764.
53 Shannon and John Ponsonby to [Lord Lieutenant], 10 Nov. 1764 (N.A.: Country Letters Miscellaneous (now destroyed), copy in Mount Melleray Abbey, Burke mss. in volume entitled 'Bishops of Waterford' (unpaginated) sub 'Peter (sic) Creagh.'
54 Ibid.
55 M. Lenihan, *Limerick, its history and antiquities* (Limerick, 1866), p. 357, n. 2.
56 *F.D.J.*, 19–23 Feb.1765.

Commons joint committee investigating the Whiteboy outbreaks), to change government opinion, previously neutral, of Sheehy for it referred to the fact that since he had gone into hiding he had engaged in 'several treasonable practices to raise a rebellion in this kingdom'. The charge of treason reflects the frustration of the gentry to convict Sheehy on a more minor charge.

Within a month of the proclamation being issued Sheehy had surrendered to Cornelius O'Callaghan who lodged him temporarily in Clonmel jail from which he was later conveyed under close guard to Dublin to stand trial.[57] His voluntary surrender can be interpreted as indicative of his belief in his own innocence. A person charged with treason and latterly murder (the latter implicit in the reward offered in March 1765), was unlikely to surrender unless he was innocent. Government conceded to Sheehy's wish to take his trial in Dublin where he expected to get justice which, as he later said himself, 'was more than he could expect in the county Tipperary'.[58]

Within a week of Sheehy's surrender the grand jury of the county issued a reward of £50 for the conviction of those who had supposedly murdered John Bridge, whose disappearance late in 1764 was equated with murder by the Whiteboys, who was one of the key informants against Sheehy, and whose non-appearance at the March assizes where he was to give evidence, raised suspicions.[59] This was a serious development for the murder charge was based merely on supposition not on hard evidence, and although Sheehy is not specifically mentioned in the reward notice, it is clear that since Bridge was a prime informant against him, the implication was that Sheehy was somehow responsible. In Curry's view it was an open invitation to anyone who was prepared to swear that Bridge was murdered by certain named persons, should receive the reward.[60] At the summer assizes of 1764, Sheehy and seven others had been indicted for assaulting Bridge in January of that year.[61]

Although Sheehy surrendered in March 1765 it was to take eleven months before he stood his trial in Dublin in February 1766.[62] In the interim he made several petitions requesting that a trial proceed and that meanwhile he be granted bail, which was given in June in the amount of £4,000 (an unusually high amount which the priest initially had difficulty raising). In addition, he made several applications to have the persons who brought the charges against him taken into custody until they gave sufficient security to prosecute. Yet when he appeared in

57 Brady, *Catholics*, pp 111–12.
58 Burke, *Clonmel*, p. 373.
59 *F.D.J.*, 12–16 Apr.1765; Burke, *Clonmel*. Curry is incorrect in giving the year of the reward as 1764 (J. Curry, *A parallel between the pretended plot in 1762 and the forgery of Titus Oates ub 1679* (Cork, 1767), p. 7.
60 Ibid., p. 7.
61 Burke, *Clonmel*, p. 370.
62 Details in the following paragraph are taken from Sheehy's petition of 25 November 1765 printed in Burke, *Clonmel*, pp 373–4.

court in early November for trial, as agreed by the bail conditions of June, it did not proceed because of the lack of readiness in the prosecution case. This delay was obviously prejudicial to Sheehy's case, and on 25 November he made a further petition that the trial proceed. These details have two points of interest: one, here we see the accused pressing the court to follow through on its commitment to grant him a fair trial; and secondly, his demand that the prosecution case be brought forward, all suggest a degree of innocence on Sheehy's part. The delay in the prosecution side bringing forward its case lends credence to Burke's view that 'The manufacture of evidence against him [Sheehy] was busily carried on'.[63]

The trial eventually came on in February 1766. The charges against him were that he had led a treasonable conspiracy and rebellion, but the prosecution witnesses proved unconvincing and Sheehy was acquitted. Bridge, a key prosecution witness, had failed to appear as he had gone missing and the grand jury in its offering of a reward for him in March 1765 had implied that Sheehy was the culprit. Sheehy's acquittal in Dublin was not entirely unforeseen by his prosecutors who immediately had a motion accepted that he be bound to appear at the next Clonmel Assizes to answer a charge of complicity in the murder of Bridge. By allowing this the government relented on its previous committment not to permit Sheehy to stand on any charge in Clonmel, again reflecting the degree to which it was now being swayed by the local gentry. Ironically, the trial came on within three weeks which contrasted sharply with the long delay in his first trial.

Unfortunately we lack an impartial account of the trial proceedings. According to Madden, many of Sheehy's parishoners were prepared to stand witness on his behalf, but this he declined fearing that they would suffer the consequences.[64] The defence case for Sheehy based itself on three main arguments. Firstly, that the status of, and evidence brought by the prosecution witnesses were of dubious authenticity. Certainly the main witnesses for the prosecution, who embarked on their action out of motives of profit, revenge, and through inducement on the part of the ultra gentry, were utterly disreputable, and though they were materially rewarded for their efforts, by tradition all three met tragic ends.[65] Specifically what appears to have been overlooked by the judges and grand jury, was the apparent contradiction in the crown evidence. Two witnesses, James Herbert and Thomas Beere, swore that Sheehy was present when Edward Meehan struck Bridge with a bill-hook; whereas, two other crown witnesses, John Toohy and Mary Brady, swore that he was not present but rather came up subsequent to the act and approved of what was done.[66]

63 Ibid., p. 374.
64 Madden, *United Irishmen*, i, p. 49.
65 Burke, *Clonmel*, pp 376–7.
66 Unsigned letter to Lord Taaffe, 1766, giving an account of the trials in *Clonmel* (R.I.A., *O'Conor papers* Ms B.1.2). See also Burke, *Clonmel*, p. 387.

Secondly, the defence had an alibi for the priest's location on the night of the supposed murder. According to Burke, in the crucial week preceding the alleged murder of Bridge on 28 October 1764, Sheehy was with his relatives in county Limerick.[67] More significantly, for the night of the murder itself Robert Keating, a wealthy Catholic middleman on Lord Cahir's estate, was able to provide an alibi for Sheehy's whereabouts. However, his evidence was rendered invalid since before it was completed Revd John Hewetson (a lowly curate seeking advancement through the presentation of the disturbances in apocalytic terms, who although resident in county Kilkenny, held the tithes of several Tipperary parishes, and who, ironically, on the question of income may have suffered as much from the rural unrest as Sheehy did),[68] stood up in the court accusing Keating of being involved in the Whiteboy affray at Newmarket, county Kilkenny in 1764, and on that basis he was taken away, which apparently deterred others from speaking on Sheehy's behalf.[69]

Thirdly, there was no firm evidence that Bridge had been murdered since the body was never located and he was later rumoured to have gone to Newfoundland.[70] The rumours of his disappearance and/or death had been in circulation since October 1764 and were heightened when the grand jury offered its reward in April 1765.

However, despite these factors, on 12 March Sheehy was convicted of the murder of Bridge after a trial of five hours, which took place in an atmosphere charged with fear and intimidation. He was executed three days later, though he protested his innocence to the end. Prior to the execution, Sheehy in a letter to Major Joseph Sirr, suggested that the real murderers of Bridge had been revealed to him in the confessional, information he could not, by virtue of his clerical office, use in his own defence.[71] Further evidence supports Sheehy's contention.[72]

From a legal perspective the irony was that the priest was found guilty on the evidence of three witnesses whose same evidence had been rejected in Dublin, thus verifying the partial nature of local justice in Tipperary. In their dying confession, Edmund Sheehy and James Buxton, who with James Farrell, a relative of Lord Cahir, were executed in May 1766 on the same charge of the murder of Bridge, both said that they had been approached by members of the faction and asked to approve and swear that 'the Priest Sheehy died with a lie in his mouth'.[73] Further, one of those who gave testimony, John Toohy, in a trial against

67 Burke, *Clonmel*, p. 385.
68 Ibid., p. 366.
69 Ibid., p. 50. Other accounts indicate that Keating was taken away before giving his evidence: Burke, *Clonmel*, p. 386n.
70 Madden, *United Irishmen*, i, pp 54–6.
71 Ibid., i, pp 57–8, 61; Burke, *Clonmel*, pp 391–2.
72 Burke, *Clonmel*, p. 395.
73 Madden, *United Irishmen*, i, p. 75, 77. It is not mentioned in James Farrell's dying declaration (ibid., pp 78–9).

Roger Sheehy in 1767, prevaricated in his evidence from what he swore against Sheehy, and a group of other Catholic gentleman were also acquitted on the same evidence as was sworn against Fr Sheehy.[74]

VI

Among Catholics, two kinds of reaction can be identified. Some saw Sheehy's execution as an extreme and devastating event, and the occasion for an increase of fear and mistrust. In 1801, Seward commenting on the event stated that 'The condemnation of Mr Sheehy occasioned great dissatisfaction and complaint amongst the Roman Catholics in general'.[75] Most believed the charge against Sheehy to be spurious.[76] They took their revenge when in September 1770 at Philipstown, King's County, several hundred gathered and stoned to death the executioner who had been responsible for hanging Fr Sheehy.[77] Others, however, while viewing the event as serious and regrettable, recognised that it held out an opportunity. Charles O'Conor, for instance, writing to John Curry in June 1766, said that: 'The Tipperary affair is, I find, become a very important one, not only to our people but to some *patriots* in particular.'[78] He suggested the necessity of having materials on the entire episode collected and published, something which Curry eventually did.

In local electoral terms, the events of the early 1760s do not appear to have had a beneficial result for Protestant extremism. Thus in the general election of 1768 for the county seats, Francis Mathew, son the Thomas Mathew, the un-seated candidate of 1761, and himself a convert, was returned for one of the seats, it was said by 'the papist int[ere]st of this Co[unty]'.[79]

Protestants outside Munster were not convinced of the charges, except perhaps county Dublin where Sir Edward Newenham's charge to the grand jury in April 1766 repeated some of the more exhorbitant claims of his Tipperary counterparts.[80] A consequence of the extreme was a discrediting of Protestant extremism. One correspondent made the point that if the Whiteboy movement was treasonable, then it would be unlikely that Protestants would have been involved in it.[81] This situation paved the way for concessions to Catholics in the late 1770s, and for the more liberal climate that prevailed at that stage.

74 *F.D.J.*, 5–8 Sept. 1767; Madden, *United Irishmen*, i, p. 82.
75 W. W. Seward, *Collectanea politica* (3 vols), i (Dublin, 1801), p. 58.
76 N.L.I., Ms 2714, p. 190.
77 *The Dublin Mercury*, 11–13 Oct. 1770.
78 C.C. Ward and R.E. Ward (ed.), *The letters of Charles O'Conor of Belanagare i: 1731–1771* (Ann Arbor, 1980), no. 148.
79 Quoted in Power, *Tipperary*, p. 271.
80 Brady, *Catholics*, p. 122.
81 B. Rivers to Lord Taaffe, 9 July 1766 (R.I.A., *O'Conor papers*, Ms B.1.1.).

VII

The impact of the Sheehy execution was to reverberate through the rest of the century and beyond. Such were the proceedings against Sheehy regarded that the term 'Sheehy's jury' became a derogatory one applied to any jury which acted in an arbitrary fashion.[82] Of the members of the grand jury that condemned Sheehy the majority are reported to have come to sad and sudden ends, which has been interpreted as divine retribution for their action.[83] Within a short time Sheehy himself became a folk-hero and martyr, and there were regular and well attended pilgrimages to his grave in Shanrahan.[84] He became the subject of a number of poems and laments.[85]

The 1770s had the potential to witness a repetition of the events of a decade earlier.[86] There was a similar background of unrest, which in the 1760s provided the canvass upon which the sectarian claims had been depicted. Yet what made the circumstances radically different was that Catholics had the opportunity of publicly attesting their loyalty under the 1774 Oath of Allegiance act, with Tipperary significantly leading the country in the number of oath-takers. The newly-appointed archbishop of Cashel, James Butler, was conspicuous in his support for the oath. His brother, Robert, was to the fore in quelling Whiteboy attacks on his lands at Ballyragget, county Kilkenny in 1775. The leadership offered by the local priest, Fr Alexander Cahill, in resisting such attacks in the area, contrasted with the perceived reverse role which Fr Sheehy had played a decade earlier. Thus widespread taking of the oath by Catholics in Munster and the active role played by Catholic clergy in resisting rural unrest, were seemingly sufficient to prevent Protestant extremists depicting the unrest as conspiratorial and treasonous in motivation.

In the 1780s, despite the unrest associated with the Rightboys, no conspiracy charges emerged. In 1787, however, the Sheehy case was cited by Fr Arthur O'Leary as part of his defence against charges that he was implicated in the Rightboy disturbances in Munster, and repeated the possibility of Bridge being still alive.[87] In reply Daniel Toler, who had been high sheriff in 1766 and was now an MP for the county, defended the action of the grand jury in condemning the priest. This in turn provoked a response from Amyas Griffith, who had been

82　Madden, *United Irishmen*, i, p. 83.

83　Ibid., i, pp 84–5; Burke, *Clonmel*, pp 397–8.

84　Maurice J. Bric, 'The Whiteboy movement in Tipperary, 1860–80' in W. Nolan and T. G. McGrath (ed.), *Tipperary: history and society* (Dublin, 1985), p. 161. See also *Bealoideas* 14 (1944), pp 82–5.

85　For a sampling see: *Feasta* (Feabhra, 1956); J.Maher, *Romantic Slievenamon* (Mullinahone, 1954), p. 95; *Irisleabhar Muighe Nuadhat* (1958), p. 62; Lonergan, 'Life and death', pp 612, 619; T. Crofton Croker, *The keen in the south of Ireland* (London, 1844), pp xxix–xxx; St Patrick's College, Maynooth: Ms C.25 (pt.); N.L.I. Ms G 582, 2–16, G 723, 83–100; R.I.A., Ms 23.C.5.

86　For what follows see Power, *Tipperary*, pp 268–71.

87　*Mr O'Leary's defence containing a vindication of his conduct and writings during the late disturbances in Munster* in A. O'Leary, *Miscellaneous tracts* (Dublin, 1791), p. 283.

an excise officer in the area at the time and was well acquainted with the facts of the case. He emphasised the role of informers, the fate of the jurors who had condemned Sheehy, and the prevalence of extremism.[88] One of the leaders of the prosecution group in the 1760s, Revd John Hewetson, had remained unrepentant in his conspiratorial analysis of events, was still alive in the 1780s and was maintaining the link between the current agrarian disturbances and the Catholic conspiracy.[89] Interestingly, the Sheehy affair and the events of the 1760s provided an introductory section to Musgrave's history of the 1798 rebellion.[90]

In 1867 a proposal by a local priest to have a monument erected on Fr Sheehy's grave at Shanrahan, was resisted by the local landlord, Lord Lismore, who was perhaps fearful that it would serve to arouse nationalist sentiment at a time when fenianism was current.[91] The memory of Fr Sheehy was perpetuated in the context of the land war of the 1880s and the campaign for home rule. A book entitled, *The fate of Father Sheehy; a tale of Tipperary eighty years ago* by Mary Anne Sadlier, originally published in 1851, was republished in New York in 1885.[92] Though highly romaniticised in its style, it emphasised the role of collective action and priestly leadership, holding up Fr Sheehy as an exemplar in this regard. The book employed the term 'Orange' to describe Maude and the rest of the ultra–Protestant faction, and the role of informers in Sheehy's fate was highlighted, something which must have had a relevance to the circumstances of the 1880s.[93] The occasion of the centenary celebrations of the 1798 rebellion in 1898, saw the erection of a memorial tablet on Sheehy's grave in Shanrahan cemetary.[94]

VIII

In conclusion it can be said that there is some credence to the charge that Fr Sheehy concurred with the validity of many of the Whiteboy grievances because they were ones which he in part felt the effects of. However, the murder charge

88 *A letter to Daniel Toler, esq., relative to the death of Rev. Nicholas Sheehy* (Dublin, 1788) cited in Burke, *Clonmel*, pp 396–9.

89 Thomas Bartlett, *The fall and rise of the Irish nation: the Catholic question, 1690–1830* (Dublin, 1992), p. 174.

90 Sir Richard Musgrave, *Memoirs of the different rebellions in Ireland* (Dublin, 1801), pp 32–5, appendix I, 1–8.

91 Power, *Waterford and Lismore*, p. 134; Maher, *Romantic Slievenamon*, p. 96. The monument was eventually erected.

92 Mary Anne Madden was born in Cootehill in 1820, in 1844 she emigrated to Canada and two years later married the American publisher D. J. Sadlier. (Brian Cleeve, *Dictionary of Irish writers: fiction* (Cork, 1967), p. 120. There is no apparent relationship with the historian R.R. Madden.

93 Mary Anne Sadlier, *The fate of Father Sheehy; a tale of Tipperary eighty years ago by Mrs. J. Sadlier* [New York, 1895 [*c*.1885]], pp 15, 23–6, 74–5, 130.

94 Nancy Murphy, 'Jospeh K. Bracken, G.A.A. founder, fenian and politician' in Nolan and McGrath, *Tipperary: history and society* (1985), p. 385.

seems highly dubious trumped up as it was in order to remove a figure of authority and standing in an area where whiteboyism was rife, and thus neutralise its virulence.

The Sheehy affair (and the other associated sectarian events of the decade in Munster), brought into sharp focus the nature of the relationship between the central administration and the local gentry. It is clear that the Tipperary gentry exploited a weakness in the central government of the early 1760s, a period characterised by a series of moderate, though lack-lustre lord lieutenants before the appointment of the more resolute Lord Townshend in 1767. In this process it was the active role of key individuals like Maude, Bagwell, the earl of Carrick, and Revd John Hewetson who forcefully made their interpretation of events prevail. By conceding to such an interpretation the central administration, which reneged on its commitment to give Sheehy justice, emerged with no credibility from the affair. Nor, obviously, did the local gentry because of the partial nature of justice which they dispensed and the reflex sectarian impulses they unleashed. Moreover, the reluctance of senior Catholic clergy in the region to intervene on Sheehy's behalf must stand as a significant indictment.

The Radical Cleric and the French Invasion of Connacht: Father Manus Sweeney (1763–99)

Sheila Mulloy

One of the most intriguing aspects of the 1798 rebellion is its entirely different guise in the three main theatres of activity – Ulster, Leinster and Connacht. While the action in Ulster was short and mainly involved the Presbyterians, that in Leinster, as it manifested itself in Wexford, was fuelled by the desperate rage of Catholic peasants led by their priests. Guerrilla warfare in the Wicklow hills under Joseph Holt and Michael Dwyer protracted the struggle, but eventually shortage of arms and provisions, and the amnesty act of 17 June, led to the surrender of the Leinster rebels. In Connacht, meanwhile, the situation had been calm. The mainly Irish-speaking population had not been politicised to the same extent as the other provinces. However, agrarian unrest was endemic and the people had responded to Defender propaganda in north and east Mayo. The influx of some 4,000 persecuted northern Catholics in 1796 had introduced a nucleus of committed radicals. At first the earl of Altamont in Westport had welcomed the northern immigrants and built houses for them on his estate, as he felt their weaving skills and habits of sober industry could not but give good example to his tenants. However, it was not long before his more suspicious brother, the Hon. Denis Browne, was reporting that Tom Paine's *Rights of man* was circulating in the area.[1] It was not too difficult for those refugees to spread a fear of avenging Orangemen among the local people, and to rekindle once more the old hopes of help from across the sea.

Connacht was different from the other provinces in that there was a comparatively large number of Catholic landowners, middlemen and minor gentry, which gave that class a self-confidence which it did not possess in other parts of the country. Many had become magistrates and had even raised companies of Volunteers and were officers in the Yeomanry, thus attaining a degree of social eminence which was the envy of their co-religionists elsewhere. Some were members of important families which had been transplanted under the

---

1   N.A., *Rebellion papers*, 620/31/70, Denis Browne to Mr Pelham, 10 June 1797. See also other letters from the Browne brothers to the government.

Cromwellian settlement, while others were descendants of the Galway tribes-men, who, through a combination of wealth and knowledge of the law, had amassed large tracts of land throughout the counties of Galway and Mayo. How-ever, Lord Carhampton's 'pacification' of Connacht in 1795, and the desire of higher-placed Catholics to hold on to their hard-won privileges, were to temper their desire for change, and only sons of gentlemen, more often second sons, who had less to lose, were to join the popular movement when the time came. Along with these were to be a number of local priests, and one of these was Fr Manus Sweeney.

I

Father Manus Sweeney was born in 1763 in the second half of the eighteenth century, that Age of Enlightenment which was to turn the rock-like certainties of the age of Louis XIV into a revolutionary melting pot before the century was over. The time-honoured order of king, lords and people was to be assailed by the rise of the middle classes. The immutable rights of the landed class were to be challenged by those who had amassed wealth through the channels of com-merce and industry. At the bottom of the heap, the urban and rural poor, whose lives had become a battle against famine, poverty and disease, were beginning to stir from their stupor and combine to improve their lot.

The accession of George III in 1767 brought new hope to the Catholics and Dissenters who had suffered the rigours of the penal code. The new king's sym-pathy for their plight, and the desire to oppose the corrupt rule of the whigs, found echoes among the Irish people. However, like similar hopes at the begin-ning of earlier reigns, such optimism was not to be justified. George felt bound by his coronation oath to maintain the Established Church, so that any relief granted to those of other faiths was doled out parsimoniously when their sup-port was needed. At the same time Protestant demands for constitutional re-form were meeting with resistance, and this, combined with repressive meas-ures in the last decade of the century, was to drive many over the brink to engage in rebellion.

Ireland could not escape the political ferment of the times any more than the American colonists or the French nation could. Liberalism became the flavour of the day, and gentlemen became amenable to new ideas filtering from America and France, as can be seen from their joining the Volunteers and subsequently (for those who were able to cross the religious divide) the United Irishmen. Propaganda of all kinds flooded the country, and the great questions of the day were debated in the coffee houses and inns of the English-speaking urban areas.

However, many of these gentleman radicals did not take the giant step from radicalism to revolution when the time came. They feared the loss of life and property, and were unhappy at current developments in France, but would have jumped on the bandwagon if French aid had turned the tide in favour of the rebels. The middle class, especially the urban middle class, was more genuinely radical, even revolutionary, having less to lose and all to gain if the rebellion was a success. In the countryside, there were some remnants of the old native gentry who believed that they could once more repossess their sequestered lands, if the seventeenth-century land settlements were set aside. As regards the rural poor, the men of no property, they were unmoved by questions of religious emancipation and parliamentary reform, but were willing to join any movement that would hold out inducements of lower rents, tithes and taxes, together with higher wages and higher prices for their produce.

Connacht would, in all probability, have remained calm but for the extraordinary arrival of General Jean-Joseph Amable Humbert, at Kilcummin near Killala on 22 August 1798 with three frigates containing 1,099 officers and men, six to eight domestic servants and two women in disguise who had concealed themselves on the vessels. The frigates had on board 3,000 flintlocks, 400 pistols, three cannon with their waggons, 30,000 lbs of powder, 66,000 ball cartridges and 1,000 uniforms. Such a happening was as unexpected in that remote corner of north Mayo as it had been in Bantry in 1796, although help from France had always been considered essential to a successful insurrection in Ireland. Captain Jobit describes the astonishment and terror of an officer who realised his mistake when he came on board with a present of fish because he believed the vessels to be English. He reports that the officer and his companions could only be revived with difficulty when they were brought into the captain's cabin. The astonishment of the local population was no less great, but their reaction was to welcome with open arms these strangers who had come from across the sea to deliver them from their abject poverty.[2]

The Revd James Little, rector of Lacken, in the diocese of Killala, since 1776, is a valuable witness to the extraordinary events then unfolding. He reports that for some time before the arrival of the French 'a considerable degree of fermentation prevailed among the inhabitants of the county of Mayo'.[3] Jobit speaks of the dreadful poverty of the people and their hatred for the rich, which combined with their religious fanaticism to foster a spirit of rebellion.[4] This would point to a certain degree of radicalism, even if it is far removed from the intellectual ferment of the United Irishmen. Little was particularly scathing in his diary of the Carmelite scapular, which was universally adopted by the Catholics of Ireland since it was introduced in 1728. He says that 'this institution was

2   Nuala Costello (ed.), 'Jean Louis Jobit, journal de l'expédition d'Irlande' in *Analecta Hibernica*, no. 11 (July, 1941), pp 12–16.
3   Nuala Costello (ed.), 'Little's diary of the French landing in 1798' in *Analecta Hibernica*, no. 11 (July, 1941), p. 63.
4   Costello, 'Jobit's journal', p. 16.

resorted to as a political weapon', and that 'certainly it was well calculated to combine and direct the efforts of the people in those districts in which it was introduced'.[5] Jobit also mentions the scapular when he writes that the people all 'wear hanging from their necks, large, nasty, dirty scapulars, as well as rosary beads'.[6] Here was a nation whose only sustenance was their faith in miracles.

II

Few of the recruits who presented themselves to General Humbert at Killala and Ballina had military experience; some had been educated in France and Belgium. Prominent among the latter group were some members of the Catholic clergy, but they were not to achieve the status of leader. Fr Manus Sweeney is typical of many of the priests who became embroiled in the insurrection in Connacht. There is a certain naïvety in their behaviour which can be attributed to their rural background and the religious zeal of their parishioners. They were carried headlong to their doom, while some of their more sophisticated colleagues were able to escape the vengeance of the authorities. Sweeney, unfortunately, lived in the sphere of influence of the Hon. Denis Browne, a great believer in the efficacy of the rope as a deterrent to would-be rebels.

At the age of thirty-five Manus Sweeney was a curate in the small town of Newport on the west coast of county Mayo.[7] His parents were Denis Sweeney and Brigid Sweeney (née Mulloy). Like most of his contemporaries in religion, he was from a reasonably comfortable farming background and had been educated in France, or perhaps in Belgium.[8] His fluency in the French language had brought him, like so many other Mayo priests, into contact with the French expeditionary force. The sounds of the French language must have awakened many memories of his student days, and the excitement of the moment would have clouded his better judgement.

The Sweeney familly was said to have come from Donegal with Rory O'Donnell. They settled at Dookinella in Achill, but Manus is believed to have been born at his grandmother's house in Rossmore near Newport. He received his early education from a wandering schoolmaster, like so many others at the time, and apparently spent several years on the continent before returning to Newport in 1798. The transfer to the poverty of the western seaboard must have been a rude awakening.

5   Costello, 'Little's diary', p. 65.
6   Costello, 'Jobit's journal', p. 16.
7   Much of the information on Father Sweeney is taken from Sheila Mulloy, 'Father Manus Sweeney, 1763–1799' in *Cathair na Mart*, no 14 (1994), pp 27–38 and Pádraig Ó Móghráin, 'Gearr-chunnas ar an Athair Mánus MacSuibhne' *Béaloideas*, xvii (1947), pp 3–57. Pádraig Ó Móghráin (Móráin), N.T., Mulrany (1880–1966) was a respected local historian and a great collector of folklore.
8   His name does not appear in the records of the Irish College in Paris.

The O'Donels were the dominant family in Newport at this time.[9] They were descended from Rory O'Donnell, a grandson of Niall Garbh O'Donnell, who had come to Newport in the seventeenth century. The pressure to conform was great, and the O'Donels, like so many others, had become members of the Established Church by 1763.[10] Neal O'Donel, grandnephew of the Jacobite, Colonel Manus, was soon to reap his reward, being made a baronet in 1780, and acquiring large tracts of land. By 1800 he had an income of £8,000 a year from 80,000 acres. Sir Neal had been captain of the Newport company of Volunteers in 1782, while his sons, James Moore and Connel, were captain and first lieutenant respectively of the Newport-Pratt yeomanry cavalry in 1798.[11]

The O'Donels, as the main ascendancy family, dominated the area economically and socially. The majority was represented by some Catholic families, much reduced from their former pre-eminence, of which perhaps the most prominent was the O'Malley family of Burrishoole. Two of their members, Colonel Austin and his brother, Joseph O'Malley, played leading parts in the rebellion and were lucky enough to escape its aftermath. Their cousins, Captain James, and his brother, Alexander of Eden Park, near Knock, were not so fortunate, James being hanged soon after the rising. Protestant cousins on the government side were Samuel O'Malley of Kilboyne and Rosehill, later to be Sir Samuel, and Captain, later Major-General, George O'Malley of Spencer Park, Castlebar, who fought with distinction at Waterloo.

This was the scene in Newport when Captain Boudet and some Irish troops came there on 28 August 1798, the day after the capture of Castlebar. No military engagement took place, for the town had already been evacuated by the yeomanry under their captain, James Moore O'Donel. Sir Neal, his father, had gone to join Cornwallis at Athlone. His early reappearance in Newport on 5 September would indicate that he was not present at the battle of Ballinamuck. However, his two sons, Lieutenant-Colonel Hugh and Neal, were at the battle, and Hugh was to die in August of the following year in Tralee.

The conduct of James Moore O'Donel and his brother, Connel, at this period was the subject of a court of inquiry which began its business at Castlebar on 1 December 1800. They had been accused by Dr Benton, an army chaplain, of being 'improper men, and unfit to hold commissions they bear in His Majesty's service'.[12] The court of inquiry was held at the insistence of James Moore, who repeatedly requested the authorities to grant the family an opportunity of vindicating its honour. The brothers' conduct was indeed somewhat ambiguous during those troubled years, but the result of the court, communicated to them in a letter of 24 January 1801, was to exonerate them completely. There is per-

9 The Newport O'Donnells spelt their name 'O'Donel'.

10 Eileen O'Byrne (ed.), *The convert rolls* (Dublin, 1891), p. 222.

11 This was the official name of the town at this time, from the former treasury official names Pratt who founded the town in the early eighteenth century.

12 *Proceedings of a court of inquiry at Castlebar, the 1st of December, 1800* (Dublin, 1801), p. v.

haps a certain element of criticism in the Lord Lieutenant's opinion that 'upon the whole Doctor Benton has entirely failed to prove the allegations which have given rise to the inquiry', but this is perhaps to put too modern a gloss on the expression 'upon the whole'. The report of the proceedings of that inquiry is one of the few printed contemporary sources we have for the situation in south Mayo during the years 1798 to 1800. It is, naturally, a somewhat tendentious document, but helps to redress the balance when piecing together the details of rebels about whom we know so little, and even that little is shrouded with the mists of tradition.

Captain Boudet found a Tree of Liberty in Newport, which had been erected by Peter Gibbons, a former yeoman, and he was greeted by the curate, Father Manus Sweeney, who was probably the only person then in town with a command of the French language.[13] It appeared to the bystanders that these two had known each other previously, but this may simply have been the result of Boudet's relief at finding someone who understood his mission, and the priest's joy at meeting a citizen of a country where he had in all probability spent many years. This fateful meeting was the beginning of a chain of events which was to lead to the priest's court-martial and death.

Humbert was to leave Castlebar a week later on 4 September, and on the following day Nemesis approached Newport in the person of Sir Neal O'Donel with his servant and John Davis of the Newport yeomanry calvary. Sir Neal was to be joined shortly afterwards by James Moore and about twenty yeomen from Tirawley. This was a remarkably sharp reaction on the part of the O'Donels to the news that the French force was leaving county Mayo.

The rebels were caught off guard and retired into the town. Captain Boudet and Fr Manus were on horseback outside the town near the Westport road, when they saw Sir Neal and his party approach the bridge from the Castlebar direction. Boudet wanted to shoot Sir Neal, but the priest prevailed on him not to do so, and as the enemy party was nearer the bridge to the town than they were, they had no option but to retreat by the steep road that led to Westport. Boudet escaped, but Fr Sweeney was not so lucky. The pursuer caught up with him after about a quarter of a mile and injured him seriously by driving the butt of his pistol through his cheek. He brought the priest back to Newport and gave orders that he should be tied up and left in the guardroom. The remaining rebels had fled by then, and Sir Neal now had the support of some of his tenants. With their help and that of his son, James Moore, the Tree of Liberty was burnt, and the houses of suspected rebels in the town and neighbourhood were searched and ransacked. The town was later to be described as being 'remarkably rebellious', with many of the local yeomanry joining the rebels or deserting.

13 Sentenced to death at a courtmartial held at Castlebar, 17 April 1799, but he appears to have escaped from prison (N.L.I., *Kilmainham papers*, 1199); *Proceedings*, p. 80.

There seems to have been good relations in the town between Protestants and Catholics, and some at least of this spirit must be credited to James and Connel O'Donel. They had banned rebel songs and insignia but had shown themselves equally adamant where Orange songs and insignia were concerned. It was naturally in their interest to have peaceful conditions prevail in their town, and they stressed their efforts to keep the peace at the court of inquiry. The humane conduct of Revd Joseph Heron towards his fellow cleric is further proof of this good relationship, although these two must have been acquaintances at least, for both were natives of the Newport area.

The Revd Mr Heron testifies at the court of inquiry that the priest's 'faintness from loss of blood, in consequence of his wound, induced me to urge his being liberated, with as little delay as might be'. In this he was supported by all the Protestants then in town, who considered 'that it would have been unwise, unsafe, and under the circumstances, an imprudent measure, to have continued Sweeney a prisoner'. They were no doubt afraid of what might happen to them should the rebels retake the town. The sympathetic clergyman was moved by higher motives and said 'it was too bad to keep a clergyman tied in a guard-room', and offered to keep him in a room in his own house, and this offer was accepted.[14] It is not clear how Sweeney subsequently succeeded in making his escape from Newport. Probably Heron and Sir Neal had decided that it would no longer be in the public interest to detain him in the minister's house.

Fr Sweeney left Newport and met Captain Boudet at a pre-arranged place. That they were able to do so is further proof of the fact that the county was still largely in the hands of the rebels. They rode to Killala, and it is apparent that, on the way there, the priest decided to throw in his lot with the rebels. He may have been sympathetic towards them all along, or his treatment at the hands of Sir Neal may have pushed him over the brink. Doubtless, the persuasive powers of Captain Boudet urged him in that direction as they rode together for the two days it took to complete the journey. It was reported that along the way Sweeney spoke to the people outside their chapels and pleaded with them to join the French troops.

The pair reached Killala on 8 September and went to Bishop Stock's house, where the priest was introduced to Col. Charost, who with two other French officers was in command of the town. Bishop Stock reports that the 'hare-brained priest', as he called him,

had a smattering of science, particularly in the antiquities of his county, of which he seemed to be passionately fond. On being introduced by Boudet to the commandant, he proferred an humble request to the officer that whereas every thing lately belonging to the Protestants must now be French property,

14 Ibid.

and inasmuch as soldiers were not usually covetous of books, he should be extremely obliged to M. Charost if he would make him a present of the bishop's library. 'The bishop's library,' answered Charost, turning from him with contempt, 'is just as much his own now, as ever it was'.[15]

The bishop must have been pleased with Charost's reaction.

The bishop, who lived in a princely fashion, with the help of a generous stipend, proceeded to wonder how priests could involve themselves in rebellion, which at that time was regarded with abhorrence by the men of property. He came to the conclusion that since Catholic priests were almost totally dependent upon their people for the means of subsistence, they 'must follow the impulse of the popular wave, or be left behind on the beach to perish'.[16] If they were to continue to exert an influence over their flock, they had to join them. Some of the restraint exercised by the Connacht rebels must be attributed to the discipline of the French troops, and some to the natural character of the Mayomen, but the role played by the priests must also be taken into account.

While in Killala, Fr Sweeney was apparently asked by Colonel Charost to translate a letter inviting the magistrates to levy money on the inhabitants for the support of the French in return for their protection, since at this stage the French funds were exhausted and there was no prospect of receiving any further supplies from France. In any event, the money was collected and sent to the French officers by the bishop's wife when they had been made prisoner afer the battle of Ballinamuck. Fr Sweeney was charged at his trial with 'levying money for the use of the French force', so he had most probably rendered this service to Colonel Charost.

This statement of Stock's, that Sweeney was passionately fond of the 'antiquities of his country', shows the priest in an agreeable light. His clumsy request for the bishop's books, probably inspired by his conversations with Boudet, does not disguise the fact that he was interested in them, and it is noteworthy that the O'Donels, and even the intemperate Dr Benton, spoke of him with a certain sympathy and respect. The charge at his trial 'of being an active rebel leader' hardly accords with our picture of him. There was certainly a moral leadership there, but also a desire on the part of the authorities to make an example of a man who by his sufferings had attracted the pity and support of the people.

The news of the defeat at Ballinamuck on 8 September did not reach Mayo for four days. Meanwhile some of the rebels from Ballina made an unsuccessful attempt on Castlebar on 12 September, while on the same day Westport was retaken by some of the local rebels. About the same time Fr Sweeney is said to have menaced the town of Newport, with the McGuires of Crossmolina and

15 Grattan Fryer, *Bishop Stock's 'narrative' of the year of the French: 1798* (Ballina, 1982), pp 19–20.
16 Ibid., pp 19–20.

Derryloughan and a company of their followers. But Sir Neal had the town in a strong state of defence and the attack was called off.

The government troops were now pouring into Mayo, and Killala was recaptured on 23 September. Fearful retribution was exacted from the Mayo insurgents, with hangings, transportations and floggings, while the soldiers robbed guilty and innocent alike and burnt the homes and crops of the country people for miles around. It was then that Sweeney, together with many others, went into hiding, being hunted like animals in the wilds of Mayo and Galway for many months. Fr Sweeney began his long agony in Glenlara, a lonely valley about six miles north-east of Newport. At that time there was only one house there belonging to a newly-married couple, Tadhg Ó Móráin and Bríghid MacFadden. Tadhg worked as a herd for Mr Roland of Glenhest. It was a safe refuge, and the priest was to spend seven weeks there, but eventually he felt it could endanger the young couple and he moved to Comcloon near Newport. There, Niall O'Donell and his brother-in-law, Séamus, made a hiding-place for him under a rick of turf. The unfortunate priest spent six harrowing weeks there, coming out at night for air and exercise. One night he was seen by a man who was regarded as being untrustworthy by the fugitive and his friends, and they advised him to move on.

All three journeyed towards Achill, the Comcloon men accompanying the priest as far as Glenamadoo. Niall O'Donell advised him to go to Ballycroy, as he would surely be hunted down in Achill, but Sweeney made for the island, probably because of his family connection with the place, and in the hope of getting passage from there to France in a smuggling boat. He made his way west via Mulrany to Belfarsad on Achill Sound. While resting in a house at the Sound, Tomás Bán Cattigan, from Cloghmore on the opposite side of the Sound, came in with the news that the water bailiffs were coming. The fugitive left the house immediately and crossed the Sound on horseback, with Tomás Bán accompanying him on foot. It is said that as they were crossing they saw a dead fish, which Cattigan interpreted as a bad omen, but the priest chided him for being superstitious. The legend relates that Tomás lived to a ripe old age, and that Fr Manus prayed for him to enjoy a long and happy life, as a reward for risking drowning when he came across the Sound with his warning.

There is a lack of information concerning the unfortunate priest's subsequent movements in Achill. He spent some time with his relatives, the Mangans, either in Keel or in Crumpaun, and later went to the village on Slievemore, the present deserted village, which at that time was the largest settlement on the island. Sweeney's final refuge was in the Valley area, where he had relations or friends. This was where Major Denis Bingham discovered him in May 1799 after pursuing him for eight months. It was an accidental discovery on Bingham's part, as according to Mr Heron he had been looking for one of the McGuires. Fifty pounds had been offered for the apprehension of Sweeney, and no doubt the major and his yeomanry corps were glad to accept the reward.[17] Nevertheless, it is likely that Bingham or any other landlord would have preferred not to have anything to do with the hunting down of a priest, for fear of the odium it would bring down on their families.

The sources differ as to who occupied the house: some say it was a family of Heneghans, while others state they were O'Malleys. The priest was hiding in the open loft when the soldiers came. They searched the house but found nothing. Then one of them fired a shot into the loft or stuck his bayonet up through the gaps between the boards. An old woman sitting in the chimney-corner, on seeing this took fright and shouted, 'You have killed the priest', and this inevitably led to his discovery and the beginning of his final agony.

Tradition relates that on the way to Castlebar he asked for a drink. A soldier went to fetch him a drink, but one of his companions deliberately spilt and broke the vessel which contained it. The first soldier then brought him a drink. The military courts were then sitting in Castlebar, and many were sentenced to death. Captain John McGuire of Derryloughlin and Peter Gibbons of Newport were sentenced in April. Hugh McGuire of Derryloughan was tried on 17 May and hanged. The following day saw the trial of George Chambers of Kilboyne near Castlebar, and he was hanged in Ballinrobe.[18] Fr James Jennings of the Neale was one of those who testified against Chambers; his name features on a secret service list as having received £50 for his trouble. Fr Michael Conway of Killala received the same amount for his testimony against Fr Sweeney, swearing that he had heard the priest preaching sedition outside a chapel on his journey there with Captain Boudet.[19] These clerics were firm supporters of the government and were totally opposed to the French because of their anti-religious stance.

Sweeney was brought before the court on 22 May, where he was charged with 'having been concerned in the late rebellion, with levying money for the use of the French force that invaded this country, and of being an active rebel leader'.[20] Sir Neal O'Donel, Fr Michael Conway and Anthony Wilkes were among those who swore against him, whilst James Moore and Connel O'Donel were active in procuring hostile witnesses. The O'Donels felt obliged to prosecute the priest, since their enemies were accusing them of being 'soft' on the rebels.

The 'unhappy man' was condemned to death, a sentence which was later confirmed by Lord Cornwallis. He was to be hanged in Newport and accordingly sent for his own horse and cart, to avoid having to walk the twelve miles from Castlebar when he was in such a wretched state after all the hardship he

17 *Proceedings*, p. 17.
18 *Kilmainham papers*, 1199, pp 87–8, 110, 194–6.
19 *Secret service list*, see Richard Hayes, *The last invasion of Ireland* (1979 edition), p. 206.
20 See Mulloy, 'Father Manus Sweeney', p. 37, for abstract of trial of George Chambers and Fr Manus Sweeney (*Kilmainham papers*, 1199), pp 211–12.

had endured over the previous eight months. The procession left Castlebar on 8 June, with Sweeney sitting on his cart surrounded by soldiers. A large crowd had assembled in Newport to greet his arrival as it was a fair day. He was to be hanged from the old crane that was within fifty yards of the little chapel where he had officiated in happier times. A table was taken from a nearby house and the priest was put standing on this. He spoke in Irish to the crowd and appealed to them not to attempt to rescue him as they had threatened to do, as he was fully prepared to meet his Maker. As the table was pushed away, a man named Lightle made an insulting remark about the priest and was answered by the deceased's sister, who said he would meet a worse fate himself.[21]

Sweeney is buried in the beautifully-situated Dominican friary at Burrishoole near Newport in county Mayo. His grave is surrounded by a distinctive iron railing where each rail terminates in a 1798 pikehead. This and the marble cross over it were unveiled on 9 June 1912. Whatever views may have been held by contemporary writers concerning the insurrection of 1798 and the radical clerics who became involved in it, there can be no doubt that the present inhabitants of Newport are proud of their patriot priest.

III

Twenty clerics, including a bishop, an administrator, four parish priests and Sweeney, were involved with the French forces. The involvement of so many senior clergy is very much in accord with the situation in the other theatres of rebellion. It can possibly be explained by the fact that the suddenness of the French invasion took the clergy by surprise, and there was no time for the hierarchy to exercise a restraining influence, as happened in some parts of the south, or for the senior clergy to have second thoughts and withdraw from the enterprise.

The priests had no place in the command in Connacht. The Presbyterian clergy had been to the fore in Ulster, and the Catholic clergy in Leinster, who supplied the deficiencies in the rebel command, but with no such deficiency in Connacht, the role of Sweeney and others was different. Humbert and his officers had nothing but contempt for the Catholic Church. They had espoused the French doctrine of equality, and no institution could claim authority over them apart from the state. Priests were banished from France, including many Irish priests who had been working there before the revolution. Religion was to be replaced by the worship of 'reason'. In Ireland, they found a poverty-stricken peasantry who looked to the priest for leadership, and to the Church for sup-

---

21 Soon afterwards Lightle was lost in a snowstorm on Cartoon Hill; a cairn marks the spot where he was found.

port. It was obvious that there could be no close fusion between such allies. The Irish officers and clergy were indispensable to the invaders and were praised for their courage, but the clergy were regarded with a mixture of contempt and pity.

The authorities suspected that a number of priests gave at least silent support for the rebellion. When every Catholic was held to be disloyal, only those who proved themselves to be otherwise could escape the wrath of the government. This disloyalty was in turn held to be fostered by the Catholic Church. Contemporary writers excel themselves in pouring venom on the Church and its priests, who kept the faithful in thrall to a foreign power and in a state of ignorance which did not allow them to recognise the benefits of the reformation and a benign government.

The priests, finding themselves distrusted by government and loyalists, and enjoying a status only slightly higher than that of their flocks, were thrown back on the people and their world. They could act with them but not against them, as they were dependent on them for their livelihood. They could hope to guide them and prevent excess, but if the current was too strong they had to move with it or get left behind.

Federalist, Social Radical and Anti-Sectarian: Thaddeus O'Malley (1797–1877)

Fergus A. D'Arcy

In 1848, three days before the last great Chartist demonstration in London on 10 April, and three months before the abortive Irish rising at Ballingarry on 22–23 July, a gathering of workers and citizens of Dublin heard a Catholic priest, Thaddeus O'Malley, call upon working men to look to France. There the workers of Paris had bravely fought for their interests and had established the rights of labour. He went on to add that they were not, as in Ireland, exclusively Catholics and Protestants, but numbered many Jews and unbelievers as well; yet, regardless of their differences about the world of spirits they stood firmly together, 'comrades and brothers all'.[1] He then called upon the workers, Protestant and Catholic alike, to take a decisive part in the great movement for the establishment of a government in this country.

O'Malley's forthright speech did not come out of the blue. Already on 7 March 1848 he had written a letter on *The rights of labour*, published in the press three days later. In this he referred to a workman's bill of rights which he had drafted and wished to see endorsed by an Irish parliament. This bill aimed to secure justice for all labour, skilled and unskilled, male and female, rural and domestic.[2]

While his April speech, in professing admiration for the French workers had not explicitly called on Irish workers to take up arms, O'Malley himself appears to have become caught up in the rapidly radicalising situation that developed between then and Smith O'Brien's abortive rising in July 1848. In June, at a meeting in the Music Hall, Abbey Street, he came as close to calling for a revolution as one could do – he urged the continued growth of Confederate Clubs and would form one himself for the poor. One police report to Dublin Castle had him stating the right of all to bear arms and when a government acted with brute force it was only right to give it a strong dose of the same physic. Another police informant at the same meeting reported that 'priest O'Malley rose and made a long-winded and determined speech telling the people they would get nothing but what they fight for and win and he called on the people above all to

---

1 *F.J.*, 7 Apr. 1848.
2 Ibid., 10 Mar. 1848.

arm'.[3] This was on 21 June: two days later the Paris workers, however armed, felt what it was like to take on the state and the middle classes and to lose when they were slaughtered in the streets of Paris. What happened to O'Malley in the immediate wake of the June days in Paris and the fiasco at Ballingarry in July is unclear. He may simply have remained in Dublin as chaplain to the nuns of the Presentation Order at George's Hill. Whatever may be the case, the little that has been revealed of him up to this point is sufficiently intriguing as to invite a more detailed attention to an undeservedly neglected figure.

I

Roy Foster has written that 'in the age of Fourier, Saint-Simon and the Spenceans there was little utopian or radical social theory in Ireland, though William Thompson should not be forgotten', and, he added, 'nor should Fintan Lalor, theoretician of a peasant revolution linked to national consciousness'.[4] Yet even in these cases the contribution was limited: Thompson's radicalism was forged in Britain and very largely worked itself out there, not in Ireland, while Foster himself admits of Lalor that he had little if any direct contact with the peasantry. In a landscape almost barren of radical theorists, or social visionaries until the close of the nineteenth century it is curious that the isolated figure of Thaddeus O'Malley has not been spotted or investigated before. In not a single survey or general history of nineteenth century Ireland does his name appear in text or footnote, while in a few specialist monographs appearing in the last fifteen years he appears occasionally, in a passing reference and almost invariably it is an adversely critical or dismissive one.[5] That apart, he appeared as an entry in Alfred Webb's biographical dictionary of 1878, where the information was based on personal knowledge and hearsay and where what little there was was incorrect in a number of important particulars.[6] At the time of his *Rights of*

---

3   TCD, Ms. S.3.5, *Police reports of Confederate Clubs*, Report of 'C.D.', 21 June 1848 and report of 'A.B.', 21 June 1848.

4   R. Foster, *Modern Ireland, 1600–1972* (London, 1989), p. 314.

5   D.A. Kerr, *Peel, Priests and Politics* (Oxford, 1982), pp 148–9, 165–70; A. Macauley, *William Crolly, archbishop of Armagh, 1835–49* (Dublin, 1994), pp 198–200, 209, 370–1, D. Bowen, *Paul Cardinal Cullen and the shaping of modern Irish Catholicism* (Dublin, 1983), pp 80, 122, 273. The most recent reference is one of the few non-dismisive ones, see E. Larkin, *The Roman Catholic Church and the Home Rule movement in Ireland, 1870–1874* (Chapel Hill and London 1990), pp 100–2.

6   A. Webb, *A compendium of Irish biography* (Dublin, 1878), pp 403–4. Others followed Webb's errors, such as W.J. Fitzpatrick in *Dictionary of national biography*, 1st ed. (London, 1909), vol. xiv, p. 1064, J.S. Crone, *A concise dictionary of Irish biography* (Dublin, 1928), p. 193, and F. Boase, *Modern English biography* (2nd impression) (London, 1965), vol. 2, p. 1243. Other brief biographical entries with some errors include R. Herbert, *Worthies of Thomond, first series* (Limerick, 1944), pp 50–1. It appears the only brief and accurate account as far as it goes is G. Oliver, *Collections illustrating the history of the Catholic religion in the counties of Cornwall, Devon, Dorset, Somerset, Wilts and Gloucester* (London, 1857), p. 369.

Labour letter in 1848 O'Malley, at fifty-one years of age was already well known in the world of working class and social politics. Born in Garryowen in county Limerick on 27 March 1797,[7] he was ordained to the priesthood in 1819 at twenty-two years of age.

From an early stage he entered the ranks of rebels and dissidents. In August 1822 he took up the pastoral care of the Catholics of Falmouth in England.[8] Twelve months later he went by invitation to the United States to serve the church in St Mary's, Philadelphia where his Limerick friend, Fr William Hogan, ministered. At the time of O'Malley's arrival a virtual schism had developed between Fr Hogan and Bishop Conwell. This arose over the issue of control of church property and it led Hogan to set up an Independent Catholic Church in February 1821. He was excommunicated by Rome in August 1822. O'Malley arrived in October-November 1823. He began intervening to attempt a reconcilation of the opposing sides, only to be excommunicated in turn by Bishop Conwell. O'Malley left Philadelphia in April 1825, and went to Rome to plead the cause of the Philadelphian schismatics.[9] Here, however, in July-August 1825 he apparently retracted and after suitable contrition and a promise never to return to Philadelphia[10] he recovered his priestly employment status but with a tarnished reputation. He went to Paris in 1827 and then to London where he appears to have made efforts to secure priestly employment. Having failed, he finally turned up in Dublin in the summer of 1830 where Archbishop Daniel Murray, having been given complete discretion by Rome, allowed him facilities to say Mass in the new metropolitan church.[11] He soon became involved in public controversy on the questions of national education and poor law. But the most remarkable and little known fact about the O'Malley of these years is that he was almost certainly the first man in modern Irish history to advocate a federal solution to the Anglo-Irish problem. That he was active in the federalist

7   Limerick Regional Archives, Parish registers, St Michael's Roman Catholic parish, Limerick city; this is the correct version of his date of birth which Webb and those who followed him presented incorrectly as the year 1796. He was the sixth child in the family of eight of John O'Malley and Bridget Behane.

8   Propaganda Fide to Murray, 9 Nov. 1830 (D.D.A., *Murray papers*); almost certainly to join his classmate and friend, Fr John McEnery, one of the founding fathers of anthropology who was ordained in Limerick city in June 1819 and spent the rest of his priestly life in Devonshire: see T. Sheehan, 'Fr John McEnery and palaeolithiic man, 1796–1841', in *Studies*, xxi (1932), pp 471–9. See also G. Oliver, *Collections* , p. 181.

9   F. Kenneally, O.F.M. (ed), *United States documents in the Propaganda Fide Archives* (1971), vol. 3, pp 299–300.

10 Propaganda Fide to Murray, dated 17 July 1830 (D.D.A., *Murray papers*) ; Kenneally (ed), *United States documents*, pp 304–9.

11 This account is based on *Records of the American Catholic historical society*, xxviii, pp 75–82; P. Guilday, *The life and times of John England, 1786–1842*, 2 vols. (New York, 1927) i, p. 421; W. Parsons, S.J., *Early Catholic Americana, 1729–1830* (New York, 1939); R. Herbert, *Worthies of Thomond*, pp 50–1; J. Begley, *The diocese of Limerick, from 1691 to the present time* (Dublin, 1938), pp 520–1; *Murray papers*, Year 1830.

episode in the history of the Repeal Association in 1843–4 is known; that he was the editor of a journal called *The Federalist* over 1871–4 in support of Isaac Butt's Home Rule movement is also well known. That Butt should have acknowledged him as the 'father of federalism' in Ireland is fact – but a curious one until it is realised that already from January 1831 he began the first number of his paper, *The Federalist*.

In this he laid down the principles that guided most of his public life thereafter – and a major one was that of reconciling Orange and Green and of accommodating the interests of Protestant and Catholic Ireland. He argued that the simple Repeal advocated by Daniel O'Connell would lead to an *imperium in imperio*, and would be a recipe for conflict between two sovereign legislatures and also could lead to the hegemony of a Catholic faction. His American experience convinced him of the superior harmony of a federal system and he specifically acknowledged the influence of Madison, Jay, Hamilton and the *The Federalist Papers*.[12] It probably was critical also in his insistence that a prerequisite to prevent a Catholic ascendancy in a new Ireland was 'the complete and absolute divorce of the connection between the Irish Church and the Irish State'.

He did not ever waver in these views. In 1836 at a time when the Tory evangelical, Sir George Sinclair, was moving a bill in the House of Commons to abolish the Maynooth Grant O'Malley wrote, remarkably for his time and cloth:

> There are very many Protestants in this country who, according to the lights that are given them, worship their God in spirit and in truth, in the unobtrusive quietness of a pure and placid conscience and in peace and charity with all mankind. These and their Catholic countrymen of a kindred spirit, though separated from each other by a slender partition, my mind delights to picture to itself as kneeling in reverend worship of our common faith in the same glorious temple of our common Christianity.[13]

He added:

> We are only cementing the union of the two countries, and what if we were to try the best cement of all – the true cement of a union of the two Churches – so long as you continue to repel us so long we repel you: so long as love rejects love, so long does bigotry on your part beget bigotry on ours.[14]

12   *The Federalist*, no. 1, Jan. 1831, p. 29.

13   T. O'Malley, *A letter to Sir George Sinclair, M.P., on his notice of motion touching Maynooth and its moralities, By a Roman Catholic priest* (Dublin, 1836), p. 30. See also, O'Malley to Archbishop Murray, 13 July 1836, enclosing the pamphlet and drawing Murray's attention specifically to this passage, 'which possibly Your Grace will not approve as implying too liberal an estimate of a Protestant's sincerity of faith ...', *Murray papers*, AB 3/31/5/7.

14   Ibid., pp 36–7.

He first gave serious thought to federalism during the Catholic emancipation struggle which he regarded as 'squandering energies upon a partial sectarian question'.[15] He would insist that an 'Irish parliament would have no power touching the establishment of religion'. He advocated separate legislatures for England and Ireland but with a separate imperial legislature composed of representatives from these separate legislatures.

O'Malley was concerned enough about the liberalism of this passage to draw Archbishop Murray's attention directly to it but it did not prevent him from proceeding further down the wayward path of liberalism in the years immediately ahead.

II

In the summer of 1839 he made a journey through France, the Low Countries and Prussia inquiring into the primary education systems that prevailed. He did so at a time when the undenominational system of primary education in Ireland, under the control of the Commissioners of National Education was experiencing increased pressure from the more stridently sectarian influence of Catholic leaders like John MacHale, Presbyterians like Henry Cooke and Anglicans like John George Beresford, archbishop of Armagh. It was also at a time when the Catholic hierarchy in Ireland became bitterly divided in itself between those like Archbishops Daniel Murray of Dublin and William Crolly of Armagh, who supported the system and those like Archbishop John MacHale of Tuam and Bishop William Higgins of Ardagh who opposed it: they were at loggerheads in private and public. Their rivalling overtures to Rome in support or against the system were to exacerbate the situation.

Whether O'Malley went on his tour as a self-appointed inspector or was put up to it by elements favourable to the national system then under threat in Ireland is unclear. The results of his tour first appeared in print as a series of four articles in the *Dublin Evening Post* in December 1839,[16] and subsequently as a substantial pamphlet.[17] What he had to say was to create a serious controversy in the public prints and to cause dismay and dissarray in the ranks of the hierarchy themselves, not least among the very bishops whose position he thought he was supporting.

There were two questions to the fore in his inquiry: one, whether the education of the people was better off under government control or not; and secondly,

---

15 *The Federalist*, no. 1 Jan. 1831, p. 30.
16 *D.E.P.* 19, 21, 26, 31 Dec. 1839 a journal which had already acted as the public forum for the differing and contending opinions of Murray and MacHale.
17 T. O'Malley, *A sketch of the state of popular education in Holland, Prussia, Belgium and France* (2nd ed., London and Dublin 1840).

could government control of education exist without prejudice to religious be-liefs.[18] Doubtless O'Malley found on the continent what he wanted to find. He formed a very favourable view of the Dutch primary national education system which, while run by government commission, was conducted in a spirit of lati-tude and proved to be one in which Catholic and Protestant pastors alike were satisfied, the latter despite the fact that 'you never see a Bible in a Dutch school'. He further alleged that he could not find one Catholic clergyman or Catholic Deputy of the States-General to complain about the system. Again, in Prussia and the other Protestant states of Germany despite close government control of education, the Roman Catholic bishops were satisfied with the primary school system and while government exercised complete control in matters of secular instruction it left the regulation of religious instruction fully in the hands of the clergy.[19]

In sharp contrast was Belgium where there was Church control of education since 1830, with no government inspection and 'anyone that likes may turn school-master in Belgium'. Yet because of the absence of government the Belgian sys-tem was completely underfunded. He deplored the absence of adequate school-ing for girls and described the Belgian primary schools for boys as 'mere Lancasterian spelling shops'.[20] In Belgium the system of education had become a party question with adverse consequences. As to Prussia he noted the hostility of the Catholic clergy to the prevailing system there and he concluded that in Ireland it was 'vital to learn that popular education was too important a matter for imtemperate views'.

He went on to deplore the fierce party spirit which infected the discussion of the subject in Ireland and referred to the scripture lessons as too little for one side and too much for the other. He suggested to the Board of National Educa-tion that they should be withdrawn altogether.

He remarked in conclusion that Rome should stay out of the debate and should not involve itself in telling governments how they should run secular education. He wanted religious instruction to be given on alternate days by al-ternate teachers to alternate groups of Catholics and Protestants at the last les-son of the day when the others would have gone home.[21] His final remarks that 'it is the duty of us all to rally round the school for the sake of the common weal of our common humanity', did not endear him to his own authorities and pro-voked a serious controversy.

His main public opponent was Bernard Kirby, parish priest of St Paul's church, Arran Quay, Dublin who took him to task in a series of letters in Janu-ary and February 1840. He called into question O'Malley's main sources for

18 O'Malley, *Sketch of the state of popular education*, p. 4.
19 Ibid., p. 4.
20 Ibid., pp 41ff.
21 Ibid., p. 74.

French churchmen's views on government control of education – individuals in debt to the government of Louis Philippe for place, pension and favours. Kirby who had been ordained in France and who spent ten years in ministry there claimed to know better the real state of things than O'Malley could hope to claim.[22] O'Malley dismissed Kirby's fantastic phillipics and misrepresentations as being those 'of a half-crown lawyer'. O'Malley demolished the ill informed arguments Kirby put forward in a way that showed a good knowledge of French revolutionary and Napoleonic history. At the same time he boldly asserted that in France the priests unfortunately did not want to have it a little more their own way but all their own way.[23]

One of his pseudonymous assailants took him to task for daring to speak of God as 'the common father' of Protestant and Catholic children.[24] 'This person, steeped in a rancorous bigotry wanted to abolish our band of enlightened and tolerant Christians and to entrust the religious education of our children to one whose largest acquaintence with religion was with its preternatural hatreds.' He was anxious that the papacy not insist on the withdrawal of the scripture lessons which attempted to be a fair compromise between contesting denominations in the matter of religion in schools for the purposes of combined instruction.[25]

While the public controversy may have been unedifying and tedious the private consternation caused by O'Malley's pamphlet was more serious. MacHale had launched an all-out attack on the system from late 1837 and brought matters to such a pass that by May 1838 Rome sought an account of the divisions from both MacHale and Murray.[26] Besides reporting to Rome they took their differences to the public press in the autumn of 1838. Even though the Sacred Congregation of Propaganda Fide in July 1838 concluded that the national education system was unacceptable, the Pope declined to promulgate this and instead, listening to a persuasive appeal from Murray, requested each side to send spokesmen to Rome.[27] While Crolly and Murray agreed on their representatives, viz., Ennis and Meagher who went in October 1839 and began making good progress between then and December, MacHale was unable to decide on a representative until he selected Martin Loftus in January 1840.

Even as he appointed Loftus he lit on O'Malley's publication of December 1839 and formally denounced O'Malley to Rome – not least because O'Malley in the pamphlet and letters to the *Dublin Evening Post* had sought to suggest limits to papal authority on the matter of the education system and because in defending the governments of Prussia and Holland in their handling of the edu-

22 *F.J.*, 7 Jan. 1840.
23 Ibid., 6 Feb 1840.
24 Ibid.
25 Macauley, *Crolly*, p. 152.
26 Ibid., p. 162.
27 D.H. Akenson, *The Irish education experiment: the national system of education in the nineteenth century* (London, Toronto, 1970), pp 202–13.

cation system that he was defending the indefensible.[28] MacHale hoped to damage the case for the national system by using the example of one of its more liberal and controversial supporters. MacHale tried to damage Murray's case not least by Murray's sheltering someone who had fallen foul of Rome fifteen years before. To his credit Murray defended his sheltering O'Malley in the pro-cathedral on the ground that 'it is hardly safe, in a country like this, to drive a priest of some talent and strong feelings to extremities without a real necessity'.[29] For all that, O'Malley's expression of views caused considerable embarrassment to the Murray camp who confessed as much to the Pope himself.[30] Just when Ennis and Meagher were making decisive progress in bringing key figures in the Curia around to a sympathetic view, notably Archbishop Cadolini, the secretary of Propaganda, Cardinals Giustiniani, Castracane and Mai,[31] there arrived in Rome O'Malley's letters as despatched by MacHale. The envoy Meagher – his own colleague in the pro-cathedral – was apoplectic at the body blow delivered by this 'wretch's cursed scribbling'. Cadolini in particular was deeply troubled by O'Malley's views and told Ennis and Meagher as much. The consequence was that Meagher implored Murray's secretary, Archdeacon Hamilton, to secure O'Malley's suspension and expulsion from the diocese.[33] Meagher was dismayed to hear that O'Malley proposed to publish his 'fantastic review of education in Holland and Prussia' – the author – 'ignorant and reckless, would cause a scandal on both sides of the Atlantic and it was appalling that he is attached to Dublin's pro-cathedral, and he was causing sinister repercussions in Rome'. He urged that a strong condemnation of O'Malley's action should appear in the public press.[33] By early February O'Malley's pamphlet had been translated into Italian and sent to Propaganda where it caused such indignation that Cadolini hurled threats at Meagher and Ennis. The unhappy delegates in an ironic defence pointed out that in the first place it was Propaganda who had foisted O'Malley on Murray's Dublin diocese, but Franzoni of Propaganda insisted that O'Malley should be silenced and publicly censured since he had not kept his promise of good behaviour after the Philadelphia episode of fifteen years before.[34]

It is not clear what happened next but on 21 February Murray told Franzoni that the order for O'Malley's silencing had been already carried out – his faculties to say Mass had been withdrawn and if Propaganda required orders Murray would see they were carried out. Meagher was relieved to hear 'O'Malley is

28 Macauley, *Crolly*, p. 198.
29 Meagher to Cullen, dated 28 Jan. 1839 (Archives of the Irish College, Rome) cited in Macauley, *Crolly*, p. 198, no. 121.
30 Macauley, *Crolly*, p. 200.
31 Ibid, p. 209.
32 Meagher to Hamilton, 11 & 25 Jan. 1840, *Arch. Hib.*, xxxviii (1983), pp 59–61.
33 Meagher to Hamilton, 11 Jan. 1840, *Arch. Hib.*, xxxviii (1983), pp 59–61.
34 Franzoni to Murray, 8 Feb. 1840, *Arch. Hib.*, xxxviii (1983), p. 65, 80.

gone' – even as he lamented with the remark 'what a curse are talents without common sense'.[35]

The damage he was perceived to have done was by no means fatal. In the end Murray's fears of a papal condemnation – anxiously shared by the British authorities – were not realised. Not least through the important influence of Paul Cullen, rector of the Irish College, the Pope decided on 10 January 1841 to leave the decisions for or against the national system up to the judgement of individual bishops. Since the majority of bishops supported the system and since McHale had set out to destroy it, the papal judgement was a victory for Murray, Crolly and if he wished, for O'Malley. But this was small consolation for him personally. The unfortunate O'Malley was never adept at promoting his personal career interests. From his first attachment to the pro-cathedral in 1830 he received no preferment. Just before the education storm reached its height in late 1839 – early 1840 an eighth curate was appointed to Murray's church and O'Malley was again passed over, greatly to his chagrin. The controversial pamphlet which soon followed ensured that he would receive no preferment from that or any other ecclesiastical quarter for a long time to come.

III

At forty-three years of age and with his career going nowhere it was in some desperation that he now appealed to Nicholas Wiseman in Birmingham for help in mending bridges with Rome and in securing some kind of position in Wiseman's diocese. Wiseman sought Murray's advice, and indicating he would be willing to accept him if he would promise to abandon pamphleteering or writing to newspapers, he expressed considerable sympathy 'at seeing Fr O'Malley driven to desperation by having every door closed against him'.[36]

If his pamphlet had outraged some authorities it had not displeased others and O'Malley was suddenly to find himself on what looked like the highroad to success. On 14 August 1841 Sir Henry Fredrick Bouverie, governor of Malta, wrote to Lord John Russell to announce that Dr Rosignaud the rector of the university there had been asked to resign due to lack of managerial ability.[37] Bouverie in a separate letter proposed as his successor the Revd Thaddeus O'Malley 'whose character and qualifications have been highly spoken of by Lord Morpeth and Mr MacDonald'. He had already spoken with and been impressed by O'Malley, a view shared by George Lewis. On 16 August Russell approved Bouverie's suggestion and O'Malley left England, arrived in Malta and took up his elevated responsibility as rector of the university on 17 Novem-

35 Meagher to Hamilton, 29 Feb. 1840, *Arch. Hib.*, xxxviii (1983), pp 61–4.
36 Wiseman to Murray, 28 Nov. 1840, *Arch. Hib.*, xxxviii (1983), p. 56. item 49.

ber 1841.[38] He was suddenly thrust from relative penury to relative prosperity at
£230 p.a. However, as he believed he was to receive the salary of £280 p.a. enjoyed by his predecessor, the unfortunate Bouverie who admitted the error of
misinformation, undertook to fund the balance from his own pocket. He was
saved this indignity by Stanley's approving the higher amount, and with the
prospect of its rising to £400 should he prove successful 'in his efforts to regen-
erate and establish on a satisfactory footing the system of education here'.[39]

Alas, the glittering prospects were speedily to dim as O'Malley's probation
proved unsatisfactory in the view of some key figures who were to determine his
fate. Lewis soon complained of O'Malley's unfitness and advised the Governor
Bouverie to recommend that he be retired. O'Malley was given leave by the
governor to visit London during the summer vacation of 1842 to see Lewis in
order to justify himself and while Bouverie considered himself more well disposed to O'Malley than most, he would not support his retention as rector against
a volume of opinion the other way.[40]

On arriving in London in August O'Malley sought an interview with Stanley
and demanded to know if his rectorship had been a failure or not[41] and suggesting that any final judgment of that was premature. Whatever about the case he
put to Stanley when he finally got to see him on 29 August, O'Malley lost the
confidence of Bouverie who accused him of bad faith: he had permitted O'Malley
to go to London to see Lewis on condition that if Lewis persisted in recom-
mending the termination of his rectorship that he, O'Malley, would accept this.
O'Malley apparently denied ever accepting this as a condition of his permission
to leave for London.[42]

Lewis confirmed to Stanley in October 1842 that he met with O'Malley to
discuss his conduct of the rectorship. Lewis made much of the point that originally he was well disposed to the priest, so much so that it was he who brought
him to the notice of the government following the suffering he endured as a
result of the pamphlet 'which had involved him in difficulties with his ecclesiastical superiors'.[43] Following O'Malley's suspension by the Church, Dr James
Kay, secretary of the Committee of the Council on Education, took up his cause
and failing to find him some employment on the Poor Law Commission recommended him for consideration to Lewis. Having been involved in a committee
of inquiry into the university education in Malta and realising that certain reforms needed to be implemented Lewis suggested O'Malley as a possible suit-

37 Bouverie to Russell, 3 Aug. 1841, (*Copies or extracts of papers relating to the removal of the Rev. Mr
     O'Malley from the office of rector of the University of Malta*, H.C. 1843 xxxiii (567), p. 1).
38 Bouverie to Stanley, 1 Dec. 1841 (ibid, p. 3).
39 Bouverie to Stanley, 2 Dec. 1841 (ibid., pp 3-4).
40 Ibid. 10 July 1842.
41 O'Malley to Stanley, 26 Aug. 1842 (ibid., pp 5-6)
42 Bouverie to Stanley, 28 Sept. 1842 (ibid, document 19, p. 135).
43 George Lewis to Stanley (ibid., 4 Oct. 1842, document 21, p. 136).

able replacement for Rosignaud, 'on account of the opinions which he entertained on the subject of education ... and his independence in avowing them'.
When Bouverie arrived in London for summer vacation in 1841 Lewis introduced O'Malley to him, and O'Malley was able to reassure the governor that
Rome's displeasure against him had mitigated.

However, on being appointed and before he had arrived on the island he had,
if Lewis is to be believed, already devised a programme of studies and a plan of
action altogether unsuited to the local conditions and which when he persisted
in introducing, brought the university into even greater confusion. Lewis felt
that the experiment with O'Malley's appointment had failed and 'I consider his
resumption of the office as a serious calamity to the island'. Precisely because
Lewis's estimate of O'Malley contained elements of the sympathetic in that he
saw him as 'zealous' and 'liberal-minded' his characterization of him as 'altogether wanting a practical skill [&] discretion' was to prove fatal. However, in
fairness to O'Malley it is also hard to avoid a conclusion that he was the victim
of a very divided government of the island, and that he was caught in crossfire
between the local government and the governor on the one hand and between
the secretary, Sir Hector Grieg, and Sir H. F. Bouverie on the other.[44] Grieg and
his officials approved the very measures which the governor had sanctioned
O'Malley in introducing.

On being informed of the recommendation that he be discontinued O'Malley
wrote to Stanley and on 15 October 1842; 'I ask to be tried by the facts and I
find myself condemned by mere opinions'.[45] However, on 21 October 1842
O'Malley was officially informed that his employment as rector had now ceased.

Unsurprisingly, O'Malley sought to appeal this decision. He sought the support of William Smith O'Brien and petitioned parliament and had the matter
raised at Westminster, the outcome of which was a committee of inquiry. Its
action however did nothing to restore him: by 1843 he was back in Dublin,
jobless save for a modest appointment as chaplain to the Presentation Nuns of
George's Hill.[46] However, he returned to a political environment of no little
interest to himself. The Repeal movement, revived actively by O'Connell from
the commencement of the 1840's was moving into its brief but interesting federalist phase.[47] A few months after his parliamentary appeal he wrote to Smith
O'Brien to congratulate him on his 'throwing himself so immediately into the
popular movement'. O'Malley confessed that he himself had resolved to do so
even before the 'additional stimulant' of Smith O'Brien's example. Like Smith
O'Brien he had not shrunk from opposing O'Connell when he thought O'Connell
was wrong, but O'Connell's recent speech on Repeal indicated the clear possi-

44 O'Malley to Wm. Smith O'Brien, n.d. 1842 (N.L.I., *William Smith O'Brien papers*, Ms. 431/876).
45 O'Malley to Stanley, dated 15 Oct. 1842 (ibid., document 24, p. 139).
46 N. Donnelly, *Short history of Dublin parishes* (Dublin, 1913), pt xii, s. 1., pp 104–6.
47 See ref. to this: by KBN & I.H.S.

bility of support, in particular because he appeared to take up 'the federal posi-tion'.[48] O'Malley was at pains to remove any impression that he supported the scheme 'because it is mine. It is Crawford's and Wyse's and Ross's and that of a great number of the thinking politicians'.

O'Malley must have been buoyed up at this time when Smith O'Brien ac-knowledged his role at a great banquet in Limerick and when he had a strong letter of support from Joseph Sturge, the Quaker leader of the Complete Suf-frage Movement in England. Sturge observed 'I know ... that there is a powerful moral force in England in favour of federalism'.[49]

Sooner than might have been expected the Federalist episode in the history of the 1840s Repeal movement fizzled out. O'Connell, who garnered widespread sympathy for his trial and imprisonment in 1844, following his release from jail and his growing conviction that Repeal was unobtainable, flirted briefly with it only to abandon it by October 1844. If O'Malley was therefore to be disap-pointed he was to be diverted simultaneously by the rise of another public issue which again placed him at odds with O'Connell and MacHale. This was the question of charitable bequests.

However greatly the Tory government abhorred O'Connell and the Repeal movement it certainly became convinced in 1843–4 of the need to offer some kind of conciliation to Ireland and in particular to Catholic Ireland. One of the minor proposals of conciliation put to cabinet in February 1844 was to arouse the greatest controversy: a proposal to revise the law governing charitable be-quests.[50] It was in one sense part of a package designed to conciliate Ireland and remove the danger of Repeal and in another a deliberate attempt to detach the Irish clergy from O'Connell.[51]

The Board of Charitable Bequests had been set up in 1800: forty years later only one of the fifty members was a Catholic although the bulk of bequests was Catholic. The bishops in 1840 had petitioned to have more Catholics on the board, to no avail. Following the dropping of a bill brought in by O'Connell in March 1844 – dropped not least because he himself was then jailed – the gov-ernment introduced its own measure in June 1844. It proposed a ten-person board of which five were to be Catholics and it facilitated private endowment of the Catholic Church.[52] It gave limited recognition to the spiritual authority of the Catholic bishops but it caused offence having been introduced without con-sultation. A key feature of the proposal by Peel and Graham would be that three

48 O'Malley to O'Brien, dated 30 Nov. 1843 (N.L.I., Ms. 433/1087, *Smith O'Brien papers*).
49 O'Malley to O'Brien, 30 Nov. 1843 (N.L.I., MS433/1091, *Smith O'Brien papers*); see also W.J. O'Neill Paunt, *Personal recollections of the late Daniel O'Connell*, M.P., 2 vols (London, 1848), pp 214–15.
50 Kerr, *Peel, Priests & Politics*, pp 110–51.
51 Ibid., p. 121.
52 Ibid, p. 124.

of the Catholics would be clergymen and Murray was to be brought on board.[53] But Catholic press opinion saw it as an attempt to bring the clergy under state control. The proposals were soon attacked by MacHale and by O'Connell from jail. By September 1844 MacHale had whipped up a considerabel lay and ecclesiastical opposition to many clauses of the bill in particular to the exculsion of religious orders from its provisions and clause 16, making any bequest under the Act invalid unless executed and registered three months before the testator's death.[54] Nevertheless the bill went through and Murray felt it was better than what they had asked for in 1840. O'Malley very ably supported the act. But as controversy raged in the autumn of 1844 that support came to be viewed as a mixed blessing. His letters to the press on the subject eventually became another pamphlet, addressed to Crolly and which went to a second edition in November.[55] Although his analysis was an extremely able one his own advocacy was presented by some as sufficient evidence against it. An extremely abusive attack was launched on O'Malley by Lucas in the *Tablet*.[56]

However, unfair and beside the point, Lucas's personal attack on O'Malley was O'Malley, still in hard circumstances, now wrote to Graham requesting to be made secretary of the Boad of Charitable Requests.[57] The government was certainly willing to offer O'Malley that position but they first consulted Murray who fearing O'Malley's reputation in Rome as well as in Ireland, advised against. That advice was taken and by way of consolation he was offered £200 out of the secret service money. O'Malley refused to accept the consolatory bribe.[58] Nevertheless, as Kerr admits, O'Malley impressed the Tory government ministers who admired his 'clear sightedness' and who were anxious 'not to lose sight of Mr O'Malley and if from time to time he will consent to receive assistance from secret service money it ought not to be witheld'.[59] Still desperate for some means of securing a decent livelihood and presumably some recognition for his talents, O'Malley sought an alternative placement in Maynooth and later in one of the Queen's Colleges that were to emerge in the wake of the next large effort of Peel's government at conciliation.

In May 1845 Graham introduced the legislation to provide for three provincial colleges which would be modelled on the example of University College London. The proposals were initially welcomed by Irish MPs although the failure to consult the Catholic Church was regretted. However, opinion against the proposals soon hardened when O'Connell and his press were to take a stance

53 Ibid., p. 129.
54 Ibid., p. 131.
55 Ibid., p. 168.
56 *Tablet*, 5, 12, 19 Oct. 1844.
57 N. A,; C. S. O., Unregistered papers, 149/1845, 23 June 1845.
58 O'Malley to Lord Lieutenant, dated 23 June 1845 (C.S.O., Unregistered papers, 149/1845).
59 Ibid.,

against them which echoed the condemnation of the Tory, Sir Robert Inglis. He had attacked the proposal as 'a gigantic scheme of Godless education'.[60]

While O'Connell and MacHale took up the theme of the godless colleges the Catholic hierarchy soon became deeply divided. A large majority of the twenty seven bishops opposed, while a minority of six, led by Crolly and Murray, supported the scheme with reservations. Over the summer and autumn of 1845 the inevitable and unseemly controversy developed in the public press, with *The Pilot* in particular endeavouring to suggest that Crolly was mad.[61] Into this controversy, unsurprisingly jumped the redoubtable O'Malley. The inevitable letters to the press were argued as ever in a clear, able and rational way out of keeping with the sectarianism of the age.[62] By September and October of 1847 cardinals and the Pope moved to condemn the colleges and to urge the institution of a separate Catholic university and reaffirmed this position in October 1848. It constituted a major blow for Crolly and for Murray; for MacHale a major victory. As for O'Malley, his efforts on behalf of the idea and of his own career got him nowhere.

On 23 June 1845 in a letter to the Lord Lieutenant he claimed to have been the only Catholic clergyman in Ireland or even in the United Kingdon to have defended the colleges.[63] He had now, as before, done the government some service and clearly expected some reward. Yet, he added, 'in very straitened circumstances I refused the compensation pressed upon me by Lord Eliot and sent back the hundred pounds enclosed to me by his undersecretary Mr Lucas', at the time of his contribution to the debate on the Charitable Bequests Act.

As before, the government sought to reward him with an appointment as vice-president of the Queen's College at Belfast.[64] Once again, however deserved an appointment might be, it would have placed the primate, Archbishop Crolly, in an embarrassing position in face of the attacks from MacHale. Consequently, no offer was made. All his efforts to secure recognition and a place had come to nought by the end of 1846. Even when Redmond Peter O'Carroll, secretary of the Charitable Bequests Commission died in 1847, Dean Meagher and the clergy of Westland Row parish signed a memorial to Lord Clarendon seeking the vacant position for O'Malley but to no avail.

He was, and for long had been, living in the kind of circumstances that enabled him to understand fairly directly the plight of the poor. Indeed, it was as early as 1831 within the pages of *The Federalist* that he first suggested the necessity of a national system of poor relief, funded in part by the transfer of tithe income and in part from progressive taxation. His social radicalism was here

60 *Hansard*, Parliamentary debates, 3rd series, lxxx (9 May 1845), vols 377–80.
61 Macauley, *Crolly*, pp 366–9.
62 O'Malley, *Letters in defence of the Queen's Colleges*, 19 May–21 November 1845.
63 O'Malley to Lord Lieutenant, dated 23 Jun. 1845 (N.A., C.S.O., Unregistered papers, 149/1845).
64 Macauley, *Crolly*, p. 371.

first evident in his remark that he was 'of such homely politics as to prefer that the rich should be deprived of some of their luxuries or even the middle classes of some of their comforts rather than that the poor should be debarred from the necessaries'.[65] His assertion of this anticipated the major conflict that arose between himself and Daniel O'Connell in 1837 which placed him strongly on the side of the workers and poor relief was not a question of moral obligation, as O'Connell suggested, but one of right. His incipient Christian socialism came out in his remark at this point that 'until the lessons of the Gospel in reference to the relations of rich and poor are adopted as the preambles to our Christian legislation, Christianity shall have failed of its purpose'. He condemned O'Connell for saying charity was the solution to unequal distribution: 'I am talking of rights, not charity'.[66] To deny the right of the poor to a poor law was to absolve the poor 'from whatever moral allegiance they owe to the laws of property'.

These sentiments, radical enough in 1831 by any Irish standards, let alone those of a Catholic priest of the Pro-Cathedral, were to be elaborated at great length six years later in O'Malley's pamphlet, *A plan of a Poor Law for Ireland*. At the time of its serial publication over the winter of 1836–7, O'Malley had become a member of O'Connell's General Association which he hoped would become the embryo of an Irish parliament.[67] Seeking to move a series of resolutions embodying his concept of poor relief brought him into headlong collision with O'Connell in the public forum.[68] That division won O'Malley an extensive notice by and support from radicals in Britain as well as workers in Ireland.[69] It brought out the fundamentally conflicting social philosophies of O'Connell's liberalism and O'Malley's collectivism. O'Connell's denial of any right of the poor to relief and his quite explicit support for the pre-eminent rights of property undoubtedly paved the way for the bitter conflict with the trade unions of Ireland which followed a few months later. Equally, it prepared O'Malley for the advance in his views which came a few years later when he delivered his *Address to mechanics, small farmers and the working classes generally*. Published in 1845 the address was actually delivered in 1844 in the Carpenters' Asylum, Gloucester Street. The date is interesting in the light of its contents. Basically it is a manifesto for co-operation as a salvation for the working classes and is based on similar principles to those which the Rochdale Pioneers were just then establishing.[70]

65 Dean Meagher to Clarendon, ? 1847 in *Arch. Hib.*, vol. xxxix (1984), p. 44, item 56, .
66 Ibid., no. 3, p. 134.
67 *The Pilot*, 18 Nov. 1836.
68 G. Lyne, 'The General Association of Ireland, 1836–7', (unpublished M.A. thesis, U.C.D. 1968) p. 43.
69 See for example *The Pilot*, 1, 15 Feb. 1837, for votes of thanks from parishioners of St Michan's Dublin, and from the Radicals of Hull, respectively.
70 S. Pollard, 'From community building to shopkeeping', in A. Briggs & J. Saville, (eds), *Essays in labour history* (London, 1971).

This is not the place for a detailed exposition of this work in the communitarian tradition. It shows the author familiar with the theories of Thomas Spence, Robert Owen, Henri St Simon and Charles Fourier and is the first and only publication in Irish history before 1880, in this writer's knowledge, that adverts to these major figures. That it should have been a theologically orthodox priest who introduced the working class of Dublin to these theories, if only to reject them, is in itself of some interest. The context of the publication of his theory of social salvation by way of family association or family community purchase of goods and communal living, was one in which the Dublin working class was organising itself into the Regular Trades Association – was beginning to articulate a language of the rights of labour and was pressing for a legislative protection against the rampages of an unbridled capitalism and industrialism. Since these workers themselves left few written records behind them we have no means of knowing how much influence O'Malley's pamphlet exerted on them, but there can be no question that he contributed something, perhaps something considerable to that growing articulation.

As the Great Famine descended upon the country and indeed affected the towns and capital as well, there was little scope for social engineering in the midst of economic catastrophe and it may well be that one of its effects was to have driven O'Malley to the extreme position the police appear to have discovered him in during the period March–June 1848. His efforts in 1847–8 to effect a reconcilation of the O'Connellites and the Young Irelanders had come to nothing.[71] By the following summer he had somehow become connected with the Chartist movement and, remarkably, on 1 May 1848 he was listed among the delegates who met to constitute the Chartist National Assembly.[72] The National Assembly ingloriously dissolved itself thirteen days later and O'Malley vanished into temporary obscurity.

Some silence descended after 1848 – for three years. Then there appeared, for at least six numbers, in November and December 1851, a Dublin newspaper called the *Christian Social Economist*, with O'Malley as founder, editor and main contributor.[73] The surviving copies reveal the only Christian socialist journal produced in Ireland in the entirety of the last century.

One does not wish to overstate its socialism: it is very much the socialism of Frederick Maurice and John Malcolm Ludlow, though without Maurice's theo-

---

71 T. O'Malley to Smith O'Brien, 22 May 1847, offering to mediate between John O'Connell and O'Brien as the leaders of the respective parties (N.L.I., *William Smith O'Brien papers*, Ms 438/1893, likewise Ms 438/1908, 1910 & 1913, O'Malley to Smith O'Brien, 10, 13 & 21 June 1847 respectively. See also, W. J. Fitzpatrick, *The life, times and contemporaries of Lord Cloncurry* (Dublin, 1855), p. 514.

72 R.G. Gammage, *History of the Chartist movement, 1837–1854* (2nd ed. 1894) (London, 1969), pp 321–4.

73 The only surviving copies known to this writer are in the newspaper collection of the British Library at Colindale.

logical complexity. Nevertheless, with its masthead slogan 'The welfare of the people is the paramount law', its mere existence points to possibilities in Irish society that were available but not availed of.

In setting out his 'mission' O'Malley identified sectarian religious strife as the primary woe and the religious press as a primary source of it. Equal rights for all was his alternative to it; he insisted that the cordial co-operation of the clergy of all classes was essential to achieving an effective amelioration 'of the condition of the masses'. Specifically he wanted a universal industrial education and a radical amendment of the useless poor law. He wanted to prevent the influence of a godless socialism upon the poor and to provide a practicable alternative. He insists on the solidarity, not of the working class, but of the interests of all classes.

Elsewhere in his first issue he wrote on socialism and how it had been disfigured by its charlatans. Defining socialism in the sense of a large programme of practical reforms designed to improve greatly the social condition of the masses he added 'in this sense it is to be hoped that we are all socialists'. He also defined it as that working-class movement of co-operative development such as he had outlined in his 1844 address. Thirdly, there was the socialism which aspired to be a science which he deplored for the reckless audacity of its logic. He insisted on the need for a Christian social philosophy – a Christian socialism – to posit against the 'atrocious political philosophy of the time which sacrificed hundreds of thousands of human victims'.[74] He urged the infusion into society of the practical social morality of the Gospel as in the work of Thomas Arnold of Rugby.

Later issues of the journal called for legislative protection against summary unfair dismissals from work and a reform of the Poor Law system.[75] Here he recalled his early support for a poor law for Ireland and deplored the defects of the system as actually introduced in 1838 'under the thraldom of certain unproved dogmas of the political economists'. He insisted that if there were a right of accumulation, its inevitable correlative was destitution. He insisted that as a law of security of life a poor law ought to be as peremptory and important as the law of security of property. He further insisted that poor rate should be a national not a local levy and that the system should cease to punish the deserving and cease to defraud the poor of their rights.

In a separate and final surviving issue, on 27 December, he took up again the theme of federalism, arguing that Irish nationality and the British connection were not incompatible. He used the example of the Scots of whom there was no people in the world so alive to feelings of nationality yet no less attached to the British connection. He now urged the institution of English, Scottish and Irish parliaments and a High Imperial Parliament to deal with the international and colonial affairs of the three kingdoms.

74 *The Christian Social Economist*, 22 Nov. 1851.
75 Ibid., 29 Nov. 1851.

Unfortunately for O'Malley, and perhaps for Ireland and its working people, the paper did not secure the support necessary to sustain its costs. Its failure silenced the radical priest as a public figure for almost a decade and a half. In the middle of the 1860s he issued a third edition of his pamphlet *Tithe rent, a poor rate, radical Poor Law reform*. If anything, while the characteristic theme remained unchanged, the tone was more radical still: he asked his readers to contrast what 'the legislature does for the security of property in favour of the upper ten thousand with what it does for securing the existence of the humbler masses'. In what was probably the first ever use of the word in Irish political discourse, he remarked of government that 'the right to live of the proletaire it surrenders to the discretion of some half-dozen gentlemen (so called) "guardians of the poor" who may too often be more truly called the guardians of their own pockets'.[76]

Privately O'Malley descended into a purgatory of penury and humiliation during the 1850s and 1860s. In a letter that was inevitably hopeless, on 5 July 1852 he detailed his past career to the new archbishop, Paul Cullen, and requested to be appointed to a parish.[77] His request apparently ignored and certainly unsuccessful, he called for the creation of a position of chaplain general to the Crown Forces and offered himself as a suitable candidate.[78] What reply he may have received is not extant but five months later he implored Cullen for a place of greater utility than his chaplaincy to the nuns of George's Hill and that he was 'ashamed of being a dumb dog in Israel'.[79] Two years later he begged Cullen for 'a more active ministry'.[80] In October 1855 he sought from Cullen the position of Inspector of Juvenile Reformatories to no avail. Finally on 31 October 1855 he asked Vicar General Meagher to put in a word for him as Roman Catholic Chaplain to the Westmoreland Lock Hospital for venereal diseases.[81] At long last humble success attended his beseechings and O'Malley wrote in grateful tones to Cullen in November 1857 thanking him for the appointment to the Lock Hospital.[82]

O'Malley managed to survive in this post for three and a half years without acrimony. But in November 1862 he was dismissed from his £50 p.a. position in a row over his refusal to celebrate Mass in conditions he felt were unworthy – a supreme irony for one of Ireland's few ecumenical spirits of that age.[83] He secured no redress from Cullen who simply nominated another Catholic chaplain

76 T. O'Malley, *Tithe-rent, a poor rate, radical poor law reform*, 3rd ed. (Dublin, 1865 ?), p. 4.
77 T. O'Malley to Cullen, dated 5 July 1852 (D.D.A., *Cullen papers*, 325/4 no. 40).
78 O'Malley to Cullen, dated 21 Feb. 1853 (ibid.,, 325/8, no. 17)
79 O'Malley to Cullen, dated 12 Jul. 1853 (ibid., 325/8, no. 46)
80 O'Malley to Cullen, dated 19 Feb. 1855 (ibid., 332/7 no. 20).
81 O'Malley to Mgr. Meagher, dated 31 Oct. 1855 (ibid., 332/7, no. 125).
82 O'Malley to Cullen, dated 9 Nov. 1857 (Ibid., 339/7, no. 107).
83 O'Malley to the governors of the Westmoreland Lock Hospital (*Cullen papers*, 340/8/1, no. 173, 28/4/1863 & 340/4, no. 140). O'Malley to Dr Emerson, Registrar of Lock Hospital, 5 De. 1862 & 340/4, No. 149, O'Malley to Cullen, 22 Dec. 1862.

in his place.[84] Three years later he was still hoping for redress against his dismissal.[85] It was however to no avail and as the 1860s came to a close he was still without preferment – his plea to be given a ministry in Avoca falling on deaf ears.[86]

He could, of course, have expected no better. Cullen had no reason to be sympathetic. O'Malley was a leading figure in a cluster of clerics who so opposed Cullen's ultramontanism and his exercise of legatine authority as to drive the archbishop and later cardinal into a trough of despair at one point in 1858:[87] and this was apart altogether from the numerous issues involving denominationalism versus interdenominationalism on which they were poles apart from the 1830s to the 1860s.

Worse horror was to follow in 1870 when O'Malley fell foul of the authorities for his alleged authorship of a book entitled *Harmony in religion*. According to some accounts its author advocated an end to clerical celibacy and 'copiously larded the text with abuse of Your Eminence and of Rome'.[88] O'Malley was suspended from his sole source of employment as chaplain to the nuns and was forbidden to exercise the sacramental functions of a Catholic priest.[89] After twenty-five years of chaplaincy to the nuns not even the kind intervention of the Mother Superior, Sister M.B. Carroll on behalf of 'Poor Fr O'Malley' could secure his reinstatement.[90] Two years later O'Malley beseeched Cullen to be at least restored to the £50 p.a. position at the Westmoreland Lock hospital, but his importunings were in vain.[91]

It was against this unhappy background, at the end of the 1860s that the Home Rule movement began to grow and O'Malley came to give it support, not least because it seemed to endorse his original position. It was typical of him that when he came now to promote the cause again it was for him inextricably linked to the cause of labour: speaking in Soho, London, in his seventy fifth year in the winter of 1872, as far as he was concerned the object of home rule was 'the greater happiness for the greater number; labour and the dignity of labour is the question of the day'.[92] Two years later he published the third edition of the substantial pamphlet *Home Rule on the basis of federalism* in which incidentally he urged that there should be a minister of labour in the national cabinets of the three kingdoms in a new federal system. It further urged the legislative institution of Courts of Arbitration with representatives of workers, employers and

---

84 O'Malley to Cullen, dated 11 Feb. 1863 (*Cullen papers*, 340/8/1, no. 24).
85 O'Malley to Cullen, dated 18 Mar. 1866 (ibid, 327/6, no. 23).
86 O'Malley to Cullen, dated 16 Apr. 1868 (ibid., 341/1, no. 37) .
87 Bowan, *Cullen and shaping of Irish Catholicism*, p. 122.
88 Conroy to Cullen, dated 7 Mar. 1870 (*Cullen papers*, 321/7, no. 25).
89 L. ? to O'Malley, 25 July 1870 (Ibid., 328/2, no 65).
90 Ibid., 328/2, no. 11, 22 Jul. 1870.
91 O'Malley to Cullen, 21 Jan. 1872 (ibid., 335/1/1).
92 *Flag of Ireland*, 21 Dec. 1872.

independent assessors. His work concluded with a plea to Fenians and Orangemen to drop their animosities and work together for the goal of a federal island.[93]

Five years later he died and has been little remembered since.[94] Yet his public
life should serve to remind us that there was an alternative possible history for
Ireland in the nineteenth century. That it was a path not followed however was
clearly due to the strong attractions of the great and destructive dual carriage-
ways of Irish nationalism and unionism which carried all before them in the end
– federalism and social vision included.

93 T. O'Malley, *Home Rule on the basis of federalism*, 3rd ed. (Dublin, 1874).
94 For obituary see *F.J.* 3 Jan. 1877, which incidentally observes that in relation to his advocacy of
    federalism O'Malley was 'pardonably vain and conceited in proclaiming himself its "father" '. This
    writer is currently preparing a biography of O'Malley.

The Radical Priest of Partry:
Fr Patrick Lavelle (1826–1885)

Gerard Moran

The history of the Catholic Church in mid-nineteenth-century Ireland has been largely examined through the careers and activities of its leading personalities, in particular Paul Cullen of Dublin, John MacHale of Tuam, Thomas Croke of Cashel, John McEvilly of Galway and Tuam and Patrick Dorrian of Down and Connor. Unfortunately, this confines the study to what Emmet Larkin has described as 'High Church Politics' and fails to consider the regionalism and low church politics which are important for our understanding of the day-to-day running of the Church and the rapport which existed between the priest and his parishioners.[1] Studies which have been undertaken on the activities of famous priests and curates, such as Fr Robert O'Keeffe in Callan and Fr Peter Daly in Galway city, which have been used to highlight how unified the Irish Church had become and how any deviation from this solidarity was not tolerated.[2] Indeed even recent examinations of Fr Patrick Lavelle by Larkin, Ó Fiaich, Norman and Bowen, have portrayed him as a tempestuous rebel, determined to undermine this unity and consolidation.[3] No attempt has been made to highlight his involvement with the radical section of the Irish Church. Indeed he served as a bridge between the pre-Famine radicalism represented by Fr John Murphy of Boolavogue, Fr Manus Sweeney of Newport in 1798 and the Young Irelander, Fr John Keynon, and that of the post-Famine Church as identified with Frs David Humpreys of Tipperary and James McFadden of Falcarragh during the Plan of Campaign, and Fr Michael O'Flanagan the vice-president of Sinn Fein during the War of Independence.

I

There is nothing in Lavelle's background or upbringing to predict his future radical or rebellious nature. Born in Mullagh at the foothills of Croagh Patrick

---

1 See Emmet Larkin, *The consolidation of the Roman Catholic Church in Ireland, 1860–70* (Chapel Hill, 1987).
2 See Patrick Hogan, 'Fr Robert O'Keeffe, parish priest and the Callan controversy, 1869–1881' in William Nolan and Kevin Whelan (eds), *Kilkenny: history and society* (Dublin, 1990), pp 507–40; James Mitchell, 'Rev. Peter Daly (c.1781–1886), in *Journal of the Galway archaeological and historical society*, xxxix (1983–4).

in county Mayo in 1825, his father, Francis, had a twenty-five acre farm from Sir Roger Palmer. Patrick's education was funded by an uncle, Patrick Lavelle, who was proprietor of the *Freeman's Journal*, the largest selling nationalist newspaper in Ireland and its first Catholic owner. In 1841 he sold the newspaper to a group of Repeal supporters, led by his fellow countryman, Sir John Gray, and made a substantial profit.[4] Patrick was educated at a local hedge school and St Jarlath's College, Tuam. He enterd Maynooth in 1844 and quickly established himself as a brilliant academic student. In October 1851 he became a Dunboyne scholar. Twenty of the College's best scholars were selected to pursue further studies and were generally regarded as superior to most seminarians, both in talent and their knowledge of theology. On 21 June 1853 he was ordained, but according to his contemporaries in the College his radical and rebellious nature was becoming evident. He quarrelled with his peers and superiors on many issues.[5] These polemical characteristics are the first indication of the attributes which were to earn him the unenviable reputation of being the most troublesome priest in the Irish Church and which certainly prevented him from achieving higher office.

II

Lavelle's fiery character first came to notice during his stay at the Irish College, Paris between 1854 and 1858. While Fergus Ó Fearghail and Emmet Larkin have recently suggested that Lavelle was the cause of the conflict, this is largely unfair and fails to take into account the bitter divisions that then existed within the Irish hierarchy.[6] One must take into consideration the difficulties that already prevailed between the College Rector, John Miley, and the Irish Board of Bishops who controlled its running and appointments. Miley wanted to run the College on his own and thus needed to control the appointments. Unfortunately Miley was a poor disciplinarian and suffered from a persecution com-

3   Larkin, *Consolidation of Roman Catholic Church*; Thomas Ó Fiaich, 'The patriot priest of Partry: Patrick Lavelle, 1825–1886' in *Journal of the Galway archaeological and historical society*, xxxv (1976), pp 129–48; E.R. Norman, *The Catholic Church and Ireland in the age of rebellion, 1859–73* (London, 1965); Desmond Bowen, *Paul Cardinal Cullen and the shaping of modern Irish catholicism* (Dublin, 1983).
4   John O'Donovan, *Ordinance survey letters, County Mayo*, vol. 3, pt. 2 (Dublin, 1938), p. 241 ref. 496; Stephen J.M. Browne, *The press in Ireland: a survey and guide* (New York, 1991).
5   E.D. D'Alton, *A history of the archdiocese of Tuam*, vol. ii (Dublin, 1928), p. 118; Ó Fiaich, 'Patriot priest of Partry', p. 130.
6   Fearghas Ó Fearghail, 'A stormy decade in the Irish College, Paris, 1849–59' in Liam Swords (ed.), *The Irish-French connection, 1578–1978* (Paris, 1978); Emmet Larkin, *The making of the Roman Catholic Church in Ireland, 1850–1860* (Chapel Hill, 1980), chpts ix, xii. For a more detailed account of the crisis at the Irish College, Paris in the 1850s see Gerard Moran, 'John Miley and the crisis at the Irish College, Paris in the 1850s' in *Arch. Hib.* (1996), pp 113–26.

plex by which he alleged that the staff opposed him, in particular Revd Thomas MacHale, the Professor of Theology and nephew of Archbishop John MacHale of Tuam. In October 1854 Miley appointed Fr John Harold to be Professor of Philosophy on a temporary basis, hoping that he would be made permanent. At the same time the Irish Board of Bishops to the Irish College appointed Lavelle and here the problems between himself and Miley had their origins. John Derry, bishop of Clonfert and secretary of the Irish Board, failed to notify Miley of the appointment, the Rector only became aware of it through the students.[7] Miley did not help the situation by refusing to accept the appointment, arguing that not a sufficient quorum of bishops were present. He regarded Lavelle's appointment as an attempt to undermine his authority, as it would strengthen the opposion grouping within the College. Thus Lavelle's arrival at the College in December 1854 set the stage for a battle between two uncompromising characters.

Both Lavelle and Miley were the cause of the problems which beset the College over the next four years, which nearly led to its total closure. Lavelle's attitude must be questioned for he never informed the Rector of the date when he intended to take up his new position. Indeed, he arrived at the College unannounced. Miley did not help matters by refusing to accept Lavelle's appointment and refusing to give him rooms upon his arrival in Paris. Lavelle had to take up residence at the nearby Hotel de Lille d'Albaon and did not assume his official duties until the end of December 1854, by which time Miley had been forced to accept the appointment by the Irish Board of Bishops.[8]

Lavelle did not endear himself to the Rector because of his readiness to go to the bishops with his grievances. He complained of Miley's failure to pay his salary for providing Irish classes at the College and of the Rector's refusal to compensate him for his hotel expenses.[9] The involvement of the Irish Board only exacerbated the tensions between the two men. The board admonished Miley and it appeared that Lavelle had won the first battle.

Lavelle now channelled his activities directly against the Rector. He obstructed Miley as he read his breviary in the courtyard, occupied his position in the choir when mass was being said, slammed doors in his face, insulted him in front of others, was generally abusive, and made his life very uncomfortable. On one occasion he went to Miley's rooms and removed pieces of furniture stating that they were his. With another staff member, Fr John Rice, he used loud whistles to greet Miley whenever possible.[10] Undoubtedly Miley exaggerated some of

7 John MIley to Paul Cullen, dated 4 Dec. 1854 (D.D.A., *Cullen papers*, Miley correspondence).
8 See Gerard Moran, *A radical priest in Mayo: Fr Patrick Lavelle, the rise and fall of an Irish nationalist, 1825–86* (Dublin, 1994), p. 6.
9 Miley to Cullen, dated 24 Feb. 1858 (D.D.A., *Cullen papers*, Miley correspondence, 1850–61).
10 Moran, 'Miley and crisis at Irish College', p. 122.

the incidents to discredit Lavelle. The most disturbing aspect was that Lavelle carried out these incidents in front of the students and the domestic staff, appearing unperturbed as to who witnessed the assaults. From this can be gauged the characteristics that were evident throughout his public life, including a violent temper which made his adversaries fearful of him. On occasions, he resorted to violence and was subject to fits of extreme anger which resulted in him assaulting his opponents. Once he hit Miley on the chin. Although small in stature he made up for his lack of height through a fiery temper and tremendous resilience.[11]

The continuing conflict resulted in a total collapse in law and order within the College, manifesting itself in a militant and undisciplined attitude among the students. While the Irish bishops were aware of the problems, no attempt was made to bring about a reconciliation, highlighting the hierarchy's own internal problems. Eventually Miley took unilateral action against Lavelle and on 24 March he and Fr John Rice were refused entry into the College after saying mass in a nearby convent. Both eventually gained entry by going to a nearby house, on the pretext that they were searching for an item that had been lost, and borrowing a ladder they climbed over the back wall. Once inside, the two professors were supported by a group of fifteen to twenty students who demanded the dismissal of those staff members who had refused them entry.[12] Miley, on the instrucaions of Cardinal Marlot of Paris, sent for the French authorities and they decided that Lavelle and Rice should leave France immediately. While the subsequent Irish bishops' inquiry exonerated Lavelle and indicated that the Rector was primarily responsible for the College's difficulties, he did not return to his old post. It was decided to reopen the College under a new administration. However, the events in Paris convinced Cullen and others who were attempting to bring about the consolidation of the Catholic Church in Ireland, that Lavelle was a troublesome rebel who could cause trouble for those advocating the ultramontanism view within the Irish Church.

III

In October 1858 Lavelle was transferred to the parish of Partry, or Ballyovey, in one of the poorest regions of Connacht. Since 1852 the local Roman Catholics had endured a relentless assault by the scripture readers employed by the Irish Church Missions Society to Roman Catholics. They were supported by the principal landowner, Lord Thomas Plunket, who was also the Church of Ireland

11   Moran, *Radical priest in Mayo*, pp 8–9.
12   Fr J. Whelan to Cullen, dated 30 Mar. 1858 (D.D.A., *Cullen papers*, Miley correspondence, 1850–61); Miley to Cullen, dated 9 Apr. 1858 (*Cullen papers*, Irish College, Paris, correspondence, 1851–83; Irish College, Paris, Archives, *O'Boyle's notes on Irish priests in France.*

bishop of Tuam, Killala and Achonry. Lavelle's predecessor, Fr Peter Ward, had failed in his encounters with the proselytisers and thus a person of tenacity and ruthlessness was required.[13] From the outset Lavelle ensured his parishioners adopted a united approach against the proselytisers. He used a strategy which increased morale within the parish and made Catholics throughout the country feel that the 'war' in Partry was also their fight. Lavelle was one of the first post-Famine clerics to realise the potential of newspapers to highlight the activities of the proselytisers. Each week he wrote to the newspapers outlining the poverty of his people and indicated how the landlord and his agents hounded them. This was at a time when Irish people were looking increasingly to the newspapers for information about what was taking place in their country. More importantly these letters appeared at critical points in the fight against the proselytisers: when the tenants were issued with notices to quit, when the Castlebar settlement was signed, which was an agreement between Bishop Plunket and himself, or when the landlord was about to evict thirteen families in November 1860. Such letters heightened awareness of the events in Partry and Catholics in Britain and Ireland came to his aid by contributing large sums of money. Lavelle also instigated a prolonged attack on the proselytisers, in particular the scripture readers. Often his methods bordered on being unlawful. Scripture readers represented the assault troops of the Irish Church Mission Society, and Lavelle's attacks on this group were particularly strong. From his arrival in Partry Lavelle used every means to exhort his parishioners to refuse to allow the scripture readers to take the children to their schools. Protestants were attacked and the area around Partry and Tourmakeady became a centre of lawlessness and outrage. While Lavelle was charged by the courts on a number of occasions he was never convicted of a serious offence. In October 1859 an evangelical clergyman, Revd Richard Goodison, was travelling through Partry when he met Lavelle and drew his pistols and threatened to shoot him. Lavelle then incited a mob to attack Goodison who was lucky to escape unharmed. Under such circumstances it was inevitable that a fatality would occur and on 31 January 1860 an innocuous Protestant, Alexander Harvison, was murdered by an unknown gunman. Tensions were heightened when one of Lavelle's parishioners, Edward Joyce, claimed that he had seen Thomas Smyth, one of Harvison's co-religionists, commit the murder.[14] These allegations were untrue and Joyce was charged with perjury. Lavelle acted as Joyce's bondsman and it was suggested that he had instigated the action against Smyth. Lavelle may have taken this approach as it removed suspicion from the Catholic community in the immediate days after the murder.

13 For the background into the crisis at Partry between the tenants and the proselytisers, see Gerard Moran, *The Mayo evictions of 1860: Fr Patrick Lavelle and the 'war' in Partry* (Westport, 1986), pp 25–35; Desmond Bowen, *Souperism: myth or reality? a study of Catholics and Protestants during the Great Famine* (Cork, 1970), pp 157–66.
14 Dublin *Daily Express*, 11 Oct. 1859; for details of the murder see Moran, *Mayo evictions*, pp 63–70.

While Lavelle was prepared to bend the law he was also prepared to use it when the necessity arose and especially when he had to subdue Plunket's supporters. From the outset *The Mayo Constitution*, the leading Conservative newspaper in Mayo, had been one of Lavelle's ardent opponents and maintained he was the cause of the trouble in Partry. Between 3 May and 11 June it carried a series of articles which tried to undermine Lavelle's popularity and were extremely caustic about his activities in Paris.[15] The accusations stopped when Lavelle threatened legal action, but he still issued a writ against its proprietor, John Bole, and sought damages of £1,000. The case was heard in Galway on 27 July 1860 and while the jury disagreed as to the verdict, the result had the desired effect. *The Mayo Constitution* ceased its personal attacks and adopted a more cautious approach towards Lavelle. It also enhanced his reputation as the uncompromising champion of the poor of Partry and increased the interest in the situation in the parish. In 1861 Lavelle instigated libel proceedings against Lord Oranmore and Browne and the Dublin *Daily Express* for making similar accusations to those in *The Mayo Constitution*. While he was successful in both cases the compensation was paltry, £15 from the *Daily Express* and 6*d.* from Oranmore and Browne, and he had to pay all of his own court costs, which he could not afford. However, he did not resort to such litigation for pure financial gain, but simply to quell opposition to him. Certainly the monetary rewards did not warrant him proceedings with litigations, but he had to pursue this course if he was to secure total control in Partry.

Nevertheless the tenants suffered the ultimate fate and on 20, 21 and 22 November 1860, thirteen families were evicted by Plunket.[16] All were associated with Lavelle's resistence which was probably the main reason for their expulsion. This approach was a major public relations disaster for Plunket and enhanced Lavelle's reputation not only in Ireland, but amongst the exiled Irish communities in Britain and the United States. Plunket had lost the propaganda war for his actions were condemned by many of fellow landlords and sections of the Conservative press, in particular the London *Times*, who stated that his actions were not those of a Christian bishop.[17] Lavelle was now seen as a radical pastor who looked after the spiritual and temporal needs of his parishioners. He arranged for the evicted tenants to be housed and cared for, food and relief was procured to help his parishioners who were constantly facing famine conditions, and schools were built as alternatives to those provided by Plunket. His contribution to the downfall of the 'Second Reformation' must not be underestimated, for the events in Partry was the last major confrontation between Catho-

---

15 *Mayo Constitution*, 3 May 1859; 5 June 1860, 31 July 1860. In the article on 3 May the editorial siad: '... it appears that this clerical firebrand is resolved on forcing himself before the public by a return to his dirty work, and the exhibition of his intolerance ...'.

16 A detailed account of the evictions can be found in Moran, *Mayo evictions*, pp 88–94; *idem*, 'The Partry evictions of 1860' in *Mayo association yearbook*, 1985 (Dublin, 1985), pp 40–1.

17 Reprinted in Nation, 1 Dec. 1860; *Mayo Constitution*, 4 Dec. 1860.

lics and Protestants. It also highlighted the increased determination of the Catholic Church to counteract the evangelical threat in all parts of the country.

Lavelle's exertions in Partry indicate a hard-working pastor who upheld the interests of his parishioners at all times. It gained him the reputation of a tough and resolute cleric who was dedicated to his flock. However, the tempestuous and fiery characteristics that were evident in Paris once again surfaced and he often lost his temper with his parishioners over their failure to carry out his instructions. John Horan had to travel to the chapel in Ballinrobe when he was condemned from the altar for having spoken to the local landlords about crime in the area.[18] Others, such as Widow Walsh were assaulted, when they failed to do as they were told. While the authorities exhorted his victims to take him to court nothing came of these requests.[19] While some of the laity may not have liked Lavelle the man, they clearly had respect for Lavelle the priest. Partry required a tenacious, ruthless and radical person and Lavelle proved to be the ideal choice. Thus Partry catapulted Lavelle onto the national scene and by the end of 1860 he had become one of the best known people in the country.

IV

Lavelle's experiences in Partry convinced him that the English would never redress Irish grievances. The land laws would only be changed when Ireland could legislate for herself. As constitutional nationalism was virtually moribund in the early 1860s Lavelle, like many of his contemporaries, felt that change could only be brought about through revolutionary action. His first contact with the Fenian movement was in November 1861 when he attended the Terence Bellew MacManus funeral.[20] Lavelle's presence indicated his support for militant nationalism. While many writers on the funeral state that Lavelle was the only cleric present, this is untrue as seven priests are listed as having attended. Lavelle did push his way forward at the graveside in Glasnevin to speak, even though it had been arranged that Col. Smyth would give the oration.[21] His pres-

---

18 N.L.I., MS7583, *Thomas Larcom papers*; *Mayo Constitution*, 23 Dec. 1862; *Connaught Patriot*, 3 Jan. 1863.

19 T.C.D., Ms 1710 (38), *Thomas Larcom papers*; *Mail*, 12 Sept. 1861; Dublin *Daily Express*, 19 Sept. 1861.

20 For accounts of the MacManus funeral see Thomas G. McAllister, *Terence Bellew MacManus, 1811–61* (Maynooth, 1972); Louis R. Bisceglia, 'The Fenian funeral of Terence Bellew MacManus', in *Eire-Ireland*, xiv (Autumn, 1979); Oliver Rafferty, 'Cardinal Cullen, early fenianism and the MacManus funeral affair' in *Recusant History*, 22, no. 4 (Oct. 1995), pp 549–63.

21 N.L.I., MS 7723, *Thomas Larcom papers*; *Nation*, 3 May 1862; *Irishman*, 3 May 1862. According to Thomas Ó Fiaich, the funeral committee had not planned on Lavelle's speech, choosing an American, Col. M.D. Smith, to give the oration, see Thomas Ó Fiaich, 'The clergy and fenianism, 1860–70' in the *Irish ecclesiastical record*, civ (Feb. 1968), p. 85.

ence may have been for financial reasons: as his association with fenianism brough
him benefits. The Fenians initiated a fund known as 'Patrick's Pence' which
Lavelle received to relieve distress in Partry.

Lavelle defended his association with the Fenians by arguing that they were
one of the few groups to have helped him in Partry between 1858 and 1862.
Contact with American Fenian leaders, like John O'Mahony, opened up new
sources of money and in 1862–3 large sums came from Britain and the United
States which helped Lavelle overcome his financial difficulties arising from court
litigations.[22] The Fenians regarded Lavelle as the symbol of Irish resistance to
British injustice, whether in his opposition to the British government or in his
attacks on landlordism.

It quickly became apparent that the MacManus affair was not an isolated
incident and that Lavelle was pursuing a radical course on the national question. Two events in particular indicated this: his lecture in Dublin on 5 February 1862 on the 'Rights of Catholics to revolt against unjust governments' and
his involvement with the National Brotherhood of St Patrick. The purpose of
the meeting on 5 February was officially to collect money for the poor of Partry,
but it developed into a political tirade with three main themes: that all governments were of human origin; that the goal of all governments was the welfare of
their people; that government forfeited its right to govern when it became ty-
rannical, so that resistance became a right and in certain circumstances a duty.[23]
Throughout the rest of the decade Lavelle adopted this line and quoted saints
and leading Catholic churchmen, like Cardinal Bellarmine, to argue that the
Church espoused the concept of the right to revolt. While Archbishop Paul
Cullen maintained that the Church had outlawed secret societies, Lavelle argued that these were not binding on the Fenians because they were not an irre-
ligious group and many were devout Catholics.

The bishops were also worried by Lavelle's involvement with the National
Brotherhood of St Patrick, which had been established on 17 March 1861 with
the aim of uniting all Irishman to win independence and to celebrate the national festival of St Patrick.[24] It was merely a loose collection of men with little
in common except the vaguest attachment to the principles of nationality. It was
closely identified with the Fenians, as many of its members expressed advanced
nationalist sentiments and it ultimately became the political wing of the Fenian
movement. Lavelle first became associated with it in March 1862 when he attended one of its functions and subsequently became a vice-president of the
brotherhood. His initial involvement was for financial reasons as it had established the Patrick's Pence Fund, organising meetings throughout Britain solic-

22 See N.L.I., MS7793, *Larcom papers*; *Nation*, 3 May 1862.
23 N.L.I., MS7723, *Larcom papers*, *Nation*, 8 Feb. 1862.
24 Thomas Neilson Underwood to William Smith O'Brien, dated 1 Jan. 1862 (N.L.I., MS 447(3557),
    William Smith O'Brien papers); letter dated April 1863 (Larcom papers, MS7517 p. 96).

iting money for the poor of Partry. They regarded Lavelle as leading the resistance to British rule as can be noted in the address of the Radcliffe Cross branch of the brotherhood:

> Irishmen, we hope that you will rally round us in your might, and respond to the call of that illustrious and patriot priest, Father Lavelle, who appeals to your sympathy knowing well that it is not, nor never was your national character to be selfish or ungrateful.[25]

Lavelle made many trips to Britain in 1862 and 1863 addressing meetings of the brotherhood which provided him with badly needed funds. He travelled there whenever he was attacked by Cullen or the officials in Rome. His visits to Britain, his radical rhetoric at meetings and his letter-writing to the local newspapers, especially in Scotland, added a further geographical dimension to the case. It was of strategic importance to Lavelle as it was away from Cullen's influence, yet near enough to continue his attacks on the archbishop. Here he tailored his speeches for his audiences. By concentrating on evictions and clearances, and suggesting seditiously that force might be necessary to save Ireland, he touched on issues of burning relevance.

The conflict between Lavelle and Cullen first became public in May 1862 when Lavelle's letter condemning the archbishop's pastoral against the Fenians was published in *The Irishman*.[26] From this point Lavelle constantly used the newspapers to defend the Fenians. Cullen was primarily annoyed with Lavelle because he had gone public on their differences by writing to the newspapers. Other clerics such as Frs Jeremiah Vaughan and John Keynon spoke at the meetings of the brotherhood, but were never admonished in the same way as Lavelle. Long after he had disappeared from public attention Lavelle still retained the reputation of a radical and maverick who was prepared to make his personal disputes public. While he gained an advantage in revealing his dispute with Plunket, the same cannot be said of his encounters with members of the Catholic Church which was becoming more intolerant of Lavelle's sort of non-conformity. Lavelle was aware of what Cullen's policy of consolidation and unity was doing to the Irish. If the Irish Church was controlled from the top the bishops and clergy could regulate the laity. His correspondence tended to be inflamatory in content when he was writing to the Irish in North America, for they were making valuable contributions towards the alleviation of his financial difficulties.

The chronology of the Lavelle–Cullen conflict in the 1860s has been well-

25 *Irishman*, 14 Jan. 1862.
26 Newspaper cutting, *Irishman*, 3 May 1862 (*Cullen papers*, laity, Jan.-Jun. 1862).

documented by Larkin, Ó Fiaich, Norman and Corish.[27] Still, it is important to point out that Cullen became obsessed with Lavelle and his activities. The clash between the two men offers us an insight into each of their personalities. Both were hard-working pastors who tended to their flocks in different ways. Lavelle did not ignore their temporal needs as when he tackled destitution and proselytism in Partry. Cullen was more concerned with pastoral issues. Otherwise they had little in common and represented contrasting strands within the Irish Church, not only in their clerical views, but also in their social and political outlooks, reflecting their different socio-economic backgrounds and pastoral training. While Cullen came from a large tenant-farmer background in Carlow, Lavelle's circumstances were humbler. Their revolutionary experiences in continental Europe affected them differently. Cullen's years in Rome left him wholly opposed to secret societies and all revolutionary movements, while Lavelle's stay in Paris in the years just after the 1848 revolution contributed towards his radical outlook. Lavelle's pastoral duties were among the poorest people in the country, while Cullen had no first-hand knowledge of any Irish parish, having served as Rector of the Irish College in Rome and then moved to the See of Armagh in 1849. This led Lavelle to say of Cullen:

> Really this comes ill from a man who never knew hunger, or thirst, or the want of a sovereign, or the approach of a bailiff, or the horror of eviction; and once more, it is only the mercy of God that such teaching does not alienate the Catholic Irish heart from the sanctuary where it emanates.[28]

The Lavelle-Cullen dispute was part of the old quarrel about the political direction of the Irish Church. Lavelle's supporters regarded it as a case of whether the Irish clergy would be permitted to become involved in political affairs, while for others the issue was the centralisation of the Irish Church, with authority coming from the top.

Cullen's problems with Lavelle emanated from his relationship with John MacHale, rather than with the priest himself. MacHale felt that Cullen was an obstacle to the kind of Church which he wanted – an independent Irish Church with minimal interference from Rome. MacHale saw in Lavelle an opportunity to embarrass Cullen, and thus did all in his power to protect his

---

27 Larkin, *Consolidation of Roman Catholic Church*, chpts. ii, iv, v, viii, x; Ó Fiaich, 'Patriot priest of partry'; Norman, *Catholic Church and age of rebellion*, pp 97–112; 121–36, 423–4; Patrick J. Corish, 'Political problems, 1860s–1878' in Patrick J. Corish (ed.), *A history of Irish Catholicism*, vol 5, no. iii (Dublin, 1967), pp 6–23.

28 *Irish People*, 12 Jan. 1867. For another letter on similar lines see *Irish People*, 16 Mar. 1867. For an account of Paul Cullen's background see Patrick Corish, 'The radical face of Paul Cullen' in P.J. Corish (ed.), *Radicals, rebels and establishments: Historical studies*, xv (Belfast, 1985), pp 174–5.

diocesan.[29] At the same time he shared a deep radical nationalism with Lavelle and any attempts to control Lavelle's overt political views would be an attempt to embarrass him. Thus he rarely punished Lavelle in the 1860s and then only when compelled by Rome. If Lavelle had been stationed in any diocese other than Tuam, he would have experienced a tighter discipline from his bishop, especially in political matters. Fr Kit Mullen, a curate in the diocese of Meath, was the only cleric besides Lavelle to express publicly his support for the Fenians and he was severely reprimanded for his 'crazed' political ideas, and moved to a parish where he could be of little harm.[30] Archdeacon James Redmond of Arklow stated in no uncertain terms: '... I have always been convinced that the Dwarf [Lavelle] felt that he had a giant at his back who would hold him harmless in his antics'.[31]

While Liam Bane argues convincingly that MacHale's support for Lavelle caused Cullen problems, this fails to take into account the archbishop of Tuam's own actions in the 1860s. Although a constitutional nationalist, he supported the broad aims of fenianism. Some bishops were convinced that Lavelle held some sway over MacHale which enabled him to escape punishment. It was suggested that Lavelle had letters belonging to MacHale and would publish them if his superior suspended him.[32] MacHale's opponents failed to comprehend the fundamental reasons why he protected Lavelle. They lacked true insight into MacHale's psychology just as they failed to understand Lavelle.

By late 1863 Lavelle's activities were causing the Roman authorities much concern and in January 1864 he was ordered to appear in Rome.[33] Here he confessed that his public writings could be interpreted as causing scandal and he promised to issue a retraction regarding his past activities. When he returned to Tuam in February he did not appear to be overawed by his Roman experiences. His retraction did not appear until 5 March, three weeks after his return to Ireland, and then it appeared in the *Connaught Patriot*, the paper that had published most of his letters attacking Cullen. Lavelle then answered eight charges against him, ranging from him being the cause of the troubles in the Irish College in Paris, and having written offensively against Cullen, to being a member

29 Liam Bane, 'John MacHale and John MacEvilly: conflict in the nineteenth century Catholic hierarchy' in *Arch. Hib.*, xxxix (1984), p. 47. For MacHale's declining influence within the Irish Church in the 1860s and 1870s, see Patrick J. Corish, *The Irish Catholic experience: a historical survey* (Dublin, 1985), p. 185.

30 Nulty to Cullen, dated 25 Nov. 1867 (D.D.A., *Cullen paper*, Roman correspondence, 1850–68), Mullen had earned the wrath of his bishop, Nulty, when he attended a Fenian council meeting in Paris in the summer of 1867, organised by Gen. Roberts from the United States, see memo to Irish government, Fenian council meeting, 18 Feb. 1868 (N.L.I., MS11,188(13), *Lord Mayo papers*).

31 Redmond to Cullen, dated 29 Oct. 1863 (*Cullen papers*, Archdeacon Redmond correspondence, 1863).

32 Ibid., Cullen to Kirby, dated 6 Aug. 1864; Norman, *Catholic Church and age of rebellion*. See also Cullen to Kirby, dated 6 Aug. 1864 (*Cullen papers*, Kirby correspondence) in Patrick Corish, 'Archives of the Irish College, Rome, Kirby papers', in *Arch. hib.*, xxx (1972), p. 43, no. 151.

of the National Brotherhood of St Patrick. He denied all of the allegations. It was clear that Lavelle's views had not changed to any great extent as a result of his Roman experiences. While Lavelle had promised the Roman officials that he would not write letters on political matters to the radical newspapers, his first act was to forward his recantation to one of these papers. It showed defiance of Papal authority and implied that he would have to be more cautious in expressing his political views in future. The letter was addressed to the people of Ireland suggesting that he was seeking the people's judgement rather than the absolution of the Roman authorities. This resulted in members of the National Brotherhood of St Patrick in Ireland and Britain rallying to his support. Meetings were held in Dublin during July and August and resolutions adopted in support of Lavelle. These stated that regardless of the directives from Cullen and the Pope, the Brotherhood accepted Lavelle as a priest and would receive the sacraments from him. In July 1864 the Committee of the Lavelle Sustainment Fund was established to support him and it declared that Lavelle was the most patriotic cleric in Ireland.[34]

By this time Lavelle was in Britain having left Ireland before the MacHale messenger had delivered the letter from Rome suspending him. He did not return to Partry until the end of August, 1864. It was probably on MacHale's advice that he came back, for the archbishop of Tuam was under pressure from Rome to suspend his diocesan. The full rigours of the suspension were not implemented, for Lavelle continued to celebrate mass at home and carried out some priestly functions, visiting and administering to the sick, hearing confessions and performing baptisms.[35] His functions were restored to him by the Papacy at the end of May 1865.

The government's attitude to Lavelle during this period is puzzling. It considered his writings and speeches to be inflammatory. While he was never prosecuted, the authorities considered bringing him before the courts on at least two occasions, in 1862 after his lecture on the 'Catholic Right to Rebel' and in 1867 when he spoke at a banquet in his honour in Dublin. They feared if he was prosecuted he would become a martyr for Irish nationalism. Generally the government was reluctant to prosecute people with high public profiles for this reason.[36] The authorities were divided about the expediency of prosecuting cler-

33 Kirby to Cullen, dated 7 Dec. 1863 (*Cullen papers*, Roman correspondence, 1850–68); Corish, 'Political problems', p. 16; Peadar MacSuibhne, *Paul Cullen and his contemporaries*, vol. iv (Naas, 1974), pp 159–60; Cullen to Gillooly, dated 12 Dec. 1863 (N.L.I., MS7622, *Laurence Gillooly papers*, pt. B).
34 *Nation*, 16 July 1864; 23 July 1864. Its leading figures were Thomas Ryan, John 'Amnesty' Nolan and James Casey, who later became famous as a member of the Invincibles who assassinated Lord Frederick Cavendish in the Phoenix Park in May 1882.
35 See *Tuam Herald*, 3 June 1865.
36 Letter dated Nov. 1862 (N.L.I., MS 7583, *Thomas Larcom papers*; National Archives, letter dated 24 Mar. 1868 (*Fenian papers*, F. Files 1866–74 (2014R); letter of A. Brewster to Lord Mayo, dated 31 Dec. 1867 (N.L.I., Ms 11,148(19), *Mayo papers*); letter of Thomas O'Hagan, (N.L.I., Ms 11,188(9) *Mayo papers*).

gymen, as in the case of Revd Jeremiah Vaughan in January 1868.[37] It suited them that the bishops and Rome would deal with clerics like Lavelle. They also felt that if he was left alone he would eventually disappear from prominence, as is evident from their decision not to prosecute him after his banquet speech in October 1867.[38] They had difficulties getting court convictions in such cases. In 1862 the information supplied by the two constables who took the notes at the Dublin meeting conflicted, while in 1868 the sympathy endemic in Ireland after the Manchester executions made it difficult to secure convictions against famous nationalists. Their refusal to arrest him denied him the fame which many lesser nationalists secured, e.g. John Martin.

Lavelle's suspension did not stop his diatribes against Cullen. He attacked him in July 1866 in an article in the New York *Irish People*, an Irish American newspaper which supported John O'Mahony and in which Lavelle wrote a weekly column. Lavelle declared that Cullen was unfair to secret societies, as he did not distinguish between those named by Rome and those which were not. He went on to state: 'Is Cardinal Cullen 'the Church? Was there ever before a fallible and fallacious cardinal? Is the history of the Cardinalate the most edifying portion of that of the Church?'[39] Cullen appeared to be unconcerned about these attacks, probably feeling that letters in a low circulation New York newspaper did not threaten the Church's authority.

The high point of Lavelle's career during these years was the banquet held in his honour on 16 October 1867 at the Rotunda when more than 160 people attended. Such functions were common in Ireland in the 1860s to acknowledge the contribution of prominent nationalists. It was organised by Thomas Ryan, a Dublin Fenian, and Peter Gill, editor of the *Tipperary Advocate*, and other advanced nationalists.

V

By 1868 there were definite signs that Lavelle's steadfast support for militant nationalism was waning, and he was moving towards constitutional nationalism. This was primarily due to his friendship with former MP, George Henry Moore, who like Lavelle had links with fenianism.[40] Neither opposed armed rebellion, providing it had reasonable grounds for success. Lavelle admired

---

37 Vaughan had written a letter to Archbishop John MacHale on the national question which was regarded as seditious, see letter of Thomas O'Hagan dated 2 Jan. 1868 (N.L.I., Ms 11, 189, *Mayo papers*).
38 See *Hansard*, 3 series, cxc [16 Mar. 1868], cols 1682–3.
39 *Irish People*, 3 Mar. 1866.
40 See David Thornley, *Isaac Butt and home rule* (London, 1964), p. 90; Joseph Hone, *The Moores of Moorehall* (London, 1939), pp 167–71; David Barr, 'George Henry Moore and his tenantry, 1840–70' in *Cathair na Mart*, viii (1988), p. 85; Desmond Ryan, *The phoenix flame* (London, 1937), p. 245.

Moore's political integrity and honesty, characteristics lacking in many Irish politicians in the 1850s and 1860s. As they discussed Irish problems Lavelle became more positive towards constitutional action. At the 1868 general election Lavelle actively supported Moore. While retaining a contempt for parliamentary methods, Lavelle felt Moore could exact concessions for Ireland from within the House of Commons. Throughout the election campaign he argued that the electoral process could improve landlord-tenant relations within the country.

At this point Lavelle cannot be classified as a totally committed constitutional nationalist, as his radical views on independence contrasted with most other nationalists. Nevertheless he was now convinced that an Irish parliament could be achieved through a programme similar to that implemented by the Hungarians against their Austrian masters.[41] The Hungarians method was too radical for some supporters of home rule. It advocated the unilateral withdrawal of Irish MPs from Westminster and the convening of an Irish parliament at College Green, Dublin. Lavelle's proposals predated Arthur Griffith's Hungarian policy by 35 years.[42] Similar thoughts preoccupied Moore before his death, for he was consulting with A.M. Sullivan and Lavelle on the formation of a new organisation which would unite all Irishmen. This was to be the Home Government Association.

Lavelle's conversion towards constitutional nationalism was not an isolated development. Other advanced nationalists were also making their peace with constitutional politics and were now turning to trusted nationalists whose loyalty to Ireland was above reproach. They were helped by the establishment of the Amnesty Association in November 1868, under Isaac Butt, to campaign for the release of the Fenian prisoners. It included Fenians and advanced nationalists, and was the first 'coalition' of militant and constitutional nationalists, preceding the more publicised 'new departures' of 1873 and 1878.[43] Amnesty symbolised all Irish grievances and not just Fenian principles in the strict ideological sense. Lavelle's involvement with the Amnesty Association, becoming a member of its executive committee, portrayed two aspects of his personality and ideology.[44] He was increasingly identifying himself with advanced nationalists rather than with the Fenians, thus rehabilitating himself further with constitutional nationalists. Lavelle also showed an awareness that the agrarian question

---

41 For Lavelle's role in the 1868 election in Mayo see Gerard Moran, 'The changing course of Mayo politics, 1868-74' in Raymond Gillespie and Gerard Moran (eds), *'A various country': essays in Mayo history, 1500–1900* (Westport, 1986), pp 137–41.

42 *Nation*, 21 May 1870. On Griffith's 'Hungarian policy' see Richard Davis, *Arthur Griffith and non-violent Sinn Fein* (Dublin, 1974), pp 21–3, 26–9; Carlton Younger, *Arthur Griffith* (Dublin, 1981), pp 222–5.

43 Maurice Johnson, 'The Fenian amnesty movement, 1869–1879' (unpublished M.A. thesis, St Patrick's College, Maynooth, 1980), pp 165–6.

44 *Irishman*, 26 June 1869.

needed an immediate settlement. He campaigned for grievances which affected all Irish people and which needed redress, avoiding the conflicts over which issues should have priority within the Amnesty movement.[45]

Lavelle's drift towards constitutional nationalism can thus be attributed to a number of factors, each complementing the other. None can be taken in isolation, but individually they indicate that he was pursuing a more moderate attitude. He adopted a more pragmatic approach to Irish independence and was prepared to support whatever group would deliver this goal.

In October 1869 Lavelle was transferred from Partry to Cong, one of the most prosperous parishes in the diocese of Tuam. Many bishops were surprised at this move. To describe Lavelle's transfer as a promotion, or, as Thomas Ó Fiaich has suggested, a financial move, overlooks the real problems in Partry.[46] While he was still in debt because of his libel actions, his difficulties with some of his parishioners made a transfer necessary. Throughout the 1860s he was in dispute with a number of them, resulting in court cases which brought the clergy into disrepute. Although he fought their cause against agrarian and pastoral aggression, his vindictiveness, quick-temper and ruthlessness had brought him into conflict with them. Cong was free from landlord-tenant friction, for the principal landlord, Sir Arthur Guinness, was an improving proprietor who had his tenants' interests at heart. As Sheridan Gilley asserts, Lavelle in Cong was less militant that the priest of Partry. He was a typical priest, but a man marked as a violent opponent of authority.[47] Still Lavelle launched his last defence of fenianism from Cong.

On 20 November 1869 Lavelle published his final letter supporting the Fenian movement in the *Irishman*. It was his most forthright declaration, and occurred while the Irish bishops were in Rome attending the First Vatican Council. He reiterated the point that the Fenians had never been condemned by name by the Papacy and they were men of stainless character. He realised this letter would determine the Church's attitude to the Fenians. His opening paragraph said it was the most responsible letter that he had ever to write, for it was of importance to his countrymen at home and abroad. The apparent swing towards fenianism, evident from the Amnesty Association and the amnesty petition of Dean O'Brien of Limerick, may have influenced his decision to write the letter, as it reflected the emotional state of the country.

Rome was finally forced into action and on 12 January 1870 Pope Pius IX

45 For the tensions within the amnesty movement on this issue see Gerard Moran, 'The difficulties of the home rule movement in south-east Ulster' in Raymond Gillespie and Harold O'Sullivan (eds), *The Borderlands: essays on the history of the Ulster-Leinster border* (Belfast, 1989), pp 130–2; T.D. Sullivan, *Recollections of troubled times in Irish politics* (Dublin, 1905), pp 129–37; Johnson, 'Fenian amnesty movement', p. 308.
46 Ó Fiaich, 'Patriot priest of Partry'. p. 145.
47 Sheridan Gilley, 'The Catholic Church and revolution' in D.G. Boyce (ed.), *The revolution in Ireland, 1879–1928* (Dublin, 1988), p. 137.

decreed that the movement in both Ireland and North America was a banned organisation and its members excommunicated. After eight years fenianism had finally been condemned and the bishops had removed Lavelle's symbolic threat to their authority. Rome had at last delivered the decisive answer to Lavelle and those others who had insisted that fenianism had never been censured.[48] Lavelle could no longer hide behind Rome's ambiguous approach to the Fenian movement. He was pragmatic enough to realise that Cullen had beaten him and he could no longer use theological arguments when the highest authority in the Church had ruled against them. Lavelle was a cleric, and while at times he implied that his religion was second to his nationalism, he would abide by the Pope's ruling. Fenianism's appeal was on the decline within Ireland, as the emphasis shifted from nationalism to agrarian issues, with the introduction of Gladstone's land bill into parliament. Fenianism had advanced as far as it could go through the process of agitation and could progress no further.

While the political situation in Ireland changed rapidly between 1868 and 1870, George Henry Moore's death on 19 April was a cruel blow to Irish nationalism, and in particular to Lavelle. Lavelle was devastated by the death and wrote: 'Our poor country! How badly you could spare your son at this juncture'.[49] It denied Lavelle a friend as well as a confidant, and it is unlikely he would have become embroiled in the confrontations of the 1874 Mayo election if Moore had been alive.

Given Lavelle's association with Moore it was inevitable that he joined the Home Government Association, when it was founded in May 1870.[50] In August 1870 he was nominated to the sixty-one man central committee which controlled the party. His attendance at meetings was erratic, missing the first annual general meeting of the party in June 1871. Nevertheless he had a positive attitude to the organisation's ideals once he committed himself to it. Since the 1850s, his political goals had not altered greatly, rather it was the methods of achieving those aims that had been modified.[51]

Lavelle took an active part in the 1872 county Galway by-election contest, which saw the home ruler, Captain Nolan, contest the seat against the Conservative, Captain Le Poer Trench. Lavelle had no alternative but to support Nolan because A.M. Sullivan, Sir John Gray and himself had acted as arbitrators in a dispute between Nolan and his Portacarron tenants, which the landlord accepted.[52] While Lavelle's role in the contest was limited, speaking at four

48 Cullen to Dr Conroy, dated 20 Jan. 1870 in Peadar MacSuibhne, *Cullen and his contemporaries*, vol. v (Naas, 1977), pp 42–3.
49 Lavelle to A.M. Sullivan, dated 19 Apr. 1870 (N.L.I., Ms 895(832) *George Henry Moore papers*).
50 See John Martin to William O'Neill Daunt, undated (N.L.I., Ms 8047(2), *W.J. O'Neill Daunt papers*).
51 John Mitchel to Daunt, undated Sept. 1870? (N.L.I., Ms 8047(2), *O'Neill Daunt papers*; Thornley, *Butt and home rule*, p. 107.
52 See Moran, *Radical priest in Mayo*, pp 136–7.

of the twelve demonstrations which the clergy organised in support of Nolan, he was severely reprimanded at the subsequent by-election petition inquiry which was presided over by Justice Keogh. Compared to the other sixty clerics who were involved in the election campaign Lavelle was harshly treated. The main case against him was that at the Gort meeting he had declared that a Catholic landowner, Sir Thomas Burke, had sounded his 'political death knell' for attempting to influence his tenants' voting intentions.[53] Keogh described Lavelle as worse than 'those profligate priests of the French Revolution'. As a result of the Keogh judgement Lavelle's open involvement in Galway elections was restricted for at least seven years.[54]

After the 1872 Galway by-election Lavelle faded from national prominence, primarily because of the changing regional base of Irish nationalism. The Home Government Association was based in Dublin and it replaced local grievances with national issues. It failed to initiate local associations which would hold demonstrations in support of the national demand. Thus personalities like Lavelle disappeared from the limelight as they no longer had an adequate vehicle to express their opinions. Only those within easy reach of Dublin and who could afford to attend the meetings and demonstrations of the Home Government Association continued to get national prominence. The movement became little more than a Dublin pressure group without a regional base.[55] Lavelle was also disadvantaged in that he had to secure permission from those bishops in whose dioceses the meetings took place. This could prove difficult as he did not have a good reputation with bishops like Cullen. Thus Lavelle regularly used the excuse of important parish duties to absent himself from many meetings.

The last major political event which involved Lavelle was the 1874 general election contest in Mayo where he championed the cause of a local landlord, Thomas Tighe, for the Home Rule nomination. In the lead-up he ensured that a leading Fenian, John O'Connor Power, abided by the decision of the county convention which selected the Home Rule candidates and was thus able to ensure that George Browne and Thomas Tighe were nominated.[56] While both these candidates were returned unopposed, they were subsequently unseated because of an objection by a fourth candidate, who had his election papers declared invalid by the County Sheriff because of an irregularity. O'Connor Power re-entered the contest and defeated Tighe for the second seat. Lavelle and O'Connor Power were enemies and their differing personalities were evident in that while Lavelle

53 *Copy of the minutes of the evidence taken at the trial of the Galway election petition, 1872, with an appendix and index*, h.c. (241–i) xviii, p. 51 q.1667.
54 *Judgement delivered by the judges selected for the trial of the county election petition*, h.c. 1872 [268] xlviii, p. 14; Emmet Larkin, *The Roman Catholic Church and the home rule movement, 1870–1874* (Chapel Hill, 1990).
55 John Ferguson to Butt, dated 14 Aug. 1872 (N.L.I., Ms 8694(8), *Butt papers*; Thornley, *Butt and home rule*, pp 94–5.
56 See Moran, 'Changing course of Mayo politics', pp 146–7.

was zealous, headstrong and determined, O'Connor Power was arrogant and ardent. Thus any reconciliation between them was impossible. During and after the contest Lavelle conducted a campaign against O'Connor Power through the newspapers, maintaining that he had no right to contest the seat because he had not suffered for his country to the same extent as John Mitchel and O'Donovan Rossa.[57] Lavelle's treatment of O'Connor Power greatly enraged the advanced section of the Home Rule movement. The Irish community in Britain was also annoyed with Lavelle who wrongly felt he had its support. His appeals to the Irish in Britain that he was the innocent party fell on deaf ears.

O'Connor Power's election ended Lavelle's importance as a political force at election time, and was the prelude to his fading from the national scene over the next decade. While he still took part in the Home Rule movement's activities, he played no role in its strategy in the west of Ireland. His political demise co-incided with a downturn in his involvement in landlord-tenant relations after his transfer to Cong. This very issue had previuosly brought him much promi-nence. There was a good rapport between the Cong tenants and their landlord, Sir Arthur Guinness.[58] As has already been pointed out, Lavelle was at his best when confronted by adversity. This did not exist in Cong and was the primary reason for his changed approach. Within a short time Lavelle had adjusted to his new lifestyle and was fraternising with the Guinness family and was heavily involved in the organisation of most of the loyalty demonstrations for Guinness. Thus Lavelle had changed from the radical revolutionary to the quiet constitu-tionalist: a transformation which many of his supporters found great difficulty in believing. In 1880 he sprang to the defence of Guinness when he was being criticised by the Land League for being an oppressive landlord. This was to be his last public act and his death on 17 November 1886 went largely unnoticed in a country that had been become totally consumed by the home rule issue. The people who attended his funeral on 19 November tell us much about Lavelle's demise in nationalist Ireland. They included Lord Ardilaun, William Jackson, JP; H.W. Jordan; J. Blake; O. Elwood and Revd Lyon, rector of Cong.[59] No rep-resentative of the Irish Parliamentary Party or the Fenian movement were in attendance. The Lavelle of the 1860s would have been shocked to learn that it was the ascendancy who turned up to his funeral.

---

57 See Moran, *Radical priest in Mayo*, pp 147–9.
58 For conditions on the Guinness estate in this period see Gerard Moran, 'Landlord and tenant relations in Ireland: Sir Arthur Guinness and his estate at Ashford Castle, 1868–1882' in *Cathair na Mart*, x (1990), pp 69–78.
59 *Tuam Herald*, 19 Nov. 1886; *Nation*, 20 Nov. 1886; *Connaught Telegraph*, 20 Nov. 1886.

VI

Patrick Corish describes Patrick Lavelle as zealous, courageous and devoted to the care of his people; but he was also outspoken, headstrong and defiant.[60] Corish might have added that he was strongly nationalist, a political pragmatist and dedicated. He came to the notice of his superiors because of his radicalism and insubordination to ecclesiastical authority. These were not acceptable traits for a priest in Cullen's Ireland. However, Lavelle cannot be regarded as a classical radical, but rather a person who thrived on conflict. Wherever he was stationed, he created conflict and indulged in confrontation. In this he has many similarities with the labour leader, James Larkin.

While Paul Cullen may have wished to limit the participation of priests in political affairs, this was impossible for people like Lavelle. The social conditions of their flocks – destitution, landlord tyranny, evictions and famine – forced many clerics to adopt radical outlooks. In many cases the priest was the only vehicle through which the people could express their difficulties and this could only be done through political channels and agitation. In the past the priest had been the natural leader of his people and this was especially the case where the landlords were absentees. If Lavelle and others did not provide their parishioners with this leadership and intercede on their behalf, they would go elsewhere for this authority. As Paul Cullen had never experienced these parochial difficulties, which were mainly found along the western seaboard, he never understood what motivated Lavelle. It is interesting that, given Cullen's preoccupation with proselytism he looked upon Lavelle so negatively; he never espoused Lavelle's position in Partry against the Evangelicals, either privately or publicly. One can only assume that Lavelle's activities in the Irish College in Paris made him deeply suspicious. This also raises an interesting point: was Cullen's fear of fenianism greater than that of proselytism? Certainly if one is to judge by his attitude towards Lavelle, there is little doubt that Cullen regarded fenianism to be a greater threat than the evangelical crusade.

Lavelle's career must be viewed in the overall context of the changing fortunes of the Irish Church. His rebellious nature had lasting implications for the political activities of that Church and was probably his greatest legacy. He set a precedent in the 1860s that was followed by other priests during the Land League and Plan of Campaign agitations and which allowed them to express their political and social concerns. In such instances the attitude of the individual bishops permitted the priests to take on these roles. Lavelle had greater difficulties to overcome as Cullen was consolidating his position as head of the Irish Church. Thus Lavelle represented the bridge between the radical Church of the pre-Famine period and that of the post-Cullen era.

60 Patrick J. Corish, 'Paul Cullen and the National Association of Ireland' in *Reportorium Novam*, iii (1961), p. 20.

Lavelle always claimed that he considered his nationalism to be more important than his clerical role. Nevertheless he respected the ultimate authority of the Church like all other clerics. His career shows up the changing nature of Irish nationalism and society between 1854 and 1886. While he was a radical to the supporters of the extreme nationalists of the 1860s, they refused to acknowledge him in the 1880s. He highlights the evolving nature of Irish nationalism between the Famine and the centralisation of Irish constitutional nationalism by Parnell in the post-1885 period. It is ironic that the sections of Irish society which he condemned so forcefully in the 1850s and 1860s – the landlords and the ascendency – were the very groups who attended his funeral. This reinforces the point that the personalities that Irish nationalists accepted in the 1860s were forgotten by the 1880s. His radical views on the political, social and economic question found a broader base of support amongst Irish exiles than within Ireland. However, this was a more fickle audience, and one that was constantly turning its attentions to new leaders with more radical ideals.

A Literary Life of a Socially and Politically Engaged Priest: Canon Patrick Augustine Sheehan (1852–1913)

Lawrence W. McBride

Patrick Augustine Sheehan, the parish priest and man of letters from Doneraile, county Cork, is best remembered for his novels that described rural life in late nineteenth- and early twentieth-century Ireland.[1] Sheehan's formative experiences – growing up in Mallow, studying at Maynooth, and working as a young priest on the English mission and in Ireland – provided a storehouse of information which stimulated his work as a novelist.[2] His literary life, however, never inhibited his pastoral or public work. He took a keen interest in the education of the children in the national and intermediate schools in his parish and he admired the local Christian Brothers school because its curriculum featured courses

---

1   Sheehan was born in Mallow, county Cork, on 17 March, 1852. His father died in 1863 and his mother followed in 1864. Young Patrick attended the local national school and was sent to St. Colman's in Fermoy for his secondary education. In 1869 he began training for the priesthood at the national seminary at Maynooth, but did not fulfill the academic potential he had previously demonstrated. He regretted that Maynooth's curriculum did not include much instruction in the humanities and he found that its emphasis on neo-scholasticism, which appealed to his philosophical temperament, was impaired by outmoded teaching methods, including the use of Latin as the language of instruction. Retreating to the library, he began an autodidactic course of study in literature and philosophy that lasted a lifetime. Ordained in 1875, Sheehan was assigned for two years to the English mission at Plymouth and Exeter. He returned to Mallow in 1877 as curate; a few years later, he was called to the cathedral at Queenstown (Cobh), where he served until 1888. Following another assignment in Mallow, Sheehan was appointed parish priest in Doneraile in 1895. He received the largely honorific title of Canon of the Cloyne Diocesan Chapter in 1903. Sheehan wrote eleven novels between 1895 and his death on 5 October, 1913. At least five of them were translated into Irish. Citations for each novel follow below as they are introduced. Sheehan's first biographer was Revd Herman Heuser, *Canon Sheehan of Doneraile* (London, 1917). Subsequent biographies include Francis Boyle, *Canon Sheehan. A sketch of his life and works* (New York, 1927); and M.P. Linehan, *Canon Sheehan of Doneraile: priest, novelist, man of letters* (Dublin, 1952). More analytical assessments of Sheehan's life and work include Brendan Clifford, *Canon Sheehan: a turbulent priest* (Irish Heritage Society in conjunction with the Aubane Historical Society, 1990); and Catherine Candy, 'Canon Sheehan: the conflicts of the priest-author', in *Religion, conflict and coexistence in Ireland*, R.V. Comerford et al. (eds) (Dublin, 1990), pp 252–77. Her most recent work on Sheehan is *Priestly fictions: popular Irish novelists of the early twentieth century* (Dublin, 1995).

2   Sheehan's remembrances of his youth in Mallow, particularly his recollections of Fenian activity, are recorded in 'The moonlight of memory', in his *The literary life and other essays* (Dublin, 1921) pp. 168–96.

in Irish history and culture.[3] He was active in Doneraile's civic affairs, helping the town secure electric lights, a water supply, and some paved streets. He assisted the local tenant farmers when they negotiated the purchase price of land under the terms of George Wyndham's land act of 1903. Typical of many parish priests, Sheehan was also an enthusiastic supporter of the local branches of the Gaelic Athletic Association and the Gaelic League.[4]

Sheehan launched his writing career anonymously, in 1881, as 'P.A.S.' with an essay, 'Religious instruction in intermediate schools', which appeared in the *Irish ecclesiastical record*.[5] His subsequent contributions to religious and literary magazines attracted attention in Ireland, England, on the continent, and in the United States.[6] He also wrote some children's stories, devotional literature, and essays on historical subjects which received widespread distribution by the Catholic Truth Society of Ireland.[7] In time, the novel came to be Sheehan's favourite medium. His first, *Geoffrey Austin*, appeared anonymously in 1895.[8] Its criticism of the education Irish Catholics received and its unkind reception by some reviewers caused a problem when he tried to publish its sequel, *The triumph of failure*.[9] The publication and immediate success in 1899 of *My new curate*, which had initially appeared as a serial in the *American ecclesiastical review*, removed the veil of anonymity.[10] With one major stroke, he joined the front rank of a host

3   For the Christian Brothers' curriculum, see Barry Coldrey, *Faith and fatherland: the Christian Brothers and the development of Irish nationalism, 1838–1921* (Dublin, 1988).
4   For Sheehan's support of the Irish cultural revival, particularly the importance of the preservation of the Irish language, see P.A. Sheehan, *Early essays and lectures* (London, 1912), pp 228–9. He wrote that the disappearance of the language would be 'a greater evil than the Penal Laws or the Act of Union, and its revival a greater blessing than emancipation'. See also, Frank Biletz, 'The boundaries of Irish identity: The emergence of the Irish-Ireland ideal, 1890–1912' (University of Chicago PhD Dissertation, 1995), pp 331–40.
5   I.E.R., vol. ii, 1881: pp 521–31.
6   Sheehan's poetry was published under the title *Cithara mea* (London, 1900). His sermons were published as *Mariae corona* (London, 1900) and as *Sermons*, edited by M.J. Phelan (ed.) (Dublin, 1920). His short stories were collected in 1905 as *A spoiled priest and other stories*; some of these were reprinted by the Catholic Truth Society of Ireland. His essays were collected in *Under the cedars and the stars* (London, 1903); *Parerga* (London, 1908); and in *The literary life and other essays*. Pope Leo XIII awarded Sheehan the title doctor of divinity in 1902 in recognition of his work as an inspirational Catholic writer.
7   See, for example, 'Our personal and social responsibilities', Dublin: The Catholic Truth Society of Ireland, Pamphlet no. 18, nd.; or 'How character is formed', CTSI Pamphlet no. 165, nd.
8   P.A. Sheehan, *Geoffrey Austin, student* (Dublin, 1895).
9   P.A. Sheehan, *The triumph of failure* (London, 1899). Irish critics occasionally commented negatively about particular aspects of Sheehan's portrayal of geographic settings or his characterizations of Irish people. One unhappy critic predicted in the June 1917 issue of *Studies* that Sheehan's novels would be forgotten during the next generation: 'He admittedly was a man of splendid talent. He was not a man of genius. The truth is, Canon Sheehan seemed to view human character, human life from the standpoint of the Pulpit, or ... the Confessional. He never discards sacerdotal spectacles for the plain vision of a man of the world ...' Cited by Clifford, pp 26–7.
10 P.A. Sheehan, *My new curate. A story gathered from the stray leaves of an old diary* (Boston, 1899).

of popular Irish novelists, including M.E. Francis, Margaret Pender, Katherine Tynan Hinkson, Standish James O'Grady, and George A. Birmingham.[11]

Sheehan's novels explored the intellectual territory that was occupied by a spectrum of characters, ranging from Christian social activists and rationalist critics, to spirited radicals and idealistic revolutionaries, to insincere cynics and lost solipsists. He approached his work with two objectives in mind. As a priest, his fundamental concern was for the safety of souls. He believed it was only through the doctrines of the Roman Catholic Church that individuals could resist the philosophical errors of modern-day rationalism. As a teacher, Sheehan tried to provide information people needed to combat the social problems of the modern world. Utilizing the medium of the printed word, Sheehan worked to achieve the spiritual and secular objectives he had set for himself as priest and teacher. His novels, therefore, generally feature two themes that create the dramatic tension in the stories. The first is secular: the protagonists attempt to advance the social welfare of the people or foster political change. The second is spiritual: they attempt to mediate between the principles of rationalism and the tenets of Christianity. As the plots unfold, Sheehan reveals the limitations of the methods the characters use to find the land of milk and honey in Ireland, but he also provides the cathartic experience that keeps them from losing their souls along the way. His message as a priest and writer was consistent: from his earliest sermons through his last novel, Sheehan taught that the divine spirit of charity, as exemplified by Christ's life among the poor, was the only infallible guide for men and women to follow as they worked to improve the human condition.[12]

In *Geoffrey Austin* and *The triumph of failure*, Sheehan created a template for characterization and plot. Geoffrey Austin is an aimless student from Doneraile who attends a lay college in Dublin to prepare for the civil service examination. Managed by 'The Grinder', the school is a horrible place, although Geoffrey enjoys his classes in rational philosophy. Sheehan, approaching his twin task of humanities teacher and priest, explicates both the content of these lessons and the fine points of the characters' discussions of them, a didactic technique he employed throughout his writings. These lessons do nothing to prepare Geoffrey for the exam, which he fails. In *The triumph of failure* – the title is an allusion to Christ's life and crucifixion – Geoffrey discovers that his education has not prepared him for any employment. He drifts from one job to another, losing

---

11 Literary critic and novelist Thomas Flanagan identifies Sheehan and Emily Lawless as the best exemplars of late nineteenth-century Irish writers of fiction in 'Literature in English, 1801–70' in *A new history of Ireland, 1870–1921, V, Ireland under the union, I*, W.E. Vaughan (ed.) (Oxford, 1989), pp. 511–14.

12 See P.A. Sheehan, 'Charity', in *Sermons*, pp 193–207 for an early formulation of Sheehan's belief in the power of charity. Sheehan believed 'The imitation of Christ and the confessions of St Augustine' provided seminal models for Christian secular life. See also, Daniel J. O'Neil, 'The cult of self-sacrifice: The Irish experience', in *Eire-Ireland*, vol. xxiv (Winter, 1989), pp 89–105.

faith in the philosophical touchstones that had guided his approach to life. His dark existence, however, is brightened by two examples: one, of Christian inno- cence and hope; the other, of Christian social activism. The former is a child, Ursula, whom he befriends. The latter is a former classmate, Charlie, now a charismatic lay preacher who works among Dublin's poorest classes. Their ex- amples lead him out despair and into the religious life. In the closing pages of *The triumph of failure*, Geoffrey finally understands how the system of Catholic philosophy, guided everywhere by the spirit of charity, must regulate the aims and methods of social reformers. 'There is a Christian realism as well as a Chris- tian idealism,' Geoffrey declares, 'that searches with no profane curiosity into hidden places, but only seeks to enlighten them; a realism, that lays bare the wounds of humanity to heal them, the sins of humanity to forgive them, the wants of humanity to relieve them.'[13]

In these two early novels, Sheehan was not a gadfly who tried to sting Irish education authorities with questions about pedagogical problems. While the quality of Irish teachers and curriculum design were important to him, Sheehan was more concerned with the principles he thought should organize the educa- tion of Irish Catholics and prepare them for spiritually meaningful and produc- tive civic lives.[14] He offered Geoffrey Austin's unsatisfying existence as proof that Irish education had failed to equip Irish men and women with the moral compass they needed to direct them to activities that would benefit the commonweal.

Sheehan's next two novels focused on the training and character of Irish priests, although social and political problems also affect their ministries. In *My new curate*, his best known work, Sheehan describes the mentoring relationship between the parish priest of Kilronan, Father Daniel Hanrahan, known affec- tionately as 'Daddy Dan', and his enthusiastic new curate, Revd Edward Letheby. Its follow-up, *Luke Delmege*, and a third novel published in 1909, *The blindness of Dr Gray*, completed a trilogy about Irish clerical life.[15] In *Luke Delmege*, Sheehan traces the career of a priest who is both intellectually troubled and inadequately prepared by Maynooth to meet his responsibilities. He completes a number of assignments, including several on the English mission, but remains perpetually unhappy. He worries about falling into heresy and he does not know how to help his parishioners improve their lot in life. The third novel in the trilogy describes the unshakable love that Irish priests have for their parishion- ers, even when the people question Dr Gray's methods in resolving issues in the parish.

---

13 Sheehan, *The triumph of failure*, p. 438.
14 For Sheehan's perspective on educational issues of the day, see his 'The American report on Irish education', in *The literary life and other essays*, pp 86–108.
15 P.A. Sheehan, *Luke Delmege* (London, 1901); *The blindness of Dr Gray*, or the final law (London, 1909).

If the priests' training and their motivations are occasionally suspect in the eyes of the people, in Sheehan's novels, their personal character and political allegiance to Irish nationalism is never in doubt.[16] Sheehan uses Father Dan's reflection on three generations of clerical personnel that had passed through the Irish Church to reassure readers that the Irish clergy were steadfast in their determination to serve and protect the people.[17] Father Dan tells a dozen priests who join him for an after dinner symposium that the generation of priests who were educated on the continent during the eighteenth century were dignified, holy, Gallican, and afraid of change; always welcome at the landlord's great house, they could hardly be called officers of the Church militant. 'Then came Maynooth,' he proudly declares, which 'poured forth from its gates the strongest, fiercest, most fearless army of priests that ever fought for the spiritual interests of the people – men of large physique and iron constitutions, who spent ten hours a day on horseback, despised French claret, loved their people and chastised them like fathers, but were prepared to defend them with their lives and the outpouring of their blood against their hereditary enemies.'[18] Father Dan notes he is a proud member of this generation, but he had also come to respect the latest cohort. Although he was concerned about their approach to the study of theology and academic training, he points out that Ireland's young priests possessed the best elements of the grand inheritance that had come down to them. 'Their passionate devotion to their faith,' he concludes, 'is only rivaled by their passionate devotion to the motherland ... And with all the ancient prejudices in favour of my own caste, I see clearly that the equipments of the new generation are best suited to modern needs.'[19] Sheehan closes this lesson in Church history on a patriotic and ultramontane note, as the older and younger priests raise their voices to sing what Father Dan calls 'genuine Irish music, with the right lilt and the right sentiment': 'I dreamt that I dwelt in marble halls', 'The west's awake', 'Dear land', and 'God bless the Pope, the great, the good'.

Sheehan's Irish priests are always challenged to find ways to improve the material and intellectual condition of their parishioners. In *The blindness of Dr Gray*, Father Henry Litton launches a branch of the Gaelic League and involves himself in other activities in the secular life of the parish. The use of physical force to solve social and political problems is often an issue that involves the priests. In *My new curate*, Father Letheby brushes aside the notion that revolutionary activity offers the best means to secure the material welfare of the peo-

16 See Sheehan's 'The Irish priesthood and politics', in *The literary life and other essays*, pp 109–20. For a modern analysis of the Maynooth-educated priest's role in fostering the development of Irish nationalism, see Seán Connolly, *Religion and society in nineteenth-century Ireland* (Dundalk, 1985), p. 40.
17 My new curate, pp 228–32.
18 Ibid., pp 232.
19 Ibid.

ple; but some of Sheehan's other priests will adopt a far more ambivalent attitude toward revolution.[20] In *My new curate*, however, Sheehan maintains the light touch that distinguishes the novel in a scene in which the young priest encounters the local hillsiders and their leader, 'Hop and Go', a lame tailor who is also an informer. Father Letheby grabs 'Hop and Go' by the nape of the neck and flings him to the ground. He then defends the clergy against the would-be revolutionary's charge that the priests are against the people, recalling that the priests and people had fought side-by-side for seven hundred years in the battle to gain Ireland's freedom from civil and religious disabilities.[21]

Sheehan offered a sterner test of character and political resolve to Father Luke Delmege, who believed that finding the best means of improving the welfare of the Irish people was an enigma, better left alone. While visiting the House of Commons, for example, he observes Charles Stewart Parnell's obstruction in the face of Benjamin Disraeli's government, but the spectacle fails to arouse any native patriotic spirit. Later, when traveling by train to a new assignment in the west of Ireland, Luke peers out the window at the evidence of Ireland's tragic past.

> Here and there they swept by the skeleton of some old ruined abbey and castle, that was just kept from falling by the tender support of the kind ivy. That was history. And here and there, more frequently, he saw standing the bare brown mud walls of an unroofed cabin, the holes that once were windows and doors, staring like the sockets of a skull.[22]

Luke decides to take drastic action: to create a new civilization that infuses English values into Irish peasants. He offers suggestions on farm management and gardening and delivers problem-solving sermons on the Victorian-era virtues of self-help and manly independence. But his English frame of reference inhibits his effectiveness because he failed to understand the people. He could not comprehend why they failed to accommodate their ideas with his or the necessity of proceeding slowly in uprooting their ancient traditions and conserving what was useful. Nevertheless, Luke's political consciousness begins to develop. Watching a poor farmer drive a heavy plow into the unyielding earth, he realizes the man is:

> labouring, not for his own little family over there in that wretched cabin – that meant only bread and potatoes – but for the agent, that he might have

---

20 For an analysis of the ambivalent attitude toward physical force that was maintained by the Irish clergy of Sheehan's generation, see Sheridan Gilley, *The Catholic Church and revolution*, in D.G. Boyce (ed.), *The revolution in Ireland, 1879–1923* (London, 1988).

21 *My new curate*, pp 131–2.

22 *Luke Delmege*, p. 224.

his brandy and cigars; and for two old ladies in a Dublin Square, that they might give steaks to their lap-dogs; and for a solicitor again above them, that he might pay for his son in Trinity; and, on the highest pinnacle of the infamous system, for the lord, that he might have a racer at the Derby and St Cloud, and a set of brilliants for Sadie at the *Opera Comique*.[23]

Yet, when he is elected president of the local branch of the Land League, Luke continues to emphasize self-help and cooperation with landlords – so much so that his parishioners begin to think he is a landlord's agent.

The novel's climax is set at the site of a violent eviction at Lisnalee, Luke's ancestral family home. His exhausted father is the last to emerge from the house. He kisses the threshold, the lintel, and the two doorposts. Lingering too long, the old man is knocked to the ground by an impatient bailiff. Luke, watching the drama with a bursting heart, rushes to aid his father only to be blocked by a cold, symbolic representation of an unfeeling legal system: the sabre of a mounted sub-inspector. As always, Luke hesitates, his habitual self-restraint calculating all the consequences.

Then, a whirlwind of celtic rage, all the greater for having been pent up so long, swept away every consideration of prudence; and with his strong hand tearing the weapon from the hands of the young officer, he smashed it to fragments across his knees, and flung them, blood-stained from his own fingers, into the officer's face.[24]

Luke is tried and found guilty of several offenses but he refuses to let his clerical status shield him from a three-month prison sentence. By taking a righteous course of action at the eviction and in court, Luke not only demonstrated he, too, was governed by the national instinct for survival, he also had lived up to the nation's ideals of heroism and self-sacrifice in the face of the enemy. The novel then closes with Luke, now serenely approaching his death, reflecting on the value system of the Irish nation and offering advice to those who might hope to develop an Irish utopia.

Let wise teachers beware of bringing down the mind of the entire nation to a common level of purely natural ambition and purely materialistic success. However necessary for the masses such efforts may be to save the race from extinction, it is not the specific genius of our people. That soars higher; and material prosperity must not be the ultimate goal of our race; but only the basis of the higher life.[25]

23 Ibid., pp 344–5.
24 Ibid., pp 532–4.
25 Ibid., pp 564–5.

Sheehan's next novel, *Glenanaar*, was a work of historical fiction he based on the records of the state trials of the so-called Doneraile Conspiracy of 1829.[26] Moving backward and forward in time, a rather innovative writing technique for the period, Sheehan included flashbacks involving Daniel O'Connell, Young Ireland, the Great Famine, and the Fenians as he traced the historical development of tensions among community members and the contemporary descendants of a man who was accused of betraying his comrades. It is a well-told tale, that also provides an opportunity to examine how Sheehan represented Irish history to his readers. In Glenanaar and most of his other novels, Sheehan wrote sparingly about the episodes and processes that constituted the nationalist interpretation of the past – invasion, conquest, expropriation, and discrimination. Taken collectively, his allusions and references to historic events and famous individuals confirmed a version of the national past that was already familiar to an informed nationalist audience. There is, however, another aspect of Sheehan's use of the past that warrants attention. Sheehan idealized the earlier generations of Ireland's Catholic peasants, maintaining that their lives had been characterized by cooperation, purity, and temperance. He believed these hardy people had relied solely on the maxims of their religion to carry them through every reverse of social and political fortune with profound and tranquil equanimity.[27] Sheehan worried that this race of peasants – the Catholic-Irish nation – was dying away under modern secular influences. In his novels, therefore, Sheehan presented his vision of a Gaelic, rural past as the model that would reverse the trends of the current generation and shape the future of an Irish state. His fictional characters had to take the first step to begin this process: they had to come to an understanding of the values that had animated the actions of these Irish people in the past and apply them to resolve their individual problems in the present. The implicit question raised by Sheehan's use of the past was whether a new generation and its leaders could embrace that particular historical view and employ it to solve the social problems affecting Ireland in the twentieth century.[28]

In 1907, Sheehan published *Lisheen*, the story of Robert Maxwell, a young landlord who seeks to emulate in Ireland the example of his hero, Tolstoy, by improving the social and intellectual life of his tenants.[29] The novel is a good example of the difficulty that urbane Irish men and women would experience in coming to terms with the peasantry and their values. Maxwell's first encounter

---

26 P.A. Sheehan, *Glenanaar, a story of Irish life* (London, 1905).
27 Sheehan, *Early essays and lectures* (London, 1919), pp 288–9.
28 For the theory that Eamon de Valera's social and economic policies were influenced by an essentially rural view of Ireland in the 1930s and 1940s, see Dermot Keogh, *Twentieth-century Ireland: nation and state* (New York, 1994), pp 71–7, 88–90.
29 P.A. Sheehan, *Lisheen or, the test of the spirits* (London, 1907).

with rural Ireland occurs at a wretched cabin – ragged thatch, mud walls, a pool of slimy water outside and a grunting pig inside. Doubtful whether he should pursue his investigation any further, he reminds himself: the deeper the degradation, the higher the resurrection. When an accident leaves the young idealist disoriented and weak, Owen McAuliffe's family gives him shelter and employment as a laborer. He comes to appreciate the physical and spiritual qualities of the Irish country people, as idealized by Sheehan:

> And these peasants! How easily, how smoothly, how deftly, they plied hand and nerve and sinew and muscle from dawn to dark, never tired, never fatigued, their whole physical system moving rhythmically at the divine call of labour. He had noticed how firm were their muscles, how broad their wrists, and how the muscles and tendons seemed to strain with the strength of whipcord when unusual pressure was placed on them. And how beautifully clean they were! Not a single scab or speck on their spotless skins. Not a trace of dust or dandruff in their hair. Their hands were hardened and enamelled by toil, their bodies were washed in sweat; but they were kept sweet and wholesome and fragrant by that daily ablution, by the free play of the pure mountain air, and the immaculate sanctity of their lives.[30]

And Robert also quickly identifies the obstacles that stand between him and the successful completion of his mission. In a conversation with other reforming landlords, he explains:

> From cock-crow to sundown, it was work, work, work, and work not for themselves but for another. Where's the use of talking about the resurrection of a people until you remove the stone from the door of their sepulchre? You cannot have a nation without manhood; you cannot have manhood without education, you cannot have education without leisure and freedom from sordid cares, and you cannot have the latter until landlordism is removed wholly and entirely from the land.[31]

Robert's reform effort collapses beneath the weight of a series of misunderstandings: he is accused of murder, is arrested, and placed in gaol. A more difficult burden is the boycott that follows the false charge that he is an evicting landlord. When the McAuliffe family is among those who are put off their land, Robert acts secretly to purchase and improve their farm and has it returned to them. But when he makes a surprise visit to the McAuliffe home, the family fails to recognize him. After an explanation of what has transpired, they still

30 *Lisheen*, pp 66–7.
31 Ibid., p. 273.

cannot overcome their suspicion that he was somehow responsible for their trouble. At the end of the novel, Robert reflects on his mistakes and the anguish of being separated from the peasants he respected and loved. Admitting that his mission had not been a total failure, he concedes that he had passed successfully through a novitiate of sorrow; he had borne well the 'test of the spirits'. But the material advancement of the tenants and his personal vindication are not enough to ease the pain in this idealist's heart. He concludes, 'There might have been something better – the farewell to a world he would have served, not under the glitter and glamour of triumph, but in the very agony of crucifixion'.[32]

Those who expected all of Sheehan's books to be as cheerful as *My new curate* were disappointed.[33] Part of the disappointment stems from the downbeat conclusion: irreconcilable differences between members of the community and a messianic deathwish were uncharacteristic elements in the denouement of Sheehan's novels, which usually left the main characters philosophically satisfied. In some respects, Sheehan had created a character who was too sympathetic: Maxwell's instincts and experiences convince him that the tenantry and landlords must be brought into communion with one another. The real obstacles in the way of achieving this goal, however, were not the mishaps that occur during the course of the story. Rather, Maxwell suffers from the sin of pride. No matter how well-intentioned, his efforts at social reform are based solely on the 'religion of humanity', which for Sheehan is at best a spurious imitation of the Church's teaching about charity and at worst pharisaic hypocrisy. In *Lisheen*, Sheehan made his point the hard way, demonstrating that success in the secular world always comes at a heavy cost, and that the resulting heartache is all the more painful if that success is not grounded in Christian self-sacrifice.

In 1910, Canon Sheehan's literary career coincided with his work in the public arena. While writing *The intellectuals*, Sheehan helped to formulate the philosophy of the All-for-Ireland League with his friend, William O'Brien, who was an independent-minded, former member of the Irish Parliamentary Party. The organizers of the league charged the party's leaders with failing to foster cooperation among Irish political groups and opposing public policy reform initiatives that would benefit all Irish citizens, not just Catholic nationalists and party sycophants. Sheehan articulated the league's position in its manifesto, which appeared in the *Cork free press* on 11 June, 1910:

> We are a generous people; and yet we are told we must keep up a sectarian bitterness to the end; and that Protestant ascendancy has been broken down,

32 Ibid., pp 453–4.
33 In a tactful letter, Sheehan's life-long friend, William O'Brien, MP, wrote, '… while the book succeeded in putting one into a cheerful mood with human nature, it did not shirk the many dark and tragic events that sometimes make the most hopeful of us a little sick at heart'. Cited in Heuser, *Canon Sheehan*, p. 207.

only to build Catholic ascendancy on its ruins. Are we in earnest about our country at all or are we seeking to perpetuate our wretchedness by refusing the honest aide of Irishmen? Why should we throw into the arms of England those children of Ireland who would be our most faithful allies, if we did not seek to disinherit them?[34]

The league enjoyed some success in Cork but it failed to loosen the grip of the Irish party elsewhere in Ireland. Nevertheless, one observer of Sheehan's public work maintains that he was the most effective liberal intellectual at the time in Irish life, applauding the priest's ill-fated attempt to make a practical accommo-dation between conflicting social and political elements in order to make Ire-land viable as a nation.[35]

The league's failure to catch the imagination of Irish men and women out-side of Cork was foreshadowed by the fate of the early serialized chapters of *The intellectuals*.[36] *The Rosary*, a Catholic periodical published by the Dominicans, dropped the work midway through its serialization; the novel appeared in 1911. With the expectation that home rule legislation would be introduced in Parlia-ment the following year, the novel envisioned the intellectually stimulating soci-ety which Sheehan hoped would take shape in an independent Ireland. The main characters include Catholics and Protestants, mostly professional men and women, from Ireland, England, and Scotland. They are organized into a club by a Cork priest named Father Dillon, a clever reference perhaps to John Dillon, a leader of the Irish Parliamentary Party and an estranged friend of O'Brien. Father Dillon turns out to be the most politically conservative member of the group. Dr James Holden serves as the exponent for Sheehan's inclusive – and, in an Irish context, radical – views.

The club convenes for thirty-seven sessions, or seminars, to discuss humani-ties and science topics. Mid-way through the series, the topic turns unexpect-edly from the migration patterns of the ancient Celts to Irish politics. A partici-pant suggests that the Irish are a feminine race, and Dr Holden improves on that observation by declaring the Irish people are anciently feminine, that is, they are led by politicians like a pack of old women or a race of docile children. To prove his point, Holden recounts a scene he had witnessed at a recent re-gional convention of the Irish party, which, he notes, did not include 'a single

---

34 *Cork free press*, 11 June 1910. The league's inaugural resolution was dated 31 March 1910. It reads in part: 'This representative meeting of the City and County of Cork hereby establishes an associa-tion to be called the All-for-Ireland League, whose primary object shall be the union and active co-operation in every department of our National life of all Irish men and women who believe in the principle of domestic self-government for Ireland.' See also, *All-for-Ireland League, The national conference of the All-for-Ireland League held at Cork May 25, 1911* (Cork, 1911); and William O'Brien, *Home rule by consent. The proposals of the All-for-Ireland League* (Cork, 1913).
35 Clifford, *Canon Sheehan*, pp 17–21.
36 P.A. Sheehan, *The intellectuals. An experiment in Irish club life* (London, 1911).

elected representative, but a melee of priests, ministers, land and labour delegates, United League representatives, Hibernians, and ultra-Hibernians – all huddled together like sheep in a pen'.[37] When a young delegate, whom Dr Holden thinks may have carried a concealed side-arm for self-defense, posed a series of awkward amendments to the resolution, 'That we renew our expression of unlimited confidence in our members of Parliament; and reiterate our resolution to maintain the unity and integrity of the Party at any cost', he was ridiculed by the chairman and laughed out of the building by the party faithful. Holden goes on to tell the seminar that he then took the convention floor, where he observed sarcastically before storming out: 'Mr. Chairman, if this deliberative and calmly consultative assemblage is to be taken as an example of what we are to expect in the near future, then God grant that we shall never see home rule in Ireland, because it would mean the total destruction of the two greatest privileges man possesses – freedom of thought and liberty of speech.' In reply, Father Dillon explains the position held by Irish party leaders and Irish priests, whom Sheehan believed had seriously misjudged the thrust of Irish political life.[38] 'When a nation is struggling onwards to freedom,' Father Dillon observes, 'the one thing absolutely necessary is discipline – the sinking of individual opinions, and accepting the verdict of the majority. We are at war, trying to recover our lost inheritance; and in war, the one thing always fatal is indiscipline – the breaking away of detachments from the main army. I think that young man should have been heard, and then, the Convention could reject his absurd proposition.' Dr Holden finds the priest's thinking absurd: 'There is little use in shaking ourselves free of England, if we are to still be slaves – without an atom of mental or moral freedom at home.'[39] He reprises the discussion in two subsequent seminars, making the final point that the typical Irishman is woefully uninformed about political and economic issues, an ignorance that he charges is intentionally abetted by the party leadership. He predicts that the uninformed citizenry will be the sport of extremists and socialists who will pass revolutionary measures without protest.[40]

37 Ibid., pp 186–9.
38 For the development of the modern Irish political system, which was based on an alliance among the Irish Parliamentary party, its leader, and the Catholic hierarchy, see Emmet Larkin, 'The Irish political tradition', in Thomas Hachey and Lawrence McCaffrey (eds), *Perspectives on Irish nationalism* (Lexington, 1989).
39 *The intellectuals*, pp 189–90.
40 See also David H Burton (ed.), *The Holmes-Sheehan correspondence. The letters of Justice Oliver Wendell Holmes and Canon Patrick Augustine Sheehan* (Port Washington, N.Y., 1976), pp 33–6, for Sheehan's private thoughts on the issue of the dangers of a one party state. Sheehan wrote to Holmes, 26 August 1910: 'Hence I have been for the last few months here in Ireland in a state of silent fury against the insolent domination of the Irish Parliamentary Party and their attempt to stamp out all political freedom'; and pp 60–1, Sheehan to Holmes, 25 February 1913: 'We are in the throes of expectation about the Home Rule Bill. It will be the best for England; the worst for Ireland since the Act of Union.'

Father Dillon breaks off the provocative discussions when emotions become too heated. The priest stands as Sheehan's warning about the dangers inherent in the political alliance that existed between the clergy and nationalist politicians, especially when compared to the powerfully self-possessed Dr Gray, or any of Sheehan's other priests for that matter. Father Dillon typically retreats to his house and frets that he may have gone too far in his attempt to bring people together. The closure in these scenes is frustrating for the reader; the novel's effectiveness is also damaged by Sheehan's penchant for seasoning the seminars with a multitiude of arcane facts from the humanities, the social and physical sciences, and philosophy. Between Sheehan's rendering of the seminars' content and the post-seminar dialogue, the academic flavor that he employed to demonstrate how people from differing traditions could discuss common interests had become instead its main course.[41]

In *Miriam Lucas*, which appeared the following year, Sheehan returned to his standard format in terms of plot development and characterization.[42] The twin issues at work in this novel were the efficacy of socialism in solving workers' discontent and the role of religion in the life of the secular humanist. Sheehan's task as teacher and priest was doubly difficult in this novel. On the one hand, he had to write convincingly about labour issues that were also being explicated by the famous Irish labour leaders, including most notably James Larkin and James Connolly. On the other hand, he had to mediate between the teachings of Pius IX in his *Syllabus of errors* (1864), with its warnings about the false doctrines of a secular age, and Leo XIII's *Rerum novarum* (1891), with its call for Catholic social activism and the formation of Christian trade unions.[43] While his use of standard late-nineteenth century melodramatic coincidences to conclude the story detracts from the novel's overall effect, Sheehan used the literary device of 'the foreign visitor to her own land' to develop one of his most interesting characters – and his only heroine.

Miriam Lucas is faced with personal, social, and spiritual difficulties. Her mother has deserted the family; her father loses his mind and disappears; a sinister advisor intends to marry her and steal her family estate in Cork. Her social problems stem from her objection to the artificial class distinctions that guide the behavior of the women who travel in Cork's elite social circles. Miriam

41 Similar criticism can be leveled at Sheehan's *The queen's fillet*, which also appeared in 1911. In this work of historical fiction, Sheehan rushed through the narrative of the French Revolution, passing judgment on the leadership skills of historical figures in this seminal event in modern European history. His objective was to warn the Irish people against the excesses of political uprisings and the disorder that follows in their wake, but the scattered paragraphs that make explicit this aim were swallowed up by the massive dose of historical trivia. He also failed to make any references to the Irish revolution of 1798, which would have made the story more immediate for his readership. P.A. Sheehan, *The queen's fillet* (London, 1911).

42 P.A. Sheehan, *Miriam Lucas* (London, 1912).

43 See Emmet Larkin, 'Socialism and Catholicism in Ireland', in *Publications in the Humanities*, Number 67, Department of Humanities, Massachusetts Institute of Technology, 1965.

has a natural goodness that everyone finds attractive; she does not, however, have faith in any particular religion. After the personal and social problems build to the breaking point, she moves to Dublin. In the metropolis she hears the fiery trumpet call of *The Watchman*, a socialist workers' magazine (modeled perhaps on Larkin's *The Irish Worker*) that describes the ceaseless war between labour and capital and arraigns society for its involvement in a criminal conspiracy against the weak and suffering. Miriam becomes the newspaper's most spirited writer, pointing out the antipathy between the classes, calling for the creation of new social systems, and demanding better working conditions. She does have some qualms: 'What if these ideas were put into practice? What if the masses rose up; and in fire and ruin taught the lessons that I am teaching in cold print?'[44]

As with Sheehan's male heroes, Miriam's attitudes undergo a transformation. Her enlightenment begins when she encounters Father Hugo, a friar who had seen socialism at work in Germany, Belgium, and America. He knew how its 'terrible, specious doctrines bore fruit; and how, commencing with the religion of humanity, it ended in the dethronement of God, the sundering of families, the breaking of all social ties, and all the other evils incident to revolution'.[45] A series of chapters narrating the course of a great strike in Dublin, which are strikingly prophetic in the light of events that took place in Dublin two years later, culminate in the description of a workers' march. The episode ends in a tremendous conflagration in which Father Hugo is accidentally burned to death. It is a sobering experience, but not enough to keep Miriam from resuming her writing when she moves to New York in an improbable, but ultimately successful, search for her mother.

The second aspect of the Miriam's enlightenment centers on her spiritual life. Father Hugo had served as a catalyst for her search for faith, and the journey ends when Miriam enters a Catholic church in New York where she listens to a succinct sermon on the great commandment: 'That you love one another, as I have loved you.' 'I shall add nothing to this,' the preacher concludes, 'but to say, that herein is contained not only the secret of eternal life, but the secret of human happiness, the welfare of the race.' Then, as if speaking directly to Miriam, he adds, 'Today, too, certain doctrinaires, well-meaning, perhaps, dream of a new world, built on cloud-castles of benevolence and well-doing. In vain!'[46]

Sheehan used the sermon on charity as a lever to redirect Miriam's socialist convictions and bring her to Catholicism. As the novel closes, Miriam understands that Christ's teaching effectively undermines the self-serving positions of both labour and capital. She also realizes that internecine class struggle and revolution can never end because they leave the struggling masses spent and

44 Sheehan, *Miriam Lucas*, p. 132.
45 Ibid., pp 152–3.
46 Ibid., p. 395.

sickened for a generation and the successful classes either paralyzed with terror or frantic for revenge. Looking ahead, Miriam decides that only the charter of everlasting peace – 'that you love one another as I have loved you' – will break the cycles of history's smoke and flame.

By the time *The intellectuals*, *The queen's fillet*, and *Miriam Lucas* appeared, Canon Sheehan was seriously ill. He had been diagnosed with cancer in 1910 but refused to undergo surgery. Perhaps the knowledge that his days were numbered explains the dull lectures in the first of these novels, the weak analysis of historical events in the second, and the contrived denouement of the third. He was also hurrying to complete the novel he knew would be his last: *The graves at Kilmorna*, a story of two friends who were Fenian officers in the rising of 1867.[47] Drawing heavily on his life experiences in England and Ireland for characters and scenes, this novel was his valedictory on Irish life.

The story opens with James Halpin, a national school teacher in Kilmorna, taking his students on an impromptu field trip for a lesson about a battle in 1690 between the Irish brigades that supported James II and William III's English armies. The spell cast by the landscape and the teacher's lesson is broken by the noisy behavior of a mob of drunken townspeople who have been hired to shout election slogans in favour of a place hunting Dublin Castle hack. The story's other hero, eighteen-year-old Myles Cogan, who has stopped to watch the mob, begins to wonder whether the people are worth dying for. The scene establishes four themes, loyalty to a political cause and blood sacrifice, that Sheehan then places in opposition to two countervailing themes, the materialistic spirit of the Irish people and their lack of political resolve.

As the date of the rising approaches, Cogan expresses his concern about the probable results: bleeding figures of a few mutilated peasants on the battlefield and a long row of prison convicts. Halpin acknowledges the risks; yet he knows they must go forward. 'The country has become plethoric,' he explains, 'and therefore indifferent to everything but bread and cheese. It needs bloodletting a little. The country is sinking into the sleep of death; and nothing can awake it but the crack of the rifle.'[48] The country is not, however, completely devoid of patriots. Sheehan idealizes the artisans and skilled workers who comprise the rank-and-file Fenian soldiers; they are anxious to follow the command of the two young idealists.

> They were strong, sinewy fellows, accustomed to bend their backs to their daily toil, and go through life without pillows beneath their elbows. There were masons, carpenters, bricklayers, shoemakers – representatives of every kind of trade amongst them, and, strange to say, many of them, who had

47 P.A. Sheehan, *The graves at Kilmorna, a story of '67* (London, 1915).
48 Ibid., p. 66.

been ploughing through life in a broken-backed, weary manner, were suddenly stiffened and strengthened into some kind of unnatural vigour, when they became soldiers of the Republic.[49]

The detachment is easily routed. Cogan and Halpin cover their comrades' retreat until Halpin is mortally wounded. Cogan gives Halpin his rosary, a bloodstained prayer book, and the Miraculous Medal of the Daughters of Charity. Halpin dies a patriot, declaring, 'I'm luckier than Sarsfield. This blood is shed for Ireland,' and in a state of grace, receiving holy communion and the last rites from a local priest.

Cogan is not so lucky; he is tried for treason. In his speech from the dock, he warns the people about the corruption that has weakened the nation and he emphasizes the necessity of the shedding of blood to stop the decomposition. 'I shall not,' he declares, 'trespass on the sacred precincts of religion to illustrate my meaning. I shall only say that as the blood of the martyrs was the seed of the saints, so the blood of the patriot is the sacred seed from which alone can spring new forces, and [instill] fresh life into a nation that is drifting into the putrescence of decay. No true Irishman sees a distinction between the battlefield and the scaffold. Both are the fields of honour for our race.'[50] Cogan is sentenced to ten years penal servitude, and much of the sentence is spent in solitary confinement.

After his return to Kilmorna, Cogan takes no part in either national or local political activities, declining the offer of a safe seat in the House of Commons because the overture comes from corrupt Nationalist party leaders. He also refuses to join with former Fenian comrades, now in the Land League, although he believed the cause was just. In any case, the land and national questions pale in significance for him compared to the problem of the debilitated moral character of the Irish people. He dreams of a united Ireland where all classes would sink their differences in a cordial acknowledgment of the nation's larger claims. His fondest hope is that Ireland will keep aloof from the materialistic aspirations that characterized the behavior of other nations and return to what she had always been: a center of spiritual and intellectual light to a world living in philosophical darkness. But four decades pass by, and his hopes and dreams are not realized.[51]

In the novel's climactic scene, Cogan finally casts aside his prohibition against public speaking and mounts an election wagon on behalf of a young Irish Unionist Party candidate. Speaking in level tones through a hail of objects and insults from a hostile crowd, he reaffirms his political principles and reiterates his concern for the character of the Irish nation: '... in building up a Nation, it is not to Acts of Parliament you must look, but to yourselves, because no material gain can compensate for moral degeneracy, and I doubt if Ireland ever sank lower in the sty of materialism than in this present age.'[52] Cogan is struck by a stone that seemed to lift his head off his shoulders. The wound is fatal; the last rites are administered.

The surviving members of his Fenian command carry his coffin to its resting place a foot away from the remains of James Halpin. As the old guard circles the patriots' graves, a priest addresses the tiny phalanx: 'There lie two Irish martyrs – one, pierced by an English bullet on the field of battle; the other, after spending the best of ten years of his life in English dungeons, done to death by his countrymen. There they lie; and with them is buried the Ireland of our dreams, our hopes, our ambitions, our love. There is no more to be said. Let us go hence!'[53]

Published posthumously in 1915, *The graves at Kilmorna* was supposedly a source of inspiration for the Irish volunteers who participated in the Easter rising the following year. Some observers maintain the novel became the bible of Sinn Féin during the war for independence.[54] Others wonder if Patrick Pearse's idea of blood sacrifice was not prophetically foreshadowed by, if not reflected in, Sheehan's last work.[55] When placed in the context of his life's work as a novelist, however, *The graves at Kilmorna* makes Sheehan's most powerful argument for the redemptive power of spiritually grounded self-sacrifice. The stories of Halpin and Cogan, in combat and in constitutional agitation, teach the greatest lesson of all about the human predicament: one must be willing to lay down one's life for the good of the commonweal.

Sheehan's objective as a priest, teacher, and novelist was to explain how Christian principles offered the best means of both solving secular problems and curing the philosophical malaise that he believed had corrupted the civility of Irish life and threatened the efficacy of a potential Irish state under home rule. He grounded his political philosophy and social activism on two principles: first, that Irish political life had to be reorganized according to democratic principles before the country could succeed as a nation-state; second, that the material and intellectual welfare of the Irish people could only advance when its members had created an inclusive social system, one that was animated by ancient Irish values and the Christian virtues of love and charity. In fiction, his characters resolved their personal and philosophical problems when they em-

---

52 Ibid., pp 365–7.
53 Ibid., p. 373.
54 Linehan, *Canon Sheehan of Doneraile*, p. 155. Boyle, *Canon Sheehan*, p. 84, writes: 'No history could give a more faithful picture of the sequence of events during Ireland's latest struggle for freedom. The military terror described in the novel, the characters portrayed, their chivalry, patriotism and general outlook class "The Graves at Kilmorna" as one of the most remarkable and prophetic works in literary history.'
55 See also, Candy, 'Canon Sheehan', p. 273, for a brief discussion of the novel's prophetic vision.

braced these principles. To solve Ireland's social ills and heal a debilitated nation, Sheehan offered the teachings of the Catholic Church on love and charity. Untimately, in two of his last novels, *The intellectuals* and *The graves at Kilmorna*, Sheehan adopted a most difficult writing technique – the voice of the prophet, not the preacher – to drive home this point.[56] As a nationalist and social critic, then, Canon Sheehan's literary life's work serves as a useful criterion for comparing the public activities and discourse of other socially and politically engaged priests of his generation.

56   See E.M. Forster, *Aspects of the novel* (New York, 1927), pp 181–212.

Soggarth Aroon and Gombeen-Priest:
Canon James MacFadden (1842–1917)

Breandán Mac Suibhne

Canon James MacFadden, parish priest of Inis Caoil, county Donegal, died on 17 April 1917. His cousin, Cardinal Michael Logue, the bishops of Derry and Dromore, his own bishop, Dr Patrick O'Donnell of Raphoe, and almost all the clergy in his diocese attended the funeral. Prominent nationalist politicians, including John Redmond and Joseph Devlin, telegrammed condolences. In a short panegyric, O'Donnell praised MacFadden's 'very remarkable and very useful career as a priest and a patriot', emphasising his success in providing schools, chapels and parochial houses and his 'efforts and suffering in Gweedore'.[1] The latter reference was an acknowledgment of MacFadden's role in the land agitation of the 1880s, when, as parish priest of Gaoth Dobhair in north west Donegal, he led a controversial campaign during which he served a gaol sentence for promoting a criminal conspiracy not to pay rent and appeared in court charged with murdering a policeman. Hailed as the 'Patriot priest of Gweedore', his political career spanned over three decades. Following his transfer to Inis Caoil in south west Donegal in 1901, he concentrated on nationalist politics and the socio-economic development of the 'congested districts', gaining national prominence in the United Irish League, Ancient Order of Hibernians and Conradh na Gaeilge.

A messianic figure, MacFadden inspired intense loyalty in Gaoth Dobhair and there is an enduring image throughout north west Donegal of a selfless clergyman who strove to improve the social condition of his parishioners, the classic 'soggarth aroon' or beloved priest. Oral tradition, a hagiographic popular biography, and several local histories of the land agitation, generally referred to as *aimsir an tSagairt 'Ic Pháidín* [trans.: Priest MacFadden's time], all cast

---

1 *Derry Standard*, 20 Apr. 1917. 'Soggarth aroon' is English orthography for Irish *a shagairt, a rúin* [trans.: O priest, dear!]. It was widely used in the nineteenth century to denote a priest regarded with great affection by his parishioners. 'Gombeen' is English orthography for Irish *gaimbín* [trans.: a small measure; interest]. It is most commonly used in the term 'gombeenman', meaning 'usurious trader'. Both phrases became the titles of popular works of fiction, see Revd Joseph Canon Guinan, *The soggarth aroon* (Dublin, 1905); 'The gombeenman' in Bram Stoker, *The snake's pass* (London, 1890), pp 32–47.

him in this heroic role.[2] Indeed, Gaoth Dobhair local histories present him as a saviour:

> Ba é seo an laoch mór oa thóg muintir Ghaoth Dobhair as an sclabhaíocht, a chuir deireadh le hocras agus anró sa pharóiste, a chuir cnámh droma iontu, a ghlac ceannaireacht orthu agus nár tharraing anáil gur chuir sé deireadh le hainchíos, le haindhlí agus le díshealbhú.[3]

> [trans.: This was the great heroic man who took the people of Gaoth Dobhair out of slavery, who ended hunger and hardship in the parish, who put backbone into them, who marshalled them and who did not draw breath until he had finished rackrents, unjust laws and eviction.]

In contrast, in his last parish, MacFadden elicited a very different response. Between 1914 and 1918, Patrick MacGill (1891–1963), a native of Inis Caoil building a literary reputation in London, published a trilogy of semi-autobiographical novels *Children of the dead end; The rat-pit* and *Glenmornan* – in which he bitterly satirised MacFadden.[4] The character based on him – 'Fr Devaney' – is among the most negative priest-characters in early twentieth-century Irish literature. In all three novels, he appears as a selfish autocrat who lived lavishly off his poor parishioners' 'offerings' and defended gombeenism (a system of usury operated by merchants and shopkeepers):

> The parish priest ... was a little pot-bellied man with white shiny false teeth, who smoked nine-penny cigars and who always travelled first-class in a railway train. Everybody feared him ... he was eternally looking for money from the people, who, although very poor, always paid when the priest commanded them. If they did not, they would go to hell as soon as they died. So Father Devaney said.[5]

---

2   Proinnsias Ó Gallchobhair, *History of landlordism in Donegal* (Ballyshannon, 1962) is essentially a biography of MacFadden; Séan Mac Fhonnlaoich, *Scéal Ghaoth Dobhair* (Bade Átha Cliath, 1983), pp 83–130. Pádraig Ua Cnáimhsí, 'Sagart 'Ac Pháidín Ghaoth Dobhair (1842–1917)' in *An tUltach*, 65, 2–9 (1988) transcends the hagiography that characterises most local historians' discussions of MacFadden's career.

3   Mac Fhionnlaoich, *Scéal*, p. 87. All translations in this chapter are my own.

4   Patrick MacGill, *Children of the dead end: the auto-biography of a navvy* (London, 1914); *The rat-pit* (London, 1915); *Glenmornan* (London, 1918). Owen Dudley Edwards, 'Patrick MacGill and the making of a historical source with a handlist of his works' in *The Innes review* (Scottish Catholic Historical Association), 37, 2 (1986), pp 73–99; Séamas Ó Catháin, 'Patrick MacGill agus an Lagán' in Nollaig Mac Conghail (ed.), *Scríbhneoireacht na gConallach* (Baile Átha Cliath, 1990), pp 241–51 consider MacGill's work as a historical source. For biographical details, see Patrick O'Sullivan, 'Patrick MacGill: the making of a writer' in Seán Hutton and Paul Stewart (eds), *Ireland's histories: aspects of state, society and ideology* (London, 1991), pp 203–22.

5   MacGill, *Children of the dead end*, pp. 11–12.

Devaney was a gombeen priest, who played on the fears and dreads of the poor and drained the needy of their last penny. For collecting stipends, offerings and plate-money, Devaney had no equal. Nothing escaped him and it was said by the people of the parish that the priest could make a corpse blush in its coffin if the offerings were small.[6]

Church historians and literary scholars have argued that MacGill was a 'dissident', a 'protester against the establishment', and that his antipathy to MacFadden stemmed from an uncommon anti-clericalism.[7] MacGill, however, was no anti-cleric. The other priests in his novels are sympathetic characters.[8] More importantly, he was not a discordant voice in Inis Caoil. In the mid-1900s Irish Folklore Commission respondents in outlying districts of the parish remembered MacFadden as a greedy autocrat with little concern for the less well-off and there remains an essentially negative image of him in these areas.[9]

This chapter reconciles these opposing images of MacFadden. Its central contention is that differences between the structure, culture and politics of the Catholic communities in Gaoth Dobhair and Inis Caoil best explain the different attitudes to the priest. In addition, by emphasising the charismatic element in MacFadden's leadership of the land agitation in Gaoth Dobhair and the success of the Land League in a neighbouring parish despite clerical opposition, it cautions against attributing nineteenth-century priests' political influence to their office.

I

James MacFadden was born in 1842 in Dunmore, near Carrigart, county Donegal, the fourth of five children. His father, John, was a comfortable farmer and his extended family included influential figures in the hierarchy: 'Long Dan'

---

6   MacGill, *Glenmornan*, p. 130. On gombeenism, see Peter Gibbon and M.D. Higgins, 'Patronage, tradition and modernisation: the case of the Irish "Gombeenman" in *Economic and Social Review*, vi, no. 1 (Oct. 1974), pp 27–44; *idem*, 'The Irish 'gombeenman': reincarnation or rehabilitation?' in *Economical and Social Review*, vii, no. 4 (July 1977), pp 313–20; Liam Kennedy, 'Farmers, traders, and agricultural politics in pre-independence Ireland' in Samuel Clark and James S. Donnelly, Jr. (eds), *Irish peasants: violence and political unrest, 1780–1914* (Dublin, 1983), pp 339–73.

7   Patrick Corish, *The Irish Catholic experience: a historical survey* (Dublin, 1985), pp 235–6; John W. Foster, *Forces and themes in Ulster fiction* (Dublin, 1974), pp 87–9; Joseph Muholland, 'Patrick MacGill: the birth of a legend' in *Donegal Annual: Bliain-Iris Thír Chonaill*, 10, 1 (1970), pp 27–35; *idem*, 'The novelist Patrick MacGill and his parish priest, Canon James McFadden' in *Derry People and Donegal News*, 3 Sept. 1983.

8   Séamus Mac Giolla Uain, 'Patrick MacGill' in Mac Conghaíl (ed.), *Scríbhneoireacht*, pp 235–7. MacGill's wife, Margaret Gibbons, was a niece of Cardinal Gibbons of Baltimore and the author of religious literature for Catholics. See Margaret Gibbons, *The life of Margaret Alyward: foundress of the Sisters of the Holy Faith* (London, 1928); *idem*, *Little Nellie of holy God: a model for first communicants* (London, 1929).

9   Áine Ní Dhíoraí (ed.), *Na Cruacha: scéalta agus seanchas* (Baile Átha Cliath, 1985), xvi.

MacGettigan, bishop of Raphoe (1861–70) and archbishop of Armagh (1870–87), and Michael Logue, bishop of Raphoe (1879–87) and cardinal archbishop of Armagh (1887–1923), were, respectively, James's uncle and cousin. In 1863, following a path increasingly well-beaten by the younger sons of the rural middle-class, he entered St Patrick's College, Maynooth. He excelled academically, continued his studies in the Dunboyne Establishment, the College's graduate school, and, on 1 January 1871, his uncle ordained him in St Patrick's Cathedral, Armagh. Appointed curate of Upper Templecrone in west Donegal, he became administrator of the parish in 1872 when the parish priest fell sick. The following year he was appointed administrator of Gaoth Dobbair, where he became parish priest two years later.[10]

An Irish-speaking, small-holding parish, Gaoth Dobhair was one of the poorest agricultural districts in Ireland. It had been largely outside the estate-system until the late 1830s when several land-speculators invested there. Before this, a few landowners who lived in north Donegal had intermittently received rent, often in the form of 'duty days' or 'duty fowl', from the occupiers but the others, despairing of regularly collecting money, had exhibited little interest in their properties. In the shadow of landlord indifference, rundale, an infield-outfield system of land-use, had survived in Gaoth Dobhair, one of the largest areas in the country where it remained in operation in the 1830s. Led by Lord George Hill, the new landlords initiated a short-lived but much publicised 'improvement' programme. They abolished key features of rundale, resettled the occupiers on squared-holdings and regularised rent collection. Hill established a 'highland' hotel, built a store and quay at An Bun Beag, and introduced a small Protestant community into what was previously an exclusively Catholic district.[11] A consummate self-publicist, Hill's success in obtaining donations from

10 Richard Griffith, *Union of Millford, valuation of the several tenements comprised in the above-named union situate in the county of Donegal* (Dublin, 1858), p. 10 returns John MacFadden as the occupier of a house, offices and 9a 2r 8p in Dunmore. The rateable valuations of the land and buildings were £3 5s. 0d. and £0 15s. 0d. respectively. The mean rateable valuation of houses in the parish was under 10s., suggesting the MacFaddens were relatively well off. Furthermore, several other MacFaddens occupied land in the same townland and it is possible these people were close relatives. The family may also have held land in other townlands. On MacFadden's family background training and clerical career see Edward Maguire, *A history of the diocese of Raphoe* (Dublin, 1920), pt i, vol. i, pp 487–90; vol. ii, pp 263–7; Leslie W. Lucas, *Mevagh down the years: a history of Carrigart, Downings, Glen and the surrounding district* (Belfast, 1983), pp 222–3. Only two of MacFadden's siblings – one brother and one sister – married: his other sister lived with him as house-keeper and his younger brother pursued a religious career at St Paul's Retreat in Mount Argus, Dublin.

11 Lord George Hill, *Facts from Gweedore, compiled from the notes of Lord George Hill: a facsimile reprint of the fifth edition (1887) with an introduction by E. Estyn Evans* (Belfast, 1971) presents the landlord version of events. For a neglected rejoinder, see Denis Holland, *The landlord in Donegal: pictures from the wilds* (Belfast, n.d. [1858]). Also see John Coll, 'Continuity and change in the parish of Gaoth Dobhair, 1850–1980' in William J. Smyth and Kevin Whelan (eds) *Common ground: essays on the historical geography of Ireland* (Cork, 1988), pp 278–95; Breandán Mac Suibhne, 'Agrarian improvement and social unrest: Lord George Hill and the Gaoth Dobhair sheep war' in William Nolan, Liam Ronayne and Mairéad Dunlevy (eds), *Donegal: history and society* (Dublin, 1995), pp 547–82.

government and charitable bodies helped to bring the parish through the Great Famine comparatively unscathed. The population increased from 3,997 in 1841 to 4,300 in 1851 and continued to rise through the 1800s. By 1881 it was 5,078.[12] No town developed, however, and subdivision accompanied this increase. By the turn of the century, Gaoth Dobhair had the dubious distinction of having the lowest poor law valuation per capita (6s. 6d.) in the west.[13]

Coupled with subdivision, mass seasonal migration underpinned demographic expansion in post-Famine Gaoth Dobhair. Children, hired at the 'rabbles' of Letterkenny and Strabane, worked on the big farms of the Lagan district of east Donegal, Derry and Tyrone, often for over six months of the year, while parties of men, single women and adolescents travelled to Scotland to work at the harvest. These annual movements involved members of almost every household in the parish: in 1896 – two decades after historians estimate seasonal migration from Ireland to Britain had peaked – the Congested Districts Board (C.D.B.) calculated that thirty-seven per cent of Gaoth Dobhair's population migrated every year. At this time, migrants' wages provided the average household with about £15, or forty per cent of their annual income, the remainder being generated by the sale of stock, kelp, fish, eggs and butter.[14] Critically, therefore, two of the small-holders' key economic relationships were with people who lived outside the parish: the farmers of the Lagan and Scotland, for whom they worked, and the landlords, to whom they paid rent. Significantly, both the farmers and landlords were predominantly Protestants. The smallholders, however, also had a subsidiary relationship with local shopkeepers who provided credit to tide them over from the exhaustion of the potato crop to the harvest and the receipt of migrants' wages.[15] With the exception of Daniel Keown, the lessee of Hill's store and mill at An Bun Beag, and John Robertson, a yarn merchant settled in the parish by Hill, by the 1870s, these shopkeepers were almost

12 Calculated for the Roman Catholic parish from townland data in *The census of Ireland for the year 1851*, H.C. 1852 (36), xcii (hereafter cited as *Census, 1851*), pp 131–2. Other factors, notably seasonal migration, the availability of 'famine foods' and the clergy's success in lobbying government for relief, were at least as important as landlord benevolence in bringing Gaoth Dobhair through the Famine.

13 'Table I. – Statistical table of the acreage, poor law valuation and population of congested districts in Ireland' in Trinity College, Dublin *Congested Districts' Board for Ireland: base-line reports*, pp 1–7.

14 *Congested Districts' Board for Ireland: base-line report: district of Gweedore, 1 March, 1896* [hereafter *Base-line report Gweedore*, 1896], p. 4. On seasonal migration, see Cormac Ó Gráda, 'Seasonal migration and post-famine adjustment in the west of Ireland' in *Studia Hibernica*, 13 (1973), pp 48–76; *idem*, 'Demographic adjustment and seasonal migration in nineteenth-century Ireland' in L. M. Cullen and F. Furet (ed.), *Ireland and France, 17th–20th centuries: towards a comparative study of rural history* (Paris, 1980), pp 181–93; Gerard P. Moran, '"A passage to Britain": seasonal migration and social change in the west of Ireland' in *Saothar: Journal of the Irish Labour History Society*, no. 13 (1988), pp 22–31; Anne O'Dowd, *Spalpeens and tattiehokers: history and folklore of the Irish migratory worker in Ireland and Britain* (Dublin, 1991).

15 *Base-line report, Gweedore*, 1896, pp 4–5 gives an account of credit dealings in the parish.

all Catholics and natives of Gaoth Dobhair. Together with teachers, publicans, and some landlord employees they constituted the parish's Catholic middle-class. A small social group, with roots no deeper than the landlord-initiated changes of the 1840s, ties of kinship, language and religion bound this class to the smallholders.[16] This common identity was the bedrock of resistance to land-lordism in the 1880s and survived into the 1900s: about 1908, in a memorandum on gombeenism submitted to the Royal Commission on Congestion, Hugh Law, MP for west Donegal, observed that while shopkeepers in a neighbouring parish brought suits 'in sheaves' every year to force smallholders to sell land to settle unpaid shop-debts, such actions were unknown in Gaoth Dobhair.[17]

In the episcopally approved history of the diocese, Canon Edward Maguire (1855–1926), administrator of Gaoth Dobhair in the late 1890s, comments candidly that its 'inferior status as a benefice did not entitle it to be looked to as the *ne plus ultra* of clerical ambition'. Once appointed here, a well-connected young clergyman would have anticipated rapid advancement. If waiting for promotion, however, MacFadden was not idle. He bought and sold property for the Church, opened a new graveyard, established several national schools and extended existing ones.[18] By now a stocky man with bull-dog features, he betrayed his comfortable background in a keen sense of etiquette and a penchant for Americanisms when speaking English. His middle-class sensibilities were also evident in the fashionable parochial house that he built in Doire Beaga. Compared by an English supporter to a 'villa at Horley', it was one of the few two-storey slate-roofed buildings in the parish, and reflected a general concern in the post-Famine Catholic Church that its clergy should be as 'respectable' as those of the Church of Ireland.[19] Still, it was a better house than most Raphoe priests would have hoped for: in the wealthier parish of Cill Chártha, for example, the parish priest had a small vernacular house with an earthen floor as late as 1893.[20] In 1888 a hostile constabulary sergeant told a journalist that MacFadden paid for the parochial house by diverting funds donated for the relief of his parishioners and by introducing the payment of 'offerings', particularly 'funeral money', to Gaoth Dobhair. The former claim is difficult to substantiate yet the latter charge has a ring of truth: in 1901–17, when parish priest of Inis

---

16 Gallchóirigh an Choitín, successful graziers, and Muintir Mhíc Ghiolla Bhrile of Baile an Droichid, Cnoc a'Stollaire who acted as bailiffs for several landlords were the most prominent families to attain middle class status before the late 1830s.

17 T.P. O'Neill, 'The food crisis of the 1890s' in E. Margaret Crawford (ed.), *Famine: the Irish experience, 900–1900: subsistence crises and famines in Ireland* (Edinburgh, 1989), pp 189–90; N.A., Royal Commission on Congestion, 1906–8, Carton 7: H.L. [Hugh Alexander Law], 'Gombeening' [n.d.; *c.*1908], p. 4. The 'neighbouring parish' is most probably Templecrone.

18 Maguire, *Diocese of Raphoe*, pt i, vol. ii, p. 267.

19 William Scawen-Blunt, *The land war in Ireland being a personal narrative of events* (London, 1912), p. 54.

20 Katharine Tynan, *The middle years* (London, 1916), p. 79.

Caoil, MacFadden operated the extremely unpopular offerings system with the implacable efficiency of an old hand.[21]

The nineteenth century, but particularly the post–Famine period, witnessed a wholescale transformation of Irish Catholicism in which chapel-centred practices displaced vernacular rituals. In explaining this 'devotional revolution', historians have pointed to the expansion of the 'plant and personnel' of the Roman Catholic Church and the decline of the rural underclass after 1845.[22] Although the Great Famine had little impact on the demographic history of Gaoth Dobhair, the parish did not become a redoubt of unorthodox belief or practice. Indeed, only thinly populated until the late 1700s, vernacular religion in Gaoth Dobhair had never been as tightly moored to the local environment as in more deeply rooted communities. In neighbouring Cloich Cheann Fhaola, for example, many placenames commemorated local patrons while wells, waterfalls, pre-Christian and Christian monuments were the foci of *turais* [trans.: pilgrimages] which nineteenth century clergymen had great difficulty in suppressing yet there were no analogous practices in Gaoth Dobhair. Still, although he had few dragons to slay, MacFadden behaved as a paragon of the post-Famine priest. He organised stations in parishioners' houses, inveighed against illicit distillation, encouraged the performance of the stations of the cross at the chapel, and insisted on attendance at Sunday mass and regular confession. A rigid disciplinarian, he punished non-conformists severely, allegedly to the point of whipping a single mother.[23]

MacFadden's effort to impose a new code of public behaviour was largely successful. In 1880, for example, a constable stationed in An Bun Beag assured a group of English visitors that there was 'little or no crime, very little drunkenness and great chastity among the women'.[24] Later, in 1896 a C.D.B. inspector reported that houses in the parish were 'superior to those in any other district in Donegal; they are kept clean outside and in, and white-washed once every year'.

21 H. F. Hurlbert, *Ireland under coercion: the diary of an American* (Edinburgh, 1888), vol. 1, pp 92; 159–63. The sergeant estimated MacFadden's income at between £1,100 and £1,200.
22 On devotional change in nineteenth-century Ireland, see Emmet Larkin, 'The devotional revolution in Ireland, 1850–75' in *American Historical Review*, lxxvii (1972), pp 625–52 [reprinted in Emmet Larkin, *The historical dimensions of Irish Catholicism* (New York, 1976), pp 57–89]; David W. Miller, 'Irish Catholicism and the Great Famine' in *Journal of Social History*, 9 (1975), pp 81–98. For excellent sub-national studies, see Kevin Whelan, 'The Catholic Church in county Tipperary, 1700–1900' in William Nolan (ed.), *Tipperary: history and society* (Dublin, 1985), pp 215–55; Lawrence J. Taylor, *Occasions of faith: an anthropology of Irish Catholics* (Dublin, 1995). Seán Connolly, *Religion and society in nineteenth-century Ireland: studies in Irish economic and social history 3* (Dublin, 1985) reviews the literature.
23 Mulholland, 'The novelist Patrick MacGill' and Noel Ó Gallchóir, 'Gan saoirse gan só' in Dónall P. Ó Baoill (ed.), *Scáthlán 3* (Béal Átha Seanaigh, 1986), p. 16 state that MacFadden made a group of schoolchildren walk to school barefoot as a punishment for an unspecified offence. However, oral and photographic sources suggest that schoolchildren were generally barefoot in Gaoth Dobhair well into the 1900s. On MacFadden and single mothers, see MacGill, *Rat-pit*, pp 29–30.
24 James H. Tuke, *Irish distress and its remedies: the land question: a visit to Donegal and Connaught in the spring of 1880* (London, 1880), p. 23.

He attributed this directly to MacFadden, 'who insists on cleanliness among his people'.[25] The clearest indicator of MacFadden's success in reconstructing popular culture, however, is his rupture of the parish's musical tradition. When he arrived in Gaoth Dobhair, the fiddle and, to a lesser extent, the warpipes were popular and house-dances were common. MacFadden condemned house-dances as 'occasions of sin', and, in his first years in the parish, vigorously broke them up with his blackthorn stick. The intensity of his opposition to dancing resonates in the strong tradition that he burned a large number of fiddles in a single night to stamp it out. Although other factors played a role, traditional music declined abruptly in Gaoth Dobhair and did not experience a revival until the 1960s.[26] In its place, MacFadden encouraged soccer – a physically draining single-sex activity which his parishioners would have encountered in Scotland – and by the mid-1890s it was 'quite an institution with them'.[27]

Almost inevitably, as the dictatorial representative of a new cultural order, MacFadden provoked a certain resentment. *Seanchas* [trans.: oral tradition] frequently opposes the bullish priest to Tarlach Mac Suibhne (*c.*1818–1916), commonly known as An Píobaire Mór, a celebrated travelling piper who was a descendant of a powerful family in the pre-conquest élite. In one of the townlands furthest from Doire Beaga chapel, the following exchange – which neatly captures the difference in *mentalité* – is attributed to MacFadden and Mac Suibhne:

MacFadden: *C'áit a raibh tú aréir?*
Mac Suibhne: *Inseoidh mé sin duit. Bhí mé thoir i mBun a'Leaca i dtigh Mháire Óige.*
MacFaddenn: *Ní raibh tú thoir i mBun a'Leaca! Ní raibh! Bhí tú ar leaca Ifrinn!*
Mac Suibhne: *Bhal, más sin an áit a raibh mé, chan iarrfainn é a fhágáil go brách!*[28]

[trans.: MacFadden: Where were you last night?; Mac Suibhne: I'll tell where I was, I was over in Bun a'Leaca [place-name meaning 'the foot of the flagstone'] in Máire Óg's house.; MacFadden: You weren't over in Bun a'Leaca! You weren't! You were on the flagstones of Hell!; Mac Suibhne: Well, if that's where I was, I wouldn't ever ask to leave it!]

25 *Base-line report Gweedore*, 1896, p. 5. The report also attributes the 'small amount of any intemperance in the district' to the clergy.
26 Caoimhín Mac Aoidh, *Between the jigs and the reels: the Donegal fiddle tradition* (Manorhamilton, 1994), pp 147–60; Kevin Whelan, 'The bases of regionalism' in Proinsias Ó Droisceoil (ed.), *Culture in Ireland – regions: identity and power* (Belfast, 1993), p. 29.
27 *Base-line report, Gweedore*, 1896, p. 5.
28 Oral communication, John Óg Hiúdaí Neidí Ó Colla, An Ghlaiseach, Gaoth Dobhair, 22 July 1995. For Mac Suibhne's career, see Mac Aoidh, *Between the jigs and the reels*, pp 151–60; Pádraig Mac Séain, 'Seanchas fá Chlainn tSuibhne agus fá Tharlach Mac Suibhne, An Píobaire Mór' in *Béaloideas*, 32 (1964), pp 71–84.

Similarly, there is a frequently-related story about MacFadden clearing a dance-house only to find Mac Suibhne sitting stoically in the centre of the deserted room. When asked what he is waiting for, he replies payment for his night's work and the priest pays him. Significantly, criticism of MacFadden is muted and the function of these anecdotes appears to be contrasting the modernity of the priest and the faded glory of the piper. A local historian finishes his version of the last story with the comment '*bhí uaisleacht na mbard sa phíobaire agus thuig an sagart sin. Níor labhair sé an dara focal ach an doras a bhaint amach*' [trans.: The piper had bardic nobility and the priest understood that without another word, he [the priest] went out the door].[29] The generally uncritical attitude of *seanchas* to the priest reflects the relative weakness of class tensions between Catholics in Gaoth Dobhair in the 1880s. In such a monolithic community, the trappings of a middle-class lifestyle were coveted rather than resented and, hence, MacFadden appeared as the embodiment of Catholic success: *his nouveau riche* house, genteel manners, and Yankee English all symbolized achievement and advancement

II

MacFadden's reputation as a radical stems from his activities during the national land agitation of 1879–93, yet he was a relative latecomer to the political platform, not committing himself until spring 1881. This initial hesitancy was not due to any absence of 'distress' in Gaoth Dobhair. Here, as elsewhere in the west, the fall of livestock prices in 1877–9 and the potato failure of 1879 had brought considerable hardship. Indeed, the smallholders were in a particularly precarious position as the demand for seasonal workers all but evaporated in 1879. That autumn, many migrants returned home with no money and they had to stretch their credit to the limit during the winter. In March 1880, the 'destitution and misery' in Gaoth Dobhair shocked James Hack Tuke, an influential English philanthropist who toured Connacht and Donegal to assess the extent of distress. After visiting smallholders with MacFadden, he described some families' condition as 'worse, if worse could be, than the bog holes of Erris with which I was familiar in 1847'.[30] A stronger explanation of MacFadden's initial reticence is that he held back from public controversy in deference to his cousin, Michael Logue, the recently appointed bishop of Raphoe. Logue had responded to the crisis of 1879–80 by establishing the Donegal Central Relief Committee which solicited aid through press appeals and then distributed money, food, and clothing via a network of local committees. In Gaoth Dobhair, perhaps the worst effected area, MacFadden formed one of these committees with the Church of Ireland minis-

29 Mac Fhionnlaoich, *Scéal*, p. 93; Mac Aoidh, *Between the jigs and the reels*, pp 157–8.
30 Tuke, *Irish distress and its remedies*, pp 27–8.

ter, Keown and several shopkeepers.[31] In the winter of 1880, however, the landlords' refusal of rent abatements starkly exposed the limits of Logue's strategy:
as long as charity paid the rent, the landlords would avoid compromise.[32]

The frustration of Logue's strategy coincided with an attempt by the Irish
National Land League, by now well established in Connacht, to mobilise support in Ulster. The league organised a series of meetings in Donegal in the winter of 1880–1 and branches appeared throughout the county. In December 1880,
nationalists formed branches in Gaoth Dobhair and Cloich Cheann Fhaola. In
MacFadden's parish, the key activists included a schoolmaster, a 'poor' small-
holder-cum-carter, a dismissed policeman and a former clerk of petty sessions
who had also worked as a process-server and cess-collector.[33] The league demanded rent reductions and boycotted the landlords, police and all who dealt
with them: the ostracised included Keown and Robertson, bailiffs, the workers
in Captain Arthur Hill's fishery and hotel, and car-men who carried constables.
There was overt intimidation, a number of minor assaults, riots with police and
several petty attacks on landlord property. Men and women trenched roads to
obstruct bailiffs and the pupils of Bun an Inbhir National School severely beat a
bailiff's son in front of the schoolmaster, Proinsias Eoghain Bháin Ó Gallchóir,
a prominent Land Leaguer who read the *Nation* and *Irish World* to their parents
at night.[34] In late May, after a crowd of 500 stoned the police for over a mile from
Doire Beaga to the barracks in An Bun Beag, the stipendiary magistrate reported
that the parish was 'on the verge of insurrection'. The government deployed one
hundred troops but failed to end boycotting.[35] In late May/early June, as part of
a national clampdown, the government interned Dónall Mac Suibhne, a wealthy
returned-emigrant who had established the league in Cloich Cheann Fhaola,
and three Gaoth Dobhair activists.[36]

31 *Londonderry Standard*, 7 Feb. 1880.
32 Logue's strategy involved a rather panglossian gambit. North west Donegal landlords had a repu-
    tation for being heavy-handed: three of the most controversial incidents in landlord-tenant rela-
    tions in Ireland between the Famine and the Land War – the Gaoth Dobhair sheep war of 1857–60;
    the Derryveagh clearances of 1861 and the troubles on Lord Leitrim's estate which began in the
    mid-1850s and culminated in his assassination in 1878 – occurred in the barony of Kilmacrenan.
33 For the Gaoth Dobhair activists, see N.A., C.S.O.R.P. 1882/25494 [Francis Gallagher, Glassagh];
    1882/3659 [Edward Coll, Glassagh; John Doherty, Knockastoller]; 1882/3660 [Hugh McBride,
    Magherclogher]. I am grateful to Dónall Ó Cnáimhsí for help in locating these files.
34 N.A., C.S.O.R.P. 1882/25494 Dungloe, 12 May 1881, Francis Campbell H.C. to Alex Reed C.I.
    'Enquiry regarding Francis Gallagher, schoolmaster'. Both Ó Gallchóir [Francis B. O'Gallagher]
    and Dónall Mac Suibhne [Daniel McSweeney] used Gaelic prefixes when signing their names in
    English. The use of prefixes with these surnames was very uncommon in the north west and may
    indicate particularly 'advanced' nationalism.
35 N.A., C.S.O.R.P. 1881/26986 Letterkenny, 24 May 1881, Alexander Reed C.I. to Inspector Gen-
    eral; Gweedore, 27 May 1881, Edmund Peel RM to Under Secretary. Lord George Hill died in
    1879 and his son, Capt. Arthur Hill, inherited the Gaoth Dobhair Estate.
36 For the warrants issued for two of those arrested, see N.A., Irish crimes records, 1881 arrests under
    the protection of persons and property (Ireland) act, 1881, carton 1: 'P.P.P. Act 1881: List of war-
    rants by counties & districts'; 'The protection of person and property (Ireland) act, 1881: List of all
    persons arrested'; carton 2: 128 [Francis Gallagher, Glassagh]; 143 [Edward Coll, Glassagh]. Hugh

By this stage, MacFadden had committed himself to the league. Several weeks before the arrests, he was addressing meetings outside his chapel, urging resistance to landlordism. Indeed, when the police were escorting Neidí Mór Ó Colla – one of the internees – to the barracks, 'thousands' of smallholders surrounded the parochial house, anticipating an attempt to arrest the priest.[37] In the following months, he consolidated his position as leader of the agitation, a position he retained after the release of the internees. Desmond Murphy has argued that MacFadden's eclipse of the lay activists can only be understood 'in the context of inactivity by other social strata in the area'. The middle class, he argues, withdrew their support in the wake of the arrests as they were reluctant to risk their newly found prosperity and respectability on behalf of people from whom 'class-and language separated them utterly'.[38] Notwithstanding MacFadden's prominence in the agitation before the arrests, the argument is weak: the parish's embryonic middle class was an ill-defined social group, a product of the massive changes of the 1840s, and intimately connected with the smallholders. Moreover, there is no evidence that middle-class support flagged following the arrests. Indeed, the league's campaign could not have continued without shopkeepers' willingness to extend credit to the smallholders, and, on one level, MacFadden's rise represented the assertion of middle-class control over the developing agitation, an effective sidelining of more volatile, less 'respectable' elements. Still, it remains necessary to explain why the parish priest, as opposed to a shopkeeper or schoolteacher, became a political leader and how he inspired such deep personal loyalty.

Max Weber's well-known distinction between traditional and charismatic authority provides a useful framework in which to examine MacFadden's political rise and the character of his leadership. Traditional authority rests upon followers' acceptance of a leader defined by an ordered tradition, or 'piety toward the possible incumbents of office fiefs and office prebends who are legitimised in their own right through privilege and conferment'. Charismatic authority is discipline 'to which the governed submit because of their belief in the extraordinary quality of the specific *person*'. It is a 'devotion born of distress and enthusiasm', most likely to arise in periods of change and uncertainty. In short, traditional authority requires a belief in the sanctity of the routine while charismatic authority requires devotion to the extraordinary person.[39] MacFadden presented himself as a traditional leader, the natural defender of an oppressed

---

McBride was also interned. On Mac Suibhne, see N.A., C.S.O.R.P. 1882/28377 Gweedore, 19 May 1882, James MacFadden P.P. to the Chief Secretary.

37 *Derry Journal*, 25 May 1881; *Londonderry Standard*, 18 June 1881.
38 Desmond Murphy, *Derry, Donegal, and modern Ulster, 1790–1921* (Derry, 1981), p. 144.
39 H. H. Gerth and C. Wright Mills (eds), *From Max Weber: essays in sociology* (London, 1947), pp 248–51; 295–301; Steve Bruce, *God save Ulster: the religion and politics of Paisleyism* (Oxford, 1986), pp 199–219 examines the charismatic and traditional bases of a contemporary Irish clergyman's political authority.

people, and this image pervades nationalist and liberal commentaries on his activities.[40] Loyalists and landlord apologists also saw him as a traditional leader, albeit one who abused his position over people whom a prominent loyalist considered to be 'as ignorant and credulous as the painted children of the prairie'.[41] Undoubtedly, MacFadden's political leadership owed much to the traditional authority of the rural priest. His office gave him considerable influence which could be used for political advantage and he often explicitly exploited it. On St Patrick's Day 1888, for example, he threatened publicans that he would make his parishioners take the temperance pledge if they served policemen. More menacingly, he used the priest's patronage powers for political ends, refusing to establish a school in Cnoc Fola as some inhabitants would not join the league and the area only got a school in 1898 when Maguire became administrator. While he made a point of addressing the smallholders on 'worldly matters' outside the chapel, he often confused the pulpit and the platform: in the speech threatening the publicans, he also condemned troops serving in the parish as bad Catholics and bad Irishmen for not attending mass.[42] Furthermore, in the absence of a significant Catholic middle class, many of his predecessors had become involved in politics, adding a political dimension to the office which legitimated his involvement with the league. For example, Fr Peadar Ó Gallchóir had been active in suppressing faction-fighting in the early 1820s; Fr Hugh O'Friel had organised resistance to the payment of tithes in the 1830s and lobbied the landlords and state for relief during the famine of 1836–7; Fr Hugh MacFadden (like James, a native of Carrigart but not a close relation) had been an eloquent spokesperson for the smallholders' during the horrors of 1846–8; and, in the 1850s, Fr John Doherty had held the reins of an anti-landlord campaign which culminated in the establishment of a parliamentary select committee to inquire into landlord-tenant relations in northwest Donegal.[43]

Nevertheless, MacFadden's authority was not simply traditional. The experience of the parish priest in Cloich Cheann Fhaola reveals the limits of the clergy's traditional authority during the land agitation. This priest, also named James MacFadden, opposed the Land League, warning his congregation against 'being led away by strangers who are coming amongst you preaching a false

40 For a striking example, see the caricature 'The fight for bare life on the Olphert Estate' in the supplement to *United Ireland*, 12 Jan. 1889. It depicts MacFadden remonstrating with armed police at an eviction. The caption reads 'For God's sake, spare my poor people!'.
41 Revd Robert Kane at a meeting in the Ulster Hall, Belfast, 14 Feb. 1889, reported in *Belfast News-letter*, 15 Feb. 1889.
42 N.A., C.S.O.R.P. 1889/11318 Speech delivered by Revd James MacFadden P.P. Gweedore at Derrybeg chapel on 17 Mar. (Patrick's Day) 1888; Maguire, *Diocese of Raphoe*, pt i, vol. ii, pp 266–7.
43 Mac Fhionnlaoich, *Scéal*, pp 47–8; *B.H.*, 24 June 1835, 19 Aug., 2 Sept. 1836; N.A., Famine relief commission: incoming correspondence [Baronial] Co. Donegal 1846–7, Kilmacrenan, 8134 Bunbeg, 9 Dec. 1846, Hugh MacFadden P.P. West Tullaghobegley to [Sir Randolph Routh?]; Mac Suibhne, 'Agrarian improvement and social unrest', pp 560–77.

doctrine'.[44] Although previously very popular with his parishioners – he had actively supported them during the protracted troubles of the 1850s – once he preached 'render unto Caesar', he quickly lost favour: Maguire, ever-frank, notes that 'his popularity suffered a violent shock'. In speeches outside the chapel in Gort a'Choirce, Mac Suibhne pilloried him as a landlord-dupe who 'perverted scripture to try and get these rotten landlords their rackrents', and his parishioners joined the league despite him.[45]

Notwithstanding its traditional elements, MacFadden's leadership was heavily charismatic. The smallholders saw him as a 'person of exceptional heroism and sanctity': a policeman reported that they regarded him with 'a reverence and awe scarcely credible'; a journalist wrote of their "almost supernatural confidence in him'; and a barrister defending him in court spoke of their 'feelings almost akin to idolatry' and claimed that they saw him as 'an earthly Providence'.[46] Indeed, MacFadden publicly acknowledged that 'they [his parishioners] are most docile to do anything I tell them to do'.[47] The depth of their faith in him is evident in the conviction that he had supernatural power. In *Eisiomláir*, a short-story based on participants' memories of the land-agitation, Séamas Ó Grianna (1889–1969) provides a revealing insight into this belief.[48] The story centres on events surrounding a rally that MacFadden had promised to address in Croithlí in defiance of an official proclamation. In Rann na Feirsde, the narrator's district, smallholders discussing the forthcoming rally were convinced that he would make an appearance. He had *cumhachtaí* [trans.: powers] that would ensure that the police would be unable to arrest him:

Bhí na daoine cinnte go rachadh ag an tSagart 'Ac Pháidín an cruinniughadh a chomóradh i gCroithlí d'aindeoin a rabh de ghunnaí is de bhaigniéidí ó chuan Dhoire go cuan na gCeall. Ní thiocfadh leo breith air. D'fhágadh sé a gcnámha marbh leis an mhuinntir a bhéarfadh iarraidh air. Dhéanfadh sé eisiomláir den chéad fhear a leagfadh barr méir air![49]

44 N.A., Irish National League papers, 1/79 D. McSweeney at Gortahork, 27 Mar. 1881.

45 Ibid., 1/77 D. McSweeney at Gortahork, 20 Mar. 1881; I/79 D. McSweeney at Gortahork, 27 Mar. 1881; W.E. Vaughan, *Sin, sheep and Scotsmen: John George Adair and the Derryveagh evictions, 1861* (Belfast, 1983), p. 63; Maguire, *Diocese of Raphoe*, pt i, vol. ii, pp 302–3.

46 N.A., Crime Branch Special papers, Divisional Commissioners' and County Inspectors' monthly confidential reports, no. 8, 19 Mar. 1889, quoted in Laurence M. Geary, *The Plan of Campaign, 1886–1891* (Cork, 1986), p. 29; *Derry Journal*, 13 Jan. 1888; R. Adams quoted in Ó Gallchobhair, *Landlordism in Donegal*, p. 78.

47 Quoted in Murphy, *Derry, Donegal and modern Ulster*, p. 147.

48 Máire (Séamas Ó Grianna), *Scéal Úr agus Sean-Scéal* (Baile Átha Cliath, 1945), pp 18–27. I am grateful to Eibhlín Ní Chnáimhsí for this reference. Tomás Ó Fiaich, 'Saothar Mháire mar fhoinse don stair shóisialta' [trans.: Máire's work as a source for social history] in Pádraig Ó Fiannachta (ed.), *Léachtaí Cholm Cille v* (Má Nuad, 1974), pp 5–30 appraises Ó Grianna's work as a source for sociohistorical research. Rann na Feirsde is in the Roman Catholic parish of Lower Templecrone, not Gaoth Dobhair.

49 Máire, *Scéal Úr agus Sean-Scéal*, pp 20–1.

[trans.: The people were certain that Priest MacFadden would manage to attend the rally in Croithlí, despite all the guns and bayonets from Derry quay to Killybegs. They [the police] wouldn't be able to capture him. He would leave dead the bones of any people who attempted to take him. He would make an *eisiomlár* of the first man who laid a finger tip on him.]

The conviction that MacFadden had the power to make an *eisiomlár* of an enemy – to deform a person in such a way that he would always be recognised as an evil-doer – was so firmly held that a rumour spread among the women, children and old men who had been unable to attend the rally that a constable had attempted to arrest the priest and had been paralysed down one side and his leg crippled:

> Acht san am chéadna bhí a ndóchas as an tSagart 'Ac Pháidín comh láidir sin agus go mb'fhuras leo an scéal fá'n eisiomláir a chreidbheáil. Ba leis a bhí siad ag dúil. Ba é a bhí i n-aice le n-a dtoil.[50]

[trans.: But at the same time, their confidence in Priest MacFadden was so strong that it was easy for them to believe the story about the *eisiomláir*. It was what they were expecting. It was what they wanted.]

This irrational faith in MacFadden – his charisma – was a product of crisis. The pile up of disasters in 1879–80 – the fall of livestock prices; the collapse of the seasonal labour market; the failure of the potato crop; the refusal of rent abatements – induced a deep fatalism in Gaoth Dobhair. In March 1880, Tuke wrote:

> There was a more depressed tone among these people than I had ever before seen. Even in the houses of the few who were rather better off, we found the same hopeless tone creeping over them.[51]

Five months later, however, fate further trampled the smallholders' confidence: on 15 August 1880 a flash flood swept through Doire Beaga chapel when MacFadden was reading mass and five members of his congregation drowned. This bizarre tragedy, all the more incomprehensible for the time and place it occurred, traumatised the parish. Sketches of the multiple drowning appeared in the Irish and British press and sympathisers raised a considerable amount of

---

50   Ibid., pp 25; 228. Also see 'example' in Michael Traynor, *The English dialect of Donegal: a glossary* (Dublin, 1953), p. 95.
51   Tuke, *Irish distress and its remedies*, p. 28.

money to renovate the chapel and reroute the river which had flooded.[52] Previously a member of a relief committee, MacFadden was now the main conduit of aid. Furthermore, his personality inspired confidence. Many acquaintances commented on his optimism and energy: the adjective 'indefatigable', first used by Tuke in March 1880, appeared with numbing regularity in newspaper accounts of his activities; William Scawen-Blunt, an English radical who met him in 1885, described him as 'filled with an unconquerable energy'; and H. E. Hurlbert, an American apologist for landlordism who interviewed him in February 1888, noted that he was 'sanguine by temperament, with an expression at once shrewd and enthusiastic, a most flexible persuasive voice'.[53] In short, optimistic and impatient, arrogant and autocratic, MacFadden was profoundly reassuring in uncertain times. A symbol of achievement in ordinary years, in the crisis of 1881 he became a saviour. Formerly admired, he was now adored. From the smallholders' perspective, his suitability to lead them against landlordism was beyond doubt.

Having assumed control of the agitation, MacFadden marshalled a campaign that continued until the capitulation of the most obstinate landlords in the early 1890s.[54] His influence extended into Cloich Cheann Fhaola, where a young curate, Daniel Stephens, became a close ally, despite his superior's opposition. Although committed to the abolition of landlordism, MacFadden's short-term objectives were rent reductions and the recognition of sub-tenancies and he organised disciplined rent strikes and civil disobedience which made it financially ruinous for the landlords to refuse to compromise. This campaign was highly successful. In 1883 he brought over 400 tenancies before the Land Court and obtained unprecedented rent reductions of 25 to 38 per cent. Nevertheless, poor harvests in 1885 and 1886 exacerbated outstanding difficulties regarding arrears and in November 1886 he introduced the Plan of Campaign – a new campaign to secure abatements, initiated in October 1886 and largely concentrated in the west – to five estates.[55] The plan was a dramatic success on the Hill

---

52 For an example of these sketches, see *Penny Illustrated Paper*, 28 Aug. 1880. Seán Ó Gallchóir and Seán MacNiallais (eds), *Scáthlán* 1 (Béal Átha Seanaigh, 1980) gives some indication of the impact of the flood in Gaoth Dobhair. In 1980 the commemoration of the flood's centenary led to the formation of an historical society in the parish.

53 Tuke, *Irish distress and its remedies*, pp 22–3; Scawen-Blunt, *Land war in Ireland*, p. 55; Hurlbert, *Coercion*, vol. 1, pp 5; 72–3. Meeting MacFadden was one of Hurlbert's main purposes in Ireland. He arrived in Ireland with Lord Ernest Hamilton, MP for north Tyrone, on 30 January 1888 and was in Gaoth Dobhair on 4 February. For a trenchant clerical rejoinder, see Revd Patrick White, *Hurlbert unmasked: an exposure of the 'thumping English lies' of William Henry Hurlbert in his 'Ireland under coercion'* (New York: Michael Walsh, 1890). The author was parish priest of Milltown-Malbay, county Clare.

54 On the land agitation in the west Ulster, see Desmond Murphy, 'The land war in Co. Donegal' in *Donegal Annual*, xxxii (1980), pp 476–86; *idem*, *Derry, Donegal and modern Ulster*, pp 138–48; 183–90; James MacFadden, *The present and past of the agrarian struggle in Gweedore with letters on railway extension in Donegal* (Derry, 1889) presents MacFadden's own analysis.

55 Geary, *Plan of Campaign*, pp 28–33 is a thorough analysis of the Plan of Campaign in north west Donegal.

estate. In November 1887, Hill accepted what the plan's historian considers 'penal terms'. He granted a rent-reduction of 30 per cent, reinstated over 130 evicted tenants, paid £900 legal costs and reduced the tenants' arrears of £3,400 by 60 per cent. The owners of the smaller estates subsequently granted sizable reductions. Wybrant Olphert, an old Colonel Blimp figure, held out longest and his heir finally reached an agreement with the tenants in 1893.[56]

From the national leadership's perspective, Gaoth Dobhair was an ideal battle-ground. The agricultural poverty of the parish was well-established and the argument that the Scottish pound, American dollar and children's wages paid the rent, rather than the produce of the land, was a strong one in the contemporary discourse on landlord rights and responsibilities. The landlords, in turn, were particularly vulnerable to rent strikes as, with the exception of Lord Leitrim, none of them were extravagantly wealthy and there were several small estates in the parish where victory could be secured quickly. Finally, that Gaoth Dobhair was in Ulster and tightly controlled by a dependable organiser added to its utility for propaganda purposes. Consequently, the leadership directed a caravan of international journalists, English politicians and radical sympathisers to the area. Scawen-Blunt, for example, arrived in Ireland on 24 March 1886 and was in Gaoth Dobhair six days later with a letter of introduction from Michael Davitt. Similarly, in 1890 when Maud Gonne, then a young socialite, asked Tim Harrington how she could participate in the 'national fight', he sent her north west, beginning a long connection with the district which inspired W.B. Yeats' *The Countess Cathleen*. On her first visit, much to Gonne's annoyance, she found the parish 'packed with English sympathisers', 'early rising ladies' with 'big serviceable boots', who 'sympathised earnestly and continuously'.[57] On the other hand, the national leadership's engagement in the local conflict allowed MacFadden to build up a network of contacts with figures such as John Dillon and John Redmond which he maintained throughout his career.

Notwithstanding the leadership's interest, MacFadden depended heavily upon the support of the local middle class, particularly shopkeepers' willingness to extend credit to the smallholders. On the rare occasions when class tensions surfaced in the movement, he acted decisively to shore up this pan-Catholic alliance. In 1885, for example, the Gaoth Dobhair branch of the National League passed the following resolution:

> That we strongly condemn the attempt in some quarters to place businessmen's accounts and landlords' rents in the same category and that we fail to discern wherein the comparison lies.[58]

---

56 Ibid., pp 29–31.
57 Scawen-Blunt, *Land war in Ireland*, pp 42–57; Maud Gonne MacBride, *A servant of the queen: her own story* (Dublin, 1938), pp 91–2; 99–112; 125–38.
58 MacFadden, *Present and past*, p. 137.

On a more general level, while professing a non-sectarian nationalism, MacFadden presented the land issue as a struggle between planted Protestants and native Catholics, making it more difficult for class fissures to develop into a split.[59] A powerful orator, he repeatedly stressed the need for Catholic unity and obedience to the priests. The argument in his speech to the Seventh Annual Reunion of Donegal People Resident in Glasgow, on 25 November 1884, is typical:

> Patriotism and religion run in the same channel. In all your undertakings look to those anointed guides, and rely on it that they will not only save you from errors and indiscretions, but they will prove your strongest stay in the fiercest winds of adversity –
>
> > For some may faint and some may stray,
> > And some may shun the pains, the loss,
> > But fearless, o'er the rugged way,
> > Will press the soldiers of the Cross.
>
> In this union between the priests and people lies the strength of the Irish Cause, and for this reason have our enemies been always trying to weaken or break the bond that unites them. But in this they have failed, and will, please God, ever fail. At no other period, perhaps, of our country's history was this union more complete than it is to-day. Bishops, priests, and people of Ireland are now banded together, under the standard kept aloft by the Irish Parliamentary Party, and the causes nearest and dearest their hearts they entrust to the care and keeping of Mr Parnell and his noble colleagues.[60]

Accepting MacFadden's sectarian analysis of the conflict, his parishioners placed intense pressure on Catholic members of the Royal Irish Constabulary. Several quit while others served gaol terms for refusing to obey orders.[61] Completing the association of Catholicism with anti-landlordism, he cultivated a quasi-religious saviour-image, pledging to lead the smallholders from the tyranny of landlordism to the promised land of owner-occupancy: the Plan of Campaign, he declared, was 'a solemn compact, made beneath the canopy of heaven in the presence of God'; 'the virtue and salvation of the people'; 'a blessed cause, a holy cause, a righteous cause and a just cause ... approved of by all the bishops and priests of Ireland with the exception of one solitary bishop, Dr O'Dwyer'.[62]

---

59 For MacFadden's nationalism, see N.A., C.S.O.R.P. 1889/11318, speech of Father MacFadden at meeting of the Young Ireland Society, St Mary's Hall, Belfast, 10 Apr. 1888. He began his speech by denouncing 'bigotry and intolerance' and stressed that many Irishmen 'who worship at another shrine' supported the land agitation but then proceeded to describe the landlords as grabbing Scotch settlers.

60 MacFadden, *Present and past*, p. 123; compare MacGill, *Glenmornan*, pp 293–5.

61 Ó Gallchobhair, *Landlordism in Donegal*, pp 58–60 mentions four cases.

62 N.A., C.S.O.R.P. 1889/11318 Bunbeg, 1 Jan. 1888, Const. James Igoe to District Inspector; Crossroads, 3 Jan. 1888, Segt. Owen Mahony to District Inspector. For MacFadden's use of biblical

MacFadden totally dominated public life in Gaoth Dobhair. He was president of the parochial branch of the National League and presided at its fortnightly meetings while his sister, Grace, who lived with him as his housekeeper, was the reluctant leader of a short-lived branch of the Ladies' Land League. When the smallholders withheld their rent, they paid a sum, set by him, into his 'war-chest' and he then negotiated with the landlords. Sympathisers' donations were also at his disposal, and he organised 'works of a public character', including road-building, for which he distributed seed and clothing and he helped an English knitwear merchant establish a factory in the parish.[63] At evictions, he personally confronted agents, bailiffs, and constables, belittling them in front of the smallholders and press, and he established 'arbitration courts' where his nominees settled disputes between parishioners before they reached the petty sessions. Although he repeatedly declared that nobody had to obey unjust laws, he generally discouraged the smallholders from stone-throwing and 'groaning' at the police and while there were some violent confrontations at evictions, they were all well-choreographed by MacFadden.[64] The need for order, particularly obedience to the clergy, was a recurrent theme in his speeches. Any lawlessness in his parish, he argued, was caused by a partisan police force.[65] The sub-text was clear: the landlords and state could not rule Gaoth Dobhair, only the priests could. MacFadden's determination to appear willing to obey 'just laws' explains his cautious behaviour in 1883 when Pat O'Donnell, a native of Gaoth Dobhair, was hanged in Newgate for assassinating James Carey, the informer whose evidence convicted and hanged five men for assassinating Lord Frederick Cavendish and Thomas H. Burke in the Phoenix Park in 1882. He studiously avoided public involvement in elaborate local commemorations (including a 'funeral', complete with a corpseless coffin, presided over by his curate on O'Donnell's month's mind); refused to allow a commemorative plaque to be erected in his chapel and only reluctantly acted as treasurer of funds raised by the *Irish World* in the United States for the erection of a monument to O'Donnell in Glasnevin Cemetery, Dublin.[66]

imagery, see ibid., Crossroads, 16 Jan. 1888, Sergt. Owen Mahony to District Inspector: report of a National League meeting, Glasshercoo, 16 Jan. 1888.

63 On the Ladies Land League and Children's Land League in Gaoth Dobhair, see N.L.I., *Land League papers Ms* 17703 Letterkenny, 17 Oct. 1881 [no name] to Miss B. Walshe; on relief works, see *Report of the evicted tenants commission*, H.C. 1893–4, xxxi, pp 378–82.

64 T.W. Russell, *Disturbed Ireland: the Plan of Campaign estates* (London, 1889), pp 53–4.

65 For examples of MacFadden's attitude to the law, see *Derry Journal*, 25 May 1881; N.A., C.S.O.R.P., 1882/28377 Gweedore,19 May 1882, James MacFadden P.P. to the Chief Secretary; ibid., 1889/11318; speech of Revd James MacFadden P.P. Gweedore, at Derrybeg chapel on 17 Mar. (Patrick's Day) 1888; n.p., 17 June 1889, Owen Mahoney to District Inspector: Revd James MacFadden P.P. at Evictions [1887–9].

66 MacFadden's limited involvement in the erection of the O'Donnell monument in Glasnevin provoked controversy, see 'Glasnevin' on 'Mr Dillon' ideal parish priest' in *Times*, 12 Oct.; 20 Oct.; 2 Nov. 1887 and MacFadden's replies 18 Oct.; 27 Oct. 1887. On O'Donnell and the assassination of Carey, see the insightful articles by Niall Ó Dónaill, Dónall P. Ó Baoill and Pádraig Ua Cnáinhsí in

Throughout the agitation, but particularly during the Plan of Campaign, MacFadden trumpeted his power in Gaoth Dobhair, with the apparent intention of drawing the government, always averse to prosecuting priests, into a propaganda ambush. In 1888 his coat-trailing finally resulted in his arrest. On 2 January, at a rally held outside Derryart chapel to extend the Plan of Campaign to north Donegal, he detailed the tactics used by his parishioners and declared himself the 'law' in the parish:

[Spoken in Irish] If ye pay behind backs, ye will be watched. If you stick together, I will give you my blessing. [Spoken in English] Mrs Boner was put out. Mrs Boner is since gone to her account and somebody must account for her death. One man had a fork, another a stone and they could only get out one that day. Now that is a sample of how you ought to conduct the campaign. Let them [constabulary note-takers] take a note of it. I don't care about all the note-takers. I am the law in Gweedore. They could not arrest any person without my consent. I despise the Coercion Act. If I got a summons, I would not reply to it. I say your methods are strictly honest. Some years there are no profits at all and that year they are entitled to no rents at all.[67]

The authorities interpreted the speech as promoting a 'criminal conspiracy' not to pay rent and arrested MacFadden in Armagh at the month's mind of his late uncle, Archbishop MacGettigan. Stephens and Alexander Blaine MP for Armagh were also arrested on similar charges. They were tried and convicted at Dunfanaghy, and sentenced to three months imprisonment. When they appealed, the judge doubled the sentences.[68] Released in October 1888, MacFadden returned in triumph to Gaoth Dobbair. 'I find my enemies almost groveling at my knees tonight,' he crowed at a rally in Dunfanaghy, 'and I am the victor'.[69]

Imprisonment confirmed MacFadden as a 'patriot priest' and he toured England in November addressing Irish workers and Liberal groups. For loyalists and Conservatives, however, a 'political priest' claiming to be the law in his parish was a portent of the Rome Rule that would follow Home Rule. Long a

Dónall P. Ó Baoill (ed.), *Scáthlán* 2 (Béal Átha Seanaigh, 1983). A 'month's mind' is a mass celebrated four weeks after a funeral for the repose of the deceased's soul.

67 N.A., C.S.O.R.P. 1889/11318 Glenveigh, 4 Jan. 1888, Stephen Cooley, Constable to Sergt. Orr Plan of Campaign meeting at Derryart chapel: Notes from speech of the Revd James McFadden P.P. Gweedore. Newspaper and police reports give the impression that MacFadden generally addressed political meetings in Gaoth Dobhair in English interspersed with Irish while his curate would then deliver a similar speech entirely in Irish. This suggests MacFadden was addressing nationalist and liberal newspaper-readers as much as his immediate audience.

68 For nationalist reaction, see the caricature of Balfour riding a horse labelled 'Toryism and bigotry' over a prostrate MacFadden in the colour supplement to *United Ireland*, 28 Apr. 1888.

69 N.A., C.S.O.R.P. 1891/11318 meeting at Dunfanaghy, county Donegal on Saturday 20 Oct. 1888: speech of the Revd James MacFadden, quoted in Geary, *Plan of Campaign*, p. 32.

bête noire for his role in the land agitation and connection with the O'Donnell monument in Glasnevin, MacFadden was now an 'apostle of anarchy'.[70] Attitudes to him hardened after the killing of District Inspector William Martin in February 1889. The events which led to Martin's death began on 19 December 1888 when MacFadden, recently returned from England, addressed a group of band boys and urged support for the plan. He ignored a summons to appear in court on Monday, 28 January, to answer a charge of incitement, and the Resident Magistrate issued a warrant for his arrest. This warrant did not allow forcible entry, and MacFadden refused to leave the parochial house. The following night when supporters gathered outside, he slipped out without the police seeing him. He returned to the house on Friday and remained there until Sunday when he left to read mass. After the service, Martin arrested him as he left the chapel. MacFadden's equal in arrogance, he brandished a naked sword as he led him away by the collar of his soutane. A woman shouted that the policeman was killing the priest and a riot broke out. Within minutes, the crowd had bludgeoned Martin to death with paling posts and stones.[71]

The killing incensed loyalists. Sir Edward Harland, Revd Hugh Hanna and Revd Richard Kane addressed a massive 'indignation meeting' in the Ulster Hall, Belfast on 14 February, which the *Belfast Newsletter* described as 'one of the finest meetings ever held in the city'.[72] The police, military and navy scoured the parish for suspects, rounding up forty eight men and women. Dubbed the 'Gweedore Terror', the government's excessive reaction outraged Liberal opinion in Britain.[73] Ten people, including MacFadden, were charged with murder and thirteen others with conspiracy. They were remanded in custody and tried at Maryborough [Port Laoise] after a long wrangle about jury selection. The Attorney General, Peter O'Brien, assisted by Edward Carson and John Ross, conducted the case for the crown, and J.E. O'Doherty MP acted for the defence, assisted by The MacDermott and Tim Healy MP. The trial, however, collapsed in the second week. Concerned that a glaringly packed jury would find at least one prisoner guilty of murder, the defence counsel reached an agreement with the Attorney General. MacFadden pleaded guilty to obstructing the

70 A dissident nationalist, F. Hugh O'Donnell, *Paraguay on Shannon: the price of a political priesthood: remarks on policy and proceedings of a Ribbonman board and a royal arranged commission* (Dublin, 1908) used the phrase 'apostles of anarchy' to describe political priests. Although coined by a nationalist, it neatly conveys loyalist perceptions of MacFadden.

71 For MacFadden's reaction to the killing, see N.L.I., *Holiday papers*, MS, 5794 Derry, 5 Apr. 1889, MacFadden to Catherine Holiday. The killing affected him deeply. Katherine Tynan devotes a chapter of her memoirs to a day spent with MacFadden – who made a very positive impression on her – in April 1893 when she was researching a series of articles on rural industries, and relates how, after a meal in his house, he emotionally re-enacted the attempt to arrest him. See Tynan, *Middle years*, pp 87–8. For propaganda photographs taken after the killing, see Ulster Folk and Transport Museum, Glass Collection (1889).

72 *Belfast Newsletter*, 25 Feb. 1889. South Donegal loyalists erected a striking memorial to Martin in the Church of Ireland church in Ballyshannon. See N.L.I. *Lawrence collection*, royal 3125.

police and was immediately released. Seven of his co-accused – six of whom pleaded guilty – were convicted of manslaughter and received sentences ranging from six months hard labour to ten years penal servitude. Nine others received short sentences for obstruction.[74] Parnellites later charged that Healy had foolishly abandoned the Gaoth Dobhair prisoners, but they cast no aspersions on MacFadden. When the Liberals returned to power in 1892, they released those still in gaol, briefly reigniting a controversy smothered in the winter of 1889–90 by the O'Shea divorce and Parnellite split. In a debate in the House of Commons on the releases, Edward Saunderson, the Unionist leader, referred to MacFadden as a 'murderous ruffian', rhetorically withdrawing the phrase in favour of 'excited politician' when pressed by the speaker.[75] Although the killing, trial and plea-bargain did not effect MacFadden's popularity in Gaoth Dobhair, they briefly weakened his hand in diocesan politics. Many Raphoe priests had long been uneasy about his activities, not least his undermining of the parish priest of Cloich Cheann Fhaola. Maud Gonne recalled that when she dined with his bishop, Patrick O'Donnell, and some priests in 1890, there was 'an awkward silence' when MacFadden was mentioned, while Maguire, who was sympathetic to the neighbouring parish priest, questions the justice of the campaign against Olphert in the diocesan history:

Lives were sacrificed, homes were wrecked, prison tortures endured; and when all was over, there was no victory for either side, and conciliation remained the only remedy. The same expenditure of life and treasure against a proved tyrant, would have proved more just and more effective.[76]

O'Donnell was fourteen years MacFadden's junior and lacked his family connections in the hierarchy: a relative of MacFadden's was bishop of either Raphoe or Armagh from 1860 to 1923. He had publicly supported MacFadden during his first term in gaol, hosted a banquet for him on his release, and stood by him through the second trial. In December 1889, however, he banned him from

---

73 For a participant's account of the police and military operation, see C.P. Crane, *Memories of a resident magistrate, 1880–1920* (Edinburgh, 1938); for English Liberal reaction, see H.W. Massingham, *The Gweedore hunt: a story of English justice in Ireland* (London, 1889).

74 Leon Ó Broin, *The prime informer: a suppressed scandal* (London, 1971), pp 45–6 argues the government were initially reluctant to charge MacFadden with either murder or manslaughter. Local histories draw heavily on reports on the trial in the nationalist press, particularly the *Derry Journal*. For unionist perspectives, see *Londonderry Sentinel*, 19 Oct., 22 Oct., 24 Oct., 26 Oct., 29 Oct., 31 Oct. 1889. John Ross, *The years of my pilgrimage: random reminiscences* (London, 1924), pp 48–9 gives a prosecutor's account of MacFadden's two trials.

75 Alvin Jackson, *Colonel Edward Saunderson: land and loyalty in Victorian Ireland* (Oxford, 1995), p. 97. Carson made his maiden speech to the House of Commons during the debate on the release of the Gaoth Dobhair prisoners, see Edward Majorbanks, *The life of Lord Carson*, vol. i (London, 1932), p. 155.

76 MacBride, *Servant of the queen*, p. 100; Maguire, *Diocese of Raphoe*, pt i, vol. ii, p. 303.

political activity for five years.[77] This ban was half-hearted. While O'Donnell took a more public role in resistance to evictions, MacFadden remained the driving force behind the agitation, organising the construction of temporary houses for evicted tenants and negotiating settlements on estates where the plan was still in force.[78] In addition, he directed road-building projects, sponsored by the C.D.B., which gave considerable employment. William Micks, the board's founder, later wrote, 'that for one important road no tender for construction was received at a reasonable amount, but Canon MacFadden took charge of the work which was completed to the satisfaction of the board's engineer. A similar result happened as regards the construction of Magheragallon pier in his parish – both striking proofs of his engineering capacity'.[79] Gradually, MacFadden re-entered politics proper. In 1896 he participated in the Conference of the Irish Race, an early attempt to re-unite constitutional nationalism, and in 1899 he joined the United Irish League (U.I.L.), a new nationalist agrarian organisation which O'Donnell supported.[80] In 1897, apparently at MacFadden's suggestion, the bishop sent him to the United States to raise funds for a cathedral in Letterkenny. The tour was highly successful and he undertook a second trip in 1900–1.[81] While in America, O'Donnell transferred MacFadden to Inis Caoil – an undoubted promotion – and, as it was also the bishop's home-parish, a further vote of confidence.[82]

III

In explaining the different images of MacFadden, the contrast between the monolithic Catholic community in Gaoth Dobhair and the high degree of social, cultural and political differentiation within the Catholic community of Inis Caoil is of crucial significance. Inis Caoil was one of the most prosperous parishes in the diocese. Since the early 1800s, its largest town, Na Gleanntaí [pop. 1841: 317; 1901: 366], had been the commercial and administrative centre of west Donegal and the hub of an extensive putting-out system for the produc-

77 Seán Ó Síoda, 'The Gweedore case' in Ó Gallchóir and MacNiallais (eds), Scáthlán 1, pp 47–51.
78 Joseph V. O'Brien, William O'Brien and the course of Irish politics (London, 1976), pp 76–7.
79 Evicted tenants commission, pp 375–82; William L. Micks, An account of the constitution, administration and dissolution of the Congested Districts' Board for Ireland from 1891 to 1923 (Dublin, 1925), pp 201–2.
80 F.J., Sept. 1896.
81 On fund-raising for the cathedral, see Maguire, Diocese of Raphoe, pt i, vol. i, pp 343–5; 489–90. The erection of this 'metropolitan cathedral in that petty town' in a county so heavily dependent on state-aid drew criticism, particularly as O'Donnell was a leading member of the C.D.B., see O'Donnell, Paraguay on Shannon, pp xvii-xviii; 91–2; Michael J.F. McCarthy, Priests and people in Ireland (Dublin, 1902), pp 89–91.
82 Ross, Years of my Pilgrimage, p. 57 mistakenly states that MacFadden's position became 'unbearable' in Gaoth Dobhair and that O'Donnell removed him to 'a poor parish in a remote part of the county'.

tion of knitwear.[83] In contrast to Gaoth Dobhair's embryonic middle class, it had a sizable, long-established class of Catholic middlemen, merchants, farmers and professionals. Some families in this class had enjoyed quiet prosperity through the 1700s, several managing to educate their sons in Irish colleges on the continent.[84] Socially secure, they had exhibited precocious political confidence in 1813 by sending representatives to the county's Catholic Committee while their co-religionists in larger towns such as Letterkenny kept their heads down. Later, they embraced O'Connellite nationalism and won control of the local Board of Guardians in the 1840s.[85] Critically, they had begun to disengage from popular culture before the Great Famine, in some instances even abandoning the language: in the 1870s John MacDevitt was astonished to hear his brother James, the bishop of Raphoe and a native of Inis Caoil, preach in Irish, as he had rarely spoken it since childhood.[86] In the hungry seasons that punctuated the decades before the blight, this social and cultural cleavage had produced violent unrest within the Catholic community as labourers and smallholders repeatedly clashed with farmers over wages and food entitlements.[87] Such was the extent of this unrest that in 1836 the middle class, alarmed at the number of 'refractory characters who have too eager a propensity for the commission of evil', twice petitioned the Lord Lieutenant to station a stipendiary magistrate in the town.[88]

The Great Famine tilted the social balance in favour of the townsman and

83 James McParlan, *Statistical survey of Donegal with observations on the means of improvement* (Dublin, 1802), p. 53.
84 Seán Ó Dómhnaill, 'County Donegal in the Catholic qualification rolls, 1778–1790' in *Journal of the County Donegal historical society*, 1, 3 (1949), pp 204–5 lists several merchants and farmers from Inis Caoil. The parish's middle-class included some descendants of the pre-conquest élite. Dálaigh na Glaisí, agents for several landlords until the mid-1800s, were the most important of these 'old-stock' families. Of the main line of the O'Donnells, they exercised a range of quasi-feudal rights until the early 1800s. For example, they would not allow priests to begin mass until they were present. On this family, see Rupert S. Ó Cochlainn, 'Captain Manus O'Donnell ('Manus a'Phíce'): a hero of '98' in *Journal of the County Donegal historical society*, 1, 3 (1949), pp 193–203; Maguire, *Diocese of Raphoe*, pt i, vol. i, pp 480–1; Ní Dhíoraí (ed.), *Na Cruacha*, pp 160–1.
85 For a wide-ranging discussion of the 'Catholic Question' in Donegal, see J.C.T. MacDonagh, 'The Catholic emancipation movement in the county of Donegal' in *Abú: 21st anniversary commemoration Cumann Thír Chonaill/Donegal Association, Dublin Branch* (Dublin, 1957), pp 43–9.
86 John MacDevitt, *The most Reverend James MacDevitt, D.D. a memoir* (Dublin, 1880), p. 329.
87 Tensions between smallholders and farmers were but one cause of unrest; sectarian and faction conflicts also generated considerable violence. For some examples of pre-Famine social unrest in Inis Caoil, see N.A., State of the country papers series I 1711/47 [1815]; 1832/5 [1817]; 1832/8 [1817]; 2187/10 [1820]; 2359/13 [1822]; 2359/23 [1822]; 2520/30 [1823]; 2520/32 [1823]; 2882/16 [1828]; 2882/17 [1828]; N.A., State of country papers series 11 [uncatalogued] box 170 letters of Revd John Barrett dated 29 Feb.; 15 Apr.; 16 May; 6 June; 29 Aug. 1822; box 176 Glenties, 6 Dec. 1830, Godfrey Hill Chief Const. to Maj. Thomas D'Arcy; N.A., Outrage Reports 1835 7/14; 7/42; 1836 7/37; 7/42; 7/48; 7/55; 7/61; 7/68; 1837 7/46; 7/47; 7/143; 7/147; 7/157; 1838 7/80; 7/1-8; 1839 7/2815; 7/4532; 7/4547; 1840 7/43863; 713925; 1842 7/14387; 1843 7/11163; 1844 7/4507; 1845 7/15463; 7/20183.
88 N.A., Official papers 1836/218 'The humble petition of the inhabitants of Glenties and vicinity ...', Dec. 1836; 'The humble petition of the inhabitants of the Barony of Boylagh ...' n.d. [Oct. 1836]. Of

comfortable farmer. Excess mortality and emigration cut the population from 7,779 in 1841 to 7,422 in 1851. In sharp contrast to Gaoth Dobhair, a secular decline in population followed the crisis as chain migration and less and later marriage depleted the lower strata of society. By 1901 the population had slipped below 5,500.[89] Social unrest – higher before the Great Famine than in the other more homogenous parishes of west Donegal – fell in the latter half of the century. Inis Caoil attracted little attention from Dublin Castle in the 1880s. Again, the contrast with MacFadden's previous parish – tranquil before the crisis and active in the 1850s and 1880s – is striking.[90] Inevitably, cultural change accompanied the depletion of the lower class. Clerically directed devotions displaced independent religious practices and Irish-speaking quickened its retreat from the town and farm to the marginal smallholdings. In 1911, 24 per cent of the population, monoglot English-speakers, could not converse with 9 per cent, monoglot Irish-speakers.[91] Traditional singing and story-telling – based on oral transmission from one performer to another – gave way to a new literary culture, which tapped the *Nation*, *Moore's Melodies*, English music halls and tinpan alley, but few local influences. Even the architecture changed: in 1866, the *Irish Builder* reported that an Italianate Gothic residence, designed by Timothy Hevey, was to be built opposite the chapel for Daniel MacDevitt, the most successful knitwear merchant in the parish.[92]

Although the *sodar i ndiaidh na n-uaisle* [trans.: traipsing after nobility] values of the market-town and the snug farm had been in the ascendancy for over half a century when MacFadden became parish priest, middle-class dominance was not absolute. Some outlying districts, most notably the mountain communities of Baile na Finne and Na Cruacha – the latter area only settled by refugees from Tyrone in the 1700s – had maintained the soul of their pre-Famine cul-

course, the appointment of a stipendiary magistrate had the added attraction to middle-class Catholics that it neutralised landlord Justices of the Peace.

89 Calculated for the Roman Catholic parish from townland data in *Census*, 1851, pp 106–14; *Census of Ireland, 1901: County of Donegal*, H.C. 1901 Cd. 1123–111, pp 24–37. The 1851 figure includes 276 inmates of the workhouse in Na Gleanntaí, many of whom were from surrounding parishes.

90 This observation is based on a close reading of N.A., State of the country papers, series I and II; Outrage reports, county Donegal 1835–52; C.S.O.R.P. for 1850–61 and a cursory examination of the C.S.O.R.P., newspapers and parliamentary papers for subsequent years.

91 Calculated from 'table XXXVI. – Showing for 1911 the number and ages of persons who spoke Irish only, and Irish and English, in each county district and district electoral division in the county of Donegal' in *Census of Ireland for the year 1911: Donegal*, pp 155–62.

92 Quoted in Alistair Rowan, *The buildings of Ireland: northwest Ulster. The counties of Londonderry, Donegal, Fermanagh, and Tyrone* (London, 1979), p. 309.

93 For rich accounts of the history and culture of one of these communities, see Seán Ó hEochaidh, *Sean-chainnt na gCruach, Co. Dhún na nGall/Alte redensarten aus den Cruacha County Donegal phonetisch-transkribiert und ins Deutsche übersetzt von Heinrich Wagner* (Tübingen, 1963); Séamas Ó Catháin (ed.), *Uair an chloig cois teallaigh/An hour by the hearth: stories told by Pádraig Eoghain Phádraig Mac an Luain, Crooveenananta, Co. Donegal* (Dublin, 1985); Ní Dhíoraí (ed.), *Na Cruacha*. Also see Seosamh Laoide (ed.), *Cruach Chonaill* (Baile Átha Cliath, 1909), an early collection of Donegal folklore which includes material from Inis Caoil.

ture.[93] Here, Irish remained the vernacular and the population included a substantial number of monoglots, ensuring the survival of a robust folk memory which nourished resentment of the lowland middle class. In some instances over ten miles from chapel, many popular religious practices had changed little since the Famine and fiddle-playing and house dances had stayed beyond the reach of clerical blackthorns much later than in the lowlands.[94] Indeed, owing to the brevity of the potato-growing season in the hills, even the diet of Na Cruacha was archaic, including a larger proportion of oatmeal bread and porridge than lower-class diets elsewhere in the county as late as the mid-1900s.[95] In terms of *mentalité*, the parish's core and periphery were worlds apart. The O'Donnells, the pre-conquest dynasty of Donegal, were key figures in the invented tradition of the nationalism which spread from the town in the 1800s but in the *seanchas* of Na Cruacha they remained harsh overlords who coerced labour to build roads and a castle.[96] For *bunadh na gcnoc* [trans.: the hill folk], Colm Cille – the West Ulster patron – remained a boisterous, irreverent, endearing, imperfect character referred to affectionately as Colm, yet in the lowlands the mutually reinforcing processes of devotional revolution and language-shift re-cast him as a cold and lonely icon – Saint Columba.[97] With obvious implications for gender roles, the same processes transformed Mary from a flesh and blood 'wailing woman' – a representation still acceptable in the outlying areas in the mid-1900s – into a blue-sashed, serene virgin.[98] Not surprisingly, attitudes to priests – addressed as 'Father' in the core but simply as '*a shagairt*' [trans.: priest] on the periphery – changed as one moved further from the town. *Seanchas* collected in the hills throughout the 1900s expresses a gentle scepticism towards the diocesan clergy, implicitly contrasting them with the colourful wandering friars of the 1700s whom they held in high esteem. Although it falls short of anti-clericalism, the

94 Even in the outlying areas, some pre-Famine religious practices declined. E J. Mullen, *Mount Silver looks down: supplement to history of Raphoe* (Glenties, 1952), pp 25; 36 notes a well-documented tradition of lay Catholics memorising and reciting Bishop Gallagher's Irish sermons, first published in 1735, petered out. The last Inis Caoil sermon reciter died in Baile na Finne in 1920. Ó hEochaidh, *Sean-chainnt na gCruach*, pp 12–13 attributes the decline of house-dances in Na Cruacha (unspecified period, but apparently in the early 1900s) to a change in '*an dligheadh*' [trans.: the law], but does not specify whether it was civil or clerical 'law' which changed. He notes the inhabitants resented this change.

95 Ó hEochaidh, *Sean-chainnt na gCruach*, p. 10.

96 Ní Dhíoraí (ed.), *Na Cruacha*, pp 142–6.

97 For the different images of the patron, contrast Ní Dhíoraí (ed.), *Na Cruacha*, pp 137–40; 166 with Edward Maguire (ed.), *Cuimhne Coluimcille or the Gartan festival being a record of the celebration held at Gartan on the 9th June, 1897, the thirteenth centennial of St Columba* (Dublin, 1898), *passim*. I am grateful to Séamas Ó Catháin for drawing my attention to the different images of Colm Cille and to the last source.

98 For examples of Marianism from the periphery of Inis Caoil, see Énrí Ó Muirgheasa (ed.), *Dánta Diadha Uladh* [trans.: The religious poetry of Ulster] (Baile Átha Cliath, 1936), pp 122–3; Angela Partridge, *Caoineadh na dtrí Miure: téama na páise i bhfilíocht bhéil na Gaeilge* [trans.: The keening of the three Marys: the theme of the passion in Irish oral poetry] (Baile Átha Cliath, 1983), p. 236; Ní Dhíoraí (ed.), *Na Cruacha*, pp 178–84. Also see Angela Partridge, 'Wild men and wailing women' in *Éigse*, xvii (1980), pp 25–37.

humour in the following apocraphy story, told by Anna John Chiot Nic a'Luain (1884–1954), Cruach Thiobraid in 1948, would have been lost on the more deferential households in the lowlands where fulfilment of 'obligations' had become confused with piety:

> Bhíodh daoine mór, ar ndóiche, san an sin nuair a théadh siad faoi lámh easpaig agus go minic bhíodh daoine thall is abhus ina seandaoine agus ina seanmhná sula dtéadh siad chuige. Chualaigh mé iomrá ar sheanduine a chuaigh ionsar an easpag sa tseanam. D'fhiafraigh an t-easpag de cé mhéad dia a bhí ann.
> 'Silim', a deir an seanduine, 'go bhfuil trí cinn ann'.
> 'Bo, bo!' a deir an t-easpag, 'caidé an t-ábhar a ndeir tú sin?'
> 'Tá mé chomh sean', a deir an seanduine, 'agus go bhfuil an tríú sagart paróiste anseo ó tháinig mé i gcuimhne agus níl sagart ar bith acu', a deir sé, 'nach raibh a dhligheadh féin aige, agus shíl mé go raibh dia ag géilleadh d'achan sagantacu!'
> Ní thearn an t-easpag faic ach ticéad a thabhairt dó. 'Seo dhuit', a deir sé,' agus bog leat'. D'aithin sé go maith go raibh an teagasc críostaí ag an tseanduine.[99]

[trans.: Of course, people were grown up when they were confirmed in those days [before the establishment of the school in Na Cruacha in 1907] and often there would be men and women here and there who were very old before they would go to the bishop. I heard tell of an old fellow who went to the bishop to be confirmed way back. The bishop asked him how many gods there were. 'I think', says the old fellow, 'that there are three'. 'Bah!' says the bishop, 'and what makes you say that?' 'I am that old', says the old fellow, 'that I can remember three parish priests here and there wasn't one of them that didn't have his own law so I thought there must be a different god following each one of them'. The bishop simply gave him a ticket. 'Here', says he, 'now get away'. He could tell that the old fellow knew his catechism.]

While still culturally autonomous, the outlying districts were enmeshed in highly exploitative relationships with the gombeenmen of Na Gleanntaí. Women of all ages knitted socks with yarn issued by several merchant houses, the largest that of the MacDevitt family. The MacDevitts' well-documented practice of refusing to settle with Rosses women for socks until the tide was turning in

---

99 Ní Dhíoraí (ed.), *Na Cruacha*, pp 164. Nic a'Luain told the story when explaining how a local woman with a rudimentary education had taught catechism in *Na Cruacha* before the establishment of the school in 1907. For perceptions of the clergy in outlying areas, also see ibid., pp 167; 176–7; Laoide (ed.), *Cruach Chonaill*, pp 106–7.

100 MacGill, *Rat-pit*, pp 1–37 is widely cited. Also see Pádraig Ua Cnáimhsí, *Róise Rua* (Baile Átha Cliath, 1988), pp 49–55; Máire, *Bean Rua de Dhálach* (Baile Átha Cliath, 1966), pp 127–37; *Congested Districts' Board for Ireland: base-line report: district of Glenties*, 28 March 1892 [hereafter *Base-line report, Glenties, 1892*], p. 10.

Gaoth Bearra, an estuary that they had to wade across at low-tide to get home, is indicative of the parasitic gombeenism in the parish.[100] Indeed, the MacDevitts were not the worst: in 1892 a C.D.B. inspector reported that they always settled in cash, while other merchants, who had a lower wholesale price, gave the women 'their money's worth, or supposed worth' in tea, sugar, tobacco and snuff. Noting the large profit on tea, he observed 'the tea is almost forced on the women and girls in exchange for the knitting'. In addition to socks, women bartered sprigging and eggs for 'all small necessities'. Credit dealing was general and, given the smallholders' dependence on knitting, the merchants were able to charge much higher interest rates than those in neighbouring parishes.[101]

Creative writers vividly evoke the tensions in the Catholic community of Inis Caoil. For the early 1900s, MacGill's poetry and autobiographical novels illuminate the exploitative nature of the putting-out system and the snobbery of the small town where 'people have got the quality toss with them and the most genteel manners'. English music hall songs are popular and the gombeenman's daughter, Gwendoline, can sing two French songs but would never condescend to sing come-all-yehs like *Nell Flaherty's Drake* or *Pat O'Donnell* which are popular in the narrator's glen. The people of the glen, in turn, look down on the 'mountainy men', a pejorative term for the Irish-speaking smallholders in the hills. The parish is so fragmented that three words are used to describe a common foodstuff: 'porridge' [town]; 'stirabout' [glen]; and *brachán réidh* [hill].[102] Similarly, in *Dancing at Lughnasa*, Brian Friel, who spent his summers on the same schizophrenic middle-ground in the 1930s, powerfully recreates the tension between the vernacular religion of the 'back hills' and the chapel-centred religion of 'Ballybeg', a pseudonym for Na Gleanntaí:

Rose: (*Quietly, resolutely*) It was last Sunday week, the first night of the Festival of Lughnasa; and they were doing what they do every year up there in the back hills.

Kate: Festival of Lughnasa! What sort of –

Rose: First they light a bonfire beside a spring well. Then they dance round it. Then they drive their cattle through the flames to banish the devil out of them.

Kate: Banish the – ! You don't know the first thing about what –

Rose: And this year there was an extra big crowd of boys and girls. And they were off their heads with drink. And young Sweeney's trousers caught fire and he went up like a torch. That's what happened.

Kate: Who filled your head with that nonsense?

Rose: They do it every Lughnasa. I'm telling you. That's what happened.

Kate: (*Very angry, almost shouting*) And they're savages! I know those

101 *Base-line report, Glenties, 1892*, pp 8–9; 14.
102 MacGill, *Glenmornan*, pp 29–30; 31–2.

people from the back hills! I've taught them! Savages – that's what
they are! And what pagan practices they have are no concern of
ours – none whatever! It's a sorry day to hear talk like that in a
Christian home, a Catholic home! All I can say is that I'm shocked
and disappointed to hear you repeating rubbish like that, Rose!

Rose: (*Quietly, resolutely*) That's what happened. I'm telling you.[103]

Although a more complex society, MacFadden conducted himself in Inis Caoil
much as he had done in Gaoth Dobhair. He remained a proponent of stations,
weekly mass-attendance and confession. What his hagiographer terms 'the dangers arising from indiscriminate dancing in country houses' continued to be a
particular bugbear and, to counter it, he purchased the Market House in Na
Gleanntaí and converted it into a dance hall where 'dancing was permitted under conditions which were more conducive to the welfare of young people than
those which might otherwise obtain'.[104] He also retained an enthusiasm for construction, building a palatial parochial house shortly after his appointment. Most
buildings he erected, however, were in outlying, disadvantaged districts: he built
the national schools of Na Cruacha [1907], Duibhbhinn [1911] and Loch Muc
[1916], renovated the chapel in Baile na Finne [c.1910] and erected a third chapel
at Éadan Anfa [1905].[105] In addition, MacFadden was still authoritarian. Following the publication of MacGill's early works with their thinly disguised attacks
on himself and local gombeenmen, he 'read him from the altar' and the young
writer – he was about twenty three – returned to England.[106]

Finally, MacFadden stayed politically active. The political landscape, however, had changed since his glory days in Gaoth Dobhair. At the national level,
the class-coalition of Catholics which had been so formidable in the 1880s was
now fragmenting.[107] Smallholders were sporadically confronting middle-class
co-religionists, particularly graziers, in bitter disputes; militant republicans were
snapping at the Parliamentary party's heels; and, even within the reunited party,
wounds inflicted in the Parnellite split still festered. Although the Catholic communities of west Donegal experienced many of these strains, MacFadden remained a party-man. He became a national figure in the Ancient Order of
Hibernians (A.O.H.), a conservative Catholic nationalist brotherhood which

103 Brian Friel, *Dancing at Lughnasa* (London, 1990), pp 16–17.
104 Ó Gallchobhair, *Landlordism in Donegal*, p. 187.
105 Ní Dhíoraí (ed.), *Na Cruacha*, xvi notes that the smallholders in Na Cruacha credited O'Donnell,
    not MacFadden, with building the chapel at Éadan Anfa.
106 MacGill, *Glenmornan*, pp 288–313 gives the young writer's version of events.
107 On the national political context, see David W. Miller, *Church, state and nation in Ireland, 1898–
    1921* (Dublin, 1973), pp 203–30; Tom Garvin, *The evolution of Irish nationalist politics* (Dublin,
    1981), pp 89–99.

provided voting fodder for the party in the north, and he served on the U.I.L's National Directory until his death.[108] A committed Devlinite, at the directory meeting of 2 July 1916 he seconded the motion calling for acceptance of Lloyd George's partition proposal as a 'temporary and provisional settlement of the Irish difficulty'.[109] In addition, in 1903 he joined Conradh na Gaeilge, the national movement for the revival of Irish-speaking, and he was co-opted on to its *Coiste Gnó* [trans.: executive committee] in 1908.[110] Local politics, however, occupied most of his time. Shortly after his appointment, he became vice-chairman of the Glenties Improvement Committee, a self-appointed development board dominated by the MacDevitts and other businessmen, and he chaired it from 1905 to 1917. This committee acquired funding from the C.D.B. for projects such as road-building, drainage, and a water supply scheme – the proverbial parish pump – for the town.[111]

Victorious in the patriotic struggle against the 'tyranny of landlordism', the Catholic middle class was now committing many sins, particularly jobbery, for which it had vilified landlords. MacFadden was no exception. For example, in 1902, the local board of guardians, predominantly 'Hibs' and U.I.L. men, resolved to appoint an Irish-speaking workhouse master but, when lobbied by MacFadden, overlooked three bilingual applicants and selected O'Donnell's nephew, a manoglot English-speaker. The letter MacFadden sent to the poor law guardians on this occasion testifies to his power and the manner he wielded it:

I shall feel exceedingly grateful to you if you will support the candidate of my choice for the mastership of the Glenties workhouse, Mr Bernard Quigley. He is highly qualified for the position, having been trained for some time as clerk in the office of the county council. On the score of family connections, being nephew of the noble bishop of the diocese, he stands high. His character, too, is blameless and irreproachable. On the matter of the medical officership, I hope you will have the kindness to hold yourself free until all the candidates are in the field, and that you will decide to support the man whom, after full and serious consideration, I shall regard best deserving of your vote.[112]

---

108 *Donegal Independent*, 24 Mar. 1905 reports MacFadden's speech at the inaugural meeting of the Na Gleanntaí lodge of the A.O.H.. MacFadden's bishop, O'Donnell, was an enthusiastic supporter of the A.O.H. while his cousin, Cardinal Logue, was a vocal opponent of it. On the revival of republicanism in Donegal, see *Sinn Féin*, 22 Dec. 1906; 18 May 1907.
109 N.L.I., Ms. 708 United Irish League, Minute book of the national directory, 10 Aug. 1904–30 Apr. 1918, pp 455–6; United Irish League thirty-fifth meeting, Monday 3 Jul. 1916.
110 For MacFadden's involvement in Conradh na Gaeilge, see N.L.I. Ms. *Fionán Mac Colaim papers* 24408, Conradh na Gaedhilge, notices and reports of meetings of An Coiste Gnótha, 1907–1910.
111 Liam Briody, *Glenties and Inniskeel* (Ballyshannon, 1986), pp 151–8 gives a brief account of the Glenties Improvement Committee. Briody's volume is a treasure-trove of information on the social history of Inis Caoil.
112 O'Donnell, *Paraguay on Shannon*, pp 108–12. O'Donnell argues that priests, through their involve-

Of course, MacFadden's recommendation of a monoglot English-speaker for a public office sat uncomfortably with his growing involvement in Conradh na Gaeilge. In 1903, when he was appointed Orator of the Oireachtas, a national cultural festival, a motion censuring the organising committee for selecting him appeared on the *Ard-fheis* [trans.: national convention] programme. Following the intervention of Pádraig Pearse, the motion was withdrawn and MacFadden spoke on '*Tír agus teanga*' [trans.: country and language].[113] MacFadden's commitment to the revival-movement, however, is difficult to assess. He regularly preached in Irish, appointed teachers – many of whom were from Gaoth Dobhair – who could speak the language and ordered that it be the medium of instruction in the schools. Indeed, even before joining Conradh na Gaeilge, he corresponded with other priests in Irish, suggesting a high level of enthusiasm.[114] Nevertheless, English continued to dominate the public sphere in the parish. His exhortations to his parishioners to speak Irish, while delivered from the pulpit in his distinctive carrot and stick style, never constituted a viable strategy to check the decline of the language:

> Gan seachrán ar bith a bheith oraibh.! Gur imigh na laetha a bhféadfaí neamhshuim a chur i dteanga na Gaeilge. Dúirt mé cheana féin agus deirim arís nach bhfaigheann aon duine, ins an pharóiste, nó as an pharóiste, post dá bhfuil faoi mo chúramsa ach Gaeilgeoirí. Mholfainn daoibh, ar mhaithe libh féin, an Ghaeilge a labhairt agus a fhoghlaim. Tá arán agus im anois inti, a chlann, agus b'fhéidir go mbrostódh seo féin sibh.[115]

> [trans.: Let none of you be mistaken! The days have gone when the Irish language could be ignored. I have said before and say again that nobody, in the parish, or from the parish, will get any job in my gift except Irish-speakers. I'd advise you, for your own sakes, to speak and learn Irish. There is bread and butter in it now, my children, and maybe this will be enough to encourage you.]

Despite his arrogance and involvement in barefaced jobbery, MacFadden retained a genuine social concern. The schools and chapel he built were in deprived districts, and it is simplistic to reduce his motivation to social control alone. Indeed, such was his commitment to improving education in the outly-

---

ment in the A.O.H. and U.I.L., were responsible for general corruption in the west, particularly in the diocese of Raphoe. Although somewhat eccentric, he presents a well-documented case.
113 Donncha Ó Súilleabháin, *Na timirí i ré tosaigh an Chonartha, 1893–1927* [trans.: The activists in the early days of Conradh na Gaeilge, 1893–1927] (Baile Átha Cliath, 1990), p. 56.
114 Maguire, (ed.), *Cuimhne Coluimcille*, pp 69–70.
115 Ó Súilleabháin, *Na timirí*, pp 55–6.

ing areas, that in 1916, after the National Education Office had refused to sanction a school for twenty five children in Loch Muc, 'in view of the limitation of expenditure imposed by the Treasury during the continuance of the war,' MacFadden brazenly flouted regulations by building the schoolhouse 'out of his own pocket', appointing a teacher and then seeking official recognition.[116] Furthermore, while MacGill portrays him – no doubt accurately – as an apologist for gombeenism who preached that shopkeepers' bills were 'lawful debts within the letter of the law', he was also conscious of the inequalities inherent in the credit system: in a preliminary written submission to the Royal Commission on Congestion he describes it as 'a ruinous system for both dealers and customers'. Finally, he continued to address many lower-class grievances. Through the U.I.L., for example, he pressed for state-funded reclamation; land-distribution; the fixing of minimum and maximum areas for holdings; compulsory purchase of property to facilitate improvement; poor law reform and the establishment of granite quarries and factories for the production of iodine from kelp.[117]

Notwithstanding his social concern, the deep-rooted antagonism between different sections of his congregation ensured that MacFadden's middle-class lifestyle and his emphasis on Catholic unity gave the impression that he was a townsman's priest. In particular, his enthusiasm for construction alienated the smallholders as they were expected to support it with 'offerings'. In his autobiographical novels, MacGill dwells on the excessive cost of the parochial house and the offerings system:

'Do you know how much the priest is going to spend on a lav-ha-thury for his new house?' asked the beansho drily.
'Lav-ha-thury?' said Judy Farrel. 'What's that?'
'Old Oiney Dinchy of Glenmornan said that it is a place for keeping holy water,' said Maire a Crick.
'Holy water, my eye!' said the beansho. 'It's the place where the priest washes himself.'

'He's going to spend two hundred and fifty pounds on his lav-ha-thury, anyway,' said the beansho. 'Two hundred and fifty pounds on one single room of his house! Ye'll not fill yer own bellies and ye'll give him a bathroom to wash his!'[118]

116 On the establishment of Loch Muc school, see N.A., E.D. 9/27165 *Glenties*, 13 Sept. 1916, James Canon MacFadden P.P. to Secretaries National Education Office, Dublin.
117 MacGill, *Children of the dead end*, pp 3–4; N.A., Royal Commission on congestion in Ireland papers, 1906–8, Carton 1: Donegal (Killybegs): 'Summary of evidence of Very Rev. James Canon MacFadden, Glenties, Oct. 1st 1906'. For MacFadden's oral submission, see *Royal commission on congestion in Ireland: second report of the commissioners*, H.C. 1907 Cd. 3318–9, xxxv, pp 102–10.
118 MacGill, *Rat-pit*, pp 30; 93–4. The 'lav-ha-thury' is now (1996) in St Conall's Museum, Na Gleanntaí.

Similarly, the water supply scheme for Na Gleanntaí – a prerequisite if MacFadden was to flush his 'lav-ha-thury' – provoked intense opposition: in December 1902 over 600 'peasant ratepayers of the mountain districts' demonstrated in the town against a proposed rate-increase to pay for a service that would only benefit the most advantaged section of the parish; they 'groaned' loudly when Hugh MacDevitt JP – a supporter of the scheme – attempted to mollify them by mentioning their parish priest's 'revered name'.[119] Even MacFadden's conversion of the Market House did not find universal favour as the English-speaking middle-class quickly appropriated this new public space. The programme for a 'Grand Concert and Dramatic Entertainment', held in January 1914, includes no material from vernacular lower-class culture other than sanitised exhibitions of the very dances which MacFadden was so eager to banish from private houses:

1 Chorus: Convent School Children.
2 The Men of the West: Mr Donoghue.
3 Eight-hand Reel: Convent School Children.
4 Angus McDonald: Miss Cannon.
5 My Dark Rosaleen: Revd M. O'Donnell.
6 Duet: Miss Lily and Master Arthur McLoone.
7 Recitation: Revd H. McDwyer.
8 Fifty Long Years Ago: Mr Eddie Kennedy.
9 Farce: Misses Lily McLoone and Maryanne Kennedy.
10 The Coulin: Convent School Children.
11 The Song that Reached My Heart: Mrs O'Donoghue.
12 Four-hand Reel: Convent School Children.
13 Comic Song: Muldoon the Solid Man: Master James McDevitt.
14 Song: Miss Cannon.
15 Song: Revd E. O'Doherty, C.C.
16 Duet: I Saw from the Beach: Mr and Mrs O'Donoghue.
17 Irish Jig: Miss May McLoone.
18 Play: The Elegant Dempsey: Arthur McLoone; Annie Sweeney; Francis McLoone; Joseph B. Gallagher; James McDevitt; Joe Gallagher; Lily McLoone.
19 Finale: A Nation Once Again.[120]

Middle-class dominance of the Market House reached its apex in the 'Swanky Ball', the nickname given a dance organised by some well-to-do women who set

119 *Derry People and Donegal News (Christmas Supplement)*, 20 Dec. 1902
120 Briody, *Glenties and Inniskeel*, pp 181–2. Significantly, a few middle-class families dominated the concert.

an extravagant price for tickets to exclude the lower-class. This snobbery provoked considerable resentment and, following what a local historian delicately terms 'serious and even somewhat unhygienic incidents', the organisers summoned the parish priest to restore order. A popular ballad conveys some sense of the controversy that it aroused:

Oh! then tell me Dan Mulhern where the gathering is to be,
Its a Swanky Ball in Glenties where the grandeur you shall see.
Oh! close up your Billiard Room, and hurry up the street,
And give the news to the would-be-swells, that you should chance to meet![121]

Resented in lower-class Inis Caoil and revered in Gaoth Dobhair, James MacFadden died on 17 April 1917. His hagiographer attributes his death to pneumonia contracted when returning from a political meeting in Belfast and, in the diocesan history, Maguire adds to the nationalist mystique by giving 17 March as the date of his death.[122] Nevertheless, in *Glenmornan*, published in 1918, MacGill's MacFadden-character meets a less appropriate end for a patriot priest. The hero has joined the British Army, having been driven from the parish by the 'old autocratic priest'. In the trenches, he receives a letter from a neighbour telling him that the priest is dead. She writes:

Father Devaney is ded, and good job too, for nobody cared very much for the man. You should hear the countrey boys talking about him and saying that he was not worthy of his coat. He met his deth in a strange way. He was at a dance in the town, and this dance was given by the quality and all the peeple with money was at it as well as the priest, him that wouldnt allow the countrey boys to have dances in their own house. But when the quality were having a dance it didnt matter. None of the countrey boys were allowed into the dance, but it was such a grand dance that the preest himself went with his sister. Well, it was a night of big snow and the countrey boys went down to the town and the would not be allowed in, but had to stand outside and freez, so the picked up snoballs and flung them thru the window of the market hall where the dance was. Then the priest came out with his stick and chased them away with a stick. So the ran off. He followed them for a bit and the somehow got angry and turned on him and began to throw snoballs at him. The knocked his hat off him, thru the snow down his back and sent him running back. As he was going into the hall again he fell and the boys covered him up with

---

121 Ibid., pp 183–4. The date on which the ball was held is difficult to establish. Briody suggests it 'may have taken place on February 9th, 1919', but see MacGill, *Glenmornan*, pp 317–18 which associates a strikingly similar event with his MacFadden-character's death.
122 Ó Gallchobhair, *Landlordism in Donegal*, pp 188–9; Maguire, *Diocese of Raphoe*, pt i, vol. i, p. 490.

snow. When he got in he was white with fright for he thought that the were
going to kill him. Next day he had a bad cold and he died from it.[123]

Within two years of MacFadden's death, the platform on which he had stood
since the 1880s – the 'union of priests and people' for Home Rule – collapsed.
Challenged by Sinn Féin and the Irish Republican Army (I.R.A.), the U.I.L
disintegrated and the A.O.H. split. Throughout west Donegal, violent clashes
between Republicans and Hibernians – the latter enjoying most 'respectable'
support – characterised the 'Tan War' of 1919–21. Indeed, MacFadden's last
parish was among the first areas in which these clashes resulted in death: in
December 1918 Anthony Heron, a Hibernian, died from a gunshot wound inflicted in a fracas after an election rally in Na Gleanntaí.[124] The Civil War proper
in 1922–3 was particularly bitter in west Donegal, not least in Inis Caoil, where,
in 1923, Republicans burned down Cardinal O'Donnell's family home when he
failed to prevent the Irish Free State executing four I.R.A. men in Drumboe.[125]
Even in Gaoth Dobhair, a model of Catholic political unity in the 1880s,
Hibernian-Republican conflict was intense during the troubles and continued
for over three decades, sporadically spiralling into violence. The split in the
parish was almost absolute: Hibernians and Republicans supported different
political parties, read different newspapers, danced in different halls and followed different marching bands at festivals. On at least one occasion their invet-
erate antagonism had fatal consequences: in 1924, during a spate of tit-for-tat
arson attacks on dance-halls, three Republicans died from burns received in an
ill-conceived attempt to torch the Hibernian hall in Middletown.[126] Tellingly,
while MacFadden had embraced Hibernianism in Inis Caoil, he was one of the
few heroes shared by both political groups in Gaoth Dobhair: the first play
produced by Aisteoirí Ghaoth Dobhair – an amateur dramatic group established in 1935 which was supported by Hibernians and Republicans alike – was
In aimsir an Mháirtínigh [trans.: In Inspector Martin's time] and as late as the

123 MacGill, *Glenmornan*, pp 317–18.
124 Briody, *Glenties and Inniskeel*, p. 165. Throughout west Donegal, the break-up of the old Catholic-
    nationalist organisations, such as the A.O.H. and Irish National Foresters, frequently resulted in
    bitter contention for their musical instruments and halls, see Seosamh Mac Grianna, *An druma mór*
    (Baile Átha Cliath, 1969).
125 Briody, *Glenties and Inniskeel*, p. 296. Dan O'Donnell, the cardinal's brother, died several months
    later, allegedly from the effects of exposure on the night that the house was burned. Jim McLoughlin,
    'The politics of nation-building in post-famine Donegal' in Nolan, Ronayne and Dunlevy (eds),
    Donegal, pp 583–624 presents an interesting analysis of early twentieth-century nationalism in Don-
    egal. Based exclusively on English language sources, it ignores acute ideological divisions between
    different nationalist groups and the social bases of those divisions.
126 Many Hibernians became involved with the fascist Blueshirt movement in the 1930s. For a Repub-
    lican account of a clash between Gaoth Dobhair Republicans and Cloich Cheann Fhaola Blueshirts,
    see 'The northwest Tirconaill boys' in *Derry Journal, Old 'come-all-ye's': the finest collection of northern
    ballads and folk poems: second and enlarged edition with many additional ditties* (Derry, n.d. [c.1940]),
    p. 37.

1980s, when the split had lost almost all its venom, a local history society let its oars drift after publishing three excellent collections of essays which concentrated on events in the 1880s.[127]

IV

The different images of MacFadden in Gaoth Dobhair and Inis Caoil – soggarth aroon and gombeen-priest – resulted from the acute differences between the social structure, culture and politics of their Catholic communities. In Gaoth Dobhair the Catholic community was virtually monolithic. The middle class was small and, having roots scarcely deeper than the Great Famine, strong ties of language, kinship and identity bound it to the smallholders. As social tensions between his parishioners were weak, MacFadden's middle-class culture and lifestyle were admired more than resented. In the massive crisis of 1879–81, the relative unity of the Catholic community in Gaoth Dobhair, the attractiveness of MacFadden's lifestyle and the strength of his personality facilitated his emergence as a political leader: his arrogance and optimism appeared as virtues and his insistence that Catholic unity would advance the smallholders' position was convincing. In Inis Caoil, however, internal social, cultural and political differentiation had characterised the Catholic community since the eighteenth-century. Two key features of the local economy, the protoindustrial system for the production of knitwear and the credit system were transparently exploitative. Consequently, by pursuing the same agenda that he had pursued in Gaoth Dobhair, MacFadden allied himself with the farmer and the townsman against the hand-knitter and 'mountainy man'.

After his death, MacFadden remained a 'patriot priest' for nationalists and an apostle of anarchy' for loyalists. In Fermanagh in the 1920s, Hibernian schoolboys sang ballads exulting in Martin's death to provoke Protestant neighbours and polemical loyalist literature, particularly popular biographies of Carson, frequently recalled the murder trial and the 'arrogant, vain' priest at the centre of it.[128] Ironically, MacFadden was neither the radical patriot nor anarchistic demon which these images suggest. While loyalists cited his activities in Gaoth

---

127 Ó Gallchóir and MacNiallais (eds), *Scáthlán 1, passim*; Ó Baoill (ed.), *Scáthlán 2, passim*; Ó Baoill (ed.), *Scáthlán 3, passim*. Aisteoirí Ghaoth Dobhair developed out of an earlier group, Aisteoirí Dhoire Beaga (1931–5), which met in the republican hall in Doire Beaga.

128 Paddy Tunney, *The stone fiddle: my way to traditional song* (Belfast, 1991), pp 13–14; H. Montgomery Hyde, *Carson: the life of Sir Edward Carson, Lord Carson of Duncairn* (London, 1953), pp 83–4; 104–8; Marjoribanks, *Life of Lord Carson*, vol. i, p. 155. MacFadden's involvement in the A.O.H. also attracted comment in loyalist polemical literature, see Anon. [Lord Ashtown], *The unknown power behind the Irish nationalist party: its present work and criminal history* (London, 1907), pp 7–8; 14.

Dobhair as evidence of the power of the Catholic clergy, his political prominence there owed as much to his charisma as the priest's traditional authority.
Moreover, as the antipathy to him in lower-class Inis Caoil indicates, not all
lower-class Catholics were 'as ignorant and credulous as the painted children of
the prairie'. Finally, contrary to nationalist images of a radical patriot,
MacFadden's radicalism was limited to evicting the landlords and state-aided
development of the west. On other issues, he was conservative. The Devil was in
any house where there was a fiddle; the gombeenman's bills were 'lawful debts
within the letter of the law' and constitutional activity alone would deliver Home
Rule.[129]

129 Tá an chaibidil seo bunaithe ar thaighde a rinne mé fé stiúir Tom Garvin agus David W. Miller. Tá
    me buíoch daofasan agus do na daoine seo leanar a léigh direachtaí garbha di agus a mhol athruithe:
    Steve Ball; Enda Delaney; Katrina Goldstone; Tim McMahon; Willie Nolan; Séamas Ó Catháin;
    Tim O'Neill; Kevin Whelan.

The Stone of Destiny: Father John Fahy (1894–1969), Lia Fáil and Smallholder Radicalism in Modern Irish Society

Brian S. Murphy

'When a man becomes a priest he does not cease to be a citizen, and, being a citizen, he has a right to his own opinions like every other citizen.'

Archbishop Daniel Mannix, 1925

In 1957, Fr John Fahy's newly-founded radical smallholders' movement, established in the wake of Fianna Fáil's return to power amid the smallholders' precipitate post-war decline, portentuously appropriated an ancient symbol of Irish nationality. This was the ancient inaugural stone called the Lia Fáil at the symbolic site of the overkingship of Ireland on the hill of Tara, county Meath, brought there by the legendary Tuatha Dé Danaan centuries before Christ, and said by the late tenth- and early eleventh-century poet Cuán Ua Lotháin to be the stone 'that roared under the feet of each king that took possession of the throne of Ireland'.[1] But the roots of its appropriation in the 1950s lay in developments in Irish nationalism since the eighteenth century. Scottish and Irish historians since the Middle Ages had keenly contested its authenticity. John of Fordun, Andrew of Wyntoun and particularly Hector Boece, and the early seventeenth-century Irish Jacobite historian, Geoffrey Keating who followed Boece, claimed the fifth century Fergus Mór mac Eirc, first of the Dalraidic kings, moved the Lia Fáil to Scotland for his coronation as king of Scotland from where Edward I took it to London in 1296 and James I and all subsequent monarchs used it for their coronation. But John O'Donovan and George Petrie, two of the great pioneering nineteenth-century Irish antiquarians, convincingly argued in the 1830s that there was no basis to these claims because no Irish sources before the sixteenth century supported them, that Keating followed Boece to support Charles I's

---

1   George Petrie, 'On the history and antiquities of Tara hill', *Transactions of the Royal Irish Academy*, xviii (1839), section 3, p. 159. The Lia Fáil, in Petrie's description, is 'a large obeliscal pillar-stone' made of granular limestone, and stands vertically less than five feet above ground. Its original site was at the Mound of the Hostages, probably lying horizontal, but it was moved to its present site and upright position in the Rath to mark the graves of 1798 rebels killed nearby.

claim to the crown, and that tenth-, eleventh- and twelfth-century Irish writers referred to the Lia Fáil *in situ* centuries after its putative removal.[2] This then was a major discovery of antiquarian scholarship that found its way into the cultural nationalist firmament that was one of the mainsprings leading to the creation of the modern Irish state: the touchstone of the Irish race almost since the dawn of history was the stone at Tara.[3]

To contest Fianna Fáil's claims to still embody the true spirit of Irish nationality after its betrayals of republicans and the increasingly enfeebled, threadbare performance of its post-war administrations, in 1957 Fr John Fahy, a radical Clonfert priest, named his newly-founded radical smallholders' movement Lia Fáil. In the midst of the gloom of the late fifties, Fr Fahy hoped this beacon could point the way to the nation's manifold destiny.[4]

In 1982, Professor Gearóid Ó Tuathaigh called for 'serious attention' to Fr Fahy's 'life and work'.[5] Indeed, Fr Fahy was one of the most radical priests of his

2   John O'Donovan, *Letters containing information relative to the antiquities of the County of Meath* (1836; n.p., 1927), p.97; Petrie, 'History and antiquities of Tara', p. 160. Cf. R.A.S. Macalister, 'Temair Breg: a study of the remains and traditions of Tara', *R.I.A., Procs,* xxxiv c (1917–19), pp 231–399; Geoffrey Keating, *The history of Ireland (c.*1634), vol. 1, trans. David Comyn (London, 1902), pp 100–1 & 206–9; Brendan Bradshaw, 'Geoffrey Keating: apologist of Gaelic Ireland', in Brendan Bradshaw, Andrew Hadfield & Willy Malley (eds), *Representing Ireland: literature and the origins of conflict, 1534–1660* (Cambridge, 1993), pp 166–90, especially pp 170–2. For samples of the debate about its authenticity, see J. O'R[ourke], 'The Lia Fáil, or stone of destiny', *I.E.R.* (September, 1880), pp 441–53; P.J. O'Reilly, 'Notes on the coronation stone at Westminster, and the Lia Fáil at Tara', *Journal of the Royal Society of Antiquaries of Ireland,* pt 1, xxxii (March 1902), pp 77–92. For a more recent contribution, see Tomás Ó Broin, 'Lia Fáil: fact and fiction in the tradition', *Celtica,* 21 (1990), pp 393–401. And for a useful bibliography, see Edel Bhreathnach, *Tara: a select bibliography* (Dublin, 1995), pp 134–7 & *passim.* Macalister's paper read on 28 January 1918 brusquely dismissed the dispute on its authenticity as '... not worth the expense of a drop of printer's ink'. Macalister, 'Temair Breg', p. 251.
3   Consequently, in the early years of the Free State it was used as a symbol of national rebirth by Douglas Hyde when he named a newly-founded UCD Irish journal after the Lia Fáil. *Lia Fáil,* i–iv (1927–32).
4   Although some believed that Fianna Fáil was a cognate of Lia Fáil, in fact the etymology of both is very uncertain. See Donal O'Sullivan *The Irish Free State and its Senate: a study in contemporary politics* (London, 1940), p. 187.
5   Gearóid Ó Tuathaigh, 'The land question, politics and Irish society, 1922–1960', in P.J. Drudy (ed.), *Ireland: land, politics and society, Irish studies* 2 (Cambridge, 1982), p. 189, n. 28. At least five other historical accounts mention Fr Fahy. Brian O'Neill's *The war for the land in Ireland* (London, 1933), p. 111 mentions Fr Fahy's prosecution in 1929; D.R. O'Connor Lysaght's useful Trotskyist *The Republic of Ireland* (Cork, 1970), pp 203–4, associates Lia Fáil's protest with Sinn Féin's populism; Michael McInerney's *Peadar O'Donnell: Irish social rebel* (Dublin, 1974), p. 126 describes Fr Fahy, in connection with his land annuities campaign, as 'as radical a man as ever had been seen in Ireland'; Conor Foley's *Legion of the rearguard: the I.R.A. and the modern Irish state* (London, 1992), p. 74, mentions Fr Fahy's 1928 popular annuities 'catechism' and his 1929 annuities campaign; and Uinseann MacEoin's *The I.R.A. in the twilight years 1923–1948* (Dublin, 1997), pp 865–6 mentions the land annuities campaign and Lia Fáil. Finally, a Lusmagh parochial publication with biographical assessments of its priests contains a delicate portrait: not only did Fr Fahy put Lusmagh 'on the map' for his book *The sacrifice of the Mass* (1957), but for 'his active involvement in all the problems of his parishioners'. Thomas J. Kennedy, 'Lusmagh down the years', in *The Lusmagh herb: portrait of a country parish* (Lusmagh, Co. Offaly, 1982), p. 7.

day and his movement one of the most radical smallholders' movements in the history of the state, and for these reasons his 'life and work' amply repay scholarly attention.

I

Even more conspicuously than most people, Fr John Fahy's birth marked him from the start: he was born to an east Galway smallholder and Land Leaguer from Kilnadeema, near Loughrea, county Galway, in 1894.[6] Not that east Galway's particularly intense post-famine agrarian radical and secret society tradition made this background unusual. But his father's bravado in single-handedly charging and routing a line of mounted R.I.C. men at a proclaimed Land League meeting outside Loughrea was the stuff of legend.[7] Everything Fr Fahy subsequently did drew deeply from these Land League, smallholding, devoutly Catholic ideals.

Fr Fahy's education took place first at a local national school, and then at the diocesan seminary, St Joseph's, the Pines, Ballinasloe.[8] In September 1911, he entered the national seminary, St Patrick's College, Maynooth, for eight cloistered years; after 1916 most students defiantly supported Sinn Féin.[9] On 28 September 1919, he was ordained at Loughrea Cathedral by Bishop Thomas O'Doherty of Clonfert.[10] Like many other newly ordained priests whose dioceses were full, his first appointment was on loan, and he went to Dunkeld, Scotland, serving at St Joseph's, Dundee, and St Andrew's Cathedral, Dundee, in 1919–21 at the height of the Anglo-Irish war.[11] His lifelong radicalism began in earnest there: he was chaplain of the 4th Battalion of the Scottish Brigade of the I.R.A.; in November 1920 he returned to Loughrea to attend the funeral of Fr Michael Griffin, killed by the Black and Tans; his attendance at speeches by

6 J. Bernard Canning, *Irish-born secular priests in Scotland, 1829–1979* (n.p., 1979), p. 96.
7 Fr Kevin Egan interview, 9 August 1995, St Brigid's, Portumna, Co. Galway. The *East Galway Democrat* also claimed that his uncle was Fr John Bowes of Woodford evictions fame during the Plan of Campaign. *East Galway Democrat*, 27 Feb. 1937. In 1927, Fr Bowes colourfully opposed the Shannon hydroelectric scheme because 'it would turn one-eight of what used to be Ireland by law as well as creation, that is one-sixth of what is known as the Free State, over four thousand square miles – the very heart of the country – into a Dutch marsh and leave the inhabitants of that vast territory at the mercy of machinery and embankments'. Ibid., 28 May 1927. Later, Fr Fahy commended Fr Bowes's actions during the Woodford evictions. 'Lessons of the Lusmagh operation', *Lia Fáil*, no. 8, n.d., p. 1.
8 *Connacht Tribune*, 25 July 1969.
9 P.J. Corish, *Maynooth College, 1795–1995* (Dublin, 1995), pp 302–4. John Fahy matriculated on 12 September 1911, spending two years in the third year class, passing into theology in 1914–15, and becoming a subdeacon in his final year. Personal communication, Revd Professor P.J. Corish to the author, 10 November 1995.
10 *Irish Catholic Directory*, 1920, p. 479.
11 Canning, *Irish-born secular priests in Scotland*, p. 96. Cf. Stephen Coyle letter, *Saoirse* (journal of Republican Sinn Féin), January, 1993, p. 8.

Dundee's leading communist, Robert Stewart, mirrored the post-war leftward drift of the Dundee Irish; and he was said to have been too active in the Scottish Nationalists.[12] However, later in 1921 he left Scotland to take up his first Clonfert appointment at Eyrecourt, county Galway, in 1921–2, this was followed by Closetoken, 1923–5, during which he heckled Patrick Hogan, Free State minister for agriculture and a Galway T.D., at a pro-treaty election meeting in Loughrea in August 1923, and by Bullaun, New Inn, in 1926, where he first came to national attention.[13]

Two years later in 1928, his support for local ratepayers objections to an ex-R.I.C. man and another man's application to Galway County Council's Board of Health to erect a pump at Bullaun was pithily expressed by writing that as far as he knew nobody either wanted the pump or needed it, except 'a teacher and an ex-peeler'.[14] In these circumstances, the board discreetly abandoned the project.

If this pithy objection to an ex-R.I.C. man contained more than a hint of chauvinism, then Fr Fahy's conspicuous friendship with a leading unionist locally meant he was nothing so straightforward. Major Jackson and he regularly hunted together and were firm friends. But much mischievous gossip was made of the magnetic attraction of these opposites. The I.R.A.'s suspicions led to an

12 *Connacht Telegraph*, 25 July 1969; personal communication, Mrs Cathleen Knowles to the author, 14 Mar. 1996; personal communication, Stephen Coyle to the author, 9 May 1996; John Cooney in *Irish Times*, 8 Apr. 1989; Robert Stewart, *Breaking the fetters* (London, 1967), pp 152–3. In 1920, on behalf of the Dundee Sinn Féin club Fr Fahy and another priest, Fr Durand, condemned the British government's refusal to permit Archbishop Mannix to land in Ireland, and later in 1920 Fr Fahy challenged Fr Bernard Vaughan, after he had said that Terence MacSwiney should be refused the sacraments because he was deliberately on hunger strike, to a public debate about the morality of this hunger strike. ('I hold that the action of the Lord Mayor is not only moral, but heroically moral.') *Glasgow Observer*, 21 Aug. 1920; ibid., 11 Sept. 1920. The *Glasgow Observer* of 18 June 1921 reported that Fr Fahy had been recalled to Ireland. (I am grateful to Mr. Stephen Coyle of Glasgow for these three references.) Although he argues that Dundee Sinn Féin's leadership was 'indistinct and undistinguished', William M. Walker nevertheless says Fr Fahy was a 'possible exception': 'Dundee's disenchantment with Churchill', *Scottish Historical Review*, vol.49, no. 147, p. 98 & n. 4. Canning, *Irish-born secular priests in Scotland*, p. 96, quotes a *Scottish Catholic Observer* obituary as saying Fr Fahy '... was prominent in the ranks of the Scottish Nationalists'. Having arrived too late for the removal of Fr Griffin, he kept an all night vigil in Loughrea cathedral. Fr Kevin Egan interview, 9 August 1995. The Galway R.I.C. complained that the county's priests had been let off the bishop's leash. Tom Garvin, *Nationalist revolutionaries in Ireland, 1858–1928* (Oxford, 1987), p. 116. In 1933, Fr Fahy was among those present at the inauguration of a memorial church to Fr Griffin at Gurteen, county Galway. *East Galway Democrat*, 23 July 1933.

13 *Irish Catholic Directory*, 1922, p. 389; ibid., 1923, p. 401; ibid., 1924, p. 405; ibid., 1925, p. 408; *Connacht Tribune*, 25 August 1923. Fr Fahy shouted out, after pro-treatyites had earlier made aspersions about the republican candidate Frank Fahy, that he '... did not sell his country, neither did Terence MacSwiney nor Mary MacSwiney'. Professor Michael Tierney retorted by asking if Fr Fahy was '... prepared to accept responsibility for all the banks and post offices that had been plundered during the last twelve months, and for the deeds committed during that period by the party he came there to represent'. I am grateful to Dr Patrick Murray for drawing my attention to this incident.

14 *East Galway Democrat*, 1 September 1928.

internal investigation of Fr Fahy – thus his links continued since his Scottish I.R.A. activities during the Anglo-Irish war. On 25 October 1928, when Major Jackson called at Fr Fahy's house a prominent local I.R.A. man, J.J. Leonard, told him that he had ascertained that the Major had been in the Auxiliaries during the Anglo-Irish war, and he should have handed him over to I.R.A. head-quarters in Dublin.[15] Two days after, Fr Fahy wrote to Major Jackson saying that besides explaining his connection with the Major to the I.R.A. he had neither 'concern nor influence in the matter' but wished him luck.

No pure-hearted bigot could simultaneously have hated the 'ex-peeler' and befriended the Major. Nothing highlights so well Fr Fahy's triumphantly free clerical spirit than this – combining Major Jackson's friendship with I.R.A. links in defiance of republican no less than local sensibilities.

II

In the event, this episode proved but a prelude to greater things. In 1929, Fr Fahy teamed up with Peadar O'Donnell to start a land annuities agitation around Bullaun which ended with his conviction for seizing impounded cattle from a bailiff. Peadar O'Donnell's subsequent assessment of Fr Fahy might stand as an epithet for this short-lived episode: a 'great gift of leadership' together with 'occasional incoherence'.[16]

Ever since the Anglo-Irish war many east Galway smallholders had defaulted on the land annuities though there was no organised campaign; and where simi-lar conditions existed in the Rosses, county Donegal, Peadar O'Donnell started a land annuities campaign in 1925–6.[17] Yet in the aftermath of the 1923 land act the Cumann na nGaedheal government with its pro-strong farmer policies could assume that only a law and order problem remained; Patrick Hogan, dynamic Free State minister for agriculture and a Galway T.D., confidently expected in 1924 'to see the land question solved in two years with, perhaps, negligible ex-ceptions'.[18] By the time he was recruited by Fr Fahy to join the Bullaun cam-

---

15 'Rev. Father Fahy, C.C., Bullaun, Loughrea', in Cabinet Memo circulated by Minister for Justice: proceedings against Father Fahy, Bullaun, county Galway, under enforcement of Court Orders Act, 1926, 26 March 1929, S 5837, N.A., D.F.A., Secretary's office files, S 4(a). This memo described Major Jackson as 'an eccentric who says he came to Craughwell, county Galway, for the hunting season ...'

16 Peadar O'Donnell, *There will be another day* (Dublin, 1963), p. 94. O'Donnell said Fr Fahy also wrote a play on the land war that was performed at Loughrea. In 1928, under a pseudonym Fr Fahy published a popular annuities catechism. 'Hy Many', 'No tribute catechism: points for the peasant farmer', *An Phoblacht*, 11 Feb. 1928.

17 O'Donnell, *Another day*, p. 94; Henry Patterson, *The politics of illusion: republicanism and socialism in modern Ireland* (London, 1989) pp 30–43.

18 *East Galway Democrat*, 2 Feb. 1924; for a penetrating analysis, see J.J. Lee, *Ireland 1912–1985: politics and society* (Cambridge, 1989) pp 112–17. See also Joan M. Cullen, 'Patrick J. Hogan, T.D., Minister for Agriculture, 1922–1932' (Ph.D., Dublin City University, 1993), *passim*.

paign, Peadar O'Donnell's own campaign in the Rosses had collapsed, and as
editor of *An Phoblacht* he was urging the I.R.A. to become involved in social
questions.[19] Fr Fahy's intention evidently was to open a second front of the
flagging campaign in the minister's own constituency. Not only was his initiative in starting the Bullaun campaign himself remarkable for a priest. So too
was his open alliance with Peadar O'Donnell, one of the leading anti-clericals of
the day. Other allies were locals including Martin Fahy, Mick Silver, John Joe
Kennedy, and Michael Sherry while veterans of the land war were also involved,
among them Tom Kenny, Pat Gannon and Eamonn Gannon.[20] Signs of tacit
I.R.A. support were apparent too. The local I.R.A. Officer Commanding was
among the committee members; significantly, Peadar O'Donnell, a member of
the Army Executive, '... never had any anxiety that he [ie. the Officer Com-
manding] would involve his local unit in any embarrassing way; they would act
as neighbours'.[21]

Seizing the opportunity of his parish priest's request to make an appeal for
funds to build a new curate's house, Fr Fahy launched his campaign from the
altar at Sunday Mass, a scene vividly recalled by Peadar O'Donnell:

> Fr John began his address quietly. He was sorry to have to ask people for
> money and indeed he might not have agreed to do it only that it had been
> made clear to him the people had money to spare ... so if they had money to
> give away would it not be a better use to make of it to build a house for him
> than to send it to Britain by way of land annuities ... The startled parish
> priest popped out of the sacristy door, but Father John had no eyes for him.
> He was too busy advising his people to make two halves of the land annuity,
> take one half of it with them into the village and buy the makings of a cel-
> ebration, and give the other half to him. The congregation, watching the
> parish priest in a dither, was in a mood to cheer by the time Father John
> finished his sermon.[22]

The campaign then came to a head in two confrontations with the authorities.
First, on the night of 18 February 1929 Fr Fahy and others allegedly retrieved

---

19 Uinseann MacEoin speculates that Fr Fahy's agitation could have been linked to Peadar O'Donnell's
    Irish Working Farmers' organisation. Mac Eoin, *I.R.A. in twilight years*, p. 865. Cf. report of Work-
    ing Farmers Galway meeting, *Connacht Tribune*, 29 Mar. 1930; *An Phoblacht*, 5 Apr. 1930.
20 O'Donnell, *Another day*, p. 94.
21 Ibid., p. 95. O'Donnell's memoir notes that the campaign would have been 'overrun' but for the
    I.R.A. Ibid., introduction, n.p.
22 Ibid., p. 96. Fr Fahy's reading of Mary MacSwiney's new January 1929 republican constitution
    from the altar suggests a certain amount of congruence between these redoubtable two; a cabinet
    memo claimed he also urged the congregation to join the I.R.A. To each member of the Executive
    Council, 26 Mar. 1929, U.C.D.A., *Fitzgerald papers*, P80/852(1) & N.A., S 5837; Cabinet memo
    circulated by Minister for Justice: proceedings against Father Fahy, Bullaun, county Galway, under
    enforcement of Court Orders Act, 1926, 26 March 1929, N.A., D.F.A., Secretary's Office Files, S 4(a).

seized cattle from the pound at Galway.[23] Second, and more importantly, on 25 February a bailiff from Loughrea seized two cattle on the farm of Miss Bridget Nevin of Ballymurray, Loughrea, in lieu of unpaid annuities.[24] When the bailiff was driving the cattle towards Loughrea Fr Fahy and a crowd of fifteen to twenty men blocked his path at Bullaun. Fr Fahy urged the crowd to act but when no one made a move he seized a whip or stick from one of them and drove the cattle back. Only after he called them 'a crowd of cowards' did the men join in rescuing the cattle. Fr Fahy then threatened the bailiff not to follow the cattle otherwise 'something might happen to him'. As a result, on 11 March Fr Fahy was served with a summons to appear in court on 19 March, but declared he would not attend because he was a republican, and the case was adjourned until 2 April.

Before the case came to court, on 21 March, Bishop John Dignan of Clonfert, who had decisively nailed his colours to the republican mast at his consecration in 1924, attempted to resolve it by asking the Garda officer in charge, Superintendent Doyle of Loughrea, '... to write to his authorities to ascertain whether if Fr Fahy were to apologise publicly for his actions, either through the public press or in some other manner, the matter could be allowed to rest'.[25] He even offered 'to assist in having any reasonable demands of the government carried into effect insofar as the criminal aspect of the case is concerned'.

The Executive Council was prepared to settle the case, but not to compromise the rule of law and it was not afraid of the case coming before the public. It agreed to drop the case if Fr Fahy would apologise to the court for his contempt, pay the outstanding decree of £7.14s.10d., and also apologise from the altar. Henry O'Friel, secretary of the Department of Justice, then travelled to meet Bishop Dignan at Loughrea to secure agreement to these conditions. But afterwards he reported that there could be no agreement because '... owing to Father Fahy's eccentricity and intractability the bishop was not in a position to give the necessary assurance ...'[26] Bishop Dignan could only offer in these circumstances that if the government would drop the proceedings then 'he would act as bishop' – but he would not explain what that meant.

---

23   To each member of the Executive Council, 26 March 1929, U.C.D.A., *Fitzgerald papers*, P80/852(1) & N.A. S 5837.

24   Cabinet memo circulated by Minister for Justice: proceedings against Father Fahy, Bullaun, Co. Galway, under enforcement of Court Orders Act, 1926, 26 March 1929, N.A., D.F.A., Secretary's office files, S 4(a).

25   Ibid. Dignan was one of two Ballinasloe curates who supported Sinn Féin after 1916, he only escaped being murdered by the Black and Tans due to a R.I.C. tipoff, and made the remarkable declaration at his 1924 consecration that the republicans would be '... returned to power in a very short time' when this prospect was anything but inevitable. Patrick K. Egan, *The parish of Ballinasloe: its history from earliest times to the present day* (Dublin & London, 1960), p. 293; information from Revd Fr Kevin Egan, 9 Aug. 1995; *East Galway Democrat*, 7 Jun. 1924.

26   Einrí O'Friel to Minister [of Justice], 9 April 1929, N.A., D.F.A., Secretary's Office, S 4(a).

Moreover, Bishop Dignan frankly admitted with some weariness and exasperation that there was little he could do with such a free-spirited curate:

He admitted that Father Fahy was unlikely to attend or recognise the court, that it was unlikely he could be induced to apologise publicly or pay the amount of the seizure except possibly through ecclesiastical action of the bishop. The bishop in fact holds a written undertaking from Fr Fahy duly witnessed by two priests in which he said that in obedience to the bishop he would publicly apologise for having broken the law of the land by rescuing etc. etc. The bishop however seemed to be a bit uneasy whether he could enforce this undertaking and he certainly left no doubt in my mind that the undertaking was valueless as far as the court proceedings were concerned.[27]

Ruefully, Bishop Dignan added that if Fr Fahy ever got into prison he would probably go on hunger strike, making matters much worse.

If it wanted to deter Fr Fahy from making a repetition of this kind of incident over the land annuities, the Executive Council had no option in these circumstances but to let the prosecution proceed.[28] Fr Fahy was duly arrested at home on 13 April, creating a *cause célèbre* locally, and charged in court with obstructing the bailiff at Bullaun and unlawfully rescuing two cattle.[29] He refused on legitimist grounds to recognise the court, proudly admitted rescuing the cattle, and was returned for trial on 3 June but because he refused to accept bail was remanded to Galway jail.

Believing it would raise important church–state issues, Fr Fahy exulted in his arrest. Chief among these issues was that it would force the Free State government to deny the medieval *privilegium fori* prohibiting civil prosecution of a priest without ecclesiastical approval and which was still officially in the 1917 code of canon law. This action would definitively expose the Free State as a Protestant state under England's tutelage rather than the Catholic state it claimed to be. Hence he gleefully confided to the redoubtable legitimist Mary MacSwiney that his arrest had given the bishops 'a splendid opportunity to broach the question'.[30] Yet this claim cannot simply be dismissed as a characteristic exuberance.

27 Ibid. Bishop Dignan's attitude to the diocese's endemic land agitation was foreshadowed by his censure of it in May 1926. *East Galway Democrat*, 8 May 1926.
28 Fr Fahy claimed to know that the Executive Council voted 4 to 2 in favour of prosecution. Because the cabinet minutes are so tight-lipped, this claim can neither be confirmed nor denied. 'Copy of letter written by Father Fahy, to some person unknown' [ie. Mary MacSwiney], 11 May 1929, U.C.D.A., *Blythe papers*, P24/164(6); N.A., Cabinet Minutes, G 2/7, March–April, 1929.
29 P. Doyle, Superintendent, Loughrea, 16 April 1929, U.C.D.A., *Fitzgerald papers*, P80/852(2); *The Nation*, 27 April 1929, U.C.D.A., *O'Malley papers*, P17b/224. See for example protests by West Galway G.A.A. Later, Galway County Council Finance Committee's decision not to take part in a Catholic Emancipation centenary procession in protest earned a rebuke from Bishop Dignan for making it more difficult for Fr Fahy to recant. *East Galway Democrat*, 27 April & 25 May 1929.
30 'Copy of letter written by Father Fahy, to some person unknown' [ie. Mary MacSwiney], 11 May

For Bishop Dignan too raised the *privilegium fori* with Henry O'Friel when arguing that the government should not have acted against his errant cleric, showing that Fr Fahy actually did touch on a central unresolved issue in church-state relations in the Free State – whether or not the state was Catholic in law. Dignan's pregnant post-Lateran Treaties suggestion of a church-state concordat and O'Friel's nimble retort that the *privilegium fori* had not been legal under the British *régime* before 1921 reflected the unresolved tensions between the bishops' gimlet-eyed desire to further extend their secular authority and the Free State's fear of ceding any more precious autonomy, particularly threatening the state's security.[31]

However, these freebooting activities on Fr Fahy's part were not calculated to endear him to his ecclesiastical superiors. Before his arrest, his superiors met him twice, but Fr Fahy defended his actions as acts of 'justice and charity', denied the legitimacy of the conquest ('Unless the Church teaches *ex cathedra* that Ireland belonged and belongs to England, I will never accept it'), and the right of the Free State to legislate.[32] But such defiance was no match against the exalted authority of his bishop. As Bishop Dignan already informed Henry O'Friel, he had used his authority to extract a written undertaking from Fr Fahy to publicly apologise for his actions. Fr Fahy's attempt to decide the place, time or manner of this apology suggests that he signed only on threat of obedience. But Fr Michael Browne's friendly advice to him as professor of canon law at Maynooth was that he must nevertheless adhere to its terms, obey his bishop, and honour his word.[33] However much he strained the episcopal leash, ultimately he came to heel.

At the trial, Fr Fahy, seated at his solicitor's table, pleaded guilty, and was sentenced to six weeks imprisonment dating from his arrest and released. His solicitor apologised to the court on his behalf as Bishop Dignan had commanded.[34]

1929, U.C.D.A., *Blythe papers*, P24/164(7). In 1912, the *privilegium fori* briefly became an issue in the debate about home rule. Paul Bew, *Ideology and the Irish question: Ulster unionism and Irish nationalism 1912–1916* (Oxford, 1994), p. 33.

31 Einrí O'Friel to Minister [of Justice], 9 April 1929, N.A., D.F.A., secretary's office, S 4(a). In 1931, Archbishop Thomas Gilmartin of Tuam also suggested a concordat during the Dunbar-Harrison case to avoid such church-state conflicts in future. Dermot Keogh, *The Vatican, the Bishops and Irish politics 1919–39* (Cambridge, 1986), pp 171–2. Bishop Dignan's similar proposal two years earlier means that the suggestion that 'a concordat was not considered either necessary or relevant for Ireland' might merit further research. See Dermot Keogh, 'The role of the Catholic Church in the Republic of Ireland, 1922–1995,' in Forum for Peace and Reconciliation (ed.), *Building trust in Ireland: studies commissioned by the forum for peace and reconciliation* (Belfast, 1996), p. 115.

32 'Copy of letter written by Father Fahy, to some person unknown' [ie. Mary MacSwiney], 11 May 1929, U.C.D.A., *Blythe papers*, P24/164(6). 'Patriot priest imprisoned', May 1929, issued by Comhairle na Poblacht, 6 Gardiner's Row, Dublin. N.L.I., ILB 300 p. 11, item 74.

33 M.J. Browne to John [Fahy], 28 May 1929, N.A., D.F.A., Secretary's Office, S 4(a).

34 *East Galway Democrat*, 8 June 1929; Supt. [J. Doyle, Loughrea], 3 June 1929, *Fitzgerald papers*, U.C.D.A., P80/852(6). Legitimists such as Mary MacSwiney were delighted by Fr Fahy's defiant non-recognition of the court and resistance to episcopal pressure in order to maintain the republic. Máire Níc Suibne to An tAthair [Fahy], 4 June [1929], U.C.D.A., *MacSwiney papers*, P48a/364(90).

Thus ended the second phase of the land annuities campaign.[35]

After some time, Bishop Dignan appointed Fr Fahy as curate to Closetoken, county Galway, after solemnly binding him not to speak of politics when two or more people were present.[36] Even so, Fr Fahy's spirit was undimmed: he set up house with none other than Peadar O'Donnell.[37]

Two years later, Fr Fahy's antipathy to the Free State flared again by combining with the I.R.A. to overthrow the state, testing his previous undertaking to the limits. At Easter 1931, he tried to recruit an Athenry man into the I.R.A.[38] In May, he tried to buy machine guns from an army reservist in Loughrea.[39] In September, he told a clandestine parade of the Loughrea I.R.A. company that 'he was out for overthrowing any government that would be established in Ireland except the Irish Republican Government'.[40] In October, the Gardaí reported that he read the bishops' coruscating 'red scare' pastoral at Sunday Mass, but read it without comment.[41]

The Gardaí believed he was one of the most active I.R.A. leaders in east Galway, associating with the most prominent I.R.A. members, 'constantly going around on a motor cycle with civilian cap and overcoat apparently organising for the 'I.R.A.' and other illegal movements', associating with men allegedly committing serious crimes, even with Craughwell's Tom Kenny, the Galway delegate to the communist Saor Éire – so that his obedience must been heroic to read the 'red scare' pastoral from the altar! Even so, the Gardaí felt powerless to act against a man of the cloth, believing that Bishop Dignan's republicanism inclined him to turn a blind eye, and that Fr Fahy's heroic incorrigibility since his conviction two years previously meant the game was hardly worth the candle. In the end, Bishop Dignan, after this emphatic transgression of his previous admonition to refrain from politics, came to the rescue again by moving Fr Fahy from Clostoken to Ballinakill, county Galway.[42]

What was to prove a more radical change in unexpected ways for Fr Fahy as much as republicans generally was Fianna Fáil's narrow victory in the 1932 election, won in part on the backs of the western smallholders. The republicans unofficial alliance with Fianna Fáil during that election proved resilient when

35 Shortly afterwards, O'Donnell attempted to broker a settlement to the Donegal agitation with Paddy Hogan. In Co. Galway, non-payment continued for many years afterwards. P. Hogan, Minister for Agriculture, to Fitzgerald-Kenny, Minister for Justice, 25 June 1929, N.A., S 8336; O'Donnell, *There will be another day*, pp 69–72; *Irish Times*, 11 February 1935, in N.A., Department of Justice, E.7/35.
36 O'Donnell, *There will be another day*, p. 100.
37 Ibid.
38 'Extract from statement made by [?], Athenry', N.A., D.F.A., Secretary's Office Files, S 4(a).
39 'Statement of [?], Loughrea, Co. Galway, 19 October 1931, ibid.
40 'Extract from Statement made by one [?] Loughrea, [?], county Galway. n.d. [1931?], ibid.
41 [?] to Commissioner C.S., 20 October 1931, ibid.
42 Just as at Bullaun, hunting was among his passions at Ballinakill. Fr Kevin Egan interview, 9 August 1995.

de Valera sought his own majority after twelve months of minority, Labour-backed administration so that when Fr Fahy appeared with de Valera on a Fianna Fáil platform at Portumna, county Galway, during the January 1933 election campaign he was in all probability still in the first flushes of the republicans infatuation with the party.[43] The other mainstays of his alliance besides horror of Cumann na nGaedheal undoubtedly were the same forces of agrarian radicalism and left-leaning, physical force republicanism of his land annuities and 'red scare' activities. But the years of unbroken Fianna Fáil rule that followed in the thirties, especially 'coercion' of the I.R.A. in 1936, recognition of the king in the External Relations Act (1936), and waning of land redistribution by the war, were to severely test republican expectations. Indeed, by the forties radical republicans of Fr Fahy's sort often were so irrevocably alienated from the party that if not already in the I.R.A. they were driven into rebellion with the new agrarian and republican parties.

III

Having acted so radically during the later 1920s culminating in his I.R.A. activities during the 'red scare', Fr Fahy's retirement from politics thereafter with the exception of his Fianna Fáil platform appearance abruptly brought this cycle to a close. Twelve years of penitential-like conformity subsequently were rewarded by Bishop Dignan's appointment of him as parish priest of Lusmagh, a small parish near Banagher, county Offaly, in 1945, though it was tempered by the knowledge that it came later than he might have expected.[44] Yet despite this recognition his restless, passionate, burning exuberance of old proved incapable of dousing or sublimation; his respect for episcopal authority remained intact too. Try as he might to write generally within the ambits of conventional devotional works one of three books written around at this time proved heterodox. This was an unpublished, and now lost, utopian novel that was refused an *imprimatur*. The two other books, however, were more in step with his new-found conformity, though only one was published – an unpublished devotional typescript, 'The framework of what we believe' (1956), and an orthodox devotional work, *The sacrifice of the Mass: the greatest thing on earth*, published in 1957 (by

---

43 *Irish Press*, 16 January 1933. I am indebted, once again, to Dr Patrick Murray for drawing my attention to this reference. Later in 1933, Father Porter, P.P. of Ballinakill, presided at a protest meeting addressed by Paddy Hogan and two other pro-treaty T.D.s after shots were fired into the house of Henry Goonan, secretary of the local Cumann na nGaedheal branch, and Fr Fahy, although a curate of the parish, conspicuously did not attend. *East Galway Democrat*, 4 Nov. 1933.
44 Lusmagh was also the birthplace of one of the 'Manchester martyrs', Michael Larkin. Valentine Trodd, *Banagher on the Shannon: a historical guide to the town* (n.p., 1985), pp 34–6.

then the cold war communist suppression of religion in Eastern Europe had turned his earlier enthusiasm for the left into contempt).[45]

Twelve years after his arrival at Lusmagh, and twenty-six years after his last known radical activities, Fr Fahy started the second phase of his radical career in 1957 with the foundation of Lia Fáil, his radical smallholders' movement.[46] Why these two phases were separated by such a long hiatus is not documented, but the most probable explanation is that it was due to a decisive intervention by Bishop Dignan after the 'red scare' episode when he may have successfully bound Fr Fahy with an oath to him personally to abjure such radical politics in future. This oath would explain why Fr Fahy's radical career seemingly remained in abeyance right throughout the considerable tensions of the next two and a half decades, particularly during the 1930s, only to resume after Bishop Dignan's death in 1953. It also would help explain why anger and frustration at the small-holders' decline particularly since the war and Fianna Fáil's seeming abandon-ment of the agrarian radical programme were Lia Fáil's *leitmotif* – grievances that *à la* the civil war de Valera Fr Fahy had been compelled to watch from behind a wall of glass.

This pent-up anger and frustration of the thirties and forties all came to a head with the foundation of his own radical smallholders' movement. On 1 November 1957, Lia Fáil was founded at a parish meeting in Lusmagh about emigration with Fr Fahy presiding, and a provisional committee appointed, and seven founding aims agreed.[47] Lia Fáil's essential smallholder radical purposes were proclaimed in its aims:

> 1. To secure that all the sources of wealth in Ireland be preserved for the Irish people. 2. To make it illegal for any alien to purchase land, property or any source of wealth in Ireland. 3. To have annulled forthwith all sales of land, property and sources of wealth to aliens, contracted since the estab-lishment of the Irish Republic. 4. To have the 1924 Land Act annulled. This Land Act was ordered by Lord Midleton to secure the British garrison in

45 Fr John Fahy, 'The framework of what we believe', 1956, typescript in possession of Fr Kevin Egan; *idem, The sacrifice of the Mass: the greatest thing on earth* (Dublin, 1957); although the *nihili obstat* and *imprimatur* were granted on 3 October 1955, the book was published in January 1957. *Idem, Sacrifice of the Mass*, p. 42.

46 Before the foundation of Lia Fáil, Fr Fahy's activities included writing to the Banagher and Lusmagh Fianna Fáil cumann in support of Lusmagh members' demands for a new bridge over the Little Brosna in the parish, involvement in the Shannon Tourist Development Association, wholehearted support of electrification of the area in 1948, and support for the retention of Shannonbridge peat-fired electricity generating station in 1957 because it was based on native fuel. *Offaly Chronicle*, 24 Jan, 1946, 31 Jan, 1946, 1 June 1948 & 25 Dec, 1957.

47 'John Ireland', 'Birth of *Lia Fáil* ', *Lia Fáil*, no. 1, Aug. 1958, p. 1. For Lia Fáil see also my 'The land for the people, the road for the bullock': Lia Fáil, peasant protest and populism in Ireland, 1957–60', in Timothy P. O'Neill & William Nolan (eds), *Offaly: history and society* (Dublin: Geography publications, forthcoming).

the lands they had plundered from the Irish people. 5. To divide the land of Ireland among the young men of Ireland. 6. To limit private ownership of land to one hundred acres as long as young men have to emigrate from the countryside. 7. To re-instate the dispossessed Irish people on the good soil of Ireland from which their forefathers were driven by the robber-invaders, who are in possession still of the good land of Ireland.[48]

The concentration of these aims chiefly on the compulsory acquisition and banning of aliens suggested that the land problem was mainly a matter of cleansing the nation of these blow-ins. But foreigners were not the only ones going to be dispossessed. Nor indeed were speculators, 'landgrabbers' and Protestants ('robber-invaders'). The limitation of holdings to a 100 acres meant large Catholic nationalist farmers were going to make substantial involuntary contributions too. Smallholders' sons would be the chief beneficiaries of this redistribution, helping to stem emigration. Yet the programme's potentially pernicious effects were far-reaching. Confiscations of the large Catholic nationalist farmers could only be done by violently pitting smallholders against large farmers, potentially precipitating the kind of revolutionary upheaval of the Bulgarian and Lithuanian land reforms of the 1920s.[49]

To achieve its ambitious purposes Lia Fáil realised from the outset that a national organisation was necessary so one of its first tasks was to set about galvanising smallholders' throughout the country. Like-minded land clubs around the country were quickly recruited, a common policy was agreed, a provisional national executive was formed, and Lia Fáil became the umbrella organisation of the new movement.[50] Eleven counties were represented in the new organisation with groups such as the Kildare Land Division League, the National Land Division League in Limerick, Clare, Tipperary, and Mayo, the Bennekerry Land Division Club in Carlow, and the Land for the People League in Westmeath. Eleven thousand members were claimed, mostly '... young farmers, a few priests, office workers, tradesmen, teachers and shop workers ...', and

---

48 'John Ireland', 'Birth of Lia Fáil', *Lia Fáil*, No. 1, August 1958, p. 1.

49 See George D. Jackson, Jr, 'Peasant movements in Eastern Europe', in Henry A. Landsberger, *Rural protest: peasant movements and social change* (London, 1974), pp 259–315; 'The land reform of Fr Krupavicius', *Saoirse*, March 1997, p. 7.

50 Lia Fáil's five-fold structure comprised (1) the parish committee; (2) the district (electoral) committee; (3) the county committee; (4) the provincial committee; (5) the national executive council. Its inaugural meeting appointed a provisional committee that included: President, Fr John Fahy; secretary, Francis J. Kelly, Newtown; treasurer, Frank Larkin, Stream; committee members: Patrick Kelly, Tim Bennett, Denis Kelly, Martin Sullivan, Paddy Groomes, Kieran Donegan. William Killeen was named as a committee member in a Lia Fáil leaflet. 'Building an army', *Lia Fáil*, September, 1958, p. 5; 'Ireland for the Irish', copy in possession of Fr Kevin Egan. In addition, Lia Fáil's Sunday night card drive held in Lusmagh in March 1958 suggests not only that its fundraising was already under way, but that its organisation was being built up, centred on Lusmagh. *Offaly Chronicle*, 12 Mar. 1958.

among the closest clerical allies were Fr Thomas Burbage of Kildare and Leighlin, Fr Peadar MacSuibhne also of Kildare and Leighlin, and Fr Philip McGahey of Westmeath.[51]

The next major initiative was the launch of its splenetic journal *Lia Fáil* in August 1958 – grandiloquently describing itself as the 'Organ of the land and industrial army of Ireland (Under the Patronage of Our Lady of Victories)' – and which published ten issues up to early 1960. Fr Fahy wrote it almost single-handedly, others made occasional contributions, particularly, in the last two issues, W.H. Milner, a Portarlington farmer and prominent midlands monetary reformer.[52] The Department of Lands estimated its circulation at between three and four thousand, but it confidently decided when Lia Fáil started, although it would rue the day, to ignore its propaganda in a vain paternalistic expectation that it would wither away.[53]

But Lia Fáil's radical smallholders' were not prepared to meekly bow before the inevitability of fate as the department so hopefully assumed, fate largely consigning them to exile in England. Their grievances essentially were the grievances of the smallholder class since independence. Chief among these was the sheer scale and pace of their decline since then which belied the expected benefits of self-government, above all self-preservation.

The balance between small and large holdings decisively shifted against small holdings over the first four decades of independence. Total holdings fell 14 per cent from 336,000 to 290,000 between 1931 and 1960. Larger holdings of 50–99 acres increased 8 per cent from 50,000 to 54,000, and of 100–199 acres rose 9.5 per cent from 21,000 to 23,000. But holdings less than 30 acres fell 26 per cent from 194,000 to 144,000.[54] By 1961, holdings under 30 acres had fallen from 58 per cent to 49 per cent of total holdings, from 43 per cent to 31.1 per cent of males employed in agriculture, and from 22.5 per cent to 17.4 per cent of total acreage of crops and pasture.[55] By contrast, holdings over 100 acres increased

---

51 'Offaly shows the way', *Lia Fáil*, August 1958, p. 4. In addition to these three clerical allies, Fr Fahy commended two other midlands priests, Fr O'Connor and Fr Dempsey. 'Hypocrisy in excelsis', ibid., no. 9, n.d., p. 4. For examples of Burbage's anti-semitism, see Garvin, *Nationalist revolutionaries*, pp 76–7.

52 Department of Lands, 'Land agitation: memorandum for the government', 5 May 1959, p.2, N.A., S 6490/C/94. For examples of Milner's antecedents in monetary reform, see W.H. Milner, a member of Seamus Lennon's Irish Monetary Reform Association, in *Offaly Chronicle*, 25 Dec. 1947 & 15 Jan. 1948. The National Library and the National Archives's holdings can be combined to provide a full set of Lia Fáil: the National Library's set includes numbers 1,2,4,5,6,7,8, & 9, and the National Archives, Department of Justice, S 29/58 A, includes 3 & 10. The *Longford News* may have printed Lia Fáil in support of its objectives. *Longford News*, 9 May 1959, N.A., S 6490C/2/94; see also its supportive article, 'Offaly shows the way', *Longford News*, reprinted in *Lia Fáil*, August, 1958, p. 4.

53 Department of Lands, 'Land agitation: memorandum for the government', 5 May 1959, p. 2, N.A., S 6490/C/94.

54 James Meenan, *The Irish economy since 1922* (Liverpool, 1970), p. 109.

55 Raymond D. Crotty, *Irish agricultural production: its volume and structure* (Cork, 1966), p. 183.

from 8.7 per cent to 10.3 per cent of all holdings, from 17.3 per cent to 22 per cent of all males employed in agriculture, and 34.6 per cent to 36.2 per cent of total acreage of crops and pasture. The watershed in these changes was the war, the decline of male farmers more than doubling from 6 per cent from 1926–46 to 13 per cent afterwards in 1946–66.[56] Moreover, on larger holdings male farmers actually increased by 10 per cent after the war, but on small holdings they fell almost twice as fast, holdings less than 30 acres falling 18 per cent in 1926–46 compared with 35 per cent in 1946–66. Farmers' sons also rapidly declined in the post-war period, falling by 59 per cent between 1946 and 1961 compared with 14 per cent between 1926 and 1946.[57] On farms between 30 to 50 acres, between 1926 and 1946 the number of sons aged 25 to 34 years increased by 8 per cent, but between 1946 and 1966 their numbers declined by 67 per cent – a total change of 75 percentage points. And on holdings less than 30 acres between 1926 and 1946 farmers' sons aged 25 to 34 on fell by 19 per cent, but between 1946 and 1966 they fell drastically by 81 per cent.[58] Nothing could have been further from smallholders' expectations of self-government than that the first four decades of independence should be marked by such a precipitate decline imperilling their social reproduction.

Post-war emigration consequently assumed crisis proportions, exceeding 528,000 between 1946 and 1961 so that almost one in five people born since independence and resident in 1951 emigrated by 1961.[59] Indeed, by 1961 the population of the twenty-six counties had fallen to its lowest point since 1926 – even since the Famine.[60]

Government subsidies policies since the thirties unwittingly played a large part in the smallholders' decline, forcing them out of barley, wheat, sugar-beet and pigs and into young cattle while disproportionately benefiting larger farmers.[61] British post-war policy exacerbated the problem by its system of deficiency payments to British farmers so that during the fifties the only Irish agricultural export to grow was cattle, a large farmers' trade.[62] Reductions of labour led to smallholders withdrawing from labour intensive lines of production while

56 R. E. Kennedy, *The Irish: emigration, marriage and fertility* (Berkeley & Los Angeles, 1973), p. 101.

57 Ibid., p. 104.

58 Ibid., p. 106.

59 Ibid., pp 106–7.

60 W.E. Vaughan & A.J. Fitzpatrick, *Irish historical statistics: population, 1821–1971* (Dublin, 1978), p. 266; Meenan, *Irish economy*, p. 184; Richard Breen, Damian F. Hannan, David B. Rottman & Christopher T. Whelan, *Understanding contemporary Ireland: state, class and development in the Republic of Ireland* (London, 1990), p. 35. The emigration rate of younger age groups was nearly twice as high.

61 Crotty, *Irish agricultural production*, pp 187–8. Cf. Lee, *Ireland*, p. 186 – 'De Valera's policy probably sacrificed the small farmer to whose welfare he was genuinely dedicated, to salvage the economic interests of stronger farmers.'

62 Mary E. Daly, *Social and economic history of Ireland since 1800* (Dublin, 1981), p. 160; Garret FitzGerald, Paul Gillespie & Ronan Fanning in Paul Gillespie (ed.), *Britain's European question: the issues for Ireland* (Dublin, 1996), p. 35.

the introduction of new technology disproportionately benefited larger farmers.[63]

Changes in political debate and economic policy since the war anticipated
greater changes to come, but also signalled an increasing gulf from smallholders' concerns; Bew and Patterson observe that 'by the late 1950s and early 1960s
... the dominance of grassland production, foreign capital and economic liber-
alisation is openly recognised and avowed'.[64] Slackening of land redistribution
was among the most significant of these changes so that by the 1940s Fianna
Fáil's radical ardour of the later 1930s had been reduced to a trickle leading to
rumblings in the party among them Senator Joseph Connolly with his suggestions of a conspiracy to abandon land redistribution.[65] Setting the seal on smallholders' disenchantment Erskine Childers bluntly declared as Minister for Lands
from 1957 that the state could not afford the vast cost of land redistribution
necessary to satisfy all smallholders' claims.[66]

This smallholders' post-war crisis became Fr Fahy's cause; and typically he
declared that the issue really was '... the survival of the Irish people'.[67] But the
real power and uniqueness of his analysis was the conviction that the smallholders' survival was gravely endangered because of a dark conspiracy 'to reinvade
and reconquer the land of Ireland ... being carried out so secretly and so insidi-
ously that the Irish people seem to be unaware of the fact':

> Our traditional enemies, abetted by our treasonable government ... urged on
> and helped by the Englishman's son, Protestant Freemason Childers ... are
> out to establish a new English, Protestant Freemason land-gentry on all the

63   Crotty, *Agricultural production*, p. 188.
64   Paul Bew & Henry Patterson, *Seán Lemass and the making of modern Ireland 1945–66* (Dublin,
     1982), p. 193.
65   Joseph Connolly, *How does she stand?: an appeal to young Ireland* (Dublin, 1953), pp 42–7. 'If there
     was a change of policy the people were entitled to be told about it and the causes and reasons for it',
     Connolly declared. 'All that we know is that land division and settlement slowed down until it
     nearly reached a dead stop. Why?' Ibid., p. 41. 'Our original lines of policy seemed to have been, if
     not forgotten, at least watered down to a point of near extinction.' J. Anthony Gaughan (ed.), *Mem-
     oirs of Senator Joseph Connolly (1885–1961): a founder of modern Ireland* (Dublin, 1996) p. 406. But
     de Valera's response when directly charged by Connolly with abandoning redistribution was to
     'den[y] it vigorously'. Ibid., p. 365; Tim Pat Coogan, *De Valera: long fellow, long shadow* (London,
     1993), p. 694. Connolly's disenchantment was shared by others in Fianna Fáil. In 1946, Michael Joe
     Kennedy T.D. (Longford-Westmeath) complained that the Land Commission had effectively ceased
     to function, and that the Ministers for Lands and Agriculture were both 'proclaiming in best Hogan
     style that there are too many people on the land'. Bew & Patterson, *Lemass*, p.29. Aodh de Blacam's
     similar complaints resulted in his resignation from Fianna Fáil's National Executive in 1947 over
     rural depopulation. Dunphy, *Fianna Fáil*, pp 244–5. Nevertheless, in September 1947, de Valera
     still wanted to go ahead with land redistribution. Bew & Patterson, *Lemass*, p.39; for de Valera's
     commitment to the smallholders in 1944, see Lee, *Ireland*, p. 231.
66   See the *Connacht Tribune*'s Dublin correspondent's blow-by-blow accounts of every hint and shift
     of government land redistribution policy. For example, *Connacht Tribune*, 18 Jan. 1958 & Childers
     letter, 1 Feb. 1958.
67   'John Ireland', 'Birth of Lia Fáil', *Lia Fáil*, Aug. 1958, p. 1.

good land of Ireland, so that they will eventually own Ireland and hold it for the British Empire. Already in counties Dublin, Kildare, Louth, Meath, Westmeath, Wicklow, Carlow, Wexford, Roscommon, Sligo, etc., not to speak of Tipperary and the Golden Vale, their new colonists have taken root.[68]

One of the mainsprings of Lia Fáil's revolt against Fianna Fáil was its conviction that Irish nationalism's implicit social contract had been broken by a 'traitorous government' abandoning smallholders' to the nation's 'traditional enemies'. Profound disillusion with the party and pain at betrayal were palpable consequences, testaments to Fianna Fáil's ingenuity in previously so successfully embodying such high ideals. Tales of its perfidy were related with a mixture of horror and relish. Cases such as the Bennykerry, county Carlow's agitation to break up the Browne Hill and Oak Park estates, or a Russian Jew named Nairm's purchase of several hundred acres at Ballytore, county Kildare, and numerous others were cited as evidence of 'the reconquest of Ireland' abetted by politicians.[69] A republican who had emigrated to the United States after the civil war declared after describing on his return how the ideals he fought for had fared: '... we have drank the last dregs of disillusionment for we have definite proof that de Valera and his gang were only fooling us all the time'.[70] This 'proof' was: '... de Valera and his government has treasonably allowed an English syndicate to come in and buy the whole estate of 4,000 acres and he is using the guards to protect them'. So great was the contrast with its radical origins in the days of cattle-driving and land seizures during the civil war or its coasting to power in part on the back of the land annuities campaign that Lia Fáil believed Fianna Fáil now presented one of the greatest obstacles to the satisfaction of smallholders' land hunger.

Foreign land purchase assisted by native perfidy was not the only objection of Fr Fahy's xenophobia. Foreign capital was equally severely condemned with complaints that Seán Lemass's approval as Minister for Industry and Commerce of foreigners' purchase of Irish businesses such as the Cavan Gypsum industries was 'undisguised treason and treachery'.[71] Foreign penetration of the Irish economy of this kind simply could not be tolerated any longer.[72] The native genius required unfettered scope to reach its apogee, guaranteeing the *völk*

---

68 'Tussle with my P.P.', ibid., September 1958, p. 3; 'A complete job', ibid., Oct., 1958, p. 1.
69 'Salute to Carlow', ibid., August 1958, p. 2; 'The protest storm is mounting in Kildare', ibid., p. 3. Cf. George Russell TD (East Limerick) Dáil question about foreign land purchase. *Dáil Debates*, 28 Oct. 1959, cl. 318–19.
70 'Uncle Pat', ibid., no.8, n.d., p. 3.
71 'J.I.' [John Ireland], 'Is Lemass mad?', *Lia Fáil*, October 1958, p. 2.
72 Fr Fahy's revelation in 1957 that he himself had drawn up a Sinn Féin economic programme with Seán T. O'Kelly, Austin Stack, Mary MacSwiney and others at some unspecified date but perhaps shortly after the civil war emphasises his commitment to the traditional nationalist protectionist ideal. *Offaly Chronicle*, 25 Dec. 1957. Ernest Blythe, though his emphasis was on the language, was another advocate of this ideal who believed that 'the forsaking of our national heritage is the under-

opportunities in their own country. Sectarian and xenophobic paranoia were consequences of this view so that naturally Protestants occupied a prominent place in its demonology. The visible face of the sinister conspiracy to dispossess the Gael was said to be the Representative Church Body of the Church of Ireland which had recently purchased a 200-acre farm near Portumna, county Galway. Lia Fáil's bitter complaint at this purchase concentrated on the dispossessed *völk*, fifty unemployed men in nearby Eyrecourt. 'As mere Irish they are not entitled to anything better than the dole. Should they renounce their faith and join the Masons, they will be entitled to good jobs, or a slice of east Galway'.[73]

But the Catholic sectarianism of this sort going back to the Defenders and the second Whiteboy phase was unwittingly close to detonating something highly explosive. For the Church of Ireland had in fact secretly set up an Irish Land Finance Company, incorporated in 1913 to act as a lending agency to Church members to buy farms and with its working capital supplied by the Representative Church Body, that was active in the land market until it was wound up in 1973, a period when Church numbers nevertheless fell 40 per cent between 1926 and 1971; the result of a zealous county Kildare rector's efforts in the 1940s and 1950s to establish 'Protestant blocs' in his parish ('notching up these victories', 'out thrusting the opposition') through the Land Company was that 'blackguards' damaged his parish church in 1959 – Lia Fáil's heyday.[74] If amid the crisis of the fifties news of the Church of Ireland's secret activity in the land market had leaked, then the consequences for Church and society alike of land hunger and sectarianism fusing were potentially devastating, turning the ugly Fethard-on-Sea boycott into a trifle by comparison.

Politicians were not only guilty in Lia Fáil's view of treacherously conniving with Protestants and foreigners. They were also guilty of squandering sovereignty by failing to end emigration, one of Lia Fáil's most important issues. 'There is no reason why we should not have a population of from fifteen to twenty million people living on the land of Ireland', Fr Fahy cried amid the worst emigration since the 1880s, echoing nationalist sentiments since at least Young Ireland.[75] Emigration would have completely ended if even the modicum

lying cause of the excessive emigration and is directly responsible for partition'. Ibid., 9 May 1958. Blythe said this to the Tullamore branch of An Realt – the Irish language praesidium of the Legion of Mary. (An Realt was founded in 1945 by Nuala Moran, daughter of D.P. Moran.)

73 'Another Galway estate for the Church Body', *Lia Fáil*, October, 1958, p. 2.

74 Kathleen Annie Garvin, *The Church of Ireland as a Church in Ireland: a study of the Anglican Church in the Irish Free State, 1922–1935* (Clark University, Ph.D., 1977), pp 187–251. My thanks to Dr Peter Hart for drawing my attention to this thesis. By 1937 the Land Company had advanced £93,000. The spiritual and geographical centre of the Company's activities was county Laois, radiating out to King's, Kildare, Dublin, Wicklow, Carlow, Kilkenny, and Tipperary. More generally, see also Mike Millotte, *Banished babies: the secret history of Ireland's baby export business* (Dublin, 1997), pp 64–5.

75 'John Ireland', 'Birth of Lia Fáil', *Lia Fáil*, Oct. 1958, p. 1.

of independence since 1922 had been properly used, he believed. Instead, the limitless potential of sovereignty had been completely squandered by corrupt governments:

> They [i.e. emigrants] are in fact the victims of a power-hungry egomaniac, Eamon de Valera, a man who's life's work has been the creation of the smoothest and most ruthless political machine the world has ever known. A system which has robbed the Irish of their heritage and self-respect, one which has reduced the country to shambles and made its people the laughing stock of the world.[76]

But there was more to this conspiratorial explanation for the soaring emigration of the 1950s than simply disillusion with Fianna Fáil. Fundamentally, it rested on a paranoid view that it was really due to a Protestant conspiracy to under-mine and eradicate the nation's essence, its Catholicism, because emigration really was '... Satan's cunning in human form to banish religion from the only country where heresy was kept out'.[77]

This belief that the nation's glorious destiny had been squandered naturally led to the most vitriolic diatribes against the politicians' flowing freely from Fr Fahy's pen. De Valera was said to be illegitimate and 'a master of duplicity and evasion', Childers 'the English-bred Masonic minister for lands', and Lemass possessed by the devil.[78] Even when irony sometimes tinged its *völkisch* views the underlying sharpness of the disenfranchised smallholders still shone through:

> The mere Irish are not intelligent enough to realise that God brought the de Valeras from Spain, the Lemasses from Flanders, the Dillons from Nor-mandy, the Ryans from Herefordshire and the Childers from some other shire to keep the O'Donnells and O'Neills, the Kellys and the Murphys and all the other riff-raff natives in their *natural social lebensraum* – the moun-tains and wastelands and bogs of Ireland and the ghettos of cities in foreign lands![79]

Its anger was focused particularly on the English-educated, Protestant Minis-ter for Lands, Erskine Childers, notwithstanding that he was the son of the civil war martyr. Not only did it contemptuously reject his entreaties to land-hungry smallholders that they must wait for lawful land acquisition and division, that

76 '600,000 banished in ten years', ibid., March/April 1959, p. 1.
77 'An eyewitness', 'Jealousy', ibid., Aug. 1958, p. 4.
78 'Foreign vested interests – a country's greatest menace', ibid., November 1958, p. 3; 'Milner's triumphant return', ibid., no. 9, n.d., p. 3. Fr Fahy knew de Valera personally: his disillusion ex-plains his asperities. Fr Kevin Egan interview, 9 Aug. 1995.
79 'The protest storm is mounting in Kildare', *Lia Fáil*, August 1958, p. 3.

the Land Commission was doing a good job, and that the minister had no say in this independent process. It also alleged he was a frequent visitor to Colonel Bellingham of Glencarra, county Westmeath, who had bought thousands of acres for a Scottish agricultural company and who was deemed 'public enemy no.1 in the land-grabbing process in the midlands'.[80]

But Lia Fáil was not only about robust invective, bombast and diatribes against the politicians, Masons, foreigners, or Protestants. Fr Fahy also proposed his own typically quixotic programme as well. Pretensions of forming a populist Lia Fáil government, present from the start, were one of its most fanciful proposals.[81] Guarantees 'to put 500,000 families on the ranches and demesnes of Ireland' within a year of taking office were another.[82] Partition was to be expunged within five years, reflecting frustration with de Valera's fervent anti-partition rhetoric followed by suppression of the I.R.A.'s Border campaign.[83] 'Follow the old principle – England's difficulty is Ireland's opportunity – and watch for the fatal hour, then the 1916 Rebellion would only be a pin-prick to the Lia-Fáil rising', Lia Fáil declared.[84] Only with a completely reorganised and expanded defence force would this action take place – '... Irish army and air force (equipped with atomic bombs) would cross the Border and give the Orange mob what they have been looking for for a long time'.[85] But like the declamatory legitimists of the late 1920s and 1930s, Lia Fáil's rhetoric of revanchist belligerence compensated for its powerlessness.

Ideas about communal land ownership, land seizures and land redistribution fuelled Fr Fahy's historicist belief in the Brehon Laws.[86] Naturally, the Brehon Laws were believed to extol the Gael's pure spiritual values and genius: '... no other race of people known to history ever devised for themselves, and lived

80 'Ireland – our land', ibid., October 1958, p. 4. It repeated rumours that Colonel Bellingham had been '... closely associated, if not actually a member of the infamous auxiliaries back in the twenties'. For evidence of Childers's concern about sectarian discrimination, see Dunphy, *Fianna Fáil*, p. 130. How Lia Fáil came to this bitterly acerbic criticism of the son of one of the republicans civil war martyrs can only be explained by the unstated but obvious view held by some exotic republicans that his father had really been a British spy, probably involving complicity for the treaty split, and that this sinister design was being continued by the son.
81 'One hour's work', *Lia Fáil*, Aug. 1958, p. 1.
82 'Emigration and declining population: Lia Fáil's solution', ibid., August 1958, p. 3.
83 *Irish Independent*, 29 May 1958, in N.A., Department of Justice, S.46/58. 'The British are assisted there by the section of *our* people who do not want to join with us' (Emphasis added.) De Valera's panacea was even less appealing for impatient patriots: 'We have to wait for a considerable period until conditions are such that success will again be possible'. Mr Ruairí Ó Brádaigh said Fr Fahy was 'fulsome in his support of the internees', that *Lia Fáil* 'was sent in to us internees in the Curragh in 1958 and read avidly', but that the internees would have preferred a class confrontation to sectarianism in the journal. *Saoirse* (journal of Republican Sinn Féin), February, 1993, p. 8; Stephen Coyle letter, ibid., January, 1993, p. 8; personal communication, Ruairí Ó Brádaigh to the author, 15 January 1996.
84 'Lia Fáil and partition', *Lia Fáil*, September 1958, p. 5.
85 Ibid.
86 See, Lawrence Ginnell, *The Brehon Laws*, second edition, (Dublin, 1917).

under, a legislative system so closely in accord with God's divine and natural law'.[87] Consequently, Fr Fahy advocated that Lia Fáil take the Brehon-like step of taking over and distributing land whenever it became idle.[88] Brehon-like communal ownership with '... the land vested in the name of the people of Ireland and lent to those best fitted to get the best out of it – for the benefit of all the people of Ireland' was what he eventually wanted.[89] Indeed, he vowed to '... take over every farm of land in Ireland of 100 acres and over, and put the young men of Ireland on that land, giving every young man at least 50 statute acres of good land'.[90] But the gap between heights of *völkisch* Brehon-like communal ownership and the realities of a capitalist colonial land system was enormous with the smallholders' still being eradicated from their own country by Protestants and foreigners aided by a treasonable government:

> It is being bought up and gambled by speculators and gombeen-men at home, and, horrible-dictu, it is being purchased and monopolised by English syndicates and the Protestant Church-body, who, for centuries have tried to exterminate our race and destroy our religion, and would do the same today if they got the chance and de Valera and [his] treasonable government, as we will prove him and them (for he won't be able to suppress us as easily as he is suppressing the young patriots who are hurling themselves at the Border), are not only allowing and conniving at the sale of the land of our people to our alien enemies, but are helping that treacherous and treasonable and criminal transaction! Gaels! Arise and impeach the traitors![91]

The problem with establishing a *völkisch* social order based on indigenous Brehon Law was that before Protestants and foreigners could be expropriated and expelled first native enemies such as Fianna Fáil would have to be forcibly removed from power. Once it had charted that path to see the establishment of its vision Lia Fáil had set out on the road to revolt.

The betrayals of the *First programme for economic expansion* (1958), Fianna

---

87 'John Ireland', 'Back to the Brehon Laws', *Lia Fáil*, September 1958, p. 2.
88 'John Ireland', 'Lia Fáil opposed to all sales of land', ibid., p. 1.
89 'Aims and ideals', ibid.
90 In this context, W.H. Milner's views on land nationalisation are worth quoting: 'The land that was taken from the Irish people, even a thousand years ago, is still the property of the Irish people and the onus remains on the descendants of the original robber to make restitution. In the event the descendants of the original owners cannot be found, the wrongful occupiers must dispose of the land and distribute the proceeds to charity. This is Catholic teaching, and if it has not and does not apply to Ireland, nevertheless it is still the teaching of the Catholic Church, and since it is it should apply in Ireland and those who condemn land agitation are morally wrong.' 'Successful Emigration Action Movement meeting', ibid., no. 9, p. 4.
91 Ibid. Fr Fahy's most exotic inspiration derived from Vinoba Bhave's *bhudan*. See *Moved by love: the memoirs of Vinoba Bhave*, trans. Marjorie Sykes, (Dartington, Totnes, Devon, 1994), and V.S. Naipaul, *India: a wounded civilization* (London, 1977), pp 159–67.

Fáil's parsed version of T.K. Whitaker's *Economic development* (1958) signalling a sea-change in public policy from protectionism to free trade and economic planning, confirmed the government's treasons. Typically, Lia Fáil greeted the *First programme*'s endorsement of the comparative advantage of cattle-rearing as 'a clear statement of Fianna Fáil's diabolical policy to banish the Irish people from the land of Ireland and put bullocks in their place to supply beef to John Bull'.[92] The seeds of change may indeed have been sprouting since the late 1930s and early 1940s so that by the late 1950s there was nothing abrupt or unusual about open acknowledgement of grassland production and the failure of self-sufficiency. But to marginalised smallholders' of Lia Fáil's kind, their roots in post-Famine agrarian radicalism of the Land League and United Irish League and their numbers rapidly declining since the war particularly through consolidation and emigration, this change of public policy only too clearly confirmed their worst fears of official betrayal that led them into rebellion in the first place when what they sought at a minimum was a defence of their interests against foreign and domestic vagaries and a 'secure subsistence'.[93]

Predictably, the combined referendum to scrap proportional representation and the presidential election in June 1959 provoked another of Fahy's outbursts. Condemning the referendum because of the politicians' perfidy in daring to change the electoral system was predictable; it was 'a master stroke of diversion, a cunningly planned distraction of people's minds from the vital and urgent problems of wholesale emigration, unemployment, and reconquest which are bleeding and strangling our nation to death'.[94] Condemning de Valera's seeking a sinecure in the Park might have been expected too. But such was the loathing of de Valera now that Fr Fahy gave fulsome support to Seán Mac Eoin of Fine Gael, oblivious of any incongruities in this alliance with the large farmers' party, though it was mitigated by Mac Eoin's recent support for an agitation to break-up the Midleton Park estate at Castletown-Geoghegan, county Meath. The crispness of his indictment of de Valera contained a narrowness of analysis of the country's ills that gave it all the more power:

He will go down in history as the greatest living Machiavellian politician that ever crossed the Irish stage. He will go down as one who, more than any other, tried to crush and annihilate republican spirit in Ireland. His intolerance, bitterness and personal vanity has, over a period, atrophied political thought and prevented development – political and economic.[95]

92 'Fianna Fáil's economic policy', *Lia Fáil*, Feb. 1959, p. 1. See also, Lee, *Ireland*, p. 345.
93 'Secure subsistence' is James C. Scott's term in *The moral economy of the peasant: rebellion and subsistence in Southeast Asia* (New Haven & London, 1976), p. vii.
94 'Silence in the Dáil', *Lia Fáil*, Jan. 1959, p. 1.
95 'Very, very hot air', ibid., Feb. 1959, p. 3.
96 Confidential source, 19 August 1996; Department of Lands, 'Land agitation: memorandum for the government', 5 May 1959, p. 1, N.A., S 6490/2/94.

This indictment was a mark of the change that occurred in Fr Fahy's politics in the hiatus since the first phase of his radical career so that by 1959 de Valera had been transformed from the ally of 1933 vested with hopes of agrarian radicalism and left-leaning, physical force republicanism into the great ogre personally to blame for all the ills besetting the nation. Chief among these were crimes against the republic such as crushing the I.R.A.'s Border campaign; but earlier condemnations of the people's loss of self-respect and heritage reflected classical republican ideals too.

IV

On Friday 1 May 1959, Lia Fáil's eighteen month-long protests culminated with the start of an agitation at Lusmagh against the Land Commission's allegedly tardy and unfair redistribution. This agitation was actually supposed to be part of a simultaneous national rising, but none of the other parts rose except Hollymount, county Mayo, where locals tried to prevent the occupation of Land Commission lands by Mayo migrants. In Lusmagh, incidents occurred during May and June, Lia Fáil members were arrested, Gardaí combed the area, the parish was split, and Fr Fahy was at the centre of it all. In the event, the Lusmagh agitation proved to be like a firework suddenly exploding, momentarily illuminating everything, but leaving nothing in its wake.

Two incidents inaugurated the agitation. First, a smallholder, Patrick O'Leary, was moved by the Land Commission to another farm some miles away, and the Land Commission was about to divide his holding in three lots. Lia Fáil accepted the allocation of two out of the three lots to local smallholders. But it vehemently objected to 'a man who had plenty of land already' getting the third lot of a three-acre field because there were more deserving people available, including landless people. Consequently, Lia Fáil, as its journal explained, allocated the field itself:

> Opposite this field, Mrs Killeen, a widow with two sons and a daughter, lived in a labourer's cottage. She was paying high rent for the grass of a cow; following the law of the Brehon Code Lia Fáil entered this field, ploughed, tilled, and sowed it and gave Mrs Killeen a title deed to it.[97]

Two of Mrs Killeen's sons, Brendan and William, were Lia Fáil members.

Second, five Lia Fáil men drove thirty-two cattle off Frank Barry's lands at Cogran, Lusmagh, and ploughed a roadside field on his land in the shape of a

---

97 Lia Fáil divides land', *Lia Fáil*, no. 8, n.d., p. 1.

cross (Fr Fahy believed the cross was a symbol of their claim to the land).[98] This
protest was rooted in the Land Commission's failure to compulsorily purchase
Barry's holding in 1954 to relieve local congestion because Barry successfully
held out for a price guaranteed to maintain his income. But it was aimed as
much at Albert ('Bertie') Barry as his brother Frank. Bertie Barry originally
purchased the holding in 1934, and was a grazier, owner of three holdings locally, and a rate collector for county Offaly.[99] Indeed, Lia Fáil alleged that he had
pressed the already heavily debt encumbered owner Michael Gibbons for two
years rates in arrears 'until he forced him to sell the farm; Barry then bought
the farm for £500'. In 1937, he then sold it to his brother, and from 1950 onwards Frank let it back to him. As a result, Lia Fáil denounced Bertie Barry as 'a
real specimen of the land sharks who are gobbling up the families of rural Ireland'.[100] Significantly, the thirty-two cattle driven off Frank's land belonged to
Bertie the grazier.[101]

Several features of these two incidents should be noted. First, if the cattle
drive on Barry's land showed Lia Fáil's anger and frustration at the Land Commission's failure to purchase, then the allocation of the field to a landless widow
showed Fr Fahy's true radicalism. Indeed, the similarity between it and his seizure of a woman's impounded cattle from a bailiff thirty years earlier was striking. Both were instances of gendered radicalism benevolently conferred on de-
fenceless women. Second, Fr Fahy's radicalism and his role as a parish priest
were of course symbiotically connected. Rural priests could be quite energetic
in lobbying the government and state agencies to secure resources for their parish even if in the process they sometimes became local potentates, if not petty
tyrants.[102] But Fr Fahy appears to have been too disaffected from the system to
ever adopt this orthodox *modus operandi*. His resulting powerlessness, his sensi-
tive social conscience, and his unusually keen radicalism resulted in the creation
of Lia Fáil as an alternative and more immediate means of securing justice for
all Lusmagh's wrongs. But this proved a dangerous and a risky strategy for a
parish priest to take on his own initiative. Even if it gained some loyal supporters in the parish, his initiative alienated far more people than it ever persuaded,
and this was to be his downfall.

Later that day, the Gardaí arrested and detained five Lia Fáil men in relation
to these two incidents, and this proved to be the spark that set the situation

98 *Irish Press*, 12 May 1959; confidential source, 19 August 1996.
99 'Lia Fáil divides land', *Lia Fáil*, no. 8, n.d., p. 1.
100 Ibid.
101 Ibid.; 'John F. Barry, Record No. S 20597', Co. Offaly, N.A., S 490C/2/94. For analysis of peasant
    antipathies towards graziers, see David Seth Jones, *Graziers, land reform, and political conflict in
    Ireland* (Washington D.C., 1995), pp 232–55.
102 For example, see Fr Micheál MacGréil S.J. (ed.), *Monsignor James Horan: memoirs 1911–1986* (Dingle,
    1992), p. 111; Stephen Rynne, *Fr John Hayes: founder of Muintir na Tire* (Dublin & London, 1960),
    p. 209.

ablaze. Denis Kelly, a farmer's son working at Ferbane power station, and Brendan Killeen, a labourer with the Board of Works and a son of the widow-beneficiary of Lia Fáil's Brehon-like largesse, were committee members, and Noel Moran, a seventeen-year-old working on the hundred acre family farm, John Joe Kenny, a farmer's son, and Patrick Glynn, also a farmer's son, were members.[103] They were charged in Banagher court and detained at Banagher Garda station awaiting transfer to Mountjoy prison in Dublin, but during the afternoon a hundred people gathered in protest outside the station.[104] John Kelly, a brother of the detained Denis Kelly and of Francis Kelly, Lia Fáil's secretary, although not actually a member himself, shouted from among the crowd at the gate to the Gardaí and prisoners inside: 'I have come to lead you for Ireland: free those men'.[105] He and five other men, all brothers of the detained men but not Lia Fáil members themselves, then, as Garda S. Cox subsequently recounted, dramatically forced their way past three Gardaí at the gate and into the station:

> The cell door was open and John Kelly was standing sideways in the doorway. Speaking to the prisoners he shouted: 'We are followers of Jesus Christ, I will go with ye to prison.' He repeated this a few times and then approached witness with his hands in the air and said 'Are you a follower of Jesus Christ?' Witness did not answer him and Kelly then said: 'Anyone here who is not a follower of Jesus Christ should not be here.' He then approached Sergeant Coll and said something to the Sergeant: he appeared like a man who had gone berserk.[106]

The five prisoners and their rescuers then broke out past the Gardaí at the gate, and triumphantly marched up and down the street with a crowd. In the event, Lia Fáil's greatest triumphs were behind it, and the forces of order were about to counter-attack.

A day later, Saturday 2 May, the Gardaí arrested and charged six men with the jailbreak – John, Michael, and Francis Kelly, Lia Fáil's Secretary, and James Glynn, Patrick Killeen, and Thomas Moran – who were all brothers of the five imprisoned men, though none except Francis Kelly were actually members themselves.[107] However, on the following morning, Sunday 3 May, the five escapees openly attended 8.30 a.m. mass at Lusmagh, Fr Fahy greeted them afterwards, and they announced they were going on the run.[108]

103 *Offaly Independent*, 30 May 1959.
104 *Evening Press*, 8 May 1959.
105 Evidence of Garda B. Kehoe, *Midland Tribune*, 27 June 1959.
106 Ibid.
107 Ibid., 8 May 1959. See also, David Fitzpatrick, 'Class, family and rural unrest in nineteenth-century Ireland', in P.J. Drudy (ed.), *Ireland: land, politics and people* (Irish studies 2) (Cambridge, 1982), pp 37–75; *idem*, 'Unrest in rural Ireland', *Irish Economic & Social History*, XII (1985), pp 98–105.
108 *Irish Press*, 4 May 1959.

After the men's dramatic jailbreak, the government decided to crush the Lusmagh agitation altogether. Even so, it was careful not to arrest Fr Fahy in order to avoid creating a *cause célèbre*. Early on Tuesday 5 May, a party of Dublin Gardaí drove down to Lusmagh to search the parochial house for the five escapees and raid other premises in the vicinity.[109] They were informed where they were going only when the journey was well underway, but a reporter and photographer from the pro-Fianna Fáil *Evening Press* were already waiting when they arrived at Fr John's house at just before 5.00 a.m. Consequently, photographs of their dawn raid on the parish priest's house adorned the paper's front page that afternoon.[110] Nonetheless, the Gardaí found none of the five fugitives there, the men had been hiding elsewhere and had been tipped off in advance, and were only apprehended later. 'Since these young men started the land war, not one of them has entered the parochial lands or house', Fr Fahy gleefully told the press after the raid.[111] Later that morning, Oliver J. Flanagan, Laois-Offaly's irascible if brilliantly clientalist Fine Gael T.D., visited Fr Fahy to express sympathy at the raid, and later that day protested in the Dáil at 'a supposedly Catholic and Christian government sending squads of police in the dead of night to carry out a raid on the home of a parish priest'.[112] In reply, Oscar Traynor, Minister for Justice, unashamedly took 'full responsibility for the action taken' – a declaration which was unlikely to be made without having already secured episcopal support or acquiescence for such action against a priest.[113]

In the weeks after these events, not only did Lia Fáil's agitation simmer away in Lusmagh but it spread across the Shannon into east Galway. In three east Galway incidents, said to have been organised by members in Moate, county Westmeath, and Borrisokane, county Tipperary, further evidence of Lia Fáil's roots in the region's agrarian radical tradition was apparent. On the night of 3 June, on John Horseman's lands at Fermore, Eyrecourt, county Galway, ten cattle and fifty sheep were driven, and on the lands of Eamonn Williams and Francis Killeen, Keelogue, gates were left open to allow cattle to stray.[114] A notice was posted near the farms with an old cattle-driving slogan: 'The land for

---

109 'Phone message at 8.10 a.m. from Inspector at Banagher Garda Station (per Duty Officer at Garda Headquarters)', 5 May 1959, N.A., Department of Justice, S.29/58 A. The Gardaí acted on reports that Fr Fahy was hiding the escapees in his house; they had seen and heard him congratulating the men on their involvement in the Lusmagh incident. [Draft speech: adjournment debate, minister's reply], n.d. [c.15 May 1959], ibid. All five men were members of the local F.C.A. platoon, and an Army detail from Tullamore collected local F.C.A. rifles on the night before the raid. *Evening Press*, 5 May 1959.
110 *Evening Press*, 5 May 1959. Fr McGahey's support included devoting the proceeds of a dance at Collinstown, county Westmeath, to Lia Fáil. Erskine Childers to E. de Valera, 11 May 1959, N.A., S 6490C/2/94.
111 *Belfast Telegraph*, 6 May 1959.
112 Dáil Debates, 12 May 1959, cl.1946.
113 Ibid., cl.1948.
114 *Midland Tribune*, 6 June 1959.

the people, the road for the bullock.' Because these three large farmers, two of them, Horseman and Williams, Protestants, were allegedly descendants of long-execrated grabbers, Lia Fáil acted on long-standing local resentment at those incidents in the 1880s and on demands for their break-up and distribution. In Lusmagh meanwhile, on Sunday 7 June a thatched cottage on Patrick O'Leary's former holding, scene of Mayday Brehon-like largesse, was burnt down.[115] On 12 June, a storehouse and its contents of hay on Frank Barry's lands were burnt by Michael Brennan, Lusmagh, aged eighteen; the previous day, Brennan had discussed Lia Fáil with Jim and Pauline Glynn while thinning beet, they suggested to him to burn down the store, and Jim Glynn told him that 'Father Fahy would be proud of me when he heard I had burned the [store]house'.[116] Thomas Bailey, an agricultural contractor working on O'Leary's crops, was injured on O'Leary's former holding when a detonator attached to his tractor exploded; Lia Fáil had previously protested against the Land Commission's permitting O'Leary to crop the holding after he left.[117]

This spread across the Shannon into east Galway and continuing vitality in Lusmagh was as nothing compared to Lia Fáil's spectacular plan to blow up Bertie Barry's house at Shannongrove (Kylenaborris), a plan for which it had obtained the necessary explosives. Only that someone informed the authorities it would have gone ahead.[118] If it had indeed successfully blown up the grazier Barry's house on top of its existing agitation, Lia Fáil's action would have guaranteed its reputation as the most radical smallholders' movement in the history of the state.

During these incidents were and five weeks after Lia Fáil's agitation began, Bishop William Philbin of Clonfert, himself an advocate of greater purchasing powers for the Land Commission, delivered the episcopal *coup de grace* to Fr Fahy's activities in a pastoral letter on 7 June, read at six selected parishes, that implicitly condemned Lia Fáil; the six selected parishes where it was read suggest the geographical extent of Lia Fáil's activities in Clonfert – Lusmagh in county Offaly, and Eyrecourt, Lawrencetown, Fahy, Portumna, and Killimor in county Galway.[119] Fr Fahy himself read it at Lusmagh, but typically read it with congenial amendments.[120]

---

115 Ibid., 13 June 1959. 'No fire brigade call was made nor was the outbreak reported until late on Sunday morning.'

116 Ibid., 27 June 1959. Fr Fahy attended throughout the trial of young Michael Brennan.

117 Lusmagh and Banagher ratepayers were levied with £898 5s. 9d. in damages payable to the six people whose property was damaged. Ibid., 25 Jul. 1959. A postcript to Lia Fáil's agitation occurred one Friday night in September when the corn that it had sown on O'Leary's field on Mayday was cut with scythes and left in the field. *Offaly Chronicle*, 23 Sep. 1959.

118 Confidential source, 2 Oct. 1996.

119 *Connacht Tribune*, 10 October 1958; ibid., 13 June 1959.

120 Confidential source, 9 October 1996.

Although originally he had not been due to participate in a victory demonstration through Banagher to celebrate Denis Kelly and Brendan Killeen's release from Mountjoy prison on 15 June, Fr Fahy got involved only when the speaker, a schoolteacher from Longford named Kavanagh, withdrew.[121] A forty-three strong procession, led by a six-man band headed by John Coughlan with accordions, flutes and a drum playing Irish airs and with the two released men flanking Fr Fahy and W.H. Milner, proudly marched down the town from the square to the bridge and back again in defiance of Banagher's burghers.[122] Having reassembled at Lusmagh where it was swollen to more than a hundred people, Fahy strongly condemned the Garda searches of homes in the parish:

> Scarcely a home in this parish had not been outraged. We hold the government responsible, and they would see that those thugs responsible would be dealt with. It is horrible to be held in one of those squad cars for hours. This torture will be examined and exposed, and the one or two responsible brought to trial before the Irish nation.[123]

In the event, the only ones brought to trial were Lia Fáil members.

Three weeks after these demonstrations, Fr Fahy suddenly, and without explanation, announced his premature retirement as parish priest of Lusmagh after fourteen years. 'I have done so of my own free will', he stated laconically. 'My bishop ... has neither asked nor forced me to do this'.[124] And he informed Eric Waugh of the *Belfast Telegraph* that he had resigned as President of Lia Fáil as well.[125] But these two resignations seem to be linked with his bishop's displeasure. Bishop Philbin is said to have had representations from people in the parish, to have acted on these only after the Gardaí provided tapes of Fahy's apparently incendiary speech at the Banagher demonstration after the pastoral, and to have told Fr Fahy he must either publicly apologise to the parish or go.[126] Fahy was heart-broken to leave, but leave he did rather than recant his most cherished beliefs. In the following weeks, his followers came before the courts, were found guilty, but given suspended sentences and bound to keep the peace.[127]

121 Confidential source, 25 August 1996; confidential source, 2 October 1996.
122 *Midland Tribune*, 20 June 1959. W.H. Milner's car was thrown down to the bottom of a sandpit while the demonstration was going on. A copy of Lia Fáil was stuck into the front bumper, and 'Milner: keep out' was scrawled on the roof and bonnet. Ibid. & 25 July 1959.
123 *Irish Times*, 15 June 1959.
124 *Irish Independent*, 6 July 1959.
125 Eric Waugh, 'The seeds of wrath in Éire land', reprinted from *Belfast Telegraph*, Lia Fáil, no. 8, n.d., p. 2; *Belfast Telegraph*, 23 June 1959. Lia Fáil's new committee may have been: President, Eamon Ginnell, vice-President, Frank Kelly, chairman, Barney Kelly, treasurer, Tom Kavanagh, secretary, Denis Kelly, executive committee, W.H. Milner, Dick Power and one (illegible) other. 'Lia Fáil', ms., 1pp., copy in possession of Fr Kevin Egan.
126 Confidential source, 19 August 1996.
127 *Offaly Independent*, 30 May 1959; *Midland Tribune*, 21 Nov. 1959. Three of the five fugitives were

Although the Lusmagh agitation was over, Lia Fáil's journal published two more issues.[128] W.H. Milner played a larger role in these while Fr Fahy continued to contribute. After the government's effrontery in daring to suppress Lia Fáil, Milner's paranoia came more into the open. He now cited Fr Denis Fahey's Jewish-Masonic-Communist world domination conspiracy theories, and declared starkly 'we are resisting evil':

There is a well-prepared plan for world-conquest in existence. For a long time it has been directed against the surviving Gaelic-core in this country, but during the last decade it is being operated with such vigour, as to make it obvious to the most uninitiated. Why is the campaign aimed at the old Gaelic core in Ireland? Because Gaelicism and Catholicism are twin idealisms; they are so long intertwined that it is impossible to separate one from the other. So to kill Catholicism in Ireland it is necessary to destroy the Gael and this is being systematically done.[129]

This sinister design was being operated through masonry and communism. He revealed that Ireland had the most masonic lodges per square mile in the world. Communists had cells in every county, and seventeen in Dublin. And masonry was only the forerunner of communism, working to make the gentile the slave of the Jewish nation in a world republic banishing Christianity.

Lia Fáil's last issue developed this paranoia, although it was present from the start, even further in a millenarian vision of the brilliant achievements of a Lia Fáil government in the near future of 1960.[130] By then Lia Fáil had combined with such groups as Monetary Reform and National Action to oust the perfidious Fianna Fáil government. The self-styled Lia Fáil government sealed off the country, abolished the constitution and legislature, established 'a constitution suitable to our country', 'made laws the people could understand', cut the link with sterling, froze the banks, established a new monetary system, made

---

apprehended and tried for the jailbreak. Denis Kelly, Noel Moran, and Brendan Killeen, pleaded guilty to obstructing the Gardaí and escaping from lawful custody, and were each bound to keep the peace for two years and each pay a personal and independent sureties of £100. Seven other Lia Fáil defendants pleaded guilty and were convicted: John Joe Kenny and Patrick Glynn received a six months suspended sentence, £50 bail each and were bound to keep the peace for twelve months; and the five others received a twelve month suspended sentence, £50 bail each and were bound to keep the peace for twelve months.

128 Lia Fáil's last known activity was a ceilí held at Banagher under the auspices of the Emigration Action Movement some months after the Lusmagh agitation. 'Milner's triumphant return', *Lia Fáil*, no. 9, n.d., p. 3. The National Library copy of this issue was received on 10 March 1960.

129 'The agents of Satan', ibid., p. 2. It printed a synopsis of one of Fr Denis Fahey's articles, 'The Catholic nations must be crushed', ibid. p. 2.

130 For example, 'An Eyewitness', 'Jealousy', ibid., August 1958, p. 4 – 'It is clear from what is going on today that the powers of darkness in human form are making a last and final effort to have Ireland for themselves.'

emigration illegal, introduced compulsory military service, settled 500,000 young men on the good lands, abolished the Gardaí, civil service, embassies, and put these superfluous people to work at drainage, land reclamation, turf production and afforestation.[131] Not that Satan's agents could be permitted to slink in the shadows plotting to overthrow this earthly paradise. Fianna Fáil were tried for crimes against the nation, found guilty, and condemned to death. De Valera and his ministers were hanged, their corpses left dangling in Dublin as a warning to political adventurers and soapbox politicians. Landlords, alien-planters, ranchers, and large land owners who opposed forcible resettlement were similarly dispatched. England as a result issued a threat of war, but the Lia Fáil government boldly responded: 'Whore of Babylon ... do your damnedest!' It rearmed with planes, nuclear submarines, nuclear small arms, and when the Lia Fáil government smashed the Border and removed partition the English government withdrew its threat. Then Lia Fáil's earthly paradise would reign in perfect harmony.

Fr Fahy's resignation was followed by his move from Lusmagh to a curacy some distance away at the parish of Duniry and Kilnelahan where there was little agrarian agitation.[132] He resided at Abbey, Loughrea, county Galway, for ten years, and was active in republican politics until his death aged seventy-four on 19 July 1969. At his funeral, the Galway I.R.A. provided a guard of honour at the graveside and an officer laid a wreath, and the mourners included two brothers living locally (another, a priest, had predeceased him), Oliver J. Flanagan T.D., and former parishioners from the many parishes where he served.[133] 'In each of those parishes he became a legend in his own time', the *Connacht Tribune* obituarist stated coyly.[134]

131 'R.H.' [ie. 'Rory of the Hill' a nineteenth-century agrarian nom de guerre], 'How was it done?', ibid., no. 10, n.d., p. 2. This fantasy might be usefully compared with the much more moderate version published well before the government's crack down. See, '1980', ibid., January 1959, p. 5. The Bennekerry Land Club's once-off journal *The Crusade* took up the radical standard for one glorious issue. *The Crusade*, August 1959, N.A., Department of Justice, S 28/59.
132 Personal communication, Revd Patrick K. Egan to the author, 14 January 1996.
133 *Connacht Tribune*, 25 July 1969. One of Fr Fahy's brothers, a farmer 'in south Galway, was an active supporter of the republican movement', and the I.R.A. radio used his house to broadcast. Shortly after Fr Fahy's death, a group of land agitators in Westmeath, Offaly and Galway erected a memorial headstone over his grave and Ruairí Ó Brádaigh unveiled it. Ruairí Ó Brádaigh letter, *Saoirse*, February, 1993, p. 8; personal communication, Ruairí Ó Brádaigh to the author, 15 January 1996.
134 *Connacht Tribune*, 25 July 1969. Some years later, locals erected a commemorative plaque inside the church at Lusmagh that was unveiled by Peadar O'Donnell. Fr Kevin Egan interview, 9 August 1995.

V

In 1959 amid the ongoing crisis of the late 1950s, Geoffrey Hand ruminated about the nation's 'increasing political and social soul-searching' among which he noted the emergence of Lia Fáil:

> The terrible beauty that W.B. Yeats saw born in the fires of Easter Week, 1916, is now in an unlovely middle age. After thirty-seven years of self-government the traditional aims – unity with Northern Ireland, restoration of Gaelic culture, and a prosperity that would end the decline in population – are unfulfilled, and it is scarcely surprising that some of the younger generation doubt the sincerity of those who repeat the old slogans and, sometimes, even the wisdom and worth of the old aims themselves. Some groups merely try to give them more forceful application than those in authority are prepared to do. The members of the I.R.A. and kindred illicit organisations, fired by the glorification of past violence and by a constantly tendentious presentation of their country's history, are willing to give their lives in tragically destructive sacrifice. Cultural nationalism has been given a more modern look by *Gael-linn*, which has called in aid football pools, newsreels and even a TV project. Some curious episodes have recently followed on the revival of the spirit of the nineteenth-century agrarian agitation by a body entitled *Lia Fáil* (Stone of Destiny).[135]

However much it was characterised by conspiracy theories, eccentricities, or revolutionary millenarianism, Lia Fáil's smallholders' protest of the 1950s nevertheless cannot simply be dismissed as an inscrutably 'curious' or anachronistic recurrence of nineteenth-century agitation. Not only was it a revolt against the smallholders' precipitate decline particularly since the war and Fianna Fáil's seemingly callous indifference to their fate. It also was a revolt against the nation's failure after thirty-five years independence to create a *völkisch* social order guaranteeing opportunities in their own country for the people who were the nation's soul.

This failure finally provoked Fr Fahy's revolt, the second phase of his radical career, because it represented a negation of everything radical priests of his kind had aspired to in the days of the Anglo-Irish war. Paradoxically, the civil war intensified their aspirations for a heroic national destiny because the republicans' militarily ignominious defeat preserved them from acknowledging the

---

135 Geoffrey Hand, 'A letter from Dublin under President de Valera', *The Tablet* (18 July 1959), p. 614. Even a Church of Ireland journal, *Focus*, acknowledged, though it deprecated the sectarianism, that '... these troubles are symptomatic of a grave unrest about the state of things – emigration and unemployment, for instance ...' 'Land War', *Focus* (July 1959), p. 2.

necessity of compromise, leaving them ideologically indomitable and resolutely dedicated to working for the attainment of their ideals. It also taught them how to combine fervent republicanism with episcopal obedience and clerical discipline because not only did they endure the hierarchy's blistering anti-republican pastoral in October 1922 without demur, they also rejected a consequent proposal by six of their number to set up a national church.[136] Despite the precariousness of their position in relation to the bishops, they were by no means a negligible cohort immediately after the civil war. By openly hosting a priests' reception for the visiting republican prelate Archbishop Mannix of Melbourne in 1925, eighty republican priests together with 300 others who expressed support showed the extent of their organisation and discipline.[137] (Fr Thomas Burbage, later a close Lia Fáil ally, was secretary of this group.) Indeed, Archbishop Mannix's declaration at that time that 'a priest does not cease to be a citizen' and 'has a right to his own opinions' conferred them with episcopal sanction to defy their Free State Bishops. Long before they were uttered by the archbishop Fr Fahy had made these words his own.

These precepts of citizenship and conscience, always ultimately mitigated by deference to episcopal authority, were the basis of Fr Fahy's radical career. Three important differences between its first and second phases should be noted. Firstly, the *jacquerie* of Lia Fáil and the pretensions of a Hibernian Fr Krupavicius, radical Lithuanian Land Minister of the early 1920s, replaced the more individually, clerically-led actions of the east Galway land annuities campaign because Fr Fahy went into revolt against Fianna Fáil due to the party's seeming abandonment of agrarian radicalism while the smallholders' plight was getting steadily worse.

Secondly, the agrarian populist *via media* between socialism and capitalism and the demands for a *völkisch* social order of the 1950s supplanted the socialism of the Anglo-Irish war and early 1920s and the distinct left-leaning, physical force republicanism of the early 1930s so that by the time of the Cold War all traces of socialism had disappeared except vague aspirations of co-operation with labour and the rhetoric of totalitarian religious persecution had penetrated his vocabulary, identifying Fianna Fáil's suppression of Lia Fáil with Stalinist repression in Eastern Europe.

Thirdly, the ugly asperities towards Erskine Childers and the Church of Ireland Representative Body during the economic stagnation and smallholders' crisis of the 1950s replaced the mix of asperities towards the 'ex-peeler' at Bullaun and friendship with Major Jackson during the 1920s, though Fahy's enjoyment

---

136 For Fr O'Flanagan and the six priests's suggestion of a national church, see Peadar O'Donnell, 'The clergy and me', *Doctrine and Life*, vol. 24 (October 1974), no. 10, pp 542–4; *Catholic Bulletin*, 1925, p. 1161. My thanks to Dr Patrick Maume for drawing my attention to this latter source.
137 *Catholic Bulletin*, 1925, p. 1165.

of the company of local Protestants from Major Jackson in the 1920s to members of the Galway hounds in the 1950s meant that the logic of these asperities never outweighed a love of hunting. By contrast, Fr John Hayes of the Belgian boerenbond-modelled Muintir na Tire with his smallholding background on Lord Cloncurry's estate at Murroe, county Limerick, from which his father had been evicted in 1882 and his experience of intense sectarianism in Liverpool during the first world war, combined with his received smallholder radicalism to produce a pronounced disdain for sectarianism of any kind.[138] But Fr Fahy's politics of the 1950s drew on older, more elemental forces going back to the Defenders and second Whiteboy phase combined with East Galway's agrarian radical tradition. They also drew on wartime isolation which intensified Catholic identity and xenophobia, and the climate of Catholic Action of the forties and fifties with Fr Denis Fahey and Maria Duce's campaign to change Article 44 of the Constitution. By 1957 even a bishop with a progressive reputation such as Dr Philbin (whose injunction to practical patriotism Whitaker quoted approvingly in the preface to *Economic development* (1958)) could sound the tocsin in the premier Jesuit journal *Studies* that Protestants were in danger of taking over public life, though in 1961 numbering merely 4.6 per cent.[139]

The radical clerical tradition's leading exponents of this era certainly include Fr Michael O'Flanagan, Fr Albert O.F.M., and Dom Francis Sweetman O.S.B. each of whom earned that distinction largely for publicly falling foul of their superiors for their political commitments to the Sinn Féin movement during the revolutionary period.[140] Fr Fahy's claims to inclusion rest not so much on activities during the Anglo-Irish war or civil war as activities representing a new era of radical clerical activity against the new state and its rulers. His politics with their well-springs in the agrarian radicalism, republicanism and historicism of the revolutionary period were an attempt to finally secure those revolutionary objectives of a Gaelic society not merely sovereign but with a *völkisch*

---

138 Stephen Rynne, *Father John Hayes: founder of Muintir na Tire* (Dublin & London, 1960). Muintir na Tire's interdenominational character did not meet with approval from Archbishop John Charles McQuaid. J. Anthony Gaughan, *Alfred O'Rahilly, vol. iii: controversialist, part 1: social reformer* (Mount Merrion, Co. Dublin), p. 231.

139 William J. Philbin, 'A city on a hill', *Studies* (Autumn, 1957), p. 269; Keogh, 'Catholic Church in the republic', pp 143–4; *Economic development*, (Pr. 4803.), p. 9. See also, *The report of the working party on sectarianism: a discussion document for presentation to the Irish inter-church meeting* (Belfast, 1993); Joseph Liechty, 'The problem of sectarianism and the Church of Ireland', in Alan Ford, James McGuire & Kenneth Milne (eds.), *As by law established: the Church of Ireland since the reformation* (Dublin, 1995), pp 204–22.

140 See, Dominic Aidan Bellenger, 'An Irish Benedictine adventure: Dom Francis Sweetman (1872–1953) and Mount St Benedict, Gorey', in W.J. Sheils & Diana Wood (eds) *The churches, Ireland and the Irish* (Oxford, 1989), pp 401–15; Denis Carroll, *They have fooled you again: Michael O'Flanagan (1876–1942) Priest, republican, social critic* (Mount Merrion, Co. Dublin, 1993); Joost Augusteijn, *From public defiance to guerrilla warfare: the radicalisation of the Irish republican army – a comparative analysis, 1916–1921* 'University of Amsterdam, Ph.D., 1994', pp 283–8. By 1935, Sweetman was a social creditor. 'Monetary reform and the financial system', *Lia Fáil*, October 1958, p. 4.

social order as well that had seemingly been lost largely through native perfidy with such disastrous consequences to behold by the 1950s. His naming of his radical smallholders' movement after the ancient Lia Fáil symbolised his hopes that the smallholders' would yet find their destiny in a Gaelic pastoral society of rural, catholic, arcadian values cut off from the insidious modern world that would see the full flowering of the native genius. But Lemass and Whitaker's Great Leap Forward reinventing Ireland's destiny with free trade, foreign capital, and industrialisation, a vision shorn of the symbols that had launched the revolution, could only be successfully built on the ashes of Fr Fahy and de Valera's cherished pastoral society. Eventually the smallholders had no place.[141]

141 My thanks to those who helped in various ways, including those who helped on condition of remaining anonymous: Mr Fergus Campbell, Ms Bernadette Chambers of the Department of Foreign Affairs, Revd Professor Patrick J. Corish, Mr William Cogotono, Mr Stephen Coyle, Mr Enda Delaney, Dr Máirín Ní Dhonnachadha, Revd Fr Kevin Egan, Mr John Fahey, Mr Charles Flanagan T.D., Professor Tom Garvin, Dr Brian Girvin, Dr Peter Hart, Professor Michael Herity, Rev. Professor Donal Kerr, Dr Colin Kidd, Mrs Cathleen Knowles, Dr Michael Laffan, Professor Donal McCartney, Mr Brendán MacSuibhne, Mrs Mairéad Maume, Dr Patrick Maume, Dr Gerry Moran, Dr Gary Murphy, Dr Patrick Murray, Mr Ruairí Ó Brádaigh, Mr D.R. O'Connor Lysaght, Dr John O'Brien, Mrs Margaret hÓgartaigh, Mr & Mrs Colm Ó Laoghaire, the late Professor T.P. O'Neill, Mr Jim O'Shea of the National Library of Ireland, Fr Louis Page, and Dr Tony Varley. None of these, of course, are responsible for any errors.

Notes on Contributors

FERGUS A. D'ARCY lectures on modern history in University College, Dublin, where he specialises in labour history. He is a founding member of the Irish Labour History Society and has published on the political and social history of nineteenth-century Ireland and Britain. He is currently working on a biography of Thaddeus O'Malley.

JAMES KELLY lectures in history at St Patrick's College, Drumcondra. Specialising in the eighteenth-century his most recent book is *Henry Flood: Parties and Politics in Eighteenth-Century Ireland* (Dublin, 1998).

DONAL KERR is an Irish Marist priest and up to his retirement was Professor of Ecclesiastical History at St Patrick's College, Maynooth. His most recent book is *A nation of beggars?: Priests, people and politics in Famine Ireland, 1846–1862* (Oxford, 1994).

BREANDAN MAC SUIBHNE lectures in modern history at University College, Dublin and is completing a doctoral thesis at Carnegie Mellon University, Pittsburg. He has written on the political and social history of eighteenth- and nineteenth-century Ireland.

LAWRENCE W. MC BRIDE is Professor of History at the Illinois State University where he specialises in history education methods and Irish history. He is author of *The greening of Dublin Castle: The transformation of bureaucratic and judicial personnel in Ireland, 1892–1922* (Washington, DC, 1991).

SHEILA MULLOY is editor of *Cathair na Mart* (journal of the Westport Historical Society) and has written widely on late sixteenth and early seventeenth-century Ireland. She is editor of the *Franco-Irish Correspondence* (Irish Manuscripts Commission).

GERARD MORAN teaches history at the European School, Oxford and is associated with Wolfson College, Oxford. He has written on the political and social history of late nineteenth-century Ireland and is author of *A radical priest in Mayo: Fr Patrick Lavelle, the rise and fall of an Irish nationalist, 1825–86* (Dublin, 1994).

BRIAN S. MURPHY completed his doctorate at University College, Cork, and is currently preparing a biography on Mary McSweeney for publication. He is actively engaged in research work on the political and social history of twenti-eth-century Ireland.

EAMON Ó CIARDHA is completing a doctorate at Cambridge University and has recently been engaged in research work at the University of Aberdeen. He has published on late seventeenth- and eighteenth-century Ireland.

THOMAS POWER lives in Kitchener, Ontario, and has actively published on eight-eenth-century Ireland. He has lectured in Irish studies and Irish history at St Michael's College, University of Toronto, and at the University of New Bruns-wick. He is author of *Land, politics and society in eighteenth-century Tipperary* (Oxford, 1993).

Index